Principles of
Insurance
Law with
Case Studies

Shanmuganathan

PARTRIDGE

Copyright © 2020 by Shanmuganathan.

Library of Congress Control Number: 2019909348
ISBN: Softcover   978-1-5437-5239-7
              eBook   978-1-5437-5238-0

All rights reserved. No part of this book may be used or reproduced by any means, graphic, electronic, or mechanical, including photocopying, recording, taping or by any information storage retrieval system without the written permission of the author except in the case of brief quotations embodied in critical articles and reviews.

Because of the dynamic nature of the Internet, any web addresses or links contained in this book may have changed since publication and may no longer be valid. The views expressed in this work are solely those of the author and do not necessarily reflect the views of the publisher, and the publisher hereby disclaims any responsibility for them.

Print information available on the last page.

To order additional copies of this book, contact
Toll Free +65 3165 7531 (Singapore)
Toll Free +60 3 3099 4412 (Malaysia)
orders.singapore@partridgepublishing.com

www.partridgepublishing.com/singapore

CONTENTS

Foreword vii

Preface.. ix

Table of Cases xi

Table of Legislation lxv

Chapter 1   Contracts of Insurance 1

Chapter 2   Interpretation of Insurance Contracts............................. 71

Chapter 3   Good Faith 127

Chapter 4   Duty of Disclosure 164

Chapter 5   Fraud 244

Index 313

FOREWORD

The insurance industry is dynamic and with the changing landscape, the manner in which the applicable laws are interpreted to suit the current times is also seeing rapid development. Insurance companies are merging, policies are changing, contract terms are evolving and claims requirements are getting more stringent. Perpetrators of fraudulent claims, in particular, have become more sophisticated and fraud detection and investigation are a key focus with many insurers. Courts are called upon to interpret the law while balancing public interests.

These are some of the issues which practitioners are faced with today and consequently, it has become increasingly challenging for the stakeholders within the industry to keep up with the many cases and different interpretations of the law, both locally and abroad, which impact the industry as a whole.

This book on the Principles of Insurance Law with Case Studies by Shanmuganathan, a senior insurance professional from Kuala Lumpur, is therefore timely and relevant as he has not only provided a practical overview of the principles of insurance law but he has also pulled together a comprehensive collection of the most important cases every practitioner needs to be conversant with.

Not only does the writer provide ample illustrations from the Malaysian courts, he has also highlighted decisions from many other jurisdictions around the Commonwealth as a source of reference and comparison.

The author has succeeded in giving a clear and precise narration of the principles of insurance law from the formation of a contract of insurance, policy considerations, breach and the consequences thereof and what remedial action is open to the parties. The fundamental principle of good faith is discussed in great detail and he has shared with us his extensive experience as a specialist in insurance fraud in Chapter 5 where the subject matter is explored from various angles.

It is evident that the author has expended a lot of time and effort to conduct extensive research to analyse and collate the materials into a scholarly text which will no doubt be of great assistance to students and practitioners alike.

The author should be congratulated for this excellent effort and I believe that this book will be a welcome addition to any library.

DATO' SARANPAL SINGH GILL DIMP
(BC/S/426)
PEGUAMBELA & PEGUAMCARA
SELANGOR DARUL EHSAN

PREFACE

There are without a doubt, a number of books on Insurance Law currently available in the market. Nonetheless, over the years, there have been significant developments in this area of the law which are areas of common concern in the practice of insurance law today. It is for this reason that I decided to draw on my 20 years of experience in the industry and put pen to paper. After many nights and weekends spent poring over research materials, slowly but surely, this book, **Principles of Insurance Law with Case Studies** came together.

The book provides the reader with an overview of all the basic principles of insurance, the application of these principles based on decided cases and the law that regulates the insurance industry. Extensive research was made to gather pertinent information on decided cases not only from the courts in Malaysia but also from Commonwealth countries like the United Kingdom, Australia, New Zealand, India and our neighbour, Singapore. This will no doubt be of assistance to those wishing to make a comparative study of how the courts in the different jurisdictions have treated similar issues.

The Chapters include the formation of a contract of insurance, rights, duties and obligations of the insurer and insured as well as the consequences of any breach and the remedies available to the parties affected.

Cases of fraud are prevalent in the insurance industry and the huge claims paid out ultimately affect the premiums paid by the man on the street. Much effort is made by insurers to identify and combat fraud to ensure the authenticity of claims. Therefore, readers may find Chapter 5 of particular interest. It deals with the subject of insurance fraud touching on the Tort of Deceit, fraudulent misrepresentations and the requirements necessary to prove fraud.

It is hoped that this book will be successful in guiding practitioners and students alike to a critical and better understanding of the subject matter dealt with herein.

I would like to express my thanks to several people who helped in the completion of this book: my wife, Cindy Chan, for patiently going over the drafts and for her helpful suggestions; my editor, Sharmini Pillai, for her sharp eye for detail and efficiency; and my friends for their criticisms and comments. I am forever grateful for the support and understanding of my wife and daughter, Samantha, throughout the writing of this book.

The law discussed in this book is as of May 2019.

Shanmuganathan-LLB (Hons) UK, MBA (Veritas-BAC Edu Group), Cert in Project Management (Veritas-BAC Edu Group), Cert in Artificial Intelligence (Coursera)

TABLE OF CASES

A

Abdul Razak Bin Datuk Abu Samah v Shah Alam Properties Sdn Bhd and Anor Appeal [1999] 2 MLJ 500; [1999] 3 CLJ 231 (CA) 47, 260, 287

Absalom v TCRU Ltd [2006] 2 Lloyds Rep 129 ..... 87, 89

Abu Bakar v Oriental Fire & General Insurance Co Ltd [1974] 1 MLJ 149 ..... 188, 225, 228

Abu Dhabi National Tanker Co v Product Star Shipping Ltd (The "Product Star") [1993] 1 Lloyd's Rep 397, 404 142

Advance (NSW) Insurance Agencies Pty Ltd v Matthews [1987] NSW Lexis 7046; BC8701330 11

Aetna Universal Insurance Sdn Bhd v Fanny Foo May Wan [2001] 1 CLJ 476 (HC); [2001] 1 MLJ 227 ..... 3, 17, 18

Air Express International (M) Sdn Bhd v MISC Agencies Sdn Bhd [2012] 4 MLJ 59 309

Akerhielm v De Mare [1959] AC 789 283

Alcatel Australia Ltd v Scarcella (1998) 44
    NSWLR 349 — 136

ALW Car Workshop Sdn Bhd v Axa Affin General
    Insurance Bhd [2019] 7 CLJ 667 — 305

Amanah Raya Bhd v Jerneh Insurance Sdn Bhd
    [2005] 2 CLJ 393 (CA) — 88, 208

American Airlines Inc v Hope [1974]
    2 Lloyd's Rep 301 — 5

American Home Assurance v Saunders (1987) 11
    NSWLR 363 — 65

American International Assurance Co Ltd v See Ah Yu
    [1996] 3 CLJ 566 (HC) — 18, 53

American International Assurance Company Ltd v
    Nadarajan Subramaniam [2013] 5 CLJ 697 (CA) — 215, 217, 228, 229

AMP Fire & General Insurance Co Ltd v Miltenburg
    [1982] 1 NSWLR 391 — 82

AMP Workers' Compensation Services (NSW) Ltd v
    QBE Insurance Ltd (2003) 53 NSWLR 35 — 62

Ampthill Peerage, The [1977] AC 547; [1976] 2 All
    ER 411 (HL) — 255

Anali Marketing Sdn Bhd v Allianz General
    Insurance Malaysia Berhad [2012]
    MLJU 38 (HC) — 196, 198

Anderson Samuel v Ann Fitzgerald
    (1853) 4 HLC 484 — 17

Anderson v Morice (1875) 10 C.P. 609 (Exch Ch)	28
Ang Hiok Seng @Ang Yeok Seng v Yim Yut Kiu [1997] 2 MLJ 45 (FC)	303
Angus v Clifford [1891] 2 Ch 449 (CA)	253, 257
Antaios Compania Naviera v Salen Rederierna AB [1985] AC 191	87
Anthony Feasey v Sun Life Assurance Company of Canada [2003] Lloyd's Rep IR 637, [2003] EWCA Civ 885, [2003] 2 All ER (Comm) 587	29
Applegate v Moss [1971] 1 QB 406	256
Arab Bank Plc v Zurich Insurance Co [1999] 1 Lloyd's Rep 262	239, 241
Arasis Sdn Bhd lwn Pacific & Orient Insurance Co Bhd [2013] 1 MLJ 784 (HC)	308
Armstong v Strain [1951] 1 TLR 856	253
Aseambankers Malaysia Bhd & Ors v Shencourt Sdn Bhd & Anor [2014] 4 MLJ 619	146
Asean Securities Paper Mills Sdn Bhd v CGU Insurance Bhd [2007] 2 CLJ 1 (FC)	303
Ashby v Tolhurst [1937] 2KB 242	110
Ashfind Pty v McDonald [1990] NSW Conv R 55-509	289

Asia Hotel Sdn Bhd v Malayan Insurance (M) Sdn
    Bhd [1992] 2 CLJ 121 (Rep); [1992] 2 CLJ 1185;
    [1992] 2 MLJ 615 (HC)   18, 230, 308

Asia Insurance Co Ltd v Tat Hong Plant Leasing Pte   158, 187, 200, 201,
    Ltd [1992] 4 CLJ (Rep) 324; [1992] 1 CLJ 330   272

Assicurazioni Generali Spa v Arab Insurance Group
    [2003] 1 WLR 577   207

Assicurazioni Generali v Arab Insurance Group
    [2002] EWCA Civ 1642, [2002] All ER (D) 177   206

Attorney General for Belize v Belize Telecom Ltd
    [2009] UKPC 10, [2009] 2 All ER 1127, [2009] 1
    WLR 1988   137

Australian Gas Light Co v Valuer-General
    [1940] 40 SR (NSW) 126   75, 76

Australian Iron & Steel Ltd v Coal Mines Insurance
    Pty Ltd (1952) 52 SR (NSW) 47   63, 66

Australian Steel & Mining Corp Pty Ltd v Corben &
    Ors [1974] 2 NSWLR 202   289

Aviva Insurance Limited v Roger George Brown
    [2011] EWHC 362 (QB)   253, 305

Ayrey v British Legal and United Provident
    Assurance Co Ltd [1918] 1 KB 136 223,   226

Azizah Abdullah v Arab-Malaysian Eagles Sdn Bhd
    [1996] 3 CLJ 426; [1996] 5 MLJ 569   196, 208, 216, 218

B

Babatsikos v Car Owners' Mutual Insurance Co Ltd [1970] VR 297 — 294

Bank of Credit and Commerce International SA v Munawar Ali [2001] 2 WLR 735 — 77

Bank of New Zealand v Simpson [1900] AC 182 — 13

Bank of Nova Scotia v Hellenic Mutual War Risks Association (Bermuda) Ltd; [1988] 1 Lloyd's Rep 514; [1989] 3 All ER 628 (CA) — 55, 175, 184

Banque Financière de la Cité SA (formerly Banque Keyser Ullmann SA) v Westgate Insurance Co Ltd (formerly Hodge General & Mercantile Co Ltd) [1991] 2 AC 249; [1990] 2 All ER 947 — 155, 296

Banque Financiere de la Cite v Westgate Insurance Co [1990] 2 All ER 947 — 177

Banque Financiere vs Skandia (UK) Insurance Co Ltd [1990] 2 All ER 947 — 176

Banque Financiere vs Skandia (UK) Insurance Co Ltd [1990] 2 Lloyd's Rep 377 (HL) — 171

Banque Keyser Ullmann SA v Skandia (UK) Insurance Co Ltd [1990] 1 QB 665 — 155, 207, 296, 297

Banque Keyser Ullmann SA v Skandia (UK) Insurance Co Ltd and others and related actions [1987] 2 All ER 923 — 154, 165

Banque Nationale du Canada v Soucisse, Groulx and
    Robitaille [1981] 2 S.C.R. 339; 43 N.R. 283   148

Barclays Bank v Cole [1967] 2 QB 738, [1966] 3 All
    ER 948, [1967] 2 WLR 166   247, 276

Barratt Bros (Taxis) Ltd v Davies [1966] 1 WLR 1334   50, 92

Bates v Hewitt (1867) LR 2 QB 595, 607   130, 195, 218

Bawden v The London, Edinburgh and Glasgow
    Assurance Co [1892] 2 QB 534   223, 226, 236

BCCI v Ali [2001] UKHL 8, [2002] 1 AC 251, [2001] 1
    All ER 961   138

Bell v Lever Brothers, Ltd [1932] AC 161   40, 156

Berjaya Times Square Sdn Bhd (formerly knownas
    Berjaya Ditan Sdn Bhd) v M Concept Sdn Bhd
    [2010] 1 MLJ 597   77

Berkeley Community Villages Ltd v Pullen [2007]
    EWHC 1330 (Ch), [2007] 3 EGLR 101   140

B-Gold Interior Design & Construction Pte Ltd v
    Zurich Insurance (Singapore) Pte Ltd [2007]
    SGHC 126; [2007] 4 SLR 82   113

Biggar v Rock Life Assurance Co [1902] 1 KB 516   235

Black King Shipping Corp v Massie, The 'Litsion
    Pride' [1985] 1 Lloyd's Rep 437   155, 157

Black King Shipping Corporation And Wayang (Panama) S.A. v Mark Ranald Massie (the 'Litsion Pride') (1985) Vol. 1 Q.B. (Com. Ct.) 437(1985)	196, 198
Blackburn, Low & Co. v Vigors (1887) 12 App. Cas. 531, 542-543	220
Blanchette v CIS Ltd (1973) 36 DLR (3d) 561	226
Bobux Marketing Ltd v Raynor Marketing Ltd [2002] 1 NZLR 506	136
Boonsom Boonyanit @ Sun Yok Eng v Adorna Properties Sdn Bhd [1995] 2 MLJ 863	301
Boulton v Holder Bros (1904) 1 KB 784, 791	154
Bowes v Chaleyer (1923) 32 CLR 159	47
BP (Sabah) Sdn Bhd v Syarikat Jubrin Enterprise & Anor [1996] MLJU 449; [1997] 1 LNS 354	250
Bradford Third Equitable Benefit Building Society v Borders [1941] 2 All ER 205 (HL)	276
Bradley v Eagle Star Insurance Co Ltd [1989] 1 AC 957	61, 62
Brady (Inspector of Taxes) v Group Lotus Car Cos plc and another [1987] 3 All ER 1050	298
Braunstein v Accidental Death Insurance Co. (1861) 1 B. & S. 782	97, 103
Briess v Woolley [1954] AC. 333 (H.L.)	286

Britton v Royal Ins Co, (1866) 4 F&F 905	130
Brownlie v Campbell (1880) 5 App Cas 925	177
Brownlie v Campbell (1880) 5 App Cas 925	195, 207
Bulli Coal Mining Co v Osborne [1899] AC 351	256
Burger King Corp v Hungry Jack's Pty Ltd [2001] NWSCA 187	136

C

Cacciola v Fire and All Risks Insurance Co Ltd [1971] 1 NSWLR 691	62
Canning v Farquhar (1885-1886) 16 QBD 727	18, 19
Cantiere Meccanico Brindisino v Janson [1912] 3 KB 452	131
Capital Corp Securities Sdn Bhd v Abdul Malek Beh Bin Abdullah [2005] 7 MLJ 35	300
Capital Insurance Bhd v Cheong Heng Loong Goldsmiths (KL) Sdn Bhd [2005] 4 CLJ 1	175
Capital Insurance Bhd v Kasim Mohd Ali [1996] 2 MLJ 425; [1996] 3 CLJ 19	21
Carlingford Australia General Insurance Ltd v EZ Industries Ltd [1988] VR 349	112
Carr v Montefiore (1864) 5 B & S 408, Ex Ch	83
Carter v Boehm (1766) 3 Burr 1905	129, 130, 176, 177

Carter v Boehm (1766) 3 Burr 1905, [1558–1774] All ER Rep 183	131, 154, 165
Carter v Boehm (1766) 97 ER 1162	153, 194, 195, 198, 221, 240
Cartledge v E Jopling & Sons Ltd [1963] AC 758	65
Castellain v Preston & Ors [1883] 11 QBD 380 (CA)	23, 24, 25
Castle Insurance Co Ltd v Hong Kong Shipping Co Ltd (The Potoi Chou) [1984] 1 AC 226	67
Cavell USA, Inc and another v Seaton Insurance Co and another[2009] EWCA Civ 1363	246
CE Heath Underwriting & Insurance (Australia) Pty Ltd v. Edwards Dunlop & Co Ltd [1992] 112 ALR 161	172
Central Lorry Service Co Sdn Bhd v The American Insurance Co [1981] 2 MLJ 40	99
Chandris v Argo Insurance Co Ltd [1963] 2 Lloyd's Rep 65	67
Chang Kuo Ping v Malaysian Assurance Alliance Bhd [2008] 3 CLJ 752	200
Chapman v Pole (1870) 22 LT 306	295
Chariot Inns Ltd v Assicurazione Generali Spa [1981] IR 199	156
Chatenay v Brazilian Submarine Telegraph Co [1891] 1 QB 79	74

Cheong Bee v China Insurance Co Ltd [1974] 1 MLJ 203	94
China Insurance Co Ltd v Ngau Ah Kau [1971] 1 LNS 20; [1972] 1 MLJ 52 (FC)	11, 17, 18, 215, 216, 219, 228, 229
Ching Yik Development Sdn Bhd v Setapak Heights Development Sdn Bhd [1996] 3 MLJ 675	46
Chip Fong (Kuala Lumpur) Sdn Bhd & Ors v Guardian Royal Exchange Assurance (Malaysia) Sdn Bhd [1992] 1 MLJ 598	26
Chong Kok Hwa v Taisho Marine & Fire Insurance Co. Ltd. [1975] 1 LNS 14; [1977] 1 MLJ 244	48, 175
Chong Song @ Chong Sum & Anor v Uma Devi V Kandiah [2011] 3 CLJ 1; [2011] 2 MLJ 585	303
Chong Wai Automobile Enterprise (M) Sdn Bhd v Saga Autoparts Industries Sdn Bhd (Long Kwok Seng & Ors, third parties) [2013] 8 MLJ 850	302
Chu Choon Moi v Ngan Sew Tin [1985] 1 LNS 134; [1986] 1 MLJ 34	309
Chuan Hup Marine Ltd v Sembawang Engineering Pte Ltd [1995] 2 SLR 629	117, 266
Chung Kuo Ping v Malaysian Assurance Alliance Bhd [2008] 3 CLJ 752	238
Citizens Insurance Company of Canada v Parsons (1881), (1881–82) 7 App Cas 96	21
Clift v Schwabe (1846) 3 CB 437	83

Cold Storage Holdings Plc & Ors v The Overseas Assurance Corpn Ltd & Anor [1989] 2 MLJ 324 (HC)	35, 41
Commercial Union Assurance (Malaysia) Sdn Bhd v Pilihan Megah Bhd Sdn Bhd [1998] 7 MLJ 33	32
Condogianis v Guardian Assurance Co (1923) 29 CLR 341	102
Condogianis v Guardian Assurance Company Limited [1921] 1 A.C. 125	92, 94
Container Transport International Inc v Oceanus Mutual Underwriting Association (Bermuda) Ltd [1984] 1 Lloyds Rep 476	165, 167
Continental Illinois National Bank & Trust Co v Bathurst [1985] 1 Lloyd's Rep 625	86
Cooper v Phibbs (1867) LR 2 HL 149; 16 LT 678; 15 WR 1049, HL; 22 Digest (Repl) 156	42
Cornhill Insurance Co Ltd v L & B Assenheim [1937] 59 Ll L Rep 27	200
Cory v Patton (1872) LR 7 QB 304	183
Cory v Patton (1874) LR 9 QB 577	198
Cosmic Insurance Corporation Ltd v Ong Kah Hoe (t/a Ong Kah Hoe Industrial Supplies) & Anor [1998] 1 SLR 1044	86
CPC Group Ltd v Qatari Diar Real Estate Investment Co [2010] EWHC 1535 (Ch)	140

Croom-Johnson J in Metal Scrap & By Products Limited v Federated Conveyors Limited and Tribble (Third Party) [1953] 1 Ll LR 221	101
Curran v Norwich Union Life Insurance Society [1987] IEHC 5	168
Curtis & Sons v. Mathew [1918] 35 TLR 189 (CA)	24
Curtis v Chemical Cleaning and Dyeing Co [1951] 1 KB 805, 807	262

D

Dalby v India and London Life Assurance [1843-1860] All ER Rep 1040; [1843- 60] All ER Rep 1040	68
Dalglish v Jarvie (1850) 2 Mac & G 231	131
Dato' Toh Kian Chuan v Swee Construction and Transport Company (Malaysia) Sdn Bhd [1996] 1 MLJ 730	308
David Robert Zeller v British Caymanian Insurance Company Ltd [2008] UKPC 4 (PC)	170, 195
Dawsons Ltd v Bonnin & Ors [1922] All ER Rep 88; [1992] 2 AC 413	8, 17, 48, 56, 194, 230, 238
DBS Bank Ltd v Carrier Singapore (Pte) Ltd	281
De Hahn v Hartley [1786] 1 TR 343; 99 ER 1130	49, 51, 54
De Maurier (Jewels) Ltd v Bastion Insurance Co Ltd [1967] 2 Lloyd's Rep 550	59

Derry v Peek (1889) 14 App Cas 337	204, 251, 255, 275, 276, 280, 281, 284, 286, 295
Di Sora v Phillipps (1863) 10 HL Cas 624	74, 75
Dillingham Engineering Pty Ltd v National Employers' Mutual General Insurance Assn Ltd [1971] 1 NSWLR 578	64, 66, 82
Directors of the London Guarantee Co v Benjamin Lister Fearley Vol V The Law Reports House of Lords 911	48
Dirkje Peiternella Halma v Mohd Noor bin Baharom [1990] 3 MLJ 103	219
Distillers Co Biochemicals (Aust) Pty Ltd v Ajax Insurance Co Ltd (1974) 130 CLR 1	62, 161
Double Acres Sdn Bhd v Tiarasetia Sdn Bhd [2000] 7 CLJ 550	252, 308
Douglas Kerr v Danier Leather Inc., Irving Wortsman, Jeffrey Wortsman and Bryan Tatoff [2001] O.T.C. 181	265
Dowrick (1954) 17 MLR 36, Reynolds 94 LQR 225	222
Drake Insurance plc v Provident Insurance plc [2004] QB 601	206
Drinkwater v Corp of London Assurance [1767] 2 Wils K.B. 363	103
DSL Development Corp Sdn Bhd v Kampong Kita Sdn Bhd [2014] 11 MLJ 935 (HC)	41

Duchess of Kingston's Case [1776] 2 Smith LC 644	245
Dwyer v Broken Hill South Ltd (1928) 2 WCR 209	66

E

Eastleigh BC v Town Quay Developments Ltd [2009] EWCA Civ 1391, [2010] 2 P & CR 19	142
Ebsworth v Alliance Marine Insurance Co (1873) LR 8 CP 596	31
Economides v Commercial Assurance Co Plc [1998] QB 587	170
Edgington v Fitzmaurice (1885) 29 Ch D 459	259, 289
Edwards v Griffiths [1953] 1 WLR 1199	94
Elcock v. Thomson [1949] 2 KB 755, [1949] 2 All ER 381	24
Elizabeth Jeevamalar Ponnampalam & Ors v Karuppanan a/l Ramasamy & Anor (Sundram a/l Marappa Goundan & Anor as Interveners; Raya Realty (sued as a firm) as third party) [2007] 4 MLJ 214	308
Equitable Life Assurance Society v Hyman [2002] 1 AC 408	72
Etherington and The Lancashire and Yorkshire Accident Insurance Company [1909] 1 KB 591	179
Evans v Employers Mutual Insurance Association Ltd [1936] 1 KB 505	223, 227

Everbright Commercial Pte Ltd & Anor v AXA
 Insurance S'pore Pte Ltd [2000] 4 SLR 226   21

Exklusiv Auto Services Pte Ltd v Chan Yong Chua
 Eric [1996] 1 SLR 433   266, 276

F

Farrell v Federated Employers Insurance Association
 Ltd [1970] 1 WLR 498   50, 92

Fauziah Khanom bt Irshad Ali Khan v Pegawai
 Pejabat Pelajaran Daerah Johor Bahru & Ors
 [2013] 7 MLJ 737   154

Favelle Mort Ltd v Murray (1976) 133 CLR 580   64

FH v. McDougall [2008] SCC 53   304

Firbank's Executors v Humphreys 1887
 LR Q.B.D. 54   291

First Energy (UK) Ltd v Hungarian International
 Bank Ltd [1993] BCLC 1409, [1993] 2 Lloyd's
 Rep 194, 196; and (1997) 113 LQR 433   142

Fisher v Hebburn Ltd (1960) 105 CLR 188   64, 66

Fitton v Accidental Death Insurance Company
 (1864) 17 C.B.N.S. 122   98

Footner v Broken Hill Associated Smelters Pty Ltd
 (1983) 33 SASR 58   65

Fowkes v Manchester and London Life Assurance
 and Loan Association (1863) 3 B. & S. 917   97

Fraser v Furman (BN) (Productions) [1967] 3 All ER 57	81
Frederick E Rose (London) Ltd v William H Pim Junior & Co Ltd [1953] 2 QB 450	39, 43

G

Galloway v Guardian Royal Exchange (UK) Ltd [1999] 2 Lloyd's Rep IR 209 (CA)	93, 196, 198, 310
Gan v Tai Ping (Nos 2 & 3) [2001] Lloyd's Rep IR 667	142
Gateway Realty Ltd v Arton Holdings Ltd. and LaHave Developments Ltd. (No. 3) (1991), 106 N.S.R. (2d) 180; 288 A.P.R. 180 (T.D.)	148, 149, 150, 151
Geach v Ingall (1845) 14 M & W 95	202
General Accident, Fire and Life, Assurance Corporation Ltd v Shuttleworth & Anor (1938) 60 Ll LR 301	21
George Hunt Cranes Ltd v Scottish Boiler and General Insurance Co Ltd [2002] 1 All ER (Comm) 366	50
Geraldton Building Co Pty Ltd v May (1977) 136 CLR 379	64
GIO (NSW) v. Kimmedy [1988] 5 ANZ Insurance Cases 60-880	22, 173
Glicksman v Lancashire & General Assurance Co Ltd [1926] Lloyd LR 69; [1926] All ER 161; [1927] AC 139	272, 230

Globe Trawlers Pte Ltd v National Employers' Mutual General Insurance Association Ltd v Anor [1989] 1 MLJ 463 (HC Singapore)	233
Goh Chooi Leong v Public Life Assurance Co Ltd [1964] 1 MLJ 5	198, 200, 201, 208
Golden Bond Sdn Bhd v Sabtra Sdn Bhd & Anor [2004] 7 MLJ 493	289
Goldsmith Williams v Travellers Insurance [2010] Lloyd's Law Reports IR 309	205
Gotten v Wright 8 E.& B. 647	291
Gould v Vaggelas (1985) 157 CLR 215	290
Grant v Grant LR 5 CP 727	14
Gray v Burr [1971] 2 All ER 949	123
GRE Insurance Ltd v Bristile Ltd (1991) 6 ANZ Ins Cas 61-078	83
Greenclose Ltd v National Westminster Bank Plc [2014] EWHC 1156 (Ch)	133
Grosvenor Casinos Ltd v National Bank of Abu Dhabi [2008] 2 Lloyd's Rep 1	255
Grunther Industrial Developments Ltd v Federated Employers Insurance Association Ltd [1973] 1 Lloyd's Report 394	306
Gurdeep Singh a/l Melkha Singh v Malaysian Airline System Bhd [2015] 8 MLJ 24 (HC)	107

H

Hamlyn & Co v Wood & Co, [1891] 2 Q.B. 488	95
Hanwha Non-Life Insurance Co Ltd v Alba Pte Ltd [2011] SGHC 271; [2012] 1 SLR 941 (HC) (Singapore)	68, 79
Harrington v Pearl Life Assurance Co Ltd (1914) 30 TLR 613	18
Hartford Protection Insurance Co v Harmes 2 Ohio St. 452 (1853)	216
Hedley Byrne & Co Ltd v Heller & Partners Ltd [1964] AC 465	296
Hedley Byrne & Co v Heller & Partners Ltd [1963] 2 All E.R. 575 (HL)	166, 296
Helmut Schleich v Peri Formwork (M) Sdn Bhd [2013] 7 MLJ 112 (HC)	86
Hepburn v A Tomlinson (Hauliers) Ltd [1966] AC 451	119
Hew Soon Tai dan lain-lain (plaintif-plaintif kedua dan ketiga adalah budak-budak di bawah umur yang menuntut melalui ibu yang sah Hew Soon Tai) lwn Hong Leong Assurance Bhd Vol 7 (part 4 & 8)(2016) 1 MLRA 295-376	188
Heyman v Darwins Limited [1942] AC 356	157
Highlands Insurance Co v Continental Insurance Co [1987] 1 Lloyd's Rep 109	296

HIH Casualty and General Insurance Limited and others (Respondents) v Chase Manhattan Bank (Appellants) and others HIH Casualty and General Insurance Limited and others (Appellants) v Chase Manhattan Bank (Respondents) and others (First Appeal) HIH Casualty and General Insurance Limited and others (Appellants) v Chase Manhattan Bank (Respondents) and others (Second Appeal) (Conjoined appeals) [2001] 2 Lloyd's Rep 483) (CA)	132, 258, 296
HIH Casualty and General Insurance Limited and others (Respondents) v Chase Manhattan Bank (Appellants) and others, HIH Casualty and General Insurance Limited and others (Appellants) v Chase Manhattan Bank (Respondents) and others (First Appeal) and HIH Casualty and General Insurance Limited and others (Appellants) v Chase Manhattan Bank (Respondents) and others (Second Appeal) (Conjoined appeals) [2003] UKHL 6 (HL)	189, 193, 203, 239, 245, 291
HIH Casualty and General Insurance Ltd v New Hampshire Insurance Co [2001] EWCA Civ 735, [2001] 2 Lloyd's Rep 161	51, 106
HIH Casualty v Chase Manhattan Bank [2003] UKHL 6, [2003] 1 All ER (Comm) 349, [2003] 2 Lloyd's Rep 61	138
Hinchey v Gonda [1955] OWN 125	260
Holt's Motors Ltd v South East Lancashire Insurance (1930) 35 Com Cas 281	102

Home Insurance Company of New York v Victoria Montreal Fire Insurance Company [1907] AC 59	113
Hongkong Fir Shipping Co Ltd v Kawasaki Kisen Kaisha [1962] 2 QB 26	47
Hornal v Neuberger Products Ltd [1957] 1 QB 247	254
Hotel Ambassador (M) Sdn Bhd v Seapower (M) Sdn Bhd [1991] 1 MLJ 221	215
Houle v Banque Nationale du Canada [1990] 3 S.C.R. 122; 114 N.R. 161; 35 Q.A.C. 161	148
Hub Warrior Sdn Bhd v QBE Insurance (Malaysia) Bhd [2004] SGHC 279	38
Hydarnes Steamship Company v Indemnity Mutual Marine Assurance Company [1895] 1 QB 500	113

I

IBM Singapore Pte Ltd v UNIG Pte Ltd [2003] SGHC 71	117
In re B (Children) (Care Proceedings: Standard of Proof) (CAFCASS intervening (2008) UKHL 35	304
In re Bird's Trusts (1876) 3 Ch D 214	41
In Re Bradley and Essex and Suffolk Accident Indemnity Society [1912] 1 KB 415	179
In re Dellow's Trusts [1964] 1 WLR 451	254
In Re Donald J. Trump Casino Securities Litigation ('Trump') 7 F.3d 357 (3rd Cir.1993)	265

In re H (Minors) [1996] AC 563	254
In the matter of an arbitration between Etherington and The Lancashire and Yorkshire Accident Insurance Company [1909] 1 KB 591	179
Insurance Co of the State of Pennsylvania v Grand Union Insurance Co [1990] 1 Lloyd's Rep 208	6
Interfoto Picture Library Ltd v Stiletto Visual Programmes Ltd [1989] QB 433	133, 134, 143, 144
International Corona Resources Ltd. v. Lac Minerals Ltd. (1989), 101 N.R. 239; 36 O.A.C. 57; 61 D.L.R.(4th) 14 (S.C.C.)	148
International Times & Ors v Leong Ho Yuen [1980] 2 MLJ 86 (FC)	299, 300, 301
Investors Compensation Scheme Ltd v West Bromwich Building Society [1998] 1 All ER 98, [1998] 1 BCLC 493, [1998] 1 WLR 896	72, 77, 137
Iron Trades Mutual Insurance Co Ltd v Compania De Seguros Imperio 31/7/90 Commercial Court (unreported)	184

J

J Lowenstein & Co Ltd v Poplar Motor Transport (Lymm) (Gooda, third party) [1968] 2 Lloyd's Rep 233	86
James v British General Insurance Co. Ltd. [1927] 2 KB 311	33

Jamilah Ibrahim/Muhamad Haziq Asyraf v Liberty Insurance Bhd [2018] CLJ 1 LNS 812	11
Jason v Batten 1930 Ltd; Jason v British Traders' Insurance Company Ltd [1969] 1 QB 281	83
Jeffery Law Siew Su v PanGlobal Insurance Berhad & Other Cases [2006] MLJU 365	33
Joel v Law Union & Crown Insurance Co [1908] 2 KB 863	195, 202, 218
Johara Bi bte Abdul Kadir Marican v Lawrence Lam Kwok Fou & Anor [1981] 1 MLJ 139	299
John Driscoll v Teleplan Technology Services Sdn Bhd [2012] 10 MLJ 267	300
John v Price Waterhouse [2002] EWCA Civ 899	271
Joseph Constantine Steamship Line Ltd v Imperial Smelting Corporation Ltd, The Kingswood [1941] 2 All ER 165 179	298
Jureidini v National British and Irish Millers Insurance Co Ltd [1915] AC 499	158

K

K.R.M. Construction Ltd v British Columbia Railway Co (1982), 18 C.L.R. 277 (B.C.C.A.)	280
K/S Merc-Scandia XXXXII v Certain Lloyd's Underwriters and others [2000] 2 All ER (Comm) 731	272

Kamalul Arifin bin Yusof v Mayban Trustees Bhd & Anor [2013] 2 MLJ 526	300
Kandasami v Mohamed Mustafa [1983] 2 MLJ 85	93
Katotikidis v Mr Submarine Ltd [2002] ACWSJ 10135	157
Kausar v Eagle Star Insurance Co [2000] Lloyd's IR 154	242
Kawasaki Kisen Kaisha Ltd v Owners of the Ship or Vessel 'Able Lieutenant' [2002] 6 MLJ 433	251
Kearney v General Accident Fire and Life Assurance Corp Ltd [1968] 2 Lloyd's Rep 240	90, 107
Kelly v New Zealand Insurance Company Ltd (1996) 9 ANZ Insurance Cases 61-317	155, 161
Keongco Malaysia Sdn Bhd v Ng Seah Hai [2012] 7 MLJ 288	300
Kesatuan Kebangsaan Pekerja-Pekerja Bank & Ors v The New Straits Times Press (M) Bhd & Ors and another suit [2013] 8 MLJ 199	300
Kim Hok Yung & Ors v Cooperatieve Centrale Raiffeisen – Boerenleen bank [2000] 4 SLR 508	280
Kin Yuen Co Pte Ltd v Lombard Insurance Co Ltd & Ors [1994] 2 SLR 887 (HC)	84, 95, 105
King v Victor Parsons & Co [1973] 1 WLR 29	255
Kleinwort Benson Ltd v Lincoln City Council [1999] 2 AC 349; [1998] 4 All ER 513	35, 36, 37

Kodak (Australasia) Pty Ltd v Retail Traders Mutual Indemnity Insurance Assn (1942) 42 SR (NSW) 231	83
Kotak Malaysia (KOM) Sdn Bhd v Perbadanan Nasional Insurans Sdn Bhd [2005] 4 MLJ 402	43
KPMG Llp v Network Rail Infrastructure Ltd [2007] EWCA Civ 363	106
KS Energy Services Ltd v BR Energy (M) Sdn Bhd [2014] SGCA 16	72, 145

L

L Schuler AG v Wickman Machine Tool Sales Ltd [1974] AC 235	90, 107
L'Union Des Assurances De Paris IARD v HBZ International Exchange Co (S) Pte Ltd [1993] 3 SLR 161 (CA) (Singapore)	52
LAC Minerals Ltd v International Corona Resources Ltd [1989] 2 SCR 574	151
Lake v Simmons [1927] AC 487	86
Laker Vent Engineering Ltd v Templeton Insurance Ltd [2009] EWCA Civ 62; [2009] 2 All ER755 (Comm)	206, 207
Lambert v Co-operative Insurance Society Ltd [1975] 2 Lloyd's Rep 485	172, 195, 202
Lau Kee Ko & Anor v Paw Ngi Siu [1973] 1 LNS 71; [1974] 1 MLJ 21	302

Lau King Kieng v AXA Affin General Insurance Bhd and another suit [2014] 8 MLJ 883 (HC)	187, 188, 198, 228
Law Guarantee Trust & Accident Society v Munich Re-Insurance Company [1912]1 Ch 138 Ch D	32
Lazarus Estates Ltd v Beasley [1956] 1 All ER 341, [1956] 1 QB 702	244
LEC Contractors (M) Sdn Bhd (formerly known as Lotterworld Engineering & Construction Sdn Bhd) v Castle Inn Sdn Bhd & Anor [2000] 3 MLJ 339	211, 307
Lee Bee Soon & Ors v Malaysia National Insurance Sdn Bhd [1980] 2 MLJ 252	198, 208
Lee Chee Wei v Tan Hor Peow Victor and Others and Another Appeal [2007] SGCA 22 [2007] 3 SLR 537	266
Lee Cheong Fah v Soo Man Yoh [1996] 2 MLJ 627; [1996] 2 BLJ 356	302
Lee Kim Luang v Lee Shiah Yee [1988] 1 CLJ Rep 717; [1988] 1 MLJ 193	308
Lee You Sin v Chong Ngo Khoon [1981] 1 LNS 116; [1982] 2 MLJ 15	303
LeMesurier v. Andrus (1986), 12 O.A.C. 299; 54 O.R.(2d) 1 (C.A.)	148
Leong Chee Yeong (f) v China Insurance Co Ltd [1952] MLJ 246	32

Leong Kum Whay & Anor v American International Assurance Ltd [1999] 1 MLJ 24	212
Leong Kum Whay v QBE Insurance (M) Sdn Bhd & Ors [2006] 1 CLJ 1; [2006] 1 MLJ 710 (CA)	17, 22, 159, 174, 178, 226
Leong Luen Kiew & Anor v The New Zealand Insurance Co Ltd [1939] 1 LNS 50	96
Leppard v Excess Insurance Co Ltd [1979] 1 WLR 512; [1979] 2 All ER 668	24, 25, 26
Lie Kee Pong v Chin Chow Yoon & Anor [1998] 3 SLR 92	263
Life Insurance Co of Australia Ltd v Phillips (1925) 36 CLR 60	74
Lim Kim Hua v Ho Chui Lan & Anor [1995] 3 MLJ 165	305
Lishman v Northern Maritime Insurance Co (1875) LR 10 CP 179	180, 183
Lloyds TSB Foundation for Scotland v Lloyds Banking Group plc [2013] UKSC 3	140
Locker & Woolf Ltd v Western Australian Insurance Co [1936] 1 KB 408	201
Loh Bee Tuan v Shing Yin Construction (Kota Kinabalu) Sdn Bhd & Ors [2002] 2 MLJ 532	276
Loh Shiiun Hing v Kurnia Insurans (Malaysia) Bhd [2014] 7 CLJ 490 (CA)	23, 88, 128, 195

London & Provincial Leather Processes Ltd v Hudson (1939) 2 KB 724	33
London and North Western Railway Co v Glyn [1859] 1 EL & EL 652	118
London Assurance v Clare (1937) 57 Ll LR 254	295
London Assurance v Mansel (1879) 11 Ch D 363	131
London General Omnibus Co Ltd v Holloway [1911-13] All ER Rep 518	170
London Guarantee Company v Benjamin Lister Fearley (Vol. V - the Law Reports, House of Lords 911)	175
Lord Eldon-Ebsworth v Alliance Marine Insurance Co (1873) LR 8 CP 596	31
Lowenstein (J) & Co v Poplar Motor Transport (Lymm) and Gooda (Third Party) [1968] 2 Lloyd's Rep 223	82

M

M Ratnavale v S Lourdenadin [1988] 2 MLJ 371	310
MA Millner "Fraudulent Non-Disclosure" (1957) 76 SALJ 177	127
Mackay v Dick (1881) 6 App Cas 251, 263, 8 R 37, 29 WR 541	140

MacMillan v Kaiser Equipment Ltd [2004] BCJ 969	267
Macronet Sdn Bhd v RHB Bank Sdn Bhd [2002] 3 MLJ 11	269
Madam Loh Sai Nyah v American International Assurance Co Ltd [1998] 2 MLJ 310 (CA)	9, 19
MAE Engineering Ltd v Fire-Stop Marketing Services Pte Ltd [2005] 1 SLR 379	104
Malayan Banking Bhd v Ong Kee Chong Motors Sdn Bhd [1991] 1 CLJ 363 (HC)	307
Malayan Motor & General Underwriters Pte Ltd v Mohamad Hamid Almojil [1982- 1983] SLR 52	88
Malaysia Assurance Alliance Bhd v Chong Nyuk Lan [2003] 5 CLJ 245	210
Malaysia National Insurance Sdn Bhd v Abdul Aziz bin Mohamed Daud [1978] 1 LNS 117; [1979] 2 MLJ 29 (FC)	85, 86, 98, 100, 102, 103, 111, 118
Malaysia National Insurance Sdn Bhd v Malaysia Rubber Development Corporation [1986] 2 MLJ 124	85
Malaysian Assurance Alliance Bhd v Chong Nyuk Lan (Administrator of the Estate of Liew Kin On, deceased) [2002] 6 MLJ 648	212, 213
Manifest Shipping Co Ltd v Uni-Polaris Co Ltd & Others (The 'Star Sea') [2001] UKHL 1, [2003] 1 AC 469	156, 159

Manifest Shipping Co Ltd v Uni-Polaris Insurance Co Ltd & Others (The 'Star Sea') [2001] UKHL 1, [2003] 1 AC 469	127, 129, 131, 152, 168, 169, 180
Mann Macneal & Steeves Ltd v Capital & Counties Insurance Co Ltd [1921] 2 KB 300	177, 197
Manor Park Homebuilders Ltd v AIG Europe (Ireland) Ltd [2009] 1 ILRM 190	178
Manufacturers Mutual Insurance Ltd v National Employers' Mutual General Insurance Assn Ltd (1991) 6 ANZ Ins Cas 61-038	64
March Cabaret Club & Casino Ltd v London Assurance Ltd [1975] 1 Lloyd's Rep 169	169
Marquis of Camden v Inland Revenue Commissioners [1914] 1 KB 641	75
Martin (John) of London v Russell [1960] 1 Lloyd's Rep 554	82
Martin v Ryan [1990] 2 NZLR 209	255, 256
Martindale v Burrows [1997] 1 Qd R 243	65
Mary Colete John v South East Asia Insurance Bhd [2010] 2 MLJ 222 (CA)	3, 99
Master Strike Sdn Bhd v Sterling Heights Sdn Bhd [2005] 3 MLJ 585	268
Maye v. Colonial Mutual Life Assurance Society Limited [1924] HCA 26; (1924) 35 CLR 14	93

Mayne Nickless Ltd. v Pegler & Anor. (1974) 1 N.S.W.L.R. 228	197
Mayor v. Issac (1840) 6 M. & W. 605	97
McAleenan v AIG (Europe) Ltd [2010] IEHC 128	204
McAlpine (Alfred) plc v BAI (Run-Off) Ltd [2000] 1 All ER (Comm) 545, CA	272
McConnel v Murphy ((1873) LR 5 PC 203	74
McInerney v Schultz (1981) 28 SASR 542	50
MCST No 473 v De Beers Jewellery [2002] 2 SLR 1	35
MDIS v Swinbank [1999] 2 All ER (Comm) 722, [1999] Lloyd's Rep IR 516	87
Meacock v Bryant & Co [1942] 2 All ER 661	24
Medical Defence Union Ltd v Department of Trade [1979] 2 WLR 686	3, 27
Mesa Operating Ltd. Partnership v. Amoco Canada Resources Ltd. (1992), 129 A.R. 177 (Q.B.)	149, 151
Metal Scrap & By Products Limited v Federated Conveyors Limited and Tribble (Third Party) [1953] 1 Ll LR 221	101
Metro Gain Sdn Bhd v Commerce Assurance Bhd [2012] 9 MLJ 682	302
Mint Security Ltd v Blair, Thos R Miller & Son (Home) Ltd and EC Darwin Clayton and Co Ltd [1982] 1 Lloyd's Rep 188	47

Mithoolal v Life Insurance Corporation of India AIR (1962) SC 814	212, 213
MLC Insurance Ltd v FAI Traders Insurance Co Ltd (1994) 49 FCR 23	83
MMIP v Yadahavan Veerasamy & 2 Ors [2019] CLJ 1 LNS 606	16
Modern Universal Sdn Bhd v MSIG Insurance (M) Berhad (formerly known as Hong Leong Assurance Bhd) [2014] MLJU 99 (HC)	24
Mohamed Hijazi v New India Assurance Co Ltd (1969) 1 African L Rev Comm. 7	226
Mohamed Isa v Haji Ibrahim [1968] 1 MLJ 186	305
Mopani Copper Mines plc v Millenium Underwriting Ltd [2008] EWHC 1331 (Comm) [2008] All ER (D) 192 (June)	90
Morrison v Muspratt (1827) 4 Bing 60	202
Motor and General Insurance Co Ltd v Pavy [1994] 1 WLR 462	50, 92
Muhamad Rafiq Muiz Ahmad Hanipah v Pacific & Orient Insurance Co Berhad & 2 Ors [2018] CLJ 1 LNS 942	23, 32
Muhammad Zaihasri Hassan v Pacific & Orient Insurance Co Bhd [2019] 3 CLJ p 530	262
Mustafa bin Man & Anor v Pan Global Insurance Bhd [2003] MLJU 117; [2003] 8 CLJ 390	21, 23

Mustapha Ally v The Hand-In-Hand Fire Insurance
    Co Ltd (1965) 9 WIR 242   272

Mutual and Federal Ins Co v Oudtshoorn
    Municipality 1985 (1) SA 419   131

Mutual Life Insurance Co of New York v Ontario
    Metal Products Company Ltd. [1925] A.C. 344   197

Myers and another v Kestrel Acquistions Ltd and
    others [2015] EWHC 916 (Ch)   176

N

Nadarajan A/l Subramaniam v American
    International Assurance Co Ltd [2010]
    MLJU 1775   225, 226

Nanyang Development (1966) Sdn Bhd v How Swee
    Poh [1970] 1 MLJ 145 (FC)   299

Naomi Marble & Granite Pty Ltd v FAI General
    Insurance Co Ltd [1999] 1 Qd R 507   295

Narayanan Chettiar v Official Assignee of the High
    Court, Rangoon (28) AIR 1941   302

Narayanan v Official Assignee, Rangoon AIR
    (1941) PC 93   309

National & General Insurance Co Ltd v South British
    Insurance Co Ltd (1982) 149 CLR 327   64

National Employers' Mutual General Insurance
    Association Ltd v Globe Trawlers Pte Ltd [1991]
    2 MLJ 92   233

National Insurance Co Ltd v S Joseph [1973] 2 MLJ 195; [1973] 1 LNS 97 (HC)	11, 18, 198, 201
National Westminster Bank v Utrecht-America Finance [2001] 3 All ER 733	190
Neal v Secretary, Department of Transport, 3 A.L.D. 97 (FC)	74
Nelson Line (Liverpool) Ltd v James Nelson & Sons Ltd [1908] AC 16	86
Netherlands Insurance Co Est 1845 Ltd v Karl Ljungberg & Co [1986] 2 MLJ 321	116
New Hampshire Ins Co v MGN [1997] LRLR 24	184
New India Assurance Co Ltd v Yeo Beng Chow [1972] 1 MLJ 231	9
New India Insurance Company v Raghava Reddi AIR [1961] AP 295 (SC)	197
Newcastle Fire Insurance Co v Macmorran [1815] UKHL 3 Dow 255	51
Newnham v Baker [1989] 1 Qd R 393	163
Newsholme Brothers v Road Transport and General Insurance Co Ltd [1929] 2 KB 356	194, 223, 225, 226, 234, 236, 238
Newton Chemical Ltd v Arsenis [1989] 1 WLR 1297	276
Ng Chun Lin & Anor v Foo Lian Sin & Anor [2000] 6 MLJ 81	44

Ng Giap Hon v Westcomb Securities Pte Ltd and others [2009] 3 SLR 518	147
Ngu Siew Kong v ING Insurance Bhd [2011] MLJU 719	219, 238
Niger Co Ltd v Guardian Assurance Co Ltd (1922) 13 Ll L Rep 75	180, 184
Niru Battery [2004] QB 985	285
Niru Battery Manufacturing Co v Milestone Trading Ltd [2004] 1 Lloyd's Rep 344	285
Norton v The Royal Fire and Life Assurance C [1885] 1 TLR 460	158
Norwich Union Fire Insurance Society, Ltd v William H Price Ltd [1934] All ER Rep 352, [1934] AC 455	41
Notman v The Anchor Assurance Co (1858) C.B.N.S. 466	97
NSW Medical Defence Union v Transport Industries Ins Co (1985) 4 NSWLR 107	184
NTUC Co-operative Insurance Commonwealth Enterprise Ltd v Chiang Soong Chee [2008] 2 SLR 373	179

O

O'Connor v BDB Kirby Co [1971] 2 All ER 1415 (CA); [1972] 1 QB 90	223, 231, 232

Ogden Industries Pty Ltd v Lucas (1967) 116 CLR 537; (1968) 118 CLR 32	64, 66
Ong Boon Hua @ Chin Peng & Anor v Menteri Hal Ehwal Dalam Negeri, Malaysia [2008] 3 MLJ 625 (CA)	299, 300
Ong Eng Chai v China Insurance Co Ltd [1974] 1 MLJ 82 (HC)	11, 18
Opron Construction Co Ltd (plaintiff) v Her Majesty the Queen in Right of Alberta (1994) 151 A.R. 241.	107, 149, 263
Orica Ltd v CGU Insurance Ltd CA 40559/02, 2003 NSWCA 331	62, 82
Overseas Union Insurance Ltd v Turegum Insurance Co [2001] 3 SLR 330	4, 5

P

Paal Wilson & Co v Partenreederei Hannah Blumenthal [1983] 1 AC 854	105
Pacific & Orient Insurance Co Bhd v Vigneswaran a/l Rajarethinam & Ors [2014] 8 MLJ 423 (HC)	156
Pacific & Orient Insurance Co Sdn Bhd v Cheng Chor Tong & Ors [2006] 5 MLJ 431	20
Pacific & Orient Insurance Co Sdn Bhd v Kathirevelu [1992] 1 MLJ 249 (SC)	12, 196, 215, 216
Pacific & Orient Insurance Sdn Bhd v Lim Sew Chong & Anor [1985] 2 MLJ 60 (HC)	189

Pacific & Orient Underwriters (M) Sdn Bhd v Choo
 Lye Hock [1977] 1 MLJ 131 99

Pacific Carriers Ltd v BNP Paribas [2004] HCA 35,
 (2004) 218 CLR 451 95

Pacific Century Regional Development Ltd v
 Canadian Imperial Investment Pte Ltd [2001] 2
 SLR 443 104

Pan Atlantic Insurance Co Ltd v Pine Top Insurance
 Co Ltd 130, 202, 205, 206,
 [1994] 3 All ER 581 240, 241

Panatron Pte Ltd v Lee Cheow Lee [2001] 3 SLR
 405 (CA) 281, 286, 287

Panchanath a/l Ratnavale (suing as the beneficiary
 to the estate of Ratnavale s/o Mahalingam
 @ Mahalingam Ratnavale deceased under
 will dated 10 February 1971) v Sandra Segara
 Mahalingam (sued as the executor and trustee
 of the last will of Ratnavale s/o Mahalingam
 @ Mahalingam Ratnavale deceased dated 10
 February 1971) & Ors [2012] 5 MLJ 109 309

Pasley v Freeman (1789) 3 Term Rep 51 281, 284, 286

PCW Syndicates v PCW Reinsurers [1996] 1
 WLR 1136 131

Pelly v Royal Exchange Assurance Co. (1757) 97
 ER 342 96

Perembun Consortium (a joint venture between Perembun (M) Sdn Bhd and Road Builder (M) Sdn Bhd) & Anor v AXA Affin General Insurance Bhd (formerly known as AXA Affin Assurance Bhd) [2011] 6 MLJ 719 (HC)	86, 93
Pertab Chunder Ghose v Mohendra Purkait (1888-89) 16 IA 233	288
Petrofina (UK) Ltd & Ors v Magnaload Ltd & Ors [1983] 2 Lloyd Rep 91; [1983] 3 All ER 35	8, 9, 81
Philips Electronique Grand Public SA v British Sky Broadcasting Ltd [1995] EMLR 472	76
Phillips v Foxall (1872) LR 7 QB 666	175
Pilkington United Kingdom Ltd v CGU Insurance plc [2005] 1 All ER (Comm) 283	50
Pine Top Insurance Co Ltd [1995] 1 AC 501 (HL)	182, 287
Pioneer Concrete (UK) Ltd v National Employers Mutual General Insurance Associates Ltd [1985] 1 Lloyd's Rep 274	48, 50
PJ Carrigan Ltd v Norwich Union Fire Society Ltd 987 IR 618	31
PJTV Denson (M) Sdn Bhd & Ors v Roxy (Malaysia) Sdn Bhd [1980] 2 MLJ 136 (FC)	309, 310
Poh Siew Cheng v American International Assurance Co Ltd [2005] 1 LNS 252 (HC)	18
Poh Siew Cheng v American International Assurance Co Ltd [2006] 6 MLJ 57	12, 107, 118, 226

Poh Sin Mining Co v Welfare Insurance Co Ltd
[1971] 1 MLJ 65 — 13

Polygram Records Sdn Bhd v The Search & Anor
[1994] 3 MLJ 127; [1994] 3 CLJ 806 — 69

Post Office v Norwich Union Fire Insurance Society
Ltd [1967] 2 QB 363 — 61, 62

Power Consolidated (China) Pulp Inc v British
Columbia Resources Investment
Corp (1988) 14 ACWS (3d) 11 — 268

Prest v Prest and others [2013] 4 ALL ER 673, SC — 244

Projection v Tai Ping Insurance Co [2001] 2 SLR 399 — 4

Provincial Insurance Co Ltd v Yee Chee Swee [1984]
2 CLJ 12; [1984] 1 CLJ (Rep) 314; [1984] 2 MLJ
60 (FC) — 89, 106

Provincial Insurance Co of Canada v Leduc (1874) LR
6 PC 224 — 59

Prudential Insurance Co v Commissioners of Inland
Revenue [1904] 2 KB 658 — 2

Pub Co v East Crown Ltd [2000] 2 Lloyd's Rep 611 — 116

Putra Perdana Construction Sdn Bhd v AMI
Insurance Bhd & Ors [2005] 2 MLJ 123 — 91, 106

Q

Qualico Developments Ltd. v Calgary (City) (1987), 81 A.R. 161; 53 Alta. L.R. (2d) 129 (Q.B.)	77
Quinby Enterprises v General Accident [1995] 1 NZR 736	201

R

R (on the application of Heather Moor & Edgecomb Ltd) v Financial Ombudsman Service [2008] EWCA Civ 642, [2008] All ER (D) (CA)	127
R v Scott [1975] AC 814	249
R v Secretary of State for the Home Dept, ex p Puttick [1981] 1 All ER 776, [1981] QB 767	245
Raiffeisen Zentralbank Osterreich AG v Archer Daniels Midland Co and Ors [2006] SGHC 182; [2007] 1 SLR 196	261, 277
Rainy Sky SA v Kookmin Bank [2011] UKSC 50, [2012] 1 All ER 1137, [2012] 1 All ER (Comm) 1	140
Ram Chandra Singh v Savitri Devi & Ors (2003) 8 SCC 319	250, 262
Ratna Ammal v Tan Chow Soo [1967] 1 LNS 137; [1967] 1 MLJ 296	302
Ravichanthiran Ganesan v Percetakan Wawasan Maju Sdn Bhd & Ors [2008] MLJU 0488	264
Re Anchor Assurance Co [1870] LR 5 Ch App 632	23, 174

Re Bradley and Essex and Suffolk Accident Indemnity Society [1912] 1 KB 415 (CA)	49, 50, 96, 179
Re Calf & Sun Insurance Office's Arbitration [1920] 2 KB 366	84
Re Etherington and the Lancashire and Yorkshire Insurance Co. [1909] 1 KB 591	96
Re George and Goldsmiths' and General Burglary Insurance Association Ltd [1899] 1 QB 595	89
Re Hand Others (Minors) [1996] AC 563	305
Re Kerr [1943] SASR 8	22, 173
Re Sweeney & Kennedy's Arbitration [1950] IR 85	102
Re Yager & Guardian Assurance Co (1912) 108 LT 38	19
Re Zurich Australian Insurance Ltd (1999) 10 ANZ Ins Cas 61-429	161, 162
Re Zurich Australian Insurance Ltd [1998] QSC 209	84, 132, 162
Reardon Smith Line Ltd v Yngvar Hansen-Tangen [1976] 1 W.L.R. 989	105
Reddaway v Banham [1886] AC 199	247
Regina Fur Co v Bossom [1958] 2 Lloyd's Rep 425	201
Registrar, Workers' Compensation Commission of NSW v National Employers' Mutual General Insurance Assn (1978) 141 CLR 462	83

Rego v Fai General Insurance Company Ltd [2001] WADC 98 (Australia)	209, 277, 279, 295, 296
Reignmont Estate Sdn Bhd v Jaya Ikatan Plantations Sdn Bhd [2013] 9 MLJ 1	302
Rejfek v McElroy (1965) 39 ALJR 177	304
Renard Constructions (ME) Pty v Minister for Public Works (1992) 44 NSWLR 349	136
Reynolds and Anderson v Phoenix Assurance Co Ltd & Ors [1978] 2 Lloyds Rep 440 (QB)	26, 169
RHB Bank Bhd v Yap Ping Kon & Anor [2007] 2 MLJ 65	308
Richard Aubrey Film Productions Ltd. v Graham [1960] 2 Lloyd's Rep 101	24
Roberts v Avon Insurance Co [1956] 2 Lloyd's Rep 240	207
Robertson v French [1803] 4 East 130	83, 88
Royal Botanic Gardens and Domain Trust v Sydney City Council (2002) 186 ALR 289	136
Royal Brunei Airlines Sdn Bhd v Tan [1995] 2 AC 378, [1995] 3 All ER 97, [1995] 3 WLR 64	142, 252
Rozanes v Bowen [1928], 32 Ll.L Rep 98	178
Rust v Abbey Life Insurance Co Ltd [1979] 2 Lloyds Rep 334	3

S

S & M Hotels Ltd v Legal and General Assurance Society Ltd [1972] 1 Lloyd's Rep 157 — 96

S Pearson & Son Ltd v Dublin Corporation [1907] AC 351 (HL) — 192, 292

Saminathan v Pappa [1980] 1 LNS 174; [1981] 1 MLJ 121 — 301, 302, 309

Sandar Aung v Parkway Hospitals Singapore Pte Ltd [2007] 2 SLR(R) 891 — 72

Sawarn Singh a/l Mehar Singh (named as a nominee) v RHB Insurance Bhd [2014] 7 MLJ 416 (HC) — 9, 88, 119, 123

Sawarn Singh Mehar Singh v RHB Insurance Berhad [2013] MLJU 596 (HC) — 1

Schoolman v Hall [1951] 1 Lloyd's Rep 139 — 8, 201, 230, 231

Scotland v Lloyds Banking Group plc [2013] UKSC 3 — 140

Scott v Commissioner of Police for the Metropolis [1975] AC 819, [1974] 3 All ER 1032, [1974] 3 WLR 741 — 248

Seaton v Burnand [1900] AC135 — 265

Sembcorp Marine Ltd v PPL Holdings Pte Ltd and another and another appeal [2013] SGCA 43 (CA) — 72

Seppanen v Seppanen 59 BCLR 26 — 39

Serangoon Garden Estate v Chye Marian [1959] MLJ 113	35
Sere Holdings Limited v Volkswagen Group United Kingdom Limited [2004] EWHC 1551 (Ch)	117
Seri Mukali Sdn Bhd v Kertih Port Sdn Bhd [2012] 7 MLJ 437	302
Sharp and Roarer Investments Ltd v Sphere Drake Insurance PLC Minster Insurance Co Ltd and EC Parker Co Ltd (The Moonacre) [1992] 2 Lloyd's Rep 501	28
Shell Malaysia Trading Sdn Bhd v Tan Bee Leh @ Tan Yue Khoen & Ors [2012] 1 LNS 1071; [2013] 8 MLJ 533	303
Shell Timur Sdn Bhd v Achu Belon [1998] MLJU 476; [1998] 2 CLJ 775	41
Shipley Urban District Council v Bradford Corpn [1936] 1 Ch 375	40, 42
Sim Ah Hee @ Lim Ah Hee & Anor v Affin Bank Bhd and another appeal [2010] 5 MLJ 1 (CA)	86, 93
Sim Thong Realty Sdn Bhd v Teh Kim Dar [2003] 3 MLJ 460; [2003] 4 AMR 460 (CA)	264, 288
Simond v Boydell [1779] 1 Doug KB 268	83
Singapore Tourism Board v Children's Media Ltd and Ors [2008] SGHC 77; [2008] 3 SLR 981	287
Singatronics Ltd v Insurance Co Of North America [1994] 1 SLR 500	82

Sinnayah & Sons Sdn Bhd v Damai Setia Sdn Bhd [2015] 7 CLJ 584	304
Smackman v General Steam Navigation Co. (1908) 13 Com.Cas. 196	110
Smith v Accident Insurance Co (1870) LR 5 Exch 302	83, 102
Smith v Bank of Scotland [1997] SC (HL) 111	137
So Ka Soong v Bank Kerjasama Rakyat (M) Berhad & Lagi [1996] 1 CLJ 783	308
Société Anonymed' Intermediaries Luxembourgeois v Farex Gie [1995] LRLR 116	221
Socimer International Bank Ltd v Standard Bank London Ltd [2008] EWCA Civ 116, [2008] Bus LR 1304, [2008] 1 Lloyd's Rep 558	142
Sofi v Prudential Assurance Co. Ltd. [1993] Vol. 2 Lloyd's Reports 559	33
Soh Keng Hian v American International Assurance Co Ltd [1995] MLJU 234	210
Southern Cross Assurance Company Ltd v Australian Provincial Assurance Association Ltd, (1939) 39 S.R. (NSW) 174	197
Spearson & Son Ltd v Dublin Corporation [1907] AC 351 (HL)	291
Sri Kajang Rock Products Sdn Bhd v Mayban Finance Bhd & Ors [1992] 1 CLJ 204, [1992] 3 CLJ (Rep) 611	4

St Paul Fire and Marine Insurance Co (UK) v McConnell Dowell Constructors Ltd [1996] 1 All ER 96; [1995] 2 Lloyd's Rep 116	206
Stag Line Ltd v Tyne Shiprepair Group Ltd, The Zinnia [1984] 2 Lloyd's Rep 211	175
Standard Chartered Bank v KTS Sdn Bhd [2006] 4 MLJ 617 (FC)	118
Stanley v The Western Insurance Co (1868) LR 3 Ex Ch 71	89
State Government of Perak v Muniandy [1985] 1 LNS 11; [1986] 1 MLJ 490	209
State Mines Control Authority v Government Insurance Office of NSW (1964) 65 SR (NSW) 258	82
Stebbing's case [1917] 2 KB 433	158
Stewart v Merchants Marine Insurance Co (1885) 16 QBD 619 (CA)	83
Stokell v Heywood [1897] 1 Ch 459	22, 173
Stone v Reliance Mutual Insurance Society Ltd [1972] 1 Lloyd's Rep 469	226
Stoneham v The Ocean, Railway, and General Accident Insurance Company (1887) 19 QBD 237	101

Stork Technology Services Asia Pte Ltd (Formerly Known As Eastburn Stork Pte Ltd v First Capital Insurance Ltd) [2006] SGHC 101; [2006] 3 SLR 652   50, 67, 92, 101

Suhaimi bin Ibrahim v United Malayan Insurance Co Ltd [1966] 1 MLJ 140   48

Swan, Hunter & Wigham Richardson Ltd. v. France Fenwide Tyre & Wear Co. Ltd   110

Syarikat Bekalan Air Selangor Sdn Bhd v Kerajaan Negeri Selangor (Kerajaan Malaysia, third party) [2015] 7 MLJ 873 (HC)   16

Syarikat Cheap Hin Toy Mfe Sdn Bhd v Syarikat Perkapalan Kris Sdn Bhd & Anor [1995] 4 CLJ 84   108

Syarikat Tai Yuen Supermarket (Tawau) Sdn Bhd v Mercantile Insurance Sdn Bhd & Anor [1994] 1 CLJ 228   227

Syarikat Uniweld Trading v The Asia Insurance Co. Ltd. [1996] 3 CLJ 142; [1996] 2 MLJ 160   81, 11, 20, 90

Sydney Turf Club v Crowley [1971] 1 NSWLR 724; (1972) 126 CLR 420   82

Sze Hai Tong Bank v Rambler Cycle Co. Ltd. [1959] AC 576   110

T

Tai Lee Finance Co Sdn Bhd v Official Assignee & Ors [1983] 1 MLJ 81   301

Takako Sakao (f) v Ng Pek Yuen (f) & Anor [2009] 6 MLJ 751 (FC)	251
Talasco Insurance Bhd v Goh Thiam Hock [1999] 1 MLJ 179	3
Tan Guat Lan & Anor v Aetna Universal Insurance Sdn Bhd [2003] 1 MLJ 430; [2003] 5 CLJ 384	100, 208, 210, 211
Tan Jing Jeong v Allianz Life Assurance Malaysia [2011] 4 CLJ 710 (HC)	176, 194, 199, 272
Tan Jing Jeong v Allianz Life Insurance Malaysia Bhd & Anor [2012] 7 MLJ 179 (HC)	153, 178, 272
Tan Kang Hua v Safety Insurance Co [1973] 1 MLJ 6 (FC)	11, 189, 200, 294
Tan Kim Khuan v Tan Kee Kiat (M) Sdn Bhd [1998] 1 MLJ 697	300
Tan Kwang Chin v Public Prosecutor [1959] MLJ 253	94
Tan Mooi Sim and Anor v United Overseas Bank (Malaysia) Berhad and Anor [2010] MLJU 945 (HC)	208, 210, 218
Tan Thuan Seng v UMBC Insurans Sdn Bhd, (1997) 3 SLR (R) 725 (18) (High Court, Singapore)	92
Tang Bee Hong v American International Assurance Berhad [2012] MLJU 1386 (HC)	107, 123, 201
Tang Tung Thian & Anor v United Oriental Assurance Sdn Bhd [2000] 5 MLJ 696 (HC)	200

Tang Yoke Kheng v Lek Benedict (2005) 3 SLR 263	304
Tarleton v Staniforth [1794] 5 Term Rep 695	103
Tat Hong Plant Leasing Pte Ltd v Asia Insurance Co Ltd [1993] 3 SLR 563 (CA)	8, 9
Tay Eng Chuan v Ace Insurance Ltd [2008] 4 SLR 95	5, 179
Tay Hean Seng v China Insurance Co Ltd [1953] 1 MLJ 38 (CA) (Singapore)	13, 42
Tay Tho Bok & Anor v Segar Oil Palm Estate Sdn Bhd [1996] 3 MLJ 181; [1996] 1 LNS 60; [1997] 4 AMR 3541; [1996] 4 MLRH 452	259
Tay Wee Khyun v American International Assurance Co Ltd The 'Yuling No 2 [1971] 1 MLJ 218	52
Taylor v Eagle Star Insurance Co. Limited (1940) 67 Lloyd's List L.R. 136	94
Teck Liong (EM) Sdn Bhd v Hong Leong Assurance Sdn Bhd and Another Suit [2001] 7 CLJ 457 (HC)	18, 50
Tenaga Nasional Bhd v Perwaja Steel Sdn Bhd [1995] 4 MLJ 673 (HC)	299
Thames and Mersey Marine Insurance Co Ltd v HT Van Laun & Co [1917] 2 KB 48	200
The 'Melanie' United Oriental Assurance Sdn Bhd Kuantan v WM Mazzarol [1984] 1 MLJ 260	16, 194, 226
The 'Sino Glory' [1997] 4 AMR 3694	251

The "Nai Genova" and "Nai Superba" [1984] 1 Lloyd's Rep 353 (CA)	38
The Bedouin [1894] P 1	294
The Capricorn [1995] 1 Lloyd's Rep. 622	30
The Demetra K [2002] 2 Lloyd's Rep 581	38
The Good Luck [1989] 3 All ER 628 (CA)	55, 175
The People's Insurance Co (M) Sdn Bhd v Narayani a/p Raman (sekarang dikenali sebagai Tahan Insurance (M) Berhad) [2002] MLJU 628; [2003] 1 AMR 712	21, 23
The Puerto Buitrago [1976] 1 Lloyd's Rep 250	49
The Zephyr [1984] 1 Lloyd's Rep 58	6
Thomson v Weems [1884] 9 AC 671	59, 60
Thomson v Weems and Others [1884] 9 AC 671	55
Tierney v Etherington (1743) 97 ER 347	96
Tinline v White Cross Insurance Association Ltd. [1921] 3 KB 327	33
TKM (Singapore) Pte Ltd v Export Credit Insurance Corporation of Singapore Ltd [1993] 1 SLR 1041	100
TNT Australia Pty Ltd v Horne (1995) 36 NSWLR 630	66
TO v Australian Associated Motor Insurers Ltd (2001) 3 VR 279 (Supreme Court of Victoria)	295

Toh Kim Lian & Anor v Asia Insurance Co Ltd [1996] 1 MLJ 149 (HC); [1995] 3 AMR 2304	194, 196, 198, 219
Tokio Marine Insurans (M) Bhd v Mohd Radzi bin Zainuddin & Anor [2012] 8 MLJ 814 (HC)	21
Toll (FGCT) Pty Ltd v Alphapharm Pty Ltd [2004] HCA 52, (2004) 219 CLR	78
Transamerica Life Inc v ING Canada Inc (2003) 68 OR (3d) 457	136
Trans-World (Aluminium) Ltd v Cornelder China (Singapore) [2003] 3 SLR 501	275
Travelsight (M) Sdn Bhd & Anor v Atlas Corp Sdn Bhd [2003] 6 MLJ 658; [2003] 6 CLJ 344	262
Trollope & Colls Ltd v NW Metropolitan Regional Hospital Board [1973] 1 WLR 601	95
TSG Building Services v South Anglia Housing Ltd [2013] EWHC 1151 (TCC), 148 Con LR 228	144
Twenty-First Maylux Pty Ltd v Mercantile Mutual Insurance (Australia) Ltd [1990] VR 919	251
Twinsectra Ltd v Yardley [2002] 2 AC 164	252

U

UN Pandey v Hotel Marco Polo Pte Ltd [1980] 1 MLJ 4	299

Union Insurance Society of Canton Ltd v George Wills & Co [1916] 1 AC 281 — 59

United India Insurance Co Ltd v Pushpalaya Printers (2004) 3 SCC 694 — 93

United Malayan Insurance Co Ltd v Lee Yoon Heng [1964] 1 LNS 212 (HC) — 11, 18

V

Veheng Global Traders Sdn Bhd v AmGeneral Insurance Bhd & Anor and Another Appeal [2019] 7 CLJ 715 — 305

Vodafone Pacific Ltd v Mobile Innovations Ltd [2004] NSWCA 15 — 136

W

Waimiha Sawmilling Co Ltd v Waione Timber Co Ltd [1926] AC 101 — 310

Walford v Miles [1992] 2 AC 128, [1992] 1 All ER 453, [1992] 2 WLR 174 — 133, 146

Watford Electronics Limited v Sanderson CFL Limited [2001] EWCA Civ 317 — 270

Weir v Bell (1878) 3 Exch D 238 — 191

Weiss et al v Schad et al [1999] OTC 228 — 265

Welham v DPP [1961] AC 103, 133, [1960] 1 All ER 805, [1960] 2 WLR 669 — 247

Case	Page
Welwyn Hatfield BC v Secretary of State for Communities and Local Government [2011] UKSC 15; [2011] 4 All ER 851; [2011] 2 AC 304	245
West India and Panama Telegraph Company v Home and Colonial Marine Insurance Company, (1880) 6 Q.B.D. 51	83, 85
West v Hoyle (SC) (Hamilton) [1972] NZLR 996	79
West Wake Price & Co v Ching [1956] 3 All ER 821	24
Western Australian Insurance Co Ltd v Dayton (1924) 35 C.L.R. 355	197
Western Pastoral Co v Eyeington (1971) 125 CLR 342	66
White & Carter (Councils) Ltd v McGregor [1961] 3 All ER 1178 at 1181, [1962] AC 413	53
Wickman v Schuler, [1974] AC 235	49
Wigand v Bachmann-Bechtel Brewing Co, 222 NY 272	135
William Waters and Barnabas Steel v the Monarch Fire and Life Assurance Company [1856] 5EL & BL 870	119
Williams Bros v Ed T Agius Ltd [1914] AC 510	75
Williams v Atlantic Association Co Ltd [1933] 1 KB 81	208

Case	Page
Wilson J in Constitution Insurance Company of Canada v Kosmopoulos |(1987) 34 DLR (4th) 208	31
Wiltrading (WA) Pty Ltd v Lumley General Insurance Ltd [2005] WASCA 106; (2005) 30 WAR 290	163
Wishing Star Ltd v Jurong Town Corp [2008] SGCA 17; [2008] 2 SLR 909	277
Wong Cheong Kong Sdn Bhd v Prudential Assurance Sdn Bhd [1998] 1 CLJ 916; [1998] 3 MLJ 724 (HC)	24, 25, 158, 301
Wong Chong Chow v Pan-Malaysian Cement Works Bhd [1980] 2 MLJ 75	299
Wong Lang Hung v National Employees' Mutual General Insurance Association Ltd [1972] 2 MLJ 191; [1972] 1 LNS 167 (HC)	11, 18
Wooding v Monmouthshire and South Wales Mutual Indemnity Society Ltd [1939] 4 All ER 570	19
Woolcott v Excess Insurance Co Ltd [1979] 1 Lloyd's Rep 231	237
Woolford v Liverpool CC [1968] 2 Lloyd's Rep 256	92
Wyllie v National Mutual Life Association of Australasia Ltd (1997) 217 ALR 324	160

Y

Case	Page
Yam Seng Pte Ltd v International Trade Corporation Ltd [2011] EWHC 111	133

Yangtsze Insurance Association v Indemnity Mutual Marine Assurance Co [1908] 2 KB 504	86
Yap Boon Keng Sonny v Pacific Prince International Pte Ltd and Another [2008] SGHC 161; [2009] 1 SLR 385	275, 281
Yew Yin Lai v Teo Meng Hai & Anor [2013] 8 MLJ 78	300
Yong Fui Tong v United Oriental Assurance Sdn Bhd [1996] 1 BLJ 455; [1996] MLJU 559	21
Yong Tim v Hoo Kok Chong & Anor [2005] 3 CLJ 229	303
Yonge v Toynbee [1910] 1 K.B. 215	291
Yorke v Yorkshire Insurance Company (1918) 1 KB 662	92
Yorkshire Insurance Co Ltd v Campbell [1917] AC 218	104
Youell v Bland Welch & Co [1990] 2 Lloyd's Rep 423 (HC); [1992] 2 Lloyd's Rep 127 (CA)	7

Z

Zurich General Accident and Liability Insurance Co v Morrison & Ors [1942] 2 KB 53	195, 210, 293
Zurich Insurance (Singapore) Pte Ltd v B-Gold Interior Design & Construction Pte Ltd [2008] 3 SLR (R) 1029 (CA)	14, 72, 79

TABLE OF LEGISLATION

A

Administrative of Justice (Miscellaneous Provisions) Act 1933 (UK)
s 6(1)(a)   247

C

Civil Law Act (Cap 43) (Singapore)   37
s 5   9

Civil Law Act 1956 (Malaysia)
s 5(1)   128
s 5(2)   128

Contracts Act 1950 (Malaysia)
s 17   69, 249

E

Evidence Act (Singapore)
s 100   16, 80
s 93   15, 79
s 94   15, 16, 79, 80
s 94(f)   15, 80
s 95   16, 80
s 96   16, 80
s 97   16, 80
s 98   16, 80
s 99   16, 80

Evidence Act 1950 (Malaysia)
s 101 — 298, 299, 300
s 102 — 301
s 103 — 301
s 91 — 12, 219, 224
s 92 — 12, 219, 224

Evidence Ordinance 1950 (Malaysia)
s 92(f) — 14

F

Financial Services Act 2013 (Malaysia) — 129, 187, 211, 225, 227
s 129 — 215
para 12, sch 9, s 129 — 227
para 13(2), sch 9, s 129 — 210, 213, 214
para 4(1), sch 9, s 129 — 186, 188, 189, 217,
para 4(2), sch 9, s 129 — 187, 227
para 4(3), sch 9, s 129 — 227
para 5, sch 9, s 129 — 216, 217

I

Industrial Assurance Act 1923 (UK)
s 20(4) — 225

Insurance Act 1938 (India)
s 45 — 212

Insurance Act 1963 (Malaysia) — 187, 211
s 15C — 211
s 15C(4) — 211, 212, 213, 214, 215
s 44A — 226, 227

Insurance Act 1996 (Malaysia) — 129, 187, 211, 225, 227
s 147 — 211
s 147(4) — 210, 212, 213
s 149(4) — 217
s 150 — 186, 227
s 150(1) — 188, 189

s 150(2)	187, 227
s 150(3)	188, 227
s 151(1)	227, 228

Insurance Act 1971 (Jamaica)
s 74(1)	226

Insurance Contracts Act 1984 (Australia)
s 13	160, 161, 163
s 13(1)	160
s 14	160, 163
s 21	278
s 28	278
s 37	160

L

Life Assurance Companies (Compulsory Liquidation) Act 1962 (Malaysia) 187

Life Insurance Act 1774 (UK)
s 1	29

Limitation Act (UK)
s 29	256

M

Marine Insurance Act 1906 (UK) 57, 58, 127
s 4	129
s 5	29
s 7(1)	66
s 17	56, 131, 159, 167, 181, 182, 186, 191, 202, 222
s 18	56, 131, 167, 168, 190, 191, 195, 221
s 18(1)	9, 82, 132
s 18(2)	132, 196
s 18(3)(b)	190
s 18(3)(c)	189
s 18(4)	203
s 19	131, 168, 191, 203, 220, 221

s 20	56, 131, 168, 191
s 20(1)	221
s 20(2)	221
s 20(3)	258
s 20(4)	258
s 20(5)	258
s 20(6)	258
s 20(7)	203
s 24	164
s 24(1)	164
s 30	128
s 33	55, 56
s 33(3)	57, 60, 61
s 34(3)	56, 60
s 36	56
s 39(5)	180
s 42	56, 60
s 45	56
s 46	56
s 48	56
s 91(2)	241
s 95	28
s 97	28

Marine Insurance Act 1963 (India) 31

Misrepresentation Act 1967 (UK) 177
s 2(1)	203, 241, 296
s 2(2)	296

Misrepresentation Act (Cap 390, 1994 Rev Ed) (Singapore)
s 3	270

R

Road Traffic Act 1934 (UK) — 293

Rules of Court 2012 (Malaysia)
O 18 r 12(1)(a) — 307
O 35 r 4(6) — 306

S

Specific Relief Act 1950 (Malaysia)
s 30 — 43

U

Unfair Contract Terms Act (Cap 396, 1994 Rev Ed) (Singapore)
s 11 — 270

CHAPTER 1

CONTRACTS OF INSURANCE

INTRODUCTION

This chapter examines the formation of the insurance contract, which includes the offer and acceptance found in the proposal form, the nature of the insurance contract and its terms and conditions.

Policies or contracts of insurance are but a species of contracts. The terms and conditions of insurance contracts are frequently regarded or thought of as "standard". However, in reality, what those terms and conditions are, may be entirely a matter of agreement between the parties. For the seller or provider of the insurance cover, there would be a variety or range of policies on offer, to suit different needs or demands. For the buyer of the insurance cover, it would be a matter of what the requirement or the need for the cover is in the first place; the length or period of the cover; and sometimes, a matter of finance or the cost of the policy. Different names or descriptions are given to the array of policies of insurance that are available in the market. These policies are frequently marketed or advertised through pamphlets or brochures introducing the potential buyer to the product of insurance being sold, which in turn contains the proposal and declaration forms which, if accepted by the insurance companies, are generally incorporated into the contract of insurance, thus forming a part of that contract of insurance.[1]

There are various definitions of a contract of insurance. Some of the more recognised definitions are provided below.

---

[1] *Sawarn Singh Mehar Singh v RHB Insurance Berhad* [2013] MLJU 596 (HC).

A contract of insurance in the widest sense of the term may be defined as a contract whereby one person, called the 'Insurer', undertakes, in return for the agreed consideration, called the 'Premium', to pay to another person, called the 'Assured' or 'Insured', a sum of money, or its equivalent, on the happening of a specified event. The specified event must have some element of uncertainty to it; the uncertainty may be either (a) in the case of life insurance, the fact that although the event is bound to happen in the ordinary course of nature, the time of its happening is uncertain; or (b) where the happening of an event is due to accidental causes, it is possible that the event may never happen at all. In the latter case, the event is called an accident. The specified event must further be of a character more or less adverse to the interest of the assured, or in other words, the accident must, if it happens, be calculated to result in loss to the assured.[2]

A contract of insurance is an agreement whereby one party, generally referred to as the insurer ('the insurance company'), promises to pay the assured person a sum of money or benefits, on payment of, inter alia, a money consideration (normally referred to as the 'premium'), on the happening of an event or events covered by the agreement.[3]

Put in another way, a contract of insurance arises when one party (the insurer) promises, in return for a money consideration (the premium), to pay to the other party (the assured), a sum of money or provides him with some corresponding benefit, upon the occurrence of one or more specified events.

A contract of insurance, then, must be a contract for the payment of a sum of money, or for some corresponding benefit such as the rebuilding of a house or the repairing of a ship, to become due on the happening of an event.[4]

---

[2] ER Hardy Ivamy in 'General Principles of Insurance Law' (p 3, (4th Ed), Butterworths, 1979).

[3] *Prudential Insurance v Commissioners of Inland Revenue* [1904] 2 KB 658, Mac Gillivray on Insurance Law (9th Ed).

[4] Channeil J in *Prudential Insurance Co v Commissioners of Inland Revenue* [1904] 2 KB 658, at p 664.

Essentially, it is a contract and the rules governing contracts, in general, are applicable to it. It is usually made with reference to a specified event, the occurrence of which is uncertain. It is this uncertainty that forms the basis of the contract, in that, it insures against the risk of the occurrence of the specified event.[5]

These three things can be stated to be the characteristics of an insurance contract. First, the contract must provide that the assured will become entitled to something on the occurrence of some event, second, the event must be one which involves some element of uncertainty and third, the assured must have an insurable interest in the subject matter of the contract.[6] Suriyadi J in *Talasco Insurance Bhd v Goh Thiam Hock* [1999] 1 MLJ 179 defined what a policy of insurance was. His Lordship stated:

> Essentially, it is a contract and the rules governing contracts in general are applicable to a contract of insurance. Usually, a contract of insurance is made with reference to a specified event where the occurrence of which is uncertain. It is this uncertainty that forms the basis of the contract in that it insures against the risk of the occurrence of the specified event.

FORMATION

An insurance contract can be viewed in terms of offer and acceptance. The submission of the proposal form from the proposer to the insurer is considered to be the offer. A contract of insurance comes into being only when the proposal is accepted by the insurer. Thus, in *Rust v Abbey Life Insurance Co Ltd* [1979] 2 Lloyds Rep 334, it was decided, inter alia, by the English High Court and upheld by the Court of Appeal, that a contract between an assured and an insurer was concluded when the insurer accepted an application made by the assured.[7]

---

[5] *Talasco Insurance Bhd v Goh Thiam Hock* [1999] 1 MLJ 179.

[6] *Medical Defence Union Ltd v Department of Trade* [1979] 2 WLR 686. See also *Mary Colete John v South East Asia Insurance Bhd* [2010] 2 MLJ 222 (CA).

[7] *Aetna Universal Insurance Sdn Bhd v Fanny Foo May Wan* [2001] 1 MLJ 227.

To constitute a valid contract there must be separate and definite parties to it; those parties must be in agreement, that is, there must be a consensus *ad idem*; those parties must intend to create legal relations in the sense that the promises made by each side are to be enforceable, simply because they are contractual promises and the promises made by each party must be supported by consideration.[8]

The legal principles to be applied when one is construing the effect of negotiations between parties was explained by Her Ladyship Judith Prakash J in *Overseas Union Insurance Ltd v Turegum Insurance Co* [2001] 3 SLR 330 where it was held:

> They are set out in well-known texts such as Treitel - The Law of Contract (10th Ed) and Cheshire, Fifoot and Furmston's Law of Contract — Second Singapore and Malaysian Edition (1998) by Professor Andrew Phang. There is also a useful discussion on the principles applicable to protracted negotiations in the recent case of *Projection v Tai Ping Insurance Co* [2001] 2 SLR 399. The test for determining whether the parties have reached agreement is usually to ask whether an offer has been made by one party and whether that specific offer has been accepted by the other. Alternatively, in a situation where there have been protracted documentary negotiations with much modification of terms, it may be more useful to look at the whole correspondence and decide whether, on its true construction the parties had agreed to the same terms (see the Projection case). In either case, an objective test is applied to decide whether the parties have reached agreement. This means that an apparent intention to be bound may suffice, that is to say, a party may be bound if his conduct is such as to induce a reasonable person to believe that he intends to be bound even though he actually has no such intention. If, however, the offeree is aware that the offeror did not have an intention to be bound then an acceptance by the offeree will not bind the offeror.

---

[8] Per VC George J in *Sri Kajang Rock Products Sdn Bhd v Mayban Finance Bhd & Ors* [1992] 1 CLJ 204, [1992] 3 CLJ (Rep) 611.

[29] An offer, once made, may be terminated in various ways. One of these ways is by rejection. As Treitel states, an offeree who attempts to accept an offer on new terms, not contained in the original offer, may be rejecting the original offer and instead making a counter-offer. Such offeree cannot later accept the original offer. To accept an offer, the offeree must, as Professor Phang states 'unreservedly assent to the exact terms proposed by the offeror. If, while purporting to accept the offer as a whole, he introduces a new term which the offeror has not had a chance of examining, he is in fact making a counter-offer.' When such a counter-offer is made, no contract will result unless the counter-offer is accepted by the offeror.

However, in relation to insurance contracts it must be realised that they are invariably drafted and/or vetted by experts to protect the interests of the insurers, and the assured generally have little choice but to accept the terms thereof.[9]

Her Ladyship Judith Prakash J also had occasion to trace the formation of a specific type of contract, that is the reinsurance contract in *Overseas Union Insurance Ltd v Turegum Insurance Co* [2001] 3 SLR 330 where a very useful account was provided as to how reinsurance contracts come about. Her Ladyship stated at pp 350–351:

> The background
>
> 69 There are four reinsurance contracts which are now in issue between OUI and Turegum ...
>
> 70 Before I go on to discuss the issues relating to these contracts, it would be helpful to give a brief account of how such contracts usually come about. An insurance contract placed in the London market is initiated when an insurance broker presents a proposal for insurance or reinsurance to underwriters at Lloyds or to insurance companies. The procedure is described by Lord Diplock in *American Airlines Inc v Hope* [1974] 2 Lloyd's Rep 301 at

---

[9] *Tay Eng Chuan v Ace Insurance Ltd* [2008] 4 SLR 95.

304–305. What happens is that the broker acting for the assured prepares the slip (a folded card) and indicates in brief terms the cover the assured requires. Thereafter, as Lord Diplock says:

> '... He takes the slip ... to an underwriter whom he has selected to deal with as leading underwriter, i.e., one who has a reputation in the market as an expert in the kind of cover required and whose lead is likely to be followed by other insurers in the market. If it is the first contract of insurance covering that risk in which a particular underwriter has acted as leading underwriter it is treated as an original insurance. The broker and the leading underwriter go through the slip together. They agree on any amendments to the broker's draft and fix the premium. When agreement has been reached the leading underwriter initials the slip for his proportion of the cover and the broker then takes the initialled slip round the market to other insurers who initial it for such proportion of the cover as each is willing to accept. For practical purposes, all the negotiations about the terms of the insurance and the rate of premium are carried on between the broker and the leading underwriter alone ... After the slip has been initialled by all the insurers it is retained by the broker. In due course, often after several months, he prepares the policy from the slip. In the case of an original insurance he generally agrees the wording of the policy with the leading underwriter before taking it to Lloyd's Policy Signing Office for signature.'

71 When the slip is signed, it constitutes a binding contract. At that stage, the whole of the contract is found in the slip. It has been described as 'free-standing'. See *Insurance Co of the State of Pennsylvania v Grand Union Insurance Co* [1990] 1 Lloyd's Rep 208 and *The Zephyr* [1984] 1 Lloyd's Rep 58. OUI relies on these principles in relation to the two slips (for contracts 3TD70 and 3TG71) which it has in its possession and argues that since these slips do not contain arbitration clauses or any reference to any arbitration clause in any other document, the contracts of

insurance do not contain any agreement to submit disputes to arbitration.

72 The slip is usually only the first stage in the process. Following its signing, the broker will issue a cover note to its own client confirming the cover which has been placed on the client's behalf. As stated in The Law of Reinsurance in England and Bermuda by O'Neill and Woloniecki, the cover note is not provided to the insurer and thus cannot be a contractual document. It is, however, prima facie evidence of a contract and may be used to establish the terms of that contract when the slip is lost.

73 Further, it is often clear from the slip itself that the parties intend that a policy or treaty wording be issued subsequently. The purpose of this is to expand on the terms found in the slip which are usually short and often only titles of the clauses required. According to another text, Reinsurance Practice and The Law (1993) put out by a firm called Barlow, Lyde and Gilbert, once a wording is executed by both parties, it replaces the slip as a contract document. Should any inconsistency between the slip and the wording need to be resolved, it is the wording which is paramount. This statement was based on the holding in *Youell v Bland Welch & Co* [1990] 2 Lloyd's Rep 423 (HC); [1992] 2 Lloyd's Rep 127 (CA) which discussed the ranking of the slip versus the wording and ruled that if formal wording was subsequently issued, the slip would be inadmissible as an aid to construction of the policy. The judge at first instance, Philips J, also stated:

> 'An insurance slip customarily sets out a shorthand version of the contract of insurance, in terms which may neither be clear nor complete. Where, as here, the slip provides for the formal wording to be agreed by the leading underwriter, the other subscribers to the risk anticipate and agree that the leading underwriter will, on their behalf, agree the final wording that will spell out their rights and obligations. If differences between the wording of the slip and that of the formal contract which is embodied in the policy give rise to the possibility

that the natural meaning of the slip differs from that of the policy, the natural assumption is and should be that the wording of the policy has been designed the better to reflect the agreement between the parties. To refer to the slip as an aid to construction of the policy runs counter to one of the objects of replacing the slip with the policy.'

In the *Petrofina (UK) Ltd & Ors v Magnaload Ltd & Ors* case [1983] 2 Lloyd Rep 91, the 'insured' in the insurance policy was defined as '... Lindsey Oil Refinery and/or Foster Wheeler Ltd and/or ... sub-contractors'.[10]

The offer to enter into a contract of insurance may, as a general rule, be considered as being addressed to the insurers by the person who is seeking to protect himself against loss through insurance. He may have been invited by the insurers to put himself into communication with them; but, whether the invitation comes to him from the insurers direct, or through the medium of an agent, or whether it is given to him personally, or only as a member of the public through an advertisement, the position remains unchanged, and he must submit his proposal, which they may accept or decline at their pleasure. The offer, therefore, proceeds from the proposer when he has filled up the proposal and forwarded it to the insurers.[11]

The proposal form, in practice, originates from the insurers, and it further shows the terms upon which they are willing to contract. They are bound, therefore, after acceptance, to issue a policy in accordance with the proposal.[12] There is no presumption in insurance law that matters that are not dealt with in a proposal form are not material.[13] In *Dawson Ltd v Bonnin & Ors* [1922] 2 AC 413, it was held that where the statements contained in a proposal form formed the basis of a contract of insurance,

---

[10] *Tat Hong Plant Leasing Pte Ltd v Asia Insurance Co Ltd* [1993] 3 SLR 563 (CA).

[11] General Principles of Insurance Law (6th Ed) by ER Hardy Ivamy at p 111.

[12] General Principles of Insurance Law (6th Ed) by ER Hardy Ivamy at p 117.

[13] *Schoolman v Hall* [1951] 1 Lloyd's Rep 139, 142.

the truth of the statements in the proposal form was a condition on the liability of the insurer.

Once the terms and conditions in the contract of insurance are acceptable to both parties, it will be binding on them. As was stated by Viscount Dilhorne in *New India Assurance Co Ltd v Yeo Beng Chow* [1972] 1 MLJ 231 '... if conditions inserted by insurance companies are accepted by the insured, they are binding upon him'. See also *Sawarn Singh Mehar Singh v RHB Insurance Bhd* [2014] 7 MLJ 416 (HC).

The date of the conclusion of the insurance contract, is the date of the acceptance of the proposal or the date when the 'slip' is initialled by the insurers.[14]

PROPOSAL FORM

The proposal form, when duly filled in and signed by the proposer and forwarded to the insurers, operates as a formal offer by the proposer to the insurers to enter into a contract of insurance. The proposal form shows the terms on which the proposer is willing to contract, and if the offer is accepted, he cannot insist on having an insurance differing in its terms from those specified in the proposal.[15]

In *Madam Loh Sai Nyah v American International Assurance Co Ltd* [1998] 2 MLJ 310, Abdul Malek Ahmad JCA examined the formation of an insurance contract in relation to the proposal form and the payment of premiums. Reference was made to General Principles of Insurance Law (6th Ed) by ER Hardy Ivamy at p 111:

---

[14] See Section 18(1) of the UK Marine Insurance Act 1906. Section 18(1) is applicable in Singapore by way of Section 5 of the Civil Law Act (Cap 43). *Tat Hong Plant Leasing Pte Ltd v Asia Insurance Co Ltd* [1993] 3 SLR 563 (CA). See also *Petrofina (UK) Ltd & Ors v Magnaload Ltd & Ors* [1983] 2 Lloyd Rep 91.

[15] General Principles of Insurance Law (6th Ed) by ER Hardy Ivamy at p 111.

Thus, where the premium to be charged has to be settled by the insurers after consideration of the particulars furnished by the proposer, the offer to enter into a contract of insurance is made by the insurers when they settle the premium and inform the proposer of this fact, whilst the proposer, by tendering the premium, accepts their offer and does not merely offer to contract with them upon their terms.

The author further states at p 117 that "since the proposal form, in practice, proceeds from the insurers, it further shows the terms upon which they too are willing to contract. They are bound, therefore, after acceptance, to issue a policy in accordance with the proposal".

...A careful check of the relevant text shows that learned counsel had only chosen the excerpts which sound favourable to him. As for the first excerpt, it is actually preceded by the following passage at p 110:

> The offer to enter into a contract of insurance may, as a general rule, be considered as addressed to the insurers by the person who is seeking to protect himself by insurance against loss. He may have been invited by the insurers to put himself into communication with them; but, whether the invitation comes to him from the insurers direct, or through the medium of an agent, or whether it is given to him personally, or only as a member of the public through an advertisement, the position remains unchanged, and he must submit his proposal, which they may accept or decline at their pleasure. The offer, therefore, proceeds from the proposed assured when he has filled up the proposal and forwarded it to the insurers.

The second excerpt is also preceded by the following extract which appears at the bottom of p 116 and the top of p 117:

> The proposal form, when duly filled in and signed by the proposed assured and forwarded to the insurers,

> operates as a formal offer by the proposed assured to the insurers to enter into a contract of insurance. The proposal form shows the terms on which he is willing to contract, and if the offer is accepted, he cannot insist on having an insurance differing in its terms from those specified in the proposal.

Thus, once a person signs a proposal form, he is bound by its contents.[16]

It has been held that even though the proposal was in the English language and the insured could neither read, write nor understand the language, he was deemed to be bound by it.[17]

A court has to go through a fourfold process with respect to the construction of questions in a proposal for insurance as follows. First, the court looks at the true construction of the words, second, the court asks whether the words are ambiguous, third, it asks what the assured apparently understood by the words and last, it asks whether a reasonable person in the circumstances would have understood the question in the same way as the assured. In *Advance (NSW) Insurance Agencies Pty Ltd v Matthews* 1987 NSW Lexis 7046; BC8701330, Young J said:

> It is axiomatic that with any set of words there is only one true construction of them. The court can always say what that true construction is and often is asked by parties to exercise that power.

---

[16] *United Malayan Insurance Co Ltd v Lee Yoon Heng* [1964] MLJ 453; *Wong Lang Hung v National Employees' Mutual General Insurance Association Ltd* [1972] 2 MLJ 191, *China Insurance Co Ltd v Ngau Ah Kau* [1972] 1 MLJ 52, *Tan Kang Hua v Safety Insurance Co* [1973] 1 MLJ 6, *National Insurance Co Ltd v S Joseph* [1973] 2 MLJ 195 and *Ong Eng Chai v China Insurance Co Ltd* [1974] 1 MLJ 82).

[17] *United Malayan Insurance Co Ltd v Lee Yoon Heng* [1964] MLJ 453, *Syarikat Uniweld Trading v The Asia Insurance Co Ltd* [1996] 2 MLJ 160.(See also the case of Jamilah Ibrahim/Muhamad Haziq Asyraf v Liberty Insurance Bhd [2018] CLJ 1 LNS 812)

A fair and reasonable construction must be placed on the questions in the proposal form.[18]

Evidence cannot be introduced on the explanation by an insurance agent on how answers to certain questions in the proposal form were inserted. That would run afoul of SS 91 and 92 of the Malaysian Evidence Act 1950.

When a transaction is recorded in a document, it is not generally permissible to adduce other evidence of (a) its terms or (b) other terms not included, expressly or by reference, in the document or (c) its writer's intended meaning. There are here three distinct rules which exclude what is known as extrinsic evidence, i.e., evidence outside or extrinsic to the document. The evidence excluded is usually oral, but it may be documentary evidence. The three rules, either separately or together, are sometimes known as the parol evidence rule.

The first rule excludes a particular means of proof, namely secondary evidence of a document: where the rule applies, it prevents the contents of the document being proved by any means other than the production of the document. This is more usually known as the "best evidence rule". By the second rule, extrinsic evidence is inadmissible for the purpose of adding to, varying, contradicting or subtracting from the terms of the document: the writing is conclusive. The third rule deals with the admissibility of facts in aid of the interpretation or construction of documents.[19]

In other words, once the terms of the insurance have been recorded in a policy, there is a presumption that the policy contains all the terms of the cover, with the consequence that extrinsic evidence, whether oral or in writing, cannot be introduced to contradict, vary, add to or cut down the terms set out in the policy. There is a second rule, i.e., one on the construction of contracts, to the effect that where the words of a

---

[18] *Pacific and Orient Insurance Co Sdn Bhd v Kathirevelu* [1992] 1 MLJ 249, *Poh Siew Cheng v American International Assurance Co Ltd* [2006] 6 MLJ 57.

[19] The UK, Law Commission, Law of Contract: The Parol Evidence Rule (Law Com No 154, 1986) (Chairman: Beldam J) ("Law Com No 154") at para 1.2, the Law Commission of England and Wales ("the Law Commission").

policy or other document recording the terms of the insurance contract possesses a clear meaning, extrinsic evidence is inadmissible to show that the parties intended them to bear a different meaning.[20]

Where there is ambiguity, that would be an exception to the parol evidence rule and extrinsic evidence would be admissible. Where there is a latent ambiguity, that would also be an exception to the parol evidence rule and extrinsic evidence is admissible to identify the persons or things referred to in the document. His Lordship, Knight J in *Tay Hean Seng v China Insurance Co Ltd* [1953] 1 MLJ 38 (CA) (Singapore) commented on the admission of parol evidence where there was evidence of ambiguity:

> The appellant's case in the Court below and here has been argued on two grounds (1) that on the natural construction of the policy itself without the admission of parole evidence to vary it, the appellant's pillion passenger was clearly covered and (2) that if he was not, the policy should be rectified to cover such passenger. Parole evidence, of course, tending to vary the written contract was inadmissible on the first of those grounds but became admissible on the second as relevant to proving that the contracting parties' minds were not ad idem. As I see it, however, unless it is ambiguous, I should be wrong in construing this contract other than from its written terms and the practice of Insurance Companies in Singapore as testified to by the Company's witnesses, is not only irrelevant — but should be completely disregarded.

Extrinsic evidence is always admissible, not to contradict or vary the contract, but to apply it to the facts which the parties had in their minds and were negotiating about.[21]

Chang Min Tat J in *Poh Sin Mining Co v Welfare Insurance Co Ltd* [1971] 1 MLJ 65 was of the view that there was in existence latent ambiguity when

---

[20] MacGillivray on Insurance Law (Nicholas Legh-Jones gen ed) (Sweet & Maxwell, 10th Ed, 2003).

[21] *Bank of New Zealand v Simpson* [1900] AC 182 at page 187.

the policy was set against the surrounding circumstances. His Lordship said:

> The rule is thus stated in Taylor on Evidence, 8th ed. vol. ii, s. 1194: 'It may be laid down as a broad and distinct rule of law that extrinsic evidence of every material fact which will enable the court to ascertain the nature and qualities of the subject-matter of the instrument, or, in other words to identify the persons and things to which the instrument refers must of necessity be received.' In *Grant v Grant* LR 5 CP 727 at p 728, Blackburn J. quoted judicially the following passage from his valuable work on Contract of Sale (p. 49): 'The general rule seems to be that all facts are admissible which tend to shew the sense the words bear with reference to the surrounding circumstances of and concerning which the words were used, but that such facts as only tend to shew that the writer intended to use words bearing a particular sense are to be rejected.'
>
> ...And as a matter of construction, in the light of the evidence and the surrounding circumstances which are in my view admissible in evidence under section 92(f) of the Evidence Ordinance, I find as a fact that the insured was the plaintiff company.

It has even been held that despite clear and unambiguous wordings of a contract, extrinsic evidence could be admitted to show what really ought to be the conclusive interpretation of the wordings and intention of the parties to the contract. The Court of Appeal in Singapore in *Zurich Insurance (Singapore) Pte Ltd v B-Gold Interior Design & Construction Pte Ltd* [2008] 3 SLR (R) 1029 (CA) discussed the approach adopted in Singapore on the admissibility of extrinsic evidence and its effect on written contracts:

> (a) A court should take into account the essence and attributes of the document being examined. The court's treatment of extrinsic evidence at various stages of the analytical process may differ depending on the nature of the document. In general, the court ought to be more reluctant to allow extrinsic evidence to affect standard form contracts and commercial documents;

(b) If the court is satisfied that the parties intended to embody their entire agreement in a written contract, no extrinsic evidence is admissible to contradict, vary, add to, or subtract from its terms (see ss 93- ss 94 of the Evidence Act). In determining whether the parties so intended, our courts may look at extrinsic evidence and apply the normal objective test, subject to a rebuttable presumption that a contract which is complete on its face was intended to contain all the terms of the parties' agreement. In other words, where a contract is complete on its face, the language of the contract constitutes prima facie proof of the parties' intentions;

(c) Extrinsic evidence is admissible under proviso (f) to s 94 to aid in the interpretation of the written words. Our courts now adopt, via this proviso, the modern contextual approach to interpretation, in line with the developments in England in this area of the law to date. Crucially, ambiguity is not a prerequisite for the admissibility of extrinsic evidence under proviso (f) to s 94;

(d) The extrinsic evidence in question is admissible so long as it is relevant, reasonably available to all the contracting parties and relates to a clear or obvious context. However, the principle of objectively ascertaining contractual intention(s) remains paramount. Thus, the extrinsic evidence must always go towards proof of what the parties, from an objective viewpoint, ultimately agreed upon. Further, where extrinsic evidence in the form of prior negotiations and subsequent conduct is concerned, we find the views expressed in McMeel's article (supra) and Nicholls' article (supra) persuasive. For the reason, there should be no absolute or rigid prohibition against evidence of previous negotiations or subsequent conduct, although, in the normal case, such evidence is likely to be inadmissible for non-compliance with the requirements set out above. (We should add that the relevance of subsequent conduct remains a controversial and evolving topic that will require more extensive scrutiny by this court at a more appropriate juncture). Declarations of subjective intent remain inadmissible except for the purpose of giving meaning to terms which have been determined to be latently ambiguous;

(e) In some cases, the extrinsic evidence in question leads to possible alternative interpretations of the written words (i.e, the court determines that latent ambiguity exists). A court may give effect to these alternative interpretations, always bearing in mind s 94 of the Evidence Act. In arriving at the ultimate interpretation of the words to be construed, the court may take into account subjective declarations of intent. Furthermore, the normal canons of interpretation apply in conjunction with the relevant provisions of the Evidence Act, i.e, ss 95-100;

(f) A court should always be careful to ensure that extrinsic evidence is used to explain and illuminate the written words, and not to contradict or vary them. Where the court concludes that the parties have used the wrong words, rectification may be a more appropriate remedy.

See also *Syarikat Bekalan Air Selangor Sdn Bhd v Kerajaan Negeri Selangor (Kerajaan Malaysia, third party)* [2015] 7 MLJ 873 (HC).

An omission by the assured to state an earlier mishap in a proposal form was therefore not his fault but that of the insurance company themselves for framing ambiguous questions. Such ambiguity must be resolved, according to the *contra proferentum* rule in favour of the assured respondent.[22]

BASIS CLAUSE

A proposal form generally contains a declaration by the assured that all answers and statements made in the proposal are true in every respect. It will then contain a 'basis clause'; that is, a statement that the proposal and declaration are the basis of the policy and are considered as being incorporated into it.

---

[22] *The 'Melanie' United Oriental Assurance Sdn Bhd Kuantan v WM Mazzarol* [1984] 1 MLJ 260, Marine Insurance, Ivamy 3rd. Ed. p. 358.(*See also the case of MMIP v Yadahavan Veerasamy & 2 ors* [2019 CLJ 1 LNS 606.)

The legal effect of a basis clause in a proposal form is that it entitles the insurer to avoid the contract simply by showing that the statement was inaccurate or incorrect.[23] The effect of the basis clause was examined in *Leong Kum Whay v QBE Insurance (M) Sdn Bhd & Ors* [2006] 1 CLJ 1 (CA), where it was stated:

> Its effect is that when answers, including that in question, are declared to be the basis of the contract, this can only mean that their truth is made a condition, exact fulfilment of which is rendered by stipulation foundational to its enforceability" (per Viscount Haldane in *Dawsons Ltd v. Bonnin* [1922] 2 AC 413.) And, once parties to a policy agree that something should be the basis of their contract, it is not open to the court to consider the question of materiality". Per Suffian FJ in *China Insurance Co Ltd v Ngau Ah Kau* [1971] 1 LNS 20; [1972] 1 MLJ 52.

Where there is a 'basis clause' the usual declaration at the foot of the proposal form that the answers are true, and that they are to be the basis of the proposed contract of insurance, makes the truth of the answers a condition precedent, and the proposed assured, by signing it, signifies his agreement thereto.[24]

In *Aetna Universal Insurance Sdn Bhd v Fanny Foo May Wan* [2001] 1 MLJ 227, it was stated that the following principles applied:

> (i) There is no necessity to show that the misstatement is material to the risk insured. In *Anderson Samuel v Ann Fitzgerald* (1853) 4 HLC 484, the court held that the representation being part of the contract, its truth, not its materiality was in question;
>
> (ii) The knowledge of an insured as to the truth of a statement is irrelevant. As such, we are not concerned at all with the mens rea of the insured but only whether the alleged statement is correct.

---

[23] In *Aetna Universal Insurance Sdn Bhd v. Fanny Foo May Wan* [2001] 1 CLJ 476.

[24] Hardy Ivamy's General Principles of Insurance Law (2nd Ed) (at p 132).

The law on a basis clause in Malaysia is well settled, in that, where there is such a clause, the parties have thereby agreed that the truthfulness of the answers is the basis of the contract and, therefore, it is the condition precedent to the very existence of the contract. There are a number of authorities an insurer defendant may rely on for that proposition of the law: (1) *China Insurance Co. Ltd v Ngau Ah Kau* [1971] 1 LNS 20, FC; (2) *Wong Lang Hung v National Employees' Mutual General Insurance Association Ltd* [1972] 1 LNS 167, HC; (3) *National Insurance Co. Ltd v S. Joseph* [1973] 1 LNS 97, HC; (4) *Ong Eng Chai v China Insurance Co. Ltd* [1974] 1 MLJ 82, HC; (5) *Asia Hotel Sdn Bhd v Malayan Insurance (M) Sdn Bhd* [1992] 2 CLJ 121 (Rep), [1992] 2 CLJ 1185, HC; (6) *American International Assurance Co Ltd v See Ah Yu* [1996] 3 CLJ 566, HC; (7) *Aetna Universal Insurance Sdn Bhd v Fanny Foo May Wan* [2001] 1 CLJ 476, HC; (8) *United Malayan Insurance Co Ltd v Lee Yoon Heng* [1964] 1 LNS 212, HC; (9) *Teck Liong (EM) Sdn Bhd v Hong Leong Assurance Sdn Bhd and another suit* [2001] 7 CLJ 457, HC and (10) *Poh Siew Cheng v American International Assurance Co Ltd* [2005] 1 LNS 252 HC.

The difference between proposals containing a basis clause and ones without is that in the latter category, an insurer is obliged to show that the misstatement was of a material fact or that it was fraudulent, before he is entitled to avoid liability under the policy.[25]

PREMIUMS

When a premium is offered by the assured and accepted by the insurer, there is at once a contract of insurance in existence between the parties. A further condition may be incorporated into an insurance policy to the effect that the insurance shall not commence until the premium has actually been paid to and accepted by the insurer and until the insurer's official letter or policy has been issued.[26]

---

[25]   *Ong Eng Chai v China Insurance Co Ltd* [1974] 1 MLJ 82.

[26]   See condition 1 of the insurance policy and two cases on the subject matter, namely: *Canning v Farquhar* (1885-1886) 16 QBD 727 and *Harrington v Pearl Life Assurance Co Ltd* (1914) 30 TLR 613.

Where the nature of the risk has been altered at the time of the tender of the premium, there would be no contract binding the company to issue a policy.[27]

The acceptance of the proposal by the insurers may be more or less conclusively shown in one or other of the following ways, namely "... (2) By accepting the premium. Where no policy has been issued to the proposer before the loss, the receipt of the premium and its retention by the insurers, though by no means conclusive, may raise the presumption, in the absence of any circumstances leading to the contrary conclusion, that the insurers have definitely accepted his proposal. In such a case they are not entitled to refuse to issue a policy to him, and they are, therefore, liable to him in the event of a loss... The insurers, by accepting the payment of the premium, may, even where no policy has been issued, be estopped from denying the existence of a contract of insurance between the assured and themselves".[28]

It is common knowledge that the quantum of premium is affected by the risk involved and one of the principles is 'in the case of risks other than life, the assured is not given absolute right of renewal, the continuance of the policy being conditional not only upon payment of premium by the assured, but also upon the acceptance of it by the insurer'. In any such case the insurers may terminate the risk at each renewal period by refusing to accept the premium tendered.[29]

There is no rule of insurance law that states that there can be no binding contract of insurance until the premium has actually been paid or the policy has been issued.[30] What is important is to see whether the terms of the insurance have been agreed upon by the parties and if that has been achieved, then there is a *prima facie* binding contract of insurance,

---

[27] *Canning v Farquhar* (1885-1886) 16 QBD 727. See also *Madam Loh Sai Nyah v American International Assurance Co Ltd* [1998] 2 MLJ 310 (CA).

[28] Welford & Otter-Barry on Fire Insurance, 4th Ed. pages 80, 81 and 198.

[29] McGillivray on Insurance Law 3rd Edn. p. 464-465.

[30] *Wooding v Monmouthshire and South Wales Mutual Indemnity Society Ltd* [1939] 4 All ER 570 at p 581 and *Re Yager & Guardian Assurance Co* (1912) 108 LT 38 at p 44.

and the assured is obliged to pay a premium as agreed, while the insurer must deliver a policy containing the agreed terms.[31]

COVER NOTES

On receipt of the premium, the insurers will usually, in the interim, issue a cover note to provide the assured with temporary cover until the policy is issued. A certificate of insurance includes a cover note.[32]

The insurance contract comes into existence when the cover note is issued. The usual method in which interim insurance is granted is by a cover note which is, in practice, printed in common form. Normally, a cover note incorporates the terms and conditions of the insurers' standard form of policy, either by express reference or by reference to a signed proposal which incorporates the standard form; if the proposer is to be bound by the standard terms and conditions, it must be shown that he has agreed to accept them in some other way. Subject to such incorporation of the standard terms and conditions, a cover note is a contract of insurance, distinct from the contract comprised in the policy, where a policy is issued. The cover note is superseded by the subsequent issue of a policy, but the parties' rights and liabilities in respect of any loss which happens during the currency of the cover note, normally falls to be determined by reference to the terms of the cover note, not to the terms of the subsequent policy.[33]

In the case of fire insurance, where the insurers issue to the assured a cover note, termed as an interim receipt, pending the issuance of a proper fire insurance policy and where such an interim receipt states that the assured has proposed to effect an insurance against fire, 'subject to all the usual terms and conditions of this company' and that the property insured would be held assured under those conditions during the currency of the interim receipt, it was held that the words 'subject to all the usual terms

---

[31] *Syarikat Uniweld Trading v The Asia Insurance Co Ltd* [1996] 2 MLJ 160.
[32] *Pacific & Orient Insurance Co Sdn Bhd v Cheng Chor Tong & Ors* [2006] 5 MLJ 431.
[33] 25 Halsbury's Laws of England (4th Ed) para 386.

and conditions of this company' meant that the terms and conditions of the company's policy ought to be read into the interim receipt.[34]

Where a cover note incorporates the clauses and conditions of a policy and the assured accepts the cover note, in that form and content, both the insurers and the assured 'rendered themselves bound by those clauses and conditions'.[35]

POLICY

It is a condition precedent that before a policy of insurance becomes effective, it is necessary for a certificate of insurance to be delivered to the person by whom the policy has been effected, namely the assured.[36]

A contract will then have come into existence, even though there is an absence of a policy. Where no policy has been issued to the assured proposer before the loss, the receipt of the premium and its retention by the insurers, though by no means conclusive, may raise the presumption, in the absence of any circumstances leading to a contrary conclusion, that the insurers have definitely accepted his proposal. In such a case, they are

---

[34] *Citizens Insurance Company of Canada v Parsons (1881)*, (1881-82) 7 App Cas 96. See also *Everbright Commercial Pte Ltd & Anor v AXA Insurance S'pore Pte Ltd* [2000] 4 SLR 226.

[35] Third Edition of Ivamy's General Principles of Insurance Law at page 94 under the heading 'The Incorporation of the Terms of the Policy'. See also *Citizens Insurance Company of Canada v Parsons* (1881), (1881–82) 7 App Cas 96 and *General Accident, Fire and Life, Assurance Corporation Ltd v Shuttleworth & Anor* (1938) 60 Ll LR 301.

[36] *Capital Insurance Bhd v Kasim Mohd Ali* [1996] 2 MLJ 425; [1996] 3 CLJ 19, *The People's Insurance Co (M) Sdn Bhd v Narayani a/p Raman (sekarang dikenali sebagai Tahan Insurance (M) Berhad)* [2002] MLJU 628; [2003] 1 AMR 712, *Mustafa bin Man & Anor v Pan Global Insurance Bhd* [2003] MLJU 117; [2003] 8 CLJ 390, *Tokio Marine Insurans (M) Bhd v Mohd Radzi bin Zainuddin & Anor* [2012] 8 MLJ 814 (HC). See also *Yong Fui Tong v United Oriental Assurance Sdn Bhd* [1996] 1 BLJ 455; [1996] MLJU 559 in relation to the terms and conditions governing the contract of insurance.

not entitled to refuse to issue a policy to him, and they are, therefore, liable to him in the event of a loss.[37]

"Strictly, a 'renewal' is descriptive of a repetition of the whole arrangement by substituting the like agreement in place of that previously subsisting, to be operative over a new period, whereas an 'extension' betokens a prolongation of the subsisting contract by the exercise of a power reserved thereby to vary one of its provisions, that is, by enlarging the period. Upon a renewal similar rights revest... A contract reserving continuous rights of renewal will, if these be exercised, lead to succeeding contracts in a series, the identity of each contract (being) separate and distinct. On the other hand, the exercise of the right of extension augments the length of time over which the contract operates, without changing its identity".[38]

Whether there is a renewal or an extension of an insurance policy is a question of construction,[39] the term 'renewal' often being used to refer to both 'renewal' and 'extension' in the sense that those words are used above. It is however well established that, where a policy is renewable only by mutual consent (i.e., not as of right), the renewal results in a fresh contract rather than the extension of an existing contract.[40]

Gopal Sri Ram JCA in *Leong Kum Whay v QBE Insurance* (M) Sdn Bhd & Ors [2006] 1 CLJ 1 (CA) said:

> Of course, a policy may expressly stipulate that it is not to continue in force beyond the period of insurance, unless renewed by mutual consent. See, eg, *Stokell v Heywood* [1897] 1 Ch 459. And where a policy, such as the ordinary form of life policy, expressly provides for continuation beyond the specified period of insurance unless a particular event, such as the non-payment of the premium, takes place, the renewal is an extension of the

---

[37] General Principles of Insurance Law (6th Ed) by ER Hardy Ivamy at p 111.

[38] Mayo J in *Re Kerr* [1943] SASR 8, at 16.

[39] *GIO v Kimmedy* [1988] 5 ANZ Insurance Cases 60-880, at 75,541.

[40] See *Re Kerr* [1943] SASR 8, at 15; Halsbury's Laws of England, 4th ed, vol 25, para 494.

original contract. See *Re Anchor Assurance Co* [1870] LR 5 Ch App 632, at 638. But where a policy is silent on the question of renewal, renewal of it will generally constitute a new contract. See Ivamy, General Principles of Insurance Law, (5th ed, 1986), pp. 249-50.

In cases of vehicle insurance, a genuine insurance certificate should carry the territorial code, the year code, a number to indicate whether there was any renewal or not, the actual policy numbers, a number showing whether it was a private vehicle or commercial vehicle and finally a number to indicate whether it was a comprehensive or third-party policy.[41]

The main issue before the Court of Appeal in *Loh Shiiun Hing v Kurnia Insurans (Malaysia) Bhd* [2014] 7 CLJ 490 (CA) was the nature or the type of the policy. The High Court there held that it was a voyage policy. The appellant contended that it was a time policy. It was the view of the court that the nature of the policy must be determined by looking at the terms of the policy itself and in general, by reference to the merchant law as codified in the UK Marine Insurance Act 1906 ('MIA'). That it was essentially a matter of construction of the policy and the relevant provisions in the MIA.

A contract of insurance is essentially a contract of indemnity in insurance law. The contract not only ensures that the assured is indemnified for his loss, but it also applies to cover a situation where the assured does not make a profit from his loss. This principle that a policy of insurance is a contract of indemnity was emphatically stated by Brett LJ in *Castellain v Preston & Ors* [1883] 11 QBD 380:

> That is the fundamental principle of insurance, and if ever a proposition is brought forward which is at variance with it, that is to say, which either will prevent the assured from obtaining a

---

[41] See *The People's Insurance Co (M) Sdn Bhd (Dikenali Sebagai Tahan Insurance (M) Berhad) v Narayanan A/P Raman* [2003] 1 AMR 712 and *Mustafa Bin Man & Anor v Pan Global Insurance Bhd* [2003] MLJU 117. (See also the case of *Muhamad Rafiq Muiz Ahmad Hanipah v Pacific & Orient Insurance Co Berhad & 2 Ors* [2018] CLJ 1 LNS 942.)

full indemnity, or which will give to the assured more than a full indemnity, that proposition must certainly be wrong.

Most policies of insurance (with the exception of life or personal accident policies) are indemnity policies; that is, policies which obligate the insurer only to make good the actual losses suffered by the assured, which is in fact proved.[42]

The basis of a claim under an indemnity policy is that the assured may recover his actual loss, subject of course, to any provision in the policy as to the maximum amount recoverable. The assured may not recover more than his actual loss. In *Wong Cheong Kong Sdn Bhd v Prudential Assurance Sdn Bhd* [1998] 1 CLJ 916, His Lordship Vincent Ng J stated:

> The insured cannot recover more than the sum insured, for that sum is all that he has stipulated for by his premiums and it fixes the maximum liability of the insurers. See *Curtis & Sons v. Mathew* [1918] as reported in 35 TLR 189, CA. Even within that limit, however, he cannot recover more than what he establishes to be the actual amount of his loss. See *Richard Aubrey Film Productions Ltd. v. Graham* [1960] 2 Lloyd's Rep 101. The contract being one of indemnity, and of indemnity only, he can recover the actual amount of his loss and no more (see *Castellain v. Preston* [1883] 11 QBD 380 at 386, CA) whatever may have been his estimate of what his loss would likely be, and whatever the premiums he may have paid calculated on the basis of that estimate, unless he had taken out what is termed as valued or agreed value policy. See *Elcock v. Thomson* [1949] 2 KB 755, [1949] 2 All ER 381. In this connection, I need do no more than to quote from the speech of Megaw LJ in the Court of Appeal in *Leppard v. Excess Insu. Co. Ltd.* [1979] 1 WLR 512, where he said, at p. 518:

---

[42] *Meacock v Bryant & Co* [1942] 2 All ER 661 and *West Wake Price & Co v Ching* [1956] 3 All ER 821 at 825. See also *Modern Universal Sdn Bhd v MSIG Insurance (M) Berhad (formerly known as Hong Leong Assurance Bhd)* [2014] MLJU 99 (HC).

> Ever since the decision of this court in *Castellain v. Preston* [1883] 11 QBD 380, the general principle has been beyond dispute. Indeed, I think it was beyond dispute long before *Castellain v. Preston*. The insured may recover his actual loss, subject, of course, to any provision in the policy as to the maximum amount recoverable. The insured may not recover more than his actual loss...

> When a claim is made under an indemnity policy, questions pertaining to measurement of loss and/or the possibility of reinstatement must be resolved without undue delay to enable the parties to reach an agreement as to the amount to be paid under such a policy. Under an ordinary indemnity policy, the insurer undertakes to indemnify the insured for a loss caused by the insured.

In relation to loss of property, the insurers may opt to offer to reinstate or replace the property concerned. That is, the insurers reserve to themselves the option of reinstating the property instead of making payment in monetary terms.

'Reinstatement' means the restoration of property affected by a fire to the condition in which it was before the fire; in the case of a total loss, by rebuilding the building or replacing the goods by their equivalent, as the case may be, and in the case of a partial loss, by repairing the damage. Once an insurer has elected to reinstate a building, then the insurer must proceed with the reinstatement, even though in the process they discover that it is more difficult and more expensive than they had anticipated.[43]

In *Wong Cheong Kong Sdn Bhd v Prudential Assurance Sdn Bhd*,[44] the court was of the view that the claim was grounded on an indemnity rather than a reinstatement basis. It was held therefore that in accordance with the principles enunciated in *Leppard v Excess Insurance Co Ltd* [1979] 1 WLR 512 at p. 518 to 520) that the loss recoverable on plant and machinery

---

[43] *Wong Cheong Kong Sdn Bhd v Prudential Assurance Sdn Bhd* [1998] 3 MLJ 724; [1998] 1 CLJ 916.

[44] *Ibid* above

destroyed would not be based on the replacement value (with new machinery), but the market value of similar property at the time of the fire, bearing in mind the age, characteristics and condition of the assured items.

Vincent Ng J went on to hold that the market value, which was evaluated and pegged in light of the then prevailing market conditions, and which more closely approximated the plaintiffs' real loss, would be a fair and just approach for the court to take and that in respect of the damaged items that could be repaired, the loss would be the reasonable cost of repairs and not the market value.

In *Leppard v Excess Insurance Co Ltd* [1979] 2 All ER 668, the insurers agreed to indemnify the assured in respect of loss or damage caused by fire. In this case, Megaw LJ held:

> The 'full value' is the cost of replacement. That defines the maximum amount recoverable under the policy. The amount recoverable cannot exceed the cost of replacement. But it does not say that that maximum is recoverable if it exceeds the actual loss. There is nothing in the wording of the policy, including the declaration which is incorporated therein, which expressly or by any legitimate inference provides that the loss which is to be indemnified is agreed to be, or is to be deemed to be, the cost of reinstatement, 'the full value', even though the cost of reinstatement is greater than the actual loss. The plaintiff is entitled to recover his real loss, not exceeding the cost of replacement.

In relation to the question of reinstatement, or more precisely the cost of reinstatement, the court has to take into consideration either depreciation or betterment. In *Chip Fong (Kuala Lumpur) Sdn Bhd & Ors v Guardian Royal Exchange Assurance (Malaysia) Sdn Bhd* [1992] 1 MLJ 598, the court was of the view that on the facts, 'the relevant factor to be taken into consideration is the principle of betterment.'

The principle is simply this. An allowance must be made so that the assured is not getting something new for something old. In *Reynolds and*

Anderson v Phoenix Assurance Co Ltd & Ors, [1978] 2 Lloyds Rep 440(QB) Forbes J said:

> Now the principle of betterment is so well established in the law of insurance to be departed from at this stage even though it may sometimes work hardship on the insured. It is simply that an allowance must be made because the assured is getting something new for something old. But in this class of insurance there is no automatic or accepted percentage deduction. In some of the calculations put before me an attempt was made to establish a figure of 13.3 percent as the appropriate reduction for betterment. This figure has no validity...

MacGillivray & Parkington on Insurance Law (8th Ed) at pp 692 and 693, illustrates the principle of betterment in the following words:

> If an old house or an old article is destroyed or damaged and the assured replaces or repairs, he may end up with a house or article which is considerably better than the old and the question arises whether he should make any allowance to the insurers to the extent that he is better off after the loss than before. The conventional view is that such allowance should be made and in marine insurance custom has fixed an allowance of one-third 'new for old' which is said to be deductible. No such fixed allowance exists in non-marine insurance but an allowance is generally made to ensure that the assured does not make a profit of his contract of insurance.

Megarry VC in *Medical Defence Union Ltd v Department of Trade* [1979] 2 WLR 686 went on to say thus:

> Generally, insurance relates to matters that are entered into between an insurance company and the insured, and more often than not, a contract of liability will be agreed upon as its foundation. The policy will indicate that the insurers will undertake to indemnify the assured against legal liabilities incurred by him but within a specified range (Halsbury's Laws of England (4th Ed) p 350 para 688). The contract will alleviate a financially

weak tortfeasor from the burden of having to compensate an aggrieved party, as a result of a crippling judgment. Such a contract is the norm nowadays in a society like ours. Even though there is no privity of contract between the third party, i.e. the aggrieved party and the insurance company in common law, it does not mean that the third party is absolutely without any recourse. Section 95 of the Act in clear terms promulgates that any policy which restricts the scope of third-party risks, in certain circumstances, will be construed as void and of no effect against the injured third party. Furthermore, under Section 97 of the same Act, where a person is insured against liabilities to third parties, and he ends up bankrupt, or the insurance company gets wound up, the rights of the third party are still protected. This is so as the rights of that insured person now vest in the third party on whom the liability was so incurred.

INSURABLE INTEREST

The assured must be able to identify the insurable interest covered by the insurance policy. An assured should have an insurable interest in the insured property before he is permitted to recover under an insurance policy.[45]

Therefore, when one examines the authorities, one sees that the court is concerned to analyse, by reference to the terms of the policy, what is the subject of the insurance; to analyse what insurable interest a person has in the subject of the policy; and to consider whether the subject "embraces that insurable interest" in the words of Blackburn J in *Anderson v Morice* (1875) 10 C.P. 609 (Exch Ch) at 622. Where on the wording of the policy the subject is not absolutely clear-cut, it sometimes assists to identify the subject by asking what insurable interest the person has, but essentially the subject is defined by the words of the policy. In some cases, the subject is so clear, that even when the assured can identify some insurable interest that it might have had, it will be held that the assured has failed to

---

[45] *Sharp and Roarer Investments Ltd v Sphere Drake Insurance PLC Minster Insurance Co Ltd and EC Parker Co Ltd (The Moonacre)* [1992] 2 Lloyd's Rep 501.

cover that interest by the policy. In other cases what is "embraced" within the subject of the policy is less clear-cut, and in those circumstances the court may be able to say that the insurable interest is embraced within the subject of the insurance. The different elements of subject, insurable interest, and value are separate but have an impact one on the other.[46]

(1) It is from the terms of the policy that the subject of the insurance must be ascertained; (2) It is from all the surrounding circumstances that the nature of an assured's insurable interest must be discovered; (3) There is no hard and fast rule that because the nature of an insurable interest relates to a liability to compensate for loss, that insurable interest can only be covered by a liability policy rather than a policy insuring property or life or indeed properties or lives; (4) The question whether a policy embraces the insurable interest intended to be recovered, is a question of construction. The subject or terms of the policy may be so specific as to force a court to hold that the policy has failed to cover the insurable interest, but a court will be reluctant to so hold. (5) It is not a requirement of property insurance that the assured must have a "legal or equitable" interest in the property, as those terms might normally be understood. It is sufficient for a sub-contractor to have a contract that relates to the property and a potential liability for damage to the property, to have an insurable interest in it. It is sufficient under section 5 of the UK Marine Insurance Act 1906 for a person interested in a marine adventure to stand in a "legal or equitable" relation to the adventure". That is intended to be a broad concept. (6) In a policy on life or lives, the court should be searching for the same broad concept. It may be that on an insurance of a specific identified life, it will be difficult to establish a "legal or equitable" relation without a pecuniary liability recognised by law, arising on the death of that particular person. There is however no authority which deals with a policy on many lives and over a substantial period and where it can be seen that a pecuniary liability will arise by reference to those lives and the intention is to cover that legal liability. (7) The interest in policies falling within section 1 of the UK Life Insurance Act 1774 must exist at the time of entry into the policy, and be capable of pecuniary evaluation at that time.[47]

---

[46] *Anthony Feasey v Sun Life Assurance Company of Canada* [2003] Lloyd's Rep IR 637, [2003] EWCA Civ 885, [2003] 2 All ER (Comm) 587.

[47] *Ibid* above.

In simple terms, an insurable interest is the specific subject matter of which the assured has an interest in protecting against loss or damage.

Nature of Insurable Interest

Insurable interest may be described loosely as the assured's pecuniary interest in the subject-matter of the insurance, arising from a relationship with it recognised in law.[48]

Further at paragraph 1-75 of McGillivray on Insurance Law 10th Edition it was stated thus:

> Besides being capable of valuation, the interest must be of such a nature that the law will take cognisance of it. The assured must show that he will or may lose some legal or equitable right or be placed under the burden of some legal liability in consequence of the death of the person whose life is insured. A mere expectancy or hope of future pecuniary benefit from the prolongation of the life insured or of the fulfilment by him of moral obligations owed to the assured, are insufficient to sustain an insurable interest. If, however, the death of the life insured will involve the assured in a liability, it is no answer for the insurers to show that he will also derive some compensating benefit, since the contract is not one of indemnity and the insurers may not set off the assured's gain against his loss.

Mance J in *The Capricorn* [1995] 1 Lloyd's Rep. 622 at 641 observed that if insurers make a contract in deliberate terms which covers their assured in respect of a specific situation, a court is likely to hesitate before accepting a defence of lack of insurable interest.[49]

---

[48] McGillivray on Insurance Law 10th Edition at paragraph 1-11.

[49] Quoted in The Law of Insurance Contracts 4th Edition by Professor Malcolm Clarke.

An insurable interest exists where the assured stands in some legal relation to the subject matter of the insurance, whereby he stands to incur some legal loss if the event insured against occurs.[50]

Ellis, in Modern Irish Commercial and Consumer Law suggests a working definition of insurable interest, fusing this definition from a combination of the outcome in the case of *PJ Carrigan Ltd v Norwich Union Fire Society Ltd* 987 IR 618 (*'Carrigan case'*) and the views of Wilson J in *Constitution Insurance Company of Canada v Kosmopoulos* (1987) 34 DLR (4th) 208

Lord Eldon-*Ebsworth v Alliance Marine Insurance Co* (1873) LR 8 CP 596:

> insurable interest can be said to arise when a person stands in such relationship to the subject matter of the insurance that (1) he benefits by its continued safety (or absence from liability in the case of liability insurance); or (2) is prejudiced by its loss (or incurring of a legal liability). In short, to possess insurable interest, a person must have some financial involvement with the subject-matter of the insurance.

The Indian Marine Insurance Act 1963, has defined insurable interest as, 'a person is interested in a marine adventure where he stands in any legal or equitable relation to the adventurer to any insurable property at risk therein, in consequence of which he may benefit by the safety or due arrival of insurable property, or may be prejudiced by its loss, or by damage thereto, or by detention thereof, or may incur liability thereof'.

Shawcross on Motor Insurance (2nd edition) at page 80 said, "Insurable interest may be defined as the interest of such a nature that the occurrence of the event insured against would cause financial loss to the insured".

Lord Eldon in the case of *Ebsworth v Alliance Marine Insurance Co* (1873) *LR 8 CP 596,* defined it as "a right in the property, or a right derivable out of some contract about the property, which in either case may be lost upon some contingency affecting the possession or enjoyment of the property".

---

[50] McGillivray on Insurance Law 10th Edition

RISK

In examining any claim under an insurance policy, it is necessary to ascertain what exactly the risk is insured against. It is a 'general principle applicable in all cases of insurance that the obligation of the insurer is confined to the particular risk insured, and that if the risk in respect of which a claim is made against the insurer differs from the risk he has insured, he is not liable to make good that claim'.[51]

Any risk which does not answer to the description in the policy, is not covered by the policy and if such a risk materialises into a loss, no claim in respect of it can be made by the assured under the policy.[52]

The use of the concept of 'foreseeability' of loss or loss 'resulting directly and naturally' is wrong and unsustainable in insurance law.[53]

In cases where an assured or his personal representative are the only parties interested in the insurance policy, the rule of public policy is applied by the courts with extreme vigour, to prevent the assured or his personal representatives from benefiting from the assured's own wrongdoing. Where the assured is barred from recovering, by reason that the loss is caused by his own wrongdoing, all who claim through him as representing his estate or claiming a share of his estate as beneficiary under his will or on intestacy or as a creditor, are equally barred.[54]

The burden of proof is upon the assured to show that the losses which have taken place were caused proximately by the risk insured and he needs to show that the loss was occasioned accidentally, namely; the loss was occasioned by something fortuitous which could be regarded

---

[51] Warrington, J at p. 153 in *Law Guarantee Trust & Accident Society v Munich Re-Insurance Company* [1912] 1 Ch 138 Ch D; *Leong Chee Yeong (f) v China Insurance Co Ltd* [1952] MLJ 246.

[52] Shawcross on Insurance (2nd Edn. at p. 496).

[53] *Commercial Union Assurance (Malaysia) Sdn Bhd v Pilihan Megah Bhd Sdn Bhd* [1998] 7 MLJ 33.(See also the case of *Muhamad Rafiq Muiz Ahmad Hanipah v Pacific & Orient Insurance Co Berhad & 2 Ors* [2018] CLJ 1 LNS 942.

[54] S Santhana Dass, Law of Life Insurance in Malaysia, pp 63-64.

as a casualty within the meaning of the insurance contract and this is a question of fact. In other words, if the assured is to intentionally or deliberately bring about an insured event, he will not be entitled to recover under the policy. But if the losses suffered by him are caused by his negligence and the event causing the losses is uncertain as it is unexpected and fortuitous, he is entitled to recover under the insurance policy.[55]

The assured also has to show that the losses occurred during the currency or the period of the insurance policies.[56]

MISTAKE AND RECTIFICATION

The mistake is said to affect the intention of the parties. A mistake that leads to the formation of a contract is a vitiating factor. The issue of ambiguity will be raised due to the alleged mistake. An assured is entitled to have the policy rectified where it does not reflect the agreement reached between the parties.

Mistake and rectification were explained in McGillivray and Parkinson on Insurance Law (7th Ed) paras 1071 to 1074:

> 1071 Introductory. Where either party to a contract of insurance establishes that the policy formally embodying the terms of the parties' contract does not record the real agreement of the parties, he is entitled to have the policy rectified so that it properly

---

[55] *Jeffery Law Siew Su v PanGlobal Insurance Berhad & Other Cases* [2006] MLJU 365.

[56] See The Law of Insurance, Raoul Colinvaux, 4th Edn. at pp 86-87; Macgillivray & Parkington on Insurance Law, 6th Edn. at pp 722-724; Principles of Insurance Law (5th Edition) by Poh Chu Lai at pp 627, 647 and 648; *London & Provincial Leather Processes Ltd v Hudson* (1939) 2 KB 724 at pp 726, 728, 729 and 730; *Tinline v White Cross Insurance Association Ltd.* 1921 3 KB 327 at page 332; *James v British General Insurance Co. Ltd.* [1927] 2 KB 311 at p 323; *Sofi v Prudential Assurance Co. Ltd.* [1993] Vol. 2 Lloyd's Reports 559 at pp 560 and 566.

expresses their true agreement. 'If there be an agreement for a policy in a particular form, and the policy be drawn up by the office in a different form. Varying the right of the party assured, a court of equity will interfere and deal with the case upon the footing of the agreement, and not of the policy.' If the clerical staff in the insurance office had made a mistake to the prejudice of the company and not the assured, the company would be entitled to rectification of the policy to conform to the real agreement reached by the parties before issue of the policy.

1072 There is a presumption that a policy which is issued by the insurers and accepted by the assured contains the complete and final contract between the parties. Consequently, the courts' equitable jurisdiction to rectify insurance policies is exercised with restraint inside certain well-established limitations, or else it would tend to destroy certainty in insurance business. When a plaintiff seeks rectification, he must establish as a fact that the parties were agreed upon the point in question, and that the policy accidentally fails to record their agreement.

1073. Prior agreement. It is not necessary for the party claiming rectification to prove that there was a legally binding agreement concluded prior to the issue of the policy, although in many cases he might well be able to do so. He need only establish the fact of a common intention manifested in some form or other as to the form and terms of the contract which would be set out in the policy when issued. In other words, he must prove that a bargain was struck, even if it was unenforceable at the outset. Thus, when it is claimed that the true terms of an insurance are contained in a slip used by the brokers to submit to the insurers, it does not matter in principle whether the slip constituted a legally enforceable agreement, as in the case of a Lloyd's slip, or was only a memorandum of the agreement to be concluded later. It follows also that the slip, even if legally binding, can be called in question as being inaccurate.

1074 Evidence of common intention. A strong burden of proof lies upon the party seeking rectification. He must adduce convincing proof of the parties' outward expression of accord or common intention, so that the court is in no doubt that his contention is to be preferred to that of the opposite party alleging that the policy contains their agreement.

See also *Cold Storage Holdings Plc & Ors v The Overseas Assurance Corpn Ltd & Anor* [1989] 2 MLJ 324 (HC).

It is to be noted that the courts in England have stopped making a distinction between a mistake of fact and a mistake of law and its effect on an agreement. See *Kleinwort Benson Ltd v Lincoln City Council* [1999] 2 AC 349 where the House of Lords permitted the restitution of sums paid under a mistake of law.

The Court of Appeal of Singapore in *MCST No 473 v De Beers Jewellery* [2002] 2 SLR 1 was in agreement that the distinction between mistake of fact and law should be abrogated. Yong Pung How CJ delivering the judgment of the court said:

Present law

[17] The law in Singapore in this area, since *Serangoon Garden Estate v Chye Marian* [1959] MLJ 113, has been that money paid out under a mistake of law — as opposed to fact — is not recoverable. The key question here was whether Singapore law should follow the example of some other Commonwealth states and abrogate this rule. If the answer was in the affirmative, subsidiary questions included: whether the rule should be abrogated legislatively (as in Western Australia and New Zealand) or judicially (as in Australia, Canada, England and South Africa); and what defences, if any, should be developed.

Should the law be changed?

[18] In *Kleinwort Benson v Lincoln City Council* [1998] 4 All ER 513, the House of Lords unanimously decided that it was time to abrogate the rule; by a majority, it decided to do so judicially. Lord Goff referred to the Law Commission's Consultation Paper

No 120 on Restitution of Payments Made under a Mistake of Law (1991), which cited the following as the main criticisms of the rule:

(1) The rule was contrary to justice, which demanded that money paid under a mistake of law should be repaid unless there were special circumstances justifying its retention by the payee.

(2) The distinction between mistakes of fact and mistakes of law could lead to arbitrary results.

(3) Courts were tempted to manipulate the fact-law distinction in order to achieve practical justice. This led to uncertainty in the application of the rule.

[19] The court also held that two factors in particular did not defeat a claim: firstly, that the payment had been made as part of a transaction which was now closed; and secondly, that the payment had been made on a settled view of the law.

[20] The appellant's first objection to the abrogation of the rule was that it was well-entrenched. Such an argument had no merit because the common law is no stranger to judicial activism. The appellant's second objection was that the abrogation of the rule would undermine certainty, as closed transactions would be reopened and unscrambled. It will suffice to say here that it was not a fatal objection to the abrogation of the rule.

[21] Most judicial and academic opinion is in favour of bringing the law on mistakes of law in line with that on mistakes of fact. There does not seem to be any insurmountable objection once thought has been given to the scope of the new rule and the exceptions to it.

If the law is to be changed, how should it be done?

[22] The arguments in favour of judicial abrogation were as follows. Lord Lloyd in Kleinwort Benson (supra) gave two:

Indeed, I can imagine few areas of the law in which it would be more appropriate for the House [of Lords] to take the initiative. The mistake of law rule is judge made law. There are no considerations of social policy involved.

Firstly, as the mistake of law rule was not created by Parliament, abrogating it judicially would not amount to defeating legislative intent. Secondly, as no social policy issues were involved, abrogating the rule judicially would not amount to usurping the legislative function. Thirdly, the courts were not in a position to know if, and when, Parliament would change the law.

[23] The Law Reform Committee ('LRC') of the Singapore Academy of Law ('SAL'), like the Law Commission in England, recommended in its Paper on Reforms to the Law of Restitution on Mistakes of Law (2001) that the rule be abrogated by legislation. The key argument in favour of legislative intervention stemmed from a fear of opening the floodgates to the re-litigation of closed transactions. In particular, it was thought that Parliament would be better able to address two issues. The first was: whether the change in the law should have retrospective effect. The LRC of the SAL recommended that the Civil Law Act (Cap 43, 1999 Ed) be amended to allow this. However, a judicial abrogation of the law could achieve the same if this court followed Kleinwort Benson (supra) in holding that a payment made under a mistake of law could be recovered even if it had been made under a completed transaction.

When there is a mistake that leads to the formation of the contract, the question then is whether it can be rectified. The parties will then seek to rely on the equitable remedy of rectification. The following are the conditions which must be satisfied if rectification is to be granted on the ground of common mistake:

- Firstly, there must be a common intention with regard to the particular provisions of the agreement in question, together with some outward expression of accord;

- Secondly, this common intention must continue up to the time of execution of the instrument;

- Thirdly, there must be clear evidence that the instrument as executed does not accurately represent the true agreement of the parties at the time of its execution; and

- Fourthly, it must be shown that the instrument, if rectified as claimed, would accurately represent the true agreement of the parties at that time. [57]

As part of the process of construction, the court has the power to correct obvious mistakes in the written expression of the intention of the parties. Once corrected, the contract is interpreted in its corrected form. This principle enables the court to take background facts into account, in deciding whether a mistake has been made and, if so, what it is.[58]

The remedy of rectification allows words in the contract to be altered to reflect the true intention of the parties. Rectification is a discretionary remedy that may be available if there has been a common mistake in recording the terms agreed. The key idea here is that the contract does not accurately record what was agreed. It does not avail the innocent party if he has certain intentions that were not manifested, or if he agreed to something under a mistake. In Singapore, the High Court in *Hub Warrior Sdn Bhd v QBE Insurance (Malaysia) Bhd* [2004] SGHC 279 endorsed the criteria pronounced in *The Demetra K* [2002] 2 Lloyd's Rep 581, at [23] and [24], per Lord Phillips MR:

> The antecedent agreement need not amount to a binding contract but there must be a common accord as to what the parties' mutual rights and obligations are to be, to which they fail to give effect in their subsequent written contract ... Where the parties have recorded their agreement in a written contract, convincing evidence is necessary to discharge the burden of

---

[57] *The "Nai Genova" and "Nai Superba"* [1984] 1 Lloyd's Rep 353 at p 359. (CA).

[58] Lewison on The Interpretation of Contracts, 4th edition (2007) at pages 345 and 349.

proving that they made a common mistake in so doing, albeit that the standard of proof is the civil standard. But as the alleged common intention *ex hypothesi* contradicts the written instrument, convincing proof is required in order to counteract the cogent evidence of the parties' intention displayed by the instrument itself.

Denning LJ in *Frederick E Rose (London) Ltd v William H Pim Junior & Co Ltd* [1953] 2 QB 450, 461 added his usual lucid touch to the subject:

> Rectification is concerned with contracts and documents, not with intentions. In order to get rectification, it is necessary to show that the parties were in complete agreement on the terms of their contract, but by an error wrote them down wrongly; and in this regard, in order to ascertain the terms of the contract, you do not look into the inner minds of the parties into their intentions any more than you do in the formation of any other contract.

A policy of insurance entered into between an assured and the insurer may not accurately reflect the agreement between them, especially their common intention. Where the policy fails to do so, a party may seek the equitable remedy of rectification. The party seeking rectification has to show what the common intention of the parties was and that a mistake had been made in the executed policy. If one or both parties have been mistaken about an element of the contract, then there is no consensus *ad idem*. But that does not necessarily mean that the contract is void. Therefore, the common law has tried to develop a fairly sophisticated set of rules for dealing with mistake. In *Seppanen v Seppanen* 59 BCLR 26, British Columbia's Supreme Court summarized the law by stating:

> In common mistake, both parties make the same mistake. Each knows the intention of the other and accepts it but each is mistaken about some underlying and fundamental fact. In mutual mistake, the parties misunderstand each other and are at cross purposes. In unilateral mistake, only one of the parties is mistaken. The other knows, or must be taken to know, of his mistake.

If between the parties, the terms are clear enough, but there has been a drafting error that was not caught before signature, then there is a separate judicial procedure called 'rectification' which should be used (although the parties are better off to amend the original contract themselves then pay the cost of judicial rectification). This would not entail voiding the contract but correcting or amending it under judicial supervision.

The law excludes from the admissible background the previous negotiations of the parties and their declarations of subjective intent. They are admissible only in an action for rectification. The law makes this distinction for reasons of practical policy and, in this respect only, legal interpretation differs from the way we would interpret utterances in ordinary life. The boundaries of this exception are in some respects unclear.

A court can order rectification even if it has not been specifically pleaded. Also, although rectification is not granted when the rights of third parties are affected, this does not apply when the 'third parties' are before the court.

"The court can only act if it is satisfied beyond all reasonable doubt, that the instrument does not represent their common intention, and it is further satisfied as to what their common intention was. It is not sufficient to show that the written instrument does not represent their common intention unless one can positively also show what their common intention was".[59]

At common law such a contract or representation of someone or something of a contract will be described as void, there being in truth no intention to contract.[60]

It is true that in general, the test of intention in the formation of contracts and the transfer of property is objective, that is, intention is to be ascertained from what the parties said or did. But proof of mistake

---

[59] *Shipley Urban District Council v Bradford Corpn* [1936] Ch 375.
[60] *Bell v Lever Brothers, Ltd* [1932] AC 161.

affirmatively excludes intention. It is, however, essential that the mistake relied on should be of such a nature that it can be properly described as a mistake in respect of the underlying assumption of the contract or transaction or as being fundamental or basic. Whether the mistake does satisfy this description may often be a matter of great difficulty.

In the case of *Norwich Union Fire Insurance Society, Ltd v William H Price Ltd*, it was stated "Applying these principles to the present case, their Lordships find themselves so far in agreement with the opinions of the courts below that the money paid is recoverable at common law. That leaves for consideration the point on which the decision went against the insurers, so that this appeal is brought".[61]

It is only where the instrument or document drawn up does not accord with the true agreement between the parties that the terms of the instrument are revisited. For example, a contract, a deed or an insurance policy.[62]

However, on the facts in *DSL Development Corp Sdn Bhd v Kampong Kita Sdn Bhd* [2014] 11 MLJ 935 (HC), it was held that there was absent any mistake or fraud and therefore there was no instrument to rectify. Her Ladyship Mary Lim J stated:

> The letter(s) written by the defendant itself cannot and does not fall within the meaning of instrument as envisaged by equity. It is only where the instrument or document that was drawn up does not accord with the true agreement between the parties that the terms of the instrument are revisited.

---

[61] *Norwich Union Fire Insurance Society, Ltd v William H Price Ltd* [1934] All ER Rep 352, [1934] AC 455.

[62] See *In re Bird's Trusts* (1876) 3 Ch D 214; *Cold Storage Holdings Plc & Ors v Overseas Assurance Corpn Ltd & Anor* [1989] 2 MLJ 324; *Shell Timur Sdn Bhd v Achu Belon* [1998] MLJU 476; [1998] 2 CLJ 775).

Evidence of Common Intention

A strong burden of proof lies upon the party seeking rectification. He must adduce convincing proof of the parties' outward expression of accord or common intention, so that the court is in no doubt that his contention is to be preferred to that of the opposite party alleging that the policy contains their agreement.[63]

Rectification can only be granted where the document fails to represent the common intention of the parties, and in order to make it conform to what they have in fact agreed to. [64]

If parties contract under a mutual mistake and misapprehension as to their relative and respective rights, the result is, that that agreement is liable to be set aside as having proceeded on a common mistake.[65]

Clauson J in *Shipley Urban District Council v Bradford Corpn* [1936] 1 Ch 375 explained the circumstances under which the court will exercise its discretion to rectify a contract as follows:

> The law of rectification is not dependent on a complete antecedent concluded contract. In order that this court may exercise its jurisdiction to rectify a written instrument, it is not necessary to find a concluded and binding contract between the parties antecedent to the agreement which it is sought to rectify... it is sufficient to find a common continuing intention in regard to a particular provision or aspect of the agreement. If one finds that, in regard to a particular point, the parties were in agreement up to the moment when they executed their formal instrument, and the formal instrument does not conform with that common agreement, then this court has jurisdiction to rectify, although it

---

[63] McGillivray and Parkinson on Insurance Law (7th Ed) paras 1071 to 1074.
[64] *Tay Hean Seng v China Insurance Co Ltd* [1953] 1 MLJ 38 (CA) (Singapore).
[65] *Cooper v Phibbs* (1867) LR 2 HL 149; 16 LT 678; 15 WR 1049, HL; 22 Digest (Repl) 156, 1411 per Lord Westbury.

may be that there was, until the formal instrument was executed, no concluded and binding contract between the parties.

It is trite law that an insurance policy may be rectified after its issuance, if there was a common prior agreement between the insurer and the assured in terms that are different to that recorded in the policy. In such instances of 'mutual mistake' then the discretionary remedy of rectification would be ordered by the court. Section 30 of the Malaysian Specific Relief Act 1950, specifies the circumstances in which an instrument may be rectified.

On the facts of the appeal in *Kotak Malaysia (KOM) Sdn Bhd v Perbadanan Nasional Insurans Sdn Bhd* [2005] 4 MLJ 402, it was the view of Ramly Ali J that the Off-Cover Policy in question did not truly represent the intention of the parties, in that, it had departed from the original agreement between them. Thus, it was held that by virtue of Section 30 of the Malaysian Specific Relief Act 1950 the court was empowered to rectify the Off-Cover Policy. Ramly Ali J explained:

> The extent to which the court is prepared to lend its hand to rectify a document was considered by Denning LJ (as he then was) in *Frederick E Rose (London) Ltd v William H Pim & Co Ltd* [1953] 2 QB 450 at p 461:
>
>> In order to get rectification, it is necessary to show that the parties were in complete agreement upon the terms of their contract, but by an error wrote them down wrongly; and in this regard, in order to ascertain the terms of their contract, one does not look into the inner minds of the parties — into their intentions — any more than one does in the formation of any other contract. One looks at their outward acts that is at what they said or wrote to one another in coming to an agreement and then compares it with the document which they have signed. If one can predicate with certainty what the contract was and that it is, by a common mistake wrongly expressed in the document, then one rectifies the document; but nothing less will suffice.

This principle was earlier adopted by Kang Hwee Gee J in *Ng Chun Lin & Anor v Foo Lian Sin & Anor* [2000] 6 MLJ 81 where it was held that a policy of insurance may be rectified after its issuance and it is further supported by an instructive passage in the treatise Templeman on Marine Insurance: Its Principles and Practices:

If there is evidence, provided by the slip or by the conduct of the parties at the time of the contract was made that the parties to the contract were of one mind and clearly had a common intention which owing to an error had not been expressed unambiguously in the policy, then the policy may be rectified, in which event the ambiguity will, of course, be removed.

In the present case, the intention of the parties can be found upon a clear reading of the Marine Open-Cover which has been agreed upon by the parties to be the basis of which issuance of 'policies or certificates of insurance in respect of all shipment falling within the limits of the Open-Cover Policy'. Furthermore, PW1, the finance and administrative manager of the plaintiff, was the very person who negotiated on behalf of the plaintiff for the Marine Open-Cover Policy.

PW1 has personal knowledge of the chronology of events from the issuance of the Marine Open-Cover Policy and the Off-Cover Policy to the fire which destroyed the plaintiff's goods in Gudang 3B and to the subsequent repudiation of the insurance contract by the defendant. Contrary to that, the defendant has not led any evidence nor called any witnesses who can testify to the true intent of the parties when they negotiated the insurance contract. During cross-examination, the defendant's witness, DW2, stated that she has no personal knowledge over the matter as she was not with the defendant at the material time. She agreed that she was not present when the policy was negotiated and further did not know who was the officer-in-charge of the defendant when the policy was negotiated and issued. DW2 was not aware whether the intention was to include further destination within Malaysia after Port Klang.

The defendant did not call their employees or ex-employees who were involved or had personal knowledge of the negotiations between the plaintiff and the defendant pursuant to the Marine Open-Cover Policy. No evidence was led to show why the defendant was unable to call the employees concerned or attempt to trace any of them. In the premise, the evidence of PW1 is to be preferred over the evidence of DW2 for a simple reason that PW1 was present at the time the contract was negotiated and made and is able to testify as to the real intention of the parties. The real intention of the parties is not embodied in the Off-Cover Policy and that due to a mutual mistake between the parties, the Off-Cover Policy does not truly express their intention as stipulated in the earlier Marine Open-Cover Policy.

In further support of the plaintiff's intention the plaintiff has also led evidence that there were other bills of lading and insurance contracts made at that time which alluded the same terms as the Marine Open-Cover (see: exhs P5, P6, P7 P8 and P9 in Bundle A). All those supporting documents clearly evidenced that the plaintiff's shipments, which were of a similar nature to the goods in question, were bound for Malacca via Port Klang.

The court is satisfied that the plaintiff's evidence is more probable towards the real intention of the parties. Therefore, both on principles and on authorities the court is of the opinion that rectification of the Off-Cover Policy is necessary in order to give effect to the true intent of the parties and to the true intent and purport of the agreement between the parties. There is no evidence to show that the parties, particularly the plaintiff, has changed their intention with regard to the said voyage clause as appeared in the Off-Cover Policy.

In their submissions, the defendant submitted that they were unable to fully appreciate how the rectification of the voyage clause would precipitate in an order for compensation, especially when the defendant had not refused the plaintiff's claim on the grounds that the voyage clause was incorrect but rather that the duration of coverage had terminated. The court is of the view that in order for the plaintiff to claim for compensation or damages under the policy, the plaintiff has to prove that the policy was still in force (not yet terminated) at the time of the fire which destroyed their goods. In doing so, the plaintiff has to show that the voyage clause in the Off-Cover Policy contained a mistake and being contrary to the voyage clause in the Marine Open-Cover Policy. That being the case, it is necessary for the plaintiff to pray for an order of rectification of the said voyage clause in the Off-Cover Policy in order to prove that the said insurance coverage has not terminated on the delivery of the goods to warehouse Gudang 3B as alleged by the defendant. The goods were kept in Gudang 3B (at the time of the fire) awaiting transit to the plaintiff's warehouse in Malacca. The voyage destination was still not completed at the time of the fire and therefore the coverage was still in force then.

TERMS OF CONTRACT

As in all contracts, it is important to distinguish the nature of the terms as that, in turn, will determine the effect of the observance or non-observance of them. It may therefore be useful to distinguish conditions, warranties and representations.

The traditional method of classifying the terms of a contract is according to the degree of their importance. Stipulations that are essential are called 'conditions', while those of a secondary nature are referred to as 'warranties'. The breach of a condition entitles the innocent party to repudiate the contract, that is, to treat it as at an end as to future obligations, and to sue for damages. On the other hand, the breach of a warranty only entitles the party to a claim in damages. Whether a particular term is a condition or a warranty is a matter of judicial impression, i.e., it is a question of law.[66]

---

[66] See *Ching Yik Development Sdn Bhd v Setapak Heights Development Sdn Bhd* [1996] 3 MLJ 675.

Conditions may be sub-divided as follows, namely:

(1) Conditions precedent to the contract, the effect of which is that in case of their non-fulfilment the policy never attaches but is void *ab initio*.

(2) A condition subsequent to the contract which provides that in certain events the policy shall cease to attach. In this case the policy not being void *ab initio*, has attached, but is subsequently avoided.

(3) Conditions precedent to the liability of the insurers. These do not come into operation until after a loss has happened. The validity of the policy is not affected, but the assured is precluded from recovery under it, unless and until he has fulfilled them "where it is still possible to do so". [67]

An alternative method of classification of the terms of a contract is according to, not their relative importance, but the consequences of their breach. This approach is especially useful in cases of synallagmatic contracts.[68] Under this alternative method, if the breach of a particular term goes to the root of the contract, so as to affect its very substratum, then, the remedy of the innocent party lies in repudiation and damages. However, if its breach produces lesser consequences, the remedy of the innocent party lies in damages only.[69]

Where a term in an insurance contract was stipulated to be a condition precedent to the liability of an insurer, the insurer was not liable under the policy unless the term had been strictly complied with by the assured. The due observance and fulfilment of the terms of the policy insofar as they relate to anything to be done by the assured appellant shall be conditions

---

[67] *Mint Security Ltd v Blair, Thos R Miller & Son (Home) Ltd and EC Darwin Clayton and Co Ltd* [1982] 1 Lloyd's Rep 188. See also Ivamy, Marine Insurance 2nd Ed.

[68] A synallagmatic or bilateral contract is one by which each of the contracting parties binds himself to the other e.g. contracts of sale or hire.

[69] See *Bowes v Chaleyer* (1923) 32 CLR 159; *Hongkong Fir Shipping Co Ltd v Kawasaki Kisen Kaisha* [1962] 2 QB 26. See also *Abdul Razak Bin Datuk Abu Samah v Shah Alam Properties Sdn Bhd and Anor Appeal* [1999] 2 MLJ 500; [1999] 3 CLJ 231 (CA).

precedent to any liability of the insurer respondents to make any payment under the policy.[70]

An insurer can disclaim liability where an assured has failed to observe the said conditions precedent. In *Directors of the London Guarantee Co v Benjamin Lister Fearley* Vol V The Law Reports House of Lords 911, it was decided that non-compliance of the term in an insurance contract which is stipulated to be a condition precedent, furnishes a good defence to an action instituted against the insurers.

This is because compliance with the term has been made a condition precedent before the liability of the insurer arises under the policy.

The policy of insurance is a contractual document and the assured cannot enforce the insurer's promise as being contractual unless he, in turn, has performed any provisions which have to be performed by him, to make the contract effective.[71]

In *Pioneer Concrete (UK) Ltd v National Employers Mutual General Insurance Associates Ltd* [1985] 1 Lloyd's Rep 274 Bingham J ruled that an insurer was entitled to avoid liability under an insurance contract for breach of a condition precedent without having to show that he had been prejudiced by the breach of condition. In another case, *Suhaimi bin Ibrahim v United Malayan Insurance Co* Ltd [1966] 1 MLJ 140 Mac Intyre J held that when an assured was in breach of a warranty under an insurance contract, an insurer was entitled to avoid liability under the contract for a loss which occurred after the breach of warranty. Where the statements contained in a policy formed the basis of a contract of insurance, it was held in *Dawson Ltd v Bonnin* [1922] 2 AC 413 that the truth of the statement in the policy was a condition of the liability of the insurer.

Parties also accepted the position that in modern policies, those terms, the due observance of which, were to be a condition precedent to liability

---

[70] *Chong Kok Hwa v Taisho Marine Fire Insurance Co Ltd* [1975] 1LNS 14; [1977] 1MLJ 244.

[71] See 25 Halsbury's Laws of England (4th Ed) para 417).

or recovery, were usually described expressly as conditions precedent.[72] The other proposition was that since the breach of warranty entitles the insurer to repudiate the contract irrespective of how loss occurs, it must be the logical consequence that the insurer can at once disclaim liability under the policy for a breach of warranty before any claim is brought.[73]

Parties can, by clear words, provide that complete performance of a particular stipulation in a contract, can be a condition precedent. But in the absence of clear words the court should look to see which of the rival interpretations gives the more reasonable result.[74]

In *Wickman v Schuler*, [1974] AC 235, Lord Reid said:

> The fact that a particular construction leads to a very unreasonable result must be a relevant consideration. The more unreasonable the result, the more unlikely it is that the parties can have intended it and if they do intend it the more necessary it is they shall make that intention abundantly clear.

The assured is entitled to know by clear language those terms of the policy which are conditions precedent: In *re Bradley and Essex and Suffolk Accident Indemnity Society* [1912] 1 KB 415. At p 433 Lord Justice Farwell said:

> I think it is the duty of all insuring companies to state in clear and plain terms, as conditions precedent, those provisions only which are such, not to wrap them up in a number of clauses, which are not conditions precedent at all; and I think further that it is their duty to call attention to such conditions in their form of proposal so as to make sure that the insurers understand their liabilities.

When a term is stipulated to be a condition precedent in an insurance policy, the insurer is under no liability under the policy until such a term is

---

[72] See MacGillivray & Parkington on Insurance Law (8th Ed) para 741.

[73] MacGillivray & Parkington at para 744. See also *De Hahn v Hartley* [1786] 1 TR 343; 99 ER 1130.

[74] *The Puerto Buitrago* [1976] 1 Lloyd's Rep 250 per Lord Denning, MR, at p 253.

duly complied with by the assured.[75] A case which supports this principle is *Farrell v Federated Employers Insurance Association Ltd* [1970] 1 WLR 498 ("Farrell's case"). According to Farrell's case and *Pioneer Concrete (UK) Ltd v National Employers Mutual General Insurance Association Ltd* [1985] 1 Lloyd's Rep 274 ("Pioneer Concrete"), there was no need for the insurer to have suffered prejudice (as the plaintiff contended) before the insurer could rely on the breach of a notice provision which was a condition precedent. *Barratt Bros (Taxis) Ltd v Davies* [1966] 1 WLR 1334 (Barratt Bros' case) cited in Farrell's case, which stated otherwise, was distinguishable on its facts. The rule was affirmed by the Privy Council in *Motor and General Insurance Co Ltd v Pavy* [1994] 1 WLR 462 and more recently in *Pilkington United Kingdom Ltd v CGU Insurance plc* [2005] 1 All ER (Comm) 283.[76]

A term may be a condition precedent even though not labelled as such.[77] On the other hand, a term labelled as a condition precedent may be interpreted not to be so.[78]

The effect of a breach of a condition precedent in a policy of insurance has been stated in the following passage in Poh Chu Chai, Principles of Insurance Law (LexisNexis, 6th Ed, 2005):

> If an insurer wishes to disclaim liability when an insured breaches a term in the policy, the term has to be made a condition precedent to the liability of the insurer. When a term is stipulated as a condition precedent to the liability of an insurer, the insurer comes under no liability to the insured if he fails to observe the term.

---

[75] Poh Chu Chai, Principles of Insurance Law (LexisNexis, 6th Ed, 2005) (at p 392) and MacGillivray on Insurance Law at para 28-22.

[76] It was also applied by the Supreme Court of South Australia in *McInerney v Schultz* (1981) 28 SASR 542 and *Stork Technology Services Asia Pte Ltd (Formerly Known As Eastburn Stork Pte Ltd v First Capital Insurance Ltd)* [2006] SGHC 101; [2006] 3 SLR 652.

[77] *George Hunt Cranes Ltd v Scottish Boiler and General Insurance Co Ltd* [2002] 1 All ER (Comm) 366.

[78] *Re Bradley and Essex and Suffolk Accident Indemnity Society* [1912] 1 KB 415(CA). See also *Teck Liong (EM) Sdn Bhd v Hong Leong Assurance Sdn Bhd* [2001] 7 CLJ 457 (HC).

WARRANTY

Lord Mansfield characterised a warranty as being a term which is part of a written policy whereas a representation is external to the policy or contract. In *De Hahn v Hartley* (1786) 1 TR 343, Lord Mansfield observed that:

> There is a material distinction between a warranty and a representation. A representation may be equitably and substantially answered; but a warranty must be strictly complied with. Suppose a warranty to sail on the 1st of August, and the ship did not sail till the 2nd, the warranty would not be complied with. A warranty in a contract of insurance is a condition or a contingency and unless that be performed, there is no contract. It is perfectly immaterial for what purpose a warranty is introduced; but, being inserted, the contract does not exist unless it be literally complied with.

A representation does not become a warranty. In order to ensure compliance with any representation made by the assured, the insurer should take care that the representation is inserted into the policy and thus be converted into a warranty.[79]

It is a clear and first principle of insurance law, that when a thing is warranted to be of a particular nature or description, it must be exactly what it is stated to be.[80]

The use of the word 'warranty' is indicative but not decisive. Often the decision on whether a term is a warranty depends on the effect the courts think that the term should have. As Lord Justice Rix put it in *HIH Casualty and General Insurance Ltd v New Hampshire Insurance Co* [2001] EWCA Civ 735, [2001] 2 Lloyd's Rep 161:

---

[79] Ivamy, Marine Insurance 2nd Ed. page 302.

[80] Lord Eloon in *Newcastle Fire Insurance Co v Macmorran* [1815] UKHL 3 Dow 255.

It is a question of construction, and the presence or absence of the word 'warranty' or 'warranted' is not conclusive. One test is whether it is a term which goes to the root of the transaction; a second, whether it is descriptive or bears materially on the risk of loss; a third, whether damages would be an unsatisfactory or inadequate remedy.

Warranties, breach of which entitles the insurers to repudiate the policy, are usually statements made, or answers given, by the assured in a proposal which forms the basis of the contract of insurance.[81]

A warranty is contractual. Since a warranty is necessarily a term of the contract, as opposed to a representation, which is not, it must be found in the contractual documents evidencing the parties' agreements. Therefore, it will generally be found in the policy or in some other document which is incorporated by reference into the policy and made part of it. Usually that document is the proposal form, and the policy itself contains a recital incorporating the proposal and the proposer's declaration therein.[82]

Warranties should be read liberally in favour of the assured and against the insurance company.[83]

Every policy in which an express warranty is inserted, is a conditional contract, which may be avoided by the insurer, unless the warranty is literally complied with.[84]

An express warranty is always written on the face of the policy, while a representation seldom is. Further, while a representation may be satisfied with a substantial and equitable compliance, a warranty requires a strict

---

[81] See MacGillivray & Parkinson on Insurance Law (8th Ed) para 728.
[82] *L'Union Des Assurances De Paris IARD v HBZ International Exchange Co (S) Pte Ltd* [1993] 3 SLR 161 (CA) (Singapore).
[83] MacGillivray on Insurance, Vol 1 Para. 944 at p. 458.
[84] *Tay Wee Khyun v American International Assurance Co Ltd The 'Yuling No 2* [1971] 1 MLJ 218.

and literal fulfilment, i.e., what it avers must be literally true; what it promises must be exactly performed.[85]

A warranty, like every other part of the contract, should be construed according to the understanding of merchants. It must be construed, said Lord Esher, 'according to its ordinary acceptance among the class between whom the documents passed, unless by usage it has acquired a wider or narrower interpretation among men of that class'. 'The same broad rules of construction'; said Brown LJ, 'apply to the interpretation of a warranty as apply to all commercial documents'. Thus, a warranty does not bind the assured beyond the commercial import of the words, but it binds him to their full extent.[86]

Basis clause refers to the warranty, given by the assured, as to the accuracy of the statements contained in his proposal/application form, which in practice is incorporated into the terms of the policy. This warranty is contained in the declaration that is found at the foot of the form. The declaration that the proposer has to sign contains the elements that, first, the answers to the insurer's questions will be made the basis of the contract between the assured and the insurer, and secondly, that any untrue statement should render the insurance policy null and void.

The rule of strict compliance is, however, mitigated in practice by the rules of construction which sometimes have the effect of reducing the scope of a warranty. In this connection it may be noted that the *contra proferentum* rule is adopted by the court in interpreting the warranty. However, it has to be borne in mind that the *contra proferentum* rule is always subordinate to the rule of reasonable interpretation.[87]

The effect of a breach of condition, that is a term going to the root of a contract, is well settled. As Lord Reid stated in *White & Carter (Councils) Ltd v McGregor* [1961] 3 All ER 1178 at 1181, [1962] AC 413 at 427:

---

[85] British Shipping Laws, Volume 10, Cap. 19, Paras 643 and 644.
[86] British Shipping Laws, Volume 10, Cap. 19, paragraph 649.
[87] *American International Assurance Co Ltd v See Ah Yu* [1996] 3 CLJ 566.

> The general rule cannot be in doubt. It was settled in Scotland at least as early as 1848 and it has been authoritatively stated time and again in both Scotland and England. If one party to a contract repudiates it in the sense of making it clear to the other party that he refuses or will refuse to carry out his part of the contract, the other party, the innocent party, has an option. He may accept that repudiation and sue for damages for breach of contract whether or not the time for performance has come; or he may if he chooses disregard or refuse to accept it and then the contract remains in full effect.

In the general law of insurance, excluding marine insurance, a somewhat similar rule applies, although in this field, promissory conditions are customarily described as warranties. In the fifth report of the Law Reform Committee, Conditions and Exceptions in Insurance Policies (1957) para 8, a report signed by Lords Jenkins, Parker, Devlin and Diplock [1989] 3 All ER 628 at 651 it was stated:

> The effect of any promissory undertaking by the insured relating to the risk (in the law of insurance, contrary to general usage, always called a warranty) is perfectly clear. Ever since the time of Lord Mansfield (*De Hahn v. Hartley* ((1786) 1 Term Rep 343, 99 ER 1130) it has been consistently held that warranties must be strictly and literally complied with, and that any breach entitles the insurer to repudiate.

The word "warranty" is used in insurance law in a special sense to denote a term of the contract of insurance which must be strictly complied with and upon any breach of which, however trivial, the insurer is entitled to repudiate the policy. It follows that upon breach of a warranty, the insurer has the right to repudiate the whole contract from the date of the breach, regardless of the materiality of the term, the state of mind of the assured, or of any connection between the breach and the loss".[88]

---

[88] Insurance Law: Non-Disclosure and Breach of Warranty (Law Com no 104).

It is settled law that in the event of a breach of warranty, the insurer can repudiate liability on the policy irrespective of the issues of materiality.[89] As stated by Lord Watson in *Thomson v Weems and Others* [1884] 9 AC 671, at p. 689, "When the truth of a particular statement has been made the subject of warranty, no question can arise as to its materiality or immateriality to the risk, it being the very purpose of the warranty to exclude all controversy upon that point". Further, it has always been the law that there must be strict and exact compliance with the obligation or statement which is warranted.

A breach of warranty by the assured provides the insurer with a defence to any claim which is brought at a time subsequent to the breach. This event is frequently described by the expression that a breach of warranty "avoids the contract" or "renders the contract void". These expressions are however open to objection, because they disguise the undoubted fact that the policy is not automatically void upon the occurrence of a breach of warranty, as would seem to be implied from the use of the word "void", but would only be voided if the insurers elect to exercise their right to avoid the policy and repudiate all liability. It is always open to an insurer to waive a breach of warranty, and, indeed, it may even be held in some circumstances that, even where insurers have not expressly affirmed the contract, they are nonetheless estopped by their conduct from repudiating liability.[90]

In Chitty on Contracts (25th edn, 1983) vol 2, para 3706 it is stated that 'the effect of a breach of conditions or warranties gives the insurer the right to avoid the contract or escape liability for the claim as the case may be; it does not automatically abrogate the contract.'

In *Bank of Nova Scotia v Hellenic Mutual War Risks Association (Bermuda) Ltd; The Good Luck* [1989] 3 All ER 628, it was the view of the court that there was an absence of any difference between the law of marine insurance and insurance law generally, in relation to warranties and the effect of their breach. Section 33 of the UK Marine Insurance Act 1906 ("MIA") provides:

---

[89] See *Dawsons Limited v Bonnin & Others* [1992] 2 AC 413.

[90] MacGillivray and Parkington on Insurance Law (8th edn, 1988) para 790.

(1) A warranty, in the following sections relating to warranties, means a promissory warranty, that is to say, a warranty by which the assured undertakes that some particular thing shall or shall not be done, or that some condition be fulfilled, or whereby he affirms or negatives the existence of a particular state of facts.

(2) A warranty may be express or implied.

(3) A warranty, as above defined, is a condition which must be exactly complied with, whether it be material to the risk or not. If it be not so complied with, then, subject to any express provision in the policy, the insurer is discharged from liability as from the date of the breach of warranty, but without prejudice to any liability incurred by him before that date.

His Lordship May LJ in examining Section 33 said thus:

> Section 34(3) enacts the common law rule that a breach of warranty may be waived by the insurer. What then is the effect under the Act of a breach of an express promissory warranty, which is what is in issue here? In seeking to answer this question we are not concerned with cases (found in the authorities) where terms are or are expressed to be conditions precedent to the parties becoming bound or 'the basis of the contract' or cases where, on occurrence of the specified event, the contract is stipulated to be void. Nor are we concerned with cases (frequently found in practice) where a breach of warranty is the subject of a 'held covered' provision.

> When one asks whether a breach of warranty gives a right to avoid (as in ss 17, 18, 20, 36 and 42) or effects discharge from liability (as in ss 45, 46 and 48) the obvious answer is that it effects a discharge of liability because that is the language the 1906 Act uses and a parliamentary draftsman uses the same language to mean the same thing. The bank urges that the obvious answer is the right answer, and the judge with all his experience appears to have had no hesitation in accepting it.

It is, however, a matter of history that the 1906 Act had a more than usually protracted journey to the statute book, being introduced in 1894 and on repeated occasions thereafter. Until 1901 the predecessor of what is now s 33(3) contained as its second sentence:

> 'If it be not so complied with, the insurer may avoid the contract [as from the date of the breach of warranty, but without prejudice to any liability incurred by him before such date].'

The passage in square brackets was a point on which the law was thought to be uncertain. Otherwise the clause reflected what was understood to be the existing law. In 1903 the clause was altered to its present form although the square brackets began at the words 'but without prejudice'.

This does not of itself advance the argument very much, since the ordinary inference would be that the language was changed to effect a change in the meaning. We have, however, been referred to A Digest of the Law relating to Marine Insurance (1st edn, 1901; 2nd edn, 1903) and The Marine Insurance Act 1906 (1st edn, 1907; with subsequent editions in 1913, 1922 and 1932), the main author of all editions, save the last being Sir Mackenzie Chalmers. In all editions of both books the following commentary appears:

> 'The use of the term "warranty" as signifying a condition precedent is inveterate in marine insurance, but it is unfortunate, because, in other branches of the law of contract the term has a different meaning. It there signifies a collateral stipulation, the breach of which gives rise merely to a claim for damages and not to a right to avoid the contract ... It is often said that breach of a warranty makes the policy void. But this is not so. A void contract cannot be ratified, but a breach of warranty in insurance law appears to stand on the same footing as the breach of a condition in any other branch of contract. When a breach of warranty is proved the insurer

is discharged from further liability unless the assured proves that the breach has been waived.'

We cannot, of course, regard this commentary as a guide to the intention of the draftsman but only as the opinion of a learned author and former judge. Further, the last sentence reads somewhat inconsistently with what precedes it. It none the less appears to have been the opinion of this commentator, deeply immersed in the law on this subject as he plainly was, that a breach of an express promissory warranty did not of itself and without more bring the contract to an end and that the rule in marine insurance did not differ from that pertaining in the general law of insurance or in the law of contract generally.

Arnould Law of Marine Insurance and Average (16th edn, 1981) vol 2, pp 549–550, para 708 addresses this question only in the context of implied warranties and then in footnote 18(p 549):

> 'The statement made by Arnould that the breach of warranty avoids the policy is clearly inaccurate, since after it had been avoided it would not be possible for the insurer to affirm it, as he has always been able to do, by waiving the breach. It was no doubt for this reason that the draftsman of the Marine Insurance Act 1906, preferred to use the expression "discharged from liability". Strictly speaking, however, this is open to the same objection, since if he had once become "discharged as from the date of the breach" it would logically become impossible for the insurer to make himself liable by subsequent waiver, unless possibly he could be held estopped from pleading "the discharge". The true position appears to be that the breach of warranty gives the insurer the right to avoid the policy, and to make such avoidance operate from the time of breach...'.

In none of the authorities to which we were referred was the present question truly in issue. It scarcely could be, since an action could not ordinarily be tried without the insurer having made plain his intention to reject a claim or treat a contract as at an end. In *Provincial Insurance Co of Canada v Leduc* (1874) LR 6 PC 224, on which the club relied, the real issues were whether a provision in the policy was a limitation of the risk or (as it was held to be) a promissory warranty and whether the insurers had waived a breach of warranty. The bank relied on *Thomson v Weems* [1884] 9 AC 671 at 684, where Lord Blackburn said:

> 'In policies of marine insurance I think it is settled by authority that any statement of a fact bearing upon the risk introduced into the written policy is, by whatever words and in whatever place, to be construed as a warranty, and, primâ facie, at least that the compliance with that warranty is a condition precedent to the attaching of the risk.'

In *Union Insurance Society of Canton Ltd v George Wills & Co* [1916] 1 AC 281 at 288–289 this statement was relied on by the Privy Council with the additional comment that: 'There is no difference in principle in this respect between a statement of fact and an undertaking that some particular thing shall be done.' In Thomson, however, the assured had agreed that his answers to certain questions should be the basis of the contract and if any of these was untrue the contract was to be absolutely void. In the *Union Insurance case* the insurers declined to accept a declaration under the policy and thus made plain their intention to treat it as at an end. More importantly, there plainly is a difference between a condition precedent properly so called, non-fulfilment of which results in there being no contract, and breach of a promissory warranty which cannot be contended to have that result.

The point is most directly addressed by Donaldson J in *De Maurier (Jewels) Ltd v Bastion Insurance Co Ltd* [1967] 2 Lloyd's Rep 550 at 558–559, where he said:

> '... I also hold, as was ultimately conceded, that the warranty delimits and is part of the description of the risk and is not of a promissory character. By a warranty of

> a promissory character I mean a warranty by the assured that a particular state of affairs will exist, breach of which destroys a substratum of the contract and entitles the underwriter to decline to come on risk or, as the case may be, to terminate the risk as from the date of breach. In the marine field "warranted free from capture and seizure" is a warranty of the former character leaving the contract effective in respect of loss by other perils. "Warranted to sail on or before a particular date" is, however, of a promissory character, breach of which renders the contract voidable. The commercial reasoning behind this legal distinction is clear, namely, that breach of the former type of warranty does not affect the nature or extent of the risks falling outside the terms of the warranty; breach of a promissory warranty may, however, materially affect such risks.'

This passage is plainly obiter, but none the less in our view persuasive. To read s 33(3) as conferring a right to avoid is not inconsistent with the recognition of waiver in s 34(3), since in s 42 one finds both these conditions.

We were referred to no text and no authority which suggested any difference between the law of marine insurance and insurance law generally on this point. Indeed, in *Thomson v Weems* [1884] 9 AC 671 at 684, immediately following the passage cited above, Lord Blackburn said: 'I think that on the balance of authority the general principles of insurance law apply to all insurances, whether marine, life, or fire ...' We can see no reason why, on the present point, there should be such a difference, and we would think it unfortunate if there were. Nor, even accepting the need for exact compliance with a promissory warranty in an insurance policy, can we see any reason why the ordinary principles of contract should not apply. It would, we think, be contrary to principle if the assured were able by his unilateral act to bring the contract to an end, and it would be the more surprising if breach of a warranty (which might in itself be insignificant and immaterial) were to have this result. If breach of a warranty brought the policy automatically to an end we do not, despite the bank's argument to the contrary, see how it could be revived save by a new agreement. We do not regard these conclusions as in any way inconsistent with the manner in which, in our experience, insurers actually conduct their business.

We have for these reasons concluded that s 33(3) is to be read as enacting the same rule as that which applies, in the absence of contrary agreement, to breach of express promissory warranties in the law of non-marine insurance.

TYPES OF POLICIES

Different names or descriptions are given to the array of policies of insurances available in the market. These policies are frequently marketed or advertised through pamphlets or brochures introducing the potential buyer to the product of insurance being sold. These pamphlets or brochures contain the proposal and declaration forms which, if accepted by the insurance companies, are generally incorporated into and form part of the contract of insurance.

Liability Insurance Policy

A liability insurance policy is a contract of indemnity in which the insurer agrees to indemnify his assured for any loss suffered by reason of the assured's liability to another.[91]

In liability insurance, in which the assured insures against liability to third parties arising otherwise than from the contract, the liability insured against is the real subject-matter of insurance. The assured has no direct interest in the safety of third persons or in the preservation of their property from harm. The loss against which he seeks protection is not the injury or damage caused by the accident. It is the consequence of the fact

---

[91] *Post Office v Norwich Union Fire Insurance Society Ltd* [1967] 2 QB 363. See also *Bradley v Eagle Star Insurance Co Ltd* [1989] AC 957.

that he happens to be responsible for the accident in the circumstances in which it takes place.[92]

In *Orica Ltd v CGU Insurance Ltd* CA 40559/02, 2003 NSWCA 331, Spigelman CJ examined the nature of liability insurance policies and stated:

> There is a line of authority with respect to policies of liability insurance that the liability of the insurer arises only as and when the liability of the insured is established in the sense of being crystallised by settlement, arbitration or verdict. (See *Post Office v Norwich Union Fire Insurance Society Ltd* [1967] 2 QB 363 esp at 373-374, 377-378; *Cacciola v Fire and All Risks Insurance Co Ltd* [1971] 1 NSWLR 691 at 695 *Distillers Co Biochemicals (Aust) Pty Ltd v Ajax Insurance Co Ltd* (1974) 130 CLR 1 at 25-26 *Bradley v Eagle Star Insurance Co Ltd* [1989] 1 AC 957 at 964-966.)
>
> In *AMP Workers' Compensation Services (NSW) Ltd v QBE Insurance Ltd* (2003) 53 NSWLR 35 at [9], Handley JA, with whom Mason P and Beazley JA agreed, applied this line of authority to a New South Wales workers' compensation policy. However, at [15]-[16] Handley JA went on to refer to the consideration by Glass JA of the word "liability" in *Australian Iron and Steel v GIO*, where at 62, his Honour construed the word "liability" in the then third-party motor vehicle policy. His Honour held that in that context "against all liability ... incurred by the owner" the word did not require liability to be ascertained by judgment or settlement. 'Liability' arose at the time the cause of action arises which is when a defendant has incurred a liability in tort to pay damages.
>
> The determination of the meaning of the word 'liability' will always turn on the precise words of the policy in their context. In *Post Office v Norwich Union*, *Cacciola*, and *Distillers v Ajax*, the policy words were to the effect: "against all sums which the insured shall become legally liable to pay". The words "shall

---

[92] E R Hardy Ivamy General Principles of Insurance Law (6th Ed) Butterworths, London, 1993 at 12.

become" do suggest a process of establishing liability which is not inherent in the words "shall be so liable", in the policy under consideration.

In the present appeal, Mr G F Little SC, who appeared for the Respondent, did not put forward a contention that the policy did not respond until ascertainment of damage by verdict or judgment. He propounded a construction that liability arose when there has occurred damage which would "justify the bringing of proceedings for damages" (written submissions para [5]) or "entitling those indemnified to bring an action" (T21 line 39). In substance, this submission propounded a test of enforceability, as distinct from enforcement.

Mr M Joseph SC, who appeared for the Appellant, contended that the policy responded at the time of "injury". He submitted that injury occurred at the time of inhalation of the fibres. Alternatively, he submitted, if the test of liability required a complete enforceable cause of action there was sufficient damage at the time of inhalation.

The policy, upon payment of a single premium, extends indemnity for both an employer's liability at common law and for its obligations under the Act. It does this by one use only of the word "liable", applicable to both matters, ie "to pay compensation under the Act" and "to pay any other amount". The word "liable" must have the same meaning in both applications. Similarly, the words of indemnity are made applicable to both categories by a single clause "all such sums for which the Employer shall be so liable". Again, the word "liable" is used in the same sense with respect to both matters.

The authorities establish that an employer's liability under the Act accrues when injury occurs, not when consequential incapacity arises and, accordingly, compensation falls to be paid. The statutory policy responds at the time of injury, even if incapacity arises later. (See eg *Australian Iron & Steel Ltd v Coal Mines Insurance Pty Ltd* (1952) 52 SR (NSW) 47 at 50-51, 52, 55-6

Geraldton Building Co Pty Ltd v May (1977) 136 CLR 379 at 384, 404 *Manufacturers Mutual Insurance Ltd v National Employers' Mutual General Insurance Assn Ltd* (1991) 6 ANZ Ins Cas 61-038 at 76, 964 (hereafter " MMI v NEM"; *National & General Insurance Co Ltd v South British Insurance Co Ltd* (1982) 149 CLR 327 at 334-335; *State Mines v GIO* at 264-265, 268; *Dillingham Engineering* at 586-587.)

In contrast, liability arose at the time of incapacity in the case of a disease of gradual onset, not at the time of receipt of the injury. (See *Fisher v Hebburn Ltd* (1960) 105 CLR 188 esp at 203; State Mines Control Authority esp at 261, 265.) Furthermore, a dependent's death claim arose at the time of death, not injury. (*Ogden Industries Pty Ltd v Lucas* (1968) 118 CLR 32 at 38, 39 approving *Ogden Industries Pty Ltd v Lucas* (1967) 116 CLR 537.) Similarly, compensation under the Act turning on the worker's election, arises upon the election, not at the time of the injury. (*Geraldton Building Co Pty Ltd v May* (1977) 136 CLR 379 esp at 394-395.)

If the policy responds at the time of injury, with respect to an employer's liability to make payments under the Act, it is arguable that it should respond at the time of injury with respect to an obligation to make payments for liability at common law.

There is authority for the proposition that injury occurs upon inhalation of fibres. The reasoning in *Favelle Mort Ltd v Murray* (1976) 133 CLR 580, as Santow JA shows, is to the effect that the entry of a virus into the body is itself an "injury" within the meaning of the Act and, therefore, of the policy. In GRE, the Full Court of the Supreme Court of Western Australia applied this reasoning and concluded that the inhalation of asbestos fibres into the body was the "injury" and not the subsequent commencement of mesothelioma. (See at 77,260-77,261.)

Older authorities suggest that the injury constituted by the initial penetration of the lungs by asbestos fires is not sufficiently material to constitute damage for purposes of determining whether a cause of action in negligence is complete. (See eg *Cartledge v E Jopling & Sons Ltd* [1963] AC 758 at 774.1 and 779.3 (a pneumoconiosis case) and *Footner v Broken Hill Associated Smelters Pty Ltd* (1983) 33 SASR 58 at 74.3.) It is not necessary to decide any such question here.

The Appellant's case depends on when an "injury" has occurred within the meaning of the policy, not when damage has occurred for purposes of the law of negligence. It may be that an injury has occurred at the time of inhalation and penetration of the lungs, even if the disease of mesothelioma can only be said to have commenced at a later date, when the malignancy develops on the lung. (See *American Home Assurance v Saunders* (1987) 11 NSWLR 363 at 378 and 384 (cf 372) and *Martindale v Burrows* [1997] 1 Qd R 243 at 245.)

The policy, relevantly, relates to the occurrence of the injury in the following formulation:

> ... the Employer shall be liable ... to pay any other amount ... in respect of his liability independently of the Act for any injury to any ... worker.

I accept, for present purposes, that there may be an "injury" within the policy at the time of inhalation of the fibres. It does not follow that at that time, an employer is 'liable to pay an amount in respect of his liability' at common law 'for that injury'. Some of the observations of Santow JA are directed to rejecting a construction of the policy that would require an injury and damage to occur in the same policy period. I wish to make it clear that that is not how I construe the policy. The relevant insured peril is 'liability' rather than the occurrence of the injury.

The authorities which determine that a liability to pay compensation under the Act arises even before incapacity, do not, when properly understood, turn on the time when the injury occurs in and of itself. They turn on the fact that the statute creates a liability or right at the time of the injury.

Each of the cases turn on the particular provisions of the statute which fell to be construed. Under s 7(1) of the Act, which determined many of the cases, "A worker who has received an injury ... shall receive compensation from his employer in accordance with this Act". The cases determine that the liability to pay compensation arose immediately upon injury, because s 7(1), as properly construed, created a legal obligation arising at that time.

The rights of the worker, and the correlative obligations of the employer, were expressed in different terms in the various cases, but to the same effect. For example, "the rights and liabilities are vested" in the words of Rainbow J from *Dwyer v Broken Hill South Ltd* (1928) 2 WCR 209, quoted with approval by Street CJ in *Australian Iron & Steel v Coal Mines Insurance* at 50-51; and there is "a vested right to compensation" at the time of injury. (*Ibid* at 55.) The question is when can it be said that there are "rights in law" (*Ogden Industries* (Privy Council) at 38) or an "accrued right" or "accrued liability". (*Fisher v Hebburn* at 202-203 esp at 203.9; *Western Pastoral Co v Eyeington* (1971) 125 CLR 342 at 352; *Dillingham Engineering* at 586C-587B; *TNT Australia Pty Ltd v Horne* (1995) 36 NSWLR 630 at 637B-F.)

If the words of the policy "liable to pay" mean the same with respect to the two circumstances to which they apply ie "compensation under the Act" and "in respect of his liability independently of the Act" then the policy responds in the latter case only if the employer's liability has, within the relevant period, 'vested' or 'accrued'. In my opinion, that does not occur earlier than the time of onset of mesothelioma. Damage is the gist of the action in negligence. The "injury" occasioned at the time of penetration of the lung by a fibre, if it be injury within the meaning of the policy at all, which I doubt, is so negligible in and of itself, as distinct from its potential, that it does not constitute damage that is compensable at common law.

Accordingly, the policy did not respond during its currency. The appeal should be dismissed.

The Court of Appeal held that an assured did not suffer loss until his liability had been determined by judgment, arbitration or agreement. This approach differs from that taken by the court in *Chandris v Argo Insurance Co Ltd* [1963] 2 Lloyd's Rep 65 where it was held that an assured had suffered loss when he had incurred liability to the third party, even though the existence and amount of that liability had not yet been established.[93]

The purpose of liability insurance is not merely to protect the financial interests of the assured, but it is also to protect the interests of those to whom the assured may incur liability from. The Louisiana Direct Action Statute provides, for example, that "all liability policies ... are executed for the benefit of all injured persons ... to whom the insured is liable" and allows third parties a right of direct action against insurers, regardless of the solvency of the assured.

In liability insurance the assured is generally required to give notice of an occurrence or event likely to give rise to a claim. The word 'likely' excludes the mere possibility of a claim, so that notification is not required merely because a claim is 'possible'. However, the material words in the notice provision are 'may give rise to a claim' not 'likely to give rise to a claim'.[94]

Life Insurance Policy

The contract commonly called life assurance, when properly considered, is a mere contract to pay a certain sum of money, on the death of a person, in consideration of the due payment of a certain annuity for his life, the amount of the annuity being calculated in the first instance according to the probable duration of the person's life; when once fixed, it is constant and invariable. A stipulated amount of annuity is to be uniformly paid on one side, and the sum to be paid in the event of the death is always, except when bonuses have been given by prosperous offices, the same

---

[93] See also *Castle Insurance Co Ltd v Hong Kong Shipping Co Ltd (The Potoi Chou)* [1984] 1 AC 226.

[94] *Stork Technology Services Asia Pte Ltd (Formerly Known As Eastburn Stork Pte Ltd v First Capital Insurance Ltd* [2006] SGHC 101; [2006] 3 SLR 652.

on the other. This species of insurance in no way resembles a contract of indemnity, unlike policies of insurance, against fire and marine risks where the insurer is engaged to make good within certain limited amounts, the losses sustained by the assured in their buildings, ships, and effects.[95]

'Open Cover' Insurance Contract

The 'Open Cover' Insurance Contract was examined in *Hanwha Non-Life Insurance Co Ltd v Alba Pte Ltd* [2011] SGHC 271 where Tan Lee Meng J stated:

> The term "open cover" indicates that the reinsurance contract is open obligatory in nature.

In Robert H Brown, Dictionary of Marine Insurance Terms and Clauses (Witherby, 5th ed, 1989), the term "open cover" was explained at p 7 as follows:

> A form of long-term insurance contract whereby the insurer guarantees to accept risks when they are put forward by the assured as they arise during the period of the contract. The assured agrees to declare every item that falls within the scope of the cover and does not have the option to place such risk elsewhere should he consider it advantageous so to do. Thus, the open cover is an obligatory contract binding both parties to its terms, rates and conditions.

Similarly, in C Bennett, Dictionary of Insurance (Pitman, 1st ed, 1992), the term "open cover" was defined at p 240 as follows:

> This is a marine insurance term. When there are regular sendings of goods, it is usual to arrange an open cover to avoid the necessity of separate policies for each sending. The two most common methods are the floating policy and the open cover. The

---

[95] *Dalby v India and London Life Assurance* [1843-1860] All ER Rep 1040; [1843-60] All ER Rep 1040.

following features are common to both: The assured is bound to declare and the insurer to accept all endings coming within the scope of the contract.

CONTRACT OF INSURANCE AND VITIATING FACTORS

The general principle of law, of course, is that a party who signs a written contract is bound by the terms of the contract, except in limited cases where fraud, undue influence, or misrepresentation may be established. This rule is so strict that even if a party to a contract has not read the contents of a contract, he is held to be bound by its terms.[96]

Therefore, insurers are bound by the terms of the insurance contract unless it can be shown that the contract was tainted with fraud, misrepresentation or undue influence.

The various shades of fraud set out in (a) to (e) of Section 17 of the Malaysian Contracts Act 1950 — with illustrations (a) to (d) — would indicate that fraud in certain situations could be purely civil in nature, as the impugned act involved only obliquity in conduct or, what has been loosely termed as 'sharp practice'. The vital question to ask is whether the fraud complained of amounted to a criminal offence. Thus, the element of fraud could be civil and criminal in nature.

CONTRACTS OF INSURANCE

- Introduction

- Formation

- Proposal Form

- Basis Clause

---

[96] *Polygram Records Sdn Bhd v The Search & Anor* [1994] 3 MLJ 127; [1994] 3 CLJ 806.

- Premiums
- Cover Notes
- Policy
- Insurable Interest
    - Nature of Insurable Interest
- Risk
- Mistake and Rectification
    - Evidence of Common Intention
- Terms of Contract
- Warranty
- Types of Policies
    - Liability Insurance Policy
    - Life Insurance Policy
    - 'Open Cover' Insurance Contract
- Contract of Insurance and Vitiating Factors

CHAPTER 2

INTERPRETATION OF INSURANCE CONTRACTS

In relation to the terms of a contract or more specifically, insurance contracts, there may exist terms that require ascertaining whether they are conditions, warranties or representations. It may also entail ascertaining the intention of the parties, in spite of the labels attached to the terms.

The process of interpretation of contracts is to unearth the meaning attributed by the parties to words and clauses incorporated in it and its process of interpretation is set out below.

First, by 'interpretation', we refer to the process of ascertaining the meaning of the expressions in a contract. The presence of expressions, primarily in the form of words constituting an express term, is an essential prerequisite to invoke the process of interpretation. This view (i.e., that interpretation concerns the meaning of words) is supported by academics in the United States of America such as Prof Allan Farnsworth, Prof Arthur Corbin ("Prof Corbin") and Prof Samuel Williston.[97] Prof Corbin's explanation of the process of interpretation is particularly apt[98]:

---

[97] Allan Farnsworth, "'Meaning' in the Law of Contracts" (1966–1967) 76 Yale LJ 939 at 939–940.

[98] Margaret N Kniffin, Corbin on Contracts vol 5 (Joseph M Perillo ed) (LexisNexis Law Publishing, 1998 Rev Ed) at para 24.1

> Interpretation is the process whereby one person gives a meaning to the symbols of expression used by another person. The symbols most commonly in use are words, appearing singly or in groups, oral or written; but acts and forbearances are also symbols of expression requiring interpretation.
>
> [28] Since the process of interpretation entails ascribing meaning to the parties' contractual or contractually relevant expressions, there cannot be interpretation of a non-expression, ie, a non-existent expression. As Lord Steyn observed in *Equitable Life Assurance Society v Hyman* [2002] 1 AC 408 ("Hyman") at 458, the purpose of interpretation is "to assign to the language of the text the most appropriate meaning which the words can legitimately bear" [emphasis added]. It is through such a process of interpretation that the parties' intentions as expressed in the contract are objectively ascertained: *Sembcorp Marine Ltd v PPL Holdings Pte Ltd and another and another appeal* [2013] SGCA 43 (CA).

Contractual interpretation denotes the process of uncovering the meaning in and seeking to understand a [written contract] where there is some doubt or room for a difference of opinion.[99] In this regard, the general principle is that the court will ascertain the meaning which the expressions used in the contract in question would convey, to a reasonable person having all the background knowledge which would reasonably have been available to the parties, at the time the contract was entered in.[100]

'Interpretation', as Neil MacCormick, Rhetoric and the Rule of Law (Oxford University Press, 2005) succinctly states (at pp 121–122), usually denotes the process of uncovering meaning in and seeking to understand a text

---

[99] See *Zurich Insurance (Singapore) Pte Ltd v B-Gold Interior Design & Construction Pte Ltd* [2008] 3 SLR(R) 1029 at [41]).

[100] See, eg, *Sandar Aung v Parkway Hospitals Singapore Pte Ltd* [2007] 2 SLR(R) 891 at [35][37], citing *Investors Compensation Scheme Ltd v West Bromwich Building Society* [1998] 1 WLR 896 at 912913): *KS Energy Services Ltd v BR Energy (M) Sdn Bhd* [2014] SGCA 16.

where there is some doubt or room for a difference of opinion. In the context of contractual interpretation, the text sought to be understood is the written contract, which constitutes *prima facie* proof of the parties' intentions where the contract is complete on its face. In this regard, Prof Ronald Dworkin's comments in his seminal work, Law's Empire (Hart Publishing, 1998), at p 52 should be borne in mind: Interpretation is an activity undertaken in relation to an object or a practice already existing, and the shape of that object or practice will be a constraint upon the interpretation that can be applied to it. It should also be noted that the term 'construction' is often used interchangeably with 'interpretation', although some commentators regard these as qualitatively different processes (for examples of the latter view, see Catherine Mitchell, Interpretation of Contracts: Current controversies in law (Routledge-Cavendish, 2007) ('Mitchell') at; Phipson on Evidence (Hodge M Malek gen ed) (Sweet & Maxwell, 16th Ed, 2005) ('Phipson')).

The concept of 'interpretation' set out in Chitty namely, 'assigning a definite meaning to terms capable of such explanation or ... pointing out and connecting them with the proper subject-matter' – reflects the traditional approach to interpretation, under which ambiguity (or absurdity, or the existence of an alternative technical meaning) is a prerequisite for the admissibility of extrinsic evidence. This requirement also draws the line between interpreting and varying the terms of a contract. In the former scenario, the court is explaining the equivocal language of a contract by assigning one of a range of possible meanings to its terms. The shift towards what is often called the 'contextual' approach to contractual interpretation, however, appears to have removed this prerequisite of establishing (inter alia) ambiguity before extrinsic evidence may be considered when interpreting contracts. This has created further pressure on the *raison d'Être* of the thin definition of the parol evidence rule since, in 'interpreting' language that is clear on its face, the court sometimes veers dangerously close towards varying, adding to or subtracting from the contract. Indeed, it has recently been affirmed in Gerard McMeel, The Construction of Contracts: Interpretation, Implication, and Rectification (Oxford University Press, 2007) ('McMeel') at para 1.65 that 'the parol evidence rule [in its thin definition] ... is dead'.

Interpretation, is the ascertainment of the meaning which the document would convey to a reasonable person, having all the background knowledge which would reasonably have been available to the parties, in the situation in which they were at the time of the contract.[101]

Isaacs J in *Life Insurance Co of Australia Ltd v Phillips* (1925) 36 CLR 60 said:

> The 'meaning of the words' is what I call interpretation, whether the words to be interpreted into ordinary English are foreign words or code words or trade words or mere signs or even ordinary English words which on examination of surrounding circumstances turn out to be incomplete. Their effect when translated into complete English is construction. If that distinction be borne in mind very little difficulty remains.

In *Neal v Secretary, Department of Transport*, 3 A.L.D. 97 (FC), Franki J referred to the judgment of Isaacs J and further said:

> Isaacs J in *Life Insurance Co of Australia Ltd v Phillips* (1925) 36 CLR 60, referred (p 78) first of all to what had been said by Lindley LJ in; *Chatenay v Brazilian Submarine Telegraph Co* ([1891] 1 QB 79 at 85) namely: "The expression 'construction,' as applied to a document, at all events as used by English lawyers, includes two things: first, the meaning of the words; and, secondly, their legal effect, or the effect which is to be given to them. The meaning of the words I take to be a question of fact in all cases, whether we are dealing with a poem or a legal document. The effect of the words is a question of law.
>
> Isaacs J continued: He went on to refer (pp 78-79) to what had been said by the Privy Council in *McConnel v Murphy* ((1873) LR 5 PC 203 at 219) and continued (p 79): "Once there is established the full mutual expression of the agreement in English words, the construction of the document is, as Lindley LJ says, a pure matter of law. Lord Chelmsford in; *Di Sora v Phillipps* ((1863)

---

[101] Investors Compensation Scheme at WLR 912-13; All ER 114-5 per Lord Hoffman.

10 HL Cas 624 at 638, 639) makes this clear to demonstration, and there separates the interpretative function from that of true construction (see also per Lord Atkinson in; *Williams Bros v Ed T Agius Ltd* ([1914] AC *510 at 527)*. For this purpose, no external evidence is permissible. All preliminary operations of interpretation are assumed to have been performed and, if necessary, by appropriate evidence, as explained by Lord Chelmsford in; Di *Sora v Phillipps, and, the* judge's mind being sufficiently informed, he must be left to his own office of construing the language of the instrument in question.

What was said by Isaacs J in Phillips was specifically referred to by Jordan CJ in *Australian Gas Light Co v Valuer-General*, supra, in support of his proposition that the question of what is the meaning of an ordinary English word or phrase as used in a statute is one of fact not of law (40 SR (NSW) at 137). He ought not, therefore, to be taken as having departed at all from the views expressed by Isaacs J in the passage which I have cited. Accordingly, I would reject the respondent's submission that the applicant's principal proposition does not raise a question of law.

I turn then to deal with that proposition. The authorities to which I have referred show that before embarking on the exercise of construction, a judge needs to ascertain the meaning of the various expressions used in the instrument to be construed. Really, he needs to ascertain the meanings of which the expressions are capable. As I have earlier said, if words used are technical words or terms or art (or, I would add, expressed in a foreign language), recourse may be had to evidence to explain them. If they are ordinary English words, their meaning may only be ascertained by reference to dictionaries and other standard works. To the references earlier given I add a reference to the decision of the Court of Appeal in England in *Marquis of Camden v Inland Revenue Commissioners* [1914] 1 KB 641, particularly Cozens-Hardy MR at 647-8. The decisions to which I have referred provide clear authority for the proposition that a court concerned only with deciding a question of construction (that is a question of law) may inform itself of the meaning of ordinary English words by reference to dictionaries and other standard works notwithstanding that the meaning of such words is a question of fact. The court has to be able to take that course. Otherwise it cannot put itself in a position to construe the statute. In *Australian Gas Light Co v Valuer-General*, Davidson J, in his dissenting judgment, made this clear when he gave as an instance of the problem the determination of a demurrer which raised a question of construction for decision (40 SR (NSW) at 143). Although he dissented he did so, not on any question of principle, but on the construction of the statute which was in that case in question.

The Court's Role in Contractual Interpretation

Sir Thomas Bingham MR in *Philips Electronique Grand Public SA v British Sky Broadcasting Ltd* [1995] EMLR 472 (at 481) explained the court's role in the interpretation of contracts as follows:

> The courts' usual role in contractual interpretation is, by resolving ambiguities or reconciling apparent inconsistencies, to attribute the true meaning to the language in which the parties themselves have expressed their contract. The implication of contract terms involves a different and altogether more ambitious undertaking: the interpolation of terms to deal with matters for which, *ex hypothesi*, the parties themselves have made no provision.

Interpretation of Contracts as a Whole

The meaning of a document or a particular part of it, is to be sought from the document itself. This does not mean that one must discover the meaning of a particular word or phrase, from that word or the words of that phrase alone. The document must be read and interpreted as a whole in order to extract the meaning of any particular part or expression.

Further assistance as to what the parties intended by the words they used, can be gained from 'the matrix of facts' in which they were set.[102]

The basic principle in the interpretation of contracts is that written contracts must not be construed just by relying on the wordings of the same but must also take into account the surrounding circumstances between the parties to the agreement, leading up to the same being signed. The Federal Court in *Berjaya Times Square Sdn Bhd (formerly known as Berjaya Ditan Sdn Bhd) v M Concept Sdn Bhd* [2010] 1 MLJ 597 stated:

> Here it is important to bear in mind that a contract is to be interpreted in accordance with the following guidelines. First, a court interpreting a private contract is not confined to the four corners of the document. It is entitled to look at the factual matrix forming the background to the transaction. Second, the factual matrix which forms the background to the transaction includes all material that was reasonably available to the parties. Third, the interpreting court must disregard any part of the background that is declaratory of subjective intent only. Lastly, the court should adopt an objective approach when interpreting a private contract. See, *Investors Compensation Scheme Ltd v West Bromwich Building Society* [1998] 1 All ER 98.

Intention of the Parties

In relation to ascertaining the intention of the parties, Lord Clyde in *Bank of Credit and Commerce International SA v Munawar Ali* [2001] 2 WLR 735 said:

> The knowledge reasonably available to them (that is to say the parties to the contract) must include matters of law as well as matters of fact. The problem is not resolved by asking the parties what they thought they intended. It is the imputed intention of the parties that the court is concerned to ascertain. The

---

[102] Per Virtue J in *Qualico Developments Ltd. v. Calgary (City)* (1987), 81 A.R. 161; 53 Alta. L.R. (2d) 129 (Q.B.), at p. 138.

parties may well have never applied their minds to the particular eventuality which has subsequently arisen, so that they may never in fact have had any conscious intention in relation to that eventuality. It is an objective approach which is required and a solution should be found which is both reasonable and realistic. The meaning of the agreement is to be discovered from the words which they have used in the context of the circumstances in which they made the agreement. The exercise is not one where there are strict rules, but one where the solution is to be found by considering the language by the parties against the background of the surrounding circumstances.

Interpretation of Contracts - Principle of Objectivity

In interpreting contracts, the courts must apply the principle of objectivity. It is not the subjective belief or understanding of the parties about their rights and liabilities that govern their contractual relations. What matters is what each party by words and conduct would have led a reasonable person in the position of the other party to believe. References to the common intention of the parties to a contract, are to be understood as referring to what a reasonable person would understand, by the language in which the parties have expressed their agreement. The meaning of the terms in a contractual document is to be determined by what a reasonable person would have understood them to mean. That, normally, requires consideration not only of the text, but also of the surrounding circumstances known to the parties, and the purpose and object of the transaction.[103]

Generally, the courts must discern the meaning and intention of the contract from within the four corners of the document. In such a situation, extrinsic evidence is inadmissible to aid in the interpretation of it.

Where the parties have embodied the terms of their contract in a written document, the general rule is that extrinsic evidence is not admissible to add to, vary, subtract from or contradict the terms of the written instrument. This rule is often known as the 'parol evidence' rule. Its

---

[103] *Toll (FGCT) Pty Ltd v Alphapharm Pty Ltd* [2004] HCA 52, (2004) 219 CLR.

operation is not confined to oral evidence, but extends to extrinsic matters in writing such as drafts, preliminary agreements and letters of negotiation. The instrument itself is the only criterion of the intention of the parties; so extrinsic evidence is excluded even though such evidence might clearly show that the real intention of the parties was at variance with the particular expressions used in the written instrument.[104]

In *Zurich Insurance (Singapore) Pte Ltd v B-Gold Interior Design & Construction Pte Ltd* [2008] 3 SLR(R) 1029, the Court of Appeal endorsed the contextual approach for the interpretation of a contract with a qualification (at [122]) that when interpreting a contract, 'extrinsic evidence is only employed to illuminate the contractual language and not as a pretext to contradict or vary it'. VK Rajah JA stated (at [132]) as follows[105]:

> To summarise, the approach adopted in Singapore to the admissibility of extrinsic evidence to affect written contracts is a pragmatic and principled one. The main features of this approach are as follows:
>
> (a) A court should take into account the essence and attributes of the document being examined. The court's treatment of extrinsic evidence at various stages of the analytical process may differ depending on the nature of the document. In general, the court ought to be more reluctant to allow extrinsic evidence to affect standard form contracts and commercial documents ...
>
> (b) If the court is satisfied that the parties intended to embody their entire agreement in a written contract, no extrinsic evidence is admissible to contradict, vary, add to, or subtract from its terms (see ss 93–94 of the Evidence Act). In determining whether the parties so intended, our courts may look at extrinsic evidence and apply the normal objective test, subject to a rebuttable presumption that a contract which is complete on its face was

---

[104] *West v Hoyle* (SC) (Hamilton) [1972] NZLR 996 per Speight J.

[105] See also *Hanwha Non-Life Insurance Co Ltd v Alba Pte Ltd* [2011] SGHC 271; [2012] 1 SLR 941 (HC) (Singapore).

intended to contain all the terms of the parties' agreement ... In other words, where a contract is complete on its face, the language of the contract constitutes *prima facie* proof of the parties' intentions.

(c) Extrinsic evidence is admissible under proviso (f) to s 94 to aid in the interpretation of the written words. Our courts now adopt, via this proviso, the modern contextual approach to interpretation, in line with the developments in England in this area of the law to date. Crucially, ambiguity is not a prerequisite for the admissibility of extrinsic evidence under proviso (f) to s 94 ...

(d) The extrinsic evidence in question is admissible so long as it is relevant, reasonably available to all the contracting parties and relates to a clear or obvious context ... However, the principle of objectively ascertaining contractual intention(s) remains paramount. Thus, the extrinsic evidence must always go towards proof of what the parties, from an objective viewpoint, ultimately agreed upon ... [T]here should be no absolute or rigid prohibition against evidence of previous negotiations or subsequent conduct, although, in the normal case, such evidence is likely to be inadmissible ... (We should add that the relevance of subsequent conduct remains a controversial and evolving topic that will require more extensive scrutiny by this court at a more appropriate juncture.) Declarations of subjective intent remain inadmissible except for the purpose of giving meaning to terms which have been determined to be latently ambiguous (... see ... sub-para (e) below).

(e) In some cases, the extrinsic evidence in question leads to possible alternative interpretations of the written words (ie, the court determines that latent ambiguity exists). A court may give effect to these alternative interpretations, always bearing in mind s 94 of the Evidence Act. In arriving at the ultimate interpretation of the words to be construed, the court may take into account subjective declarations of intent ... Furthermore, the normal canons of interpretation apply in conjunction with the relevant provisions of the Evidence Act, ie, ss 95–100 ...

(f) A court should always be careful to ensure that extrinsic evidence is used to explain and illuminate the written words, and not to contradict or vary them. Where the court concludes that the parties have used the wrong words, rectification may be a more appropriate remedy ...

[33] In the present case, the parties clearly did not intend to embody their entire agreement in a written contract. That was why both parties relied on extrinsic evidence to shed light on the nature of the reinsurance policy. Such evidence would be useful if it is relevant, reasonably available to all the contracting parties and relates to a clear or obvious context.

THE INTERPRETATION OF INSURANCE CONTRACTS

The courts have construed policies of insurance to give effect to the commercial purpose and business sense of a policy.[106]

It is an accepted canon of construction that a commercial document, such as an insurance policy, should be construed in accordance with sound commercial principles and good business sense, so that its provisions receive a fair and sensible application. Several consequences flow from this principle. The literal meaning of words must not be permitted to prevail where it would produce an unrealistic and generally unanticipated result, as, for example, where it would absolve the insurer from liability on the chief risks sought to be covered by the policy. Thus, in the case of *Syarikat Uniweld Trading v The Asia Insurance Co. Ltd. [1996] 3 CLJ 142; [1996] 2 MLJ 160*, it was held that in a policy where the main purpose was to insure against damages arising from negligent acts by the insured, a condition that 'the insured shall take reasonable precautions' could not be construed to mean that every negligent act was a breach of it. By virtue of this maxim, the court should also be prepared to overlook obvious grammatical errors, such as an inadvertent negative remark obviously out

---

[106] *Syarikat Uniweld trading v The Asia Insurance Co. Ltd.* [1996] 3 CLJ 142; [1996] 2 MLJ 160; *Petrofina (UK) Ltd v Magnaload Ltd* [1983] 3 All ER 35; and *Fraser v Furman (BN) (Productions)* [1967] 3 All ER 57.

of context, and should interpret, for the purposes of the particular cover, inappropriate phrases in a standard printed policy, primarily intended for other sorts of insurance, or else disregard them as matters of surplusage to the cover in question. A further result of this maxim is that a court may imply into the express words granting cover, an extended scope beyond their strictly literal meaning, in order to give effect to the only sound interpretation of the contract.[107]

Insurance Policy in Mandatory Statutory Form

Even though an insurance policy may be in a mandatory statutory form, the policy must be constructed as a contract. In the Australian case of *Orica Ltd v CGU Insurance Ltd* CA 40559/02, 2003 NSWCA 331, the approach to the construction of a worker's compensation policy was explained by Spigelman CJ as follows:

> The words of the policy must be construed, not the section of the Act which requires the policy to exist. (*Sydney Turf Club v Crowley* [1971] 1 NSWLR 724 at 732 D; (1972) 126 CLR 420 at 426). The provisions of the Act may assist in determining the proper construction of the policy, not least because they are expressly "incorporated and form part of the policy" and s 18(1) of the Act is set out as the first recital of the policy. (*State Mines Control Authority v Government Insurance Office of NSW* (1964) 65 SR (NSW) 258 at 260-261; *Dillingham Engineering Pty Ltd v National Employers' Mutual General Insurance Assn Ltd* [1971] 1 NSWLR 578 at 582E-F and 584F-585A; *AMP Fire & General Insurance Co Ltd v Miltenburg* [1982] 1 NSWLR 391 at 396-397). The extent of the indemnity by the insurer to the employer must be found in the language of the policy, properly construed. (*State Mines*, at 261.)

---

[107] MacGillivray & Parkington on Insurance Law (8th Ed) at para. 1077; *Singatronics Ltd v Insurance Co Of North America* [1994] 1 SLR 500. See also *Martin (John) of London v Russell* [1960] 1 Lloyd's Rep 554, *Lowenstein (J) & Co v Poplar Motor Transport (Lymm) and Gooda (Third Party)* [1968] 2 Lloyd's Rep 223.

There is no policy discernible in the legislative scheme to favour employers, as distinct from employees (*Kodak (Australasia) Pty Ltd v Retail Traders Mutual Indemnity Insurance Assn* (1942) 42 SR (NSW) 231 at 233). Neither party can be said to have proffered the contract and it cannot be construed *contra proferentem*. (*Kodak v Retail Traders*, at 233; *Green v Windman* [1964] VR 297 at 298.) Insofar as *Nicholson J in GRE Insurance Ltd v Bristile Ltd* (1991) 6 ANZ Ins Cas 61-078 at 77 construed the policy *contra proferentem*, I believe his Honour erred. This Court should follow its own prior decision in Kodak. The proposition that the legislative scheme, particularly by making the insurer directly liable to the worker, evinces an intention that the insurer should be liable whenever the insured employer is liable, has not been adopted (See *Registrar, Workers' Compensation Commission of NSW v National Employers' Mutual General Insurance Assn* (1978) 141 CLR 462 at 490 and compare the analysis in *MLC Insurance Ltd v FAI Traders Insurance Co Ltd* (1994) 49 FCR 23 at 25, 34).

At the end of the day, the construction of a policy of insurance is a question for the court to decide; see (*Clift v Schwabe* (1846) 3 CB 437 (life insurance) per Parke B at p 469; and *Simond v Boydell* [1779] 1 Doug KB 268 (marine insurance) per Buller J, at p 277). The principles of construction are the same as in the case of other contracts (*Robertson v French* [1803] 4 East 130 (marine insurance) per Lord Ellenborough at p 135; *Carr v Montefiore* (1864) 5 B & S 408, Ex Ch (marine insurance); *Smith v Accident Insurance Co* (1870) LR 5 Exch 302 (accident insurance) per Martin B, at p 307; *West India Telegraph Co v Home and Colonial Insurance Co* (1880) 6 QBD 51, CA (marine insurance) per Brett LJ at p 58; and *Stewart v Merchants Marine Insurance Co* (1885) 16 QBD 619, CA (marine insurance) per Lord Esher MR at pp 626, 627).

In *Jason v Batten 1930 Ltd*; *Jason v British Traders' Insurance Company Ltd* [1969] 1 QB 281, Fisher J explained the application of the rules of construction to a policy of insurance in the following manner:

> A policy of insurance is subject to the same rules of construction as any other written contract. The words used in it must be given their plain, ordinary meaning in the context of the policy looked at as a whole, subject to any special definitions contained in the

policy. In the case of ambiguity, the *contra proferentum* rule will apply but apart from this there is no rule of law which requires me to strain any language of the policy in favour of or against the insured person.

In construing this policy (marine insurance) and ascertaining the intention of the parties, we look at the whole policy and the terms used in it in its plain, ordinary and popular sense. We also look at all the surrounding circumstances known to the parties at the time the contract of insurance was made.[108]

The reasonableness of the result is a relevant consideration in choosing between rival constructions. In *Re Zurich Australian Insurance Ltd* [1998] QSC 209, it was stated:[109]

> If the limitation applied to both categories, the condition could be used to the great detriment of an insured. An insurer could conduct the defence on behalf of an insured confidently expecting the action to fail only to find, at the trial, that the claimant's case was far stronger than realised. If Zurich's construction of the condition be right, the insurer could then pay the amount of the limit of indemnity and avoid liability for indemnifying the insured for the claimant's costs. I do not think a construction should be countenanced which gives an insurer such latitude.

Atkin LJ in *Re Calf & Sun Insurance Office's Arbitration* [1920] 2 KB 366 at 382 protested that one case of construction of an insurance policy should not be treated as an authority in another unless the language and the circumstances are substantially identical.

WORDS

It is the language of the policy that is paramount. In interpreting and construing the terms of the said policy in order to determine the intention

---

[108] See Halsbury's Laws of England (4th Ed) paras 43 and 45: *Kin Yuen Co Pte Ltd v Lombard Insurance Co Ltd* [1994] 2 SLR 887 (HC).

[109] See also Interpretation of Contracts by Lewison at pages 151-2.

of the parties, the court must always look to the whole policy. A contract of insurance is subjected to the same 'general rules of interpretation as any other written document'. The words used must *'prima facie'* be construed 'in their plain, ordinary, popular meaning, rather than their strictly precise, etymological, philosophical, or scientific meaning'. 'Only if there is a clause in the policy which is open to two constructions, the court will construe it *contra proferentum'* — per Raja Azlan Shah FJ (as His Highness then was) in *Malaysia National Insurance Sdn Bhd v Abdul Aziz bin Mohamed Daud* [1979] 2 MLJ 29 at p 31.

Policy of Insurance - Rules of Construction

Traditionally, if a court wants to go outside the policy, it must use one of three routes. The first route is the technical route, that is, although the words appear clear, they have a technical meaning that is not apparent without seeking extrinsic evidence, the second route is ambiguity, that is, the words are not clear but ambiguous and the ambiguity must be resolved by taking a wider view and the third route is absurdity, that is, a literal reading is not just unreasonable but unworkable or absurd and must be avoided by taking a wider view.[110]

Meaning of the Words Used

An English policy is to be construed according to the same rules of construction, which are applied by English Courts, to the construction of every other mercantile instrument. Each term in the policy, and each phrase in the policy, is *prima facie* to be construed according to its ordinary meaning.[111]

The interpretation of the relevant provisions of the policy would depend on the facts of the particular case.[112] There are one or two well-settled

---

[110] Malcolm A Clarke, The Law of Insurance Contracts (Informa, 5th Ed, 2006).

[111] *West India and Panama Telegraph Company v. Home and Colonial Marine Insurance Company*, (1880) 6 Q.B.D. 51, per Lord Justice Brett at p. 58.

[112] *Malaysia National Insurance Sdn Bhd v Malaysia Rubber Development Corporation* [1986] 2 MLJ 124.

rules of construction with regard to policies. One is that the construction depends not upon the presumed intention of the parties but upon the meaning of the words used.[113] The Court must construe the words as they stand, against the background of the transaction of which they form part of, and with due regard to the need to arrive at a conclusion which makes business common sense.[114]

In *Cosmic Insurance Corporation Ltd v Ong Kah Hoe (t/a Ong Kah Hoe Industrial Supplies) & Anor* [1998] 1 SLR 1044, Rubin J said[115]:

> The general rule of construction, as stated by Farwell LJ in *Yangtsze Insurance Association v Indemnity Mutual Marine Assurance Co* [1908] 2 KB 504 at p 509 is that the words used in documents must receive their primary signification unless the context of the instrument read as a whole or surrounding contemporaneous circumstances shew that the secondary meaning expresses the real intention of the parties or unless the words are used in connection with some place, trade or the like in which they have acquired the secondary meaning as their customary meaning *quoad hoc* [as to that]. In *J Lowenstein & Co Ltd v Poplar Motor Transport (Lymm) (Gooda, third party)* [1968] 2 Lloyd's Rep 233, Nield J suggested at p 238 that the words in the agreement must be construed according to the understanding of business people as to make their meaning realistic and such as to give business efficacy to the agreement. In *Lake v Simmons* [1927] AC 487, Viscount Sumner at p 509 observed:

---

[113] *Nelson Line (Liverpool) Ltd v James Nelson & Sons Ltd* [1908] AC 16 per Lord Loreburn LC at p 20.

[114] *Continental Illinois National Bank & Trust Co v Bathurst* [1985] 1 Lloyd's Rep 625 per Mr Justice Mustill at p 628.

[115] See also: *Malaysia National Insurance Sdn Bhd v Abdul Aziz bin Mohamed Daud* [1979] 2 MLJ 29 referred to in *Sim Ah Hee @ Lim Ah Hee & Anor v Affin Bank Bhd and another appeal* [2010] 5 MLJ 1 (CA); *Perembun Consortium (a joint venture between Perembun (M) Sdn Bhd and Road Builder (M) Sdn Bhd) & Anor v AXA Affin General Insurance Bhd (formerly known as AXA Affin Assurance Bhd)* [2011] 6 MLJ 719 (HC); *Helmut Schleich v Peri Formwork (M) Sdn Bhd* [2013] 7 MLJ 112 (HC).

> Everyone must agree that commercial contracts are to be interpreted with regard to the circumstances of commerce with which they deal, the language used by those who are parties to them and the objects which they are intended to secure.

In construing an insurance policy, the words used must be considered in the context of the particular clause as a whole, the clause must in turn be considered in the context of the policy as a whole, which must in its turn be set in its surrounding circumstances or factual matrix.[116]

(a) Businesslike Interpretation
It is an accepted canon of construction that a commercial document, such as an insurance policy, should be construed in accordance with sound commercial principles and good business sense, so that its provisions receive a fair and sensible application. See the words of Lord Diplock in *Antaios Compania Naviera v Salen Rederierna AB* [1985] AC 191 at 201 cited in paragraph 7(iv) by Longmore LJ: If a "detailed semantic and syntactical analysis of a word in a commercial contract is going to lead to a conclusion that flouts business common sense, it must be made to yield to business common sense".[117]

(b) Commercial Objective
The commercial objective or function of the clause in question and its relationship to the contract as a whole will be relevant in resolving any ambiguity in the wording.

(c) Construction to Avoid Unreasonable Results
If the wording of a clause is ambiguous, and one reading produces a fairer result than the alternative, the reasonable interpretation should be adopted. It is to be presumed that the parties, as reasonable men, would have intended to include reasonable stipulations in their contract.[118]

---

[116] See Clarke LJ in *MDIS v Swinbank* [1999] 2 All ER (Comm) 722, [1999] Lloyd's Rep IR 516 at 521 para 13.

[117] *Absalom v TCRU Ltd* [2006] 2 Lloyds Rep 129.

[118] *Ibid* above.

Insurance Words – Interpretation - Prior Judicial Pronouncements

The first and overriding consideration in construing any phrase or form of words in a policy is to inquire whether these have been the subject of any prior decision by the court, as the proper construction to be placed on words is a matter of law.[119]

In *Sawarn Singh a/l Mehar Singh (named as a nominee) v RHB Insurance Bhd* [2014] 7 MLJ 416 (HC), Her Ladyship Mary Lim J was of the view that "at the end of the day, the decisions turned on the language of the particular policy. It can only be on all fours if the language is the same. What, however, may be extracted would be the principles applied that may aid this court in interpreting this particular policy". [120]

Words - Plain Meaning

As was said by Lord Ellenborough CJ in *Robertson v French* [1803] 4 East 130:

> This is done by looking at the terms used in the policy, which terms are themselves to be understood in their primary, natural, ordinary and popular sense.

A similar approach was taken by the Singapore Court of Appeal in *Malayan Motor & General Underwriters Pte Ltd v Mohamad Hamid Almojil* [1982-1983] SLR 52 at 58[26].

In *Loh Shiiun Hing v Kurnia Insurans (Malaysia) Bhd* [2014] 7 CLJ 490 (CA), the court rejected the argument that seems to have assumed that some peculiar rules of construction applied to the terms of a policy of insurance which were not equally applicable to the terms of other instruments in all other cases. His Lordship Abu Samah Nordin JCA said:

---

[119] MacGillivray on Insurance Law at p 278, Para 11-12.

[120] See also *Amanah Raya Bhd v Jerneh Insurance Sdn Bhd* [2005] 2 CLJ 393 (CA).

> ...it is therefore proper to state upon this head, that the same rule of construction which applies to all other instruments applies equally to this instrument of a policy insurance, *viz* that it is to be construed according to its sense and meaning, as collected in the first place from the terms used in it, which terms are themselves to be understood in their plain, ordinary, and popular sense, unless they have generally in respect to the subject matter, as by the known usage of trade, or the like, acquired a peculiar sense distinct from the popular sense of the same words; or unless the context evidently points out that they must in the particular instance, and in order to effectuate the immediate intention of the parties to that contract, be understood in some other special and peculiar sense.

The Federal Court in *Provincial Insurance Co Ltd v. Yee Chee Swee* [1984] 2 CLJ 12; [1984] 1 CLJ (Rep) 314; [1984] 2 MLJ 60 expressed the same view.

> There is a presumption that the words to be construed should be construed in their ordinary and popular sense, since the parties to the contract must be taken to have intended, as reasonable men, to use words and phrases in their commonly understood and accepted sense. The object of the enquiry is not necessarily to probe the 'real' intention of the parties, but to ascertain what the language they used in the document would signify to a properly informed observer: Longmore LJ in *Absalom v TCRU Ltd* [2006] 2 Lloyds Rep 129.

The words of the policy are to be construed not according to their strictly philosophical or scientific meaning, but in their ordinary and popular sense.[121] Collins LJ in *Re George and Goldsmiths' and General Burglary Insurance Association Ltd* [1899] 1 QB 595, at p 610 said: "All I have to do is to look at the words which (the parties) have used, and try to give them their plain and common-sense meaning".

---

[121] Kelly CB said in *Stanley v The Western Insurance Co* (1868) LR 3 Ex Ch 71 at p 73.

Literal Meaning of Words

In *Syarikat Uniweld Trading v The Asia Insurance Co Ltd* [1996] 2 MLJ 160, it was reiterated thus:

> The literal meaning of the words in the insurance policy must not be allowed to prevail where it would produce an unrealistic and generally unanticipated result ... in the context of the present appeal would be to absolve the respondent as an insurer from liability on the chief risks sought to be covered by the insurance policy. It is not out of place to mention that in interpreting any clause of an insurance policy, one must bear in mind the commercial object or function of the clause and its apparent relation to the contract as a whole (*Kearney v General Accident Fire and Life Assurance Corp* [1968] 2 Lloyd's Rep 240; and *L Schuler AG v Wickman Machine Tool Sales Ltd* [1974] AC 235 at pp 251 and 265). In adopting this approach, it becomes apparent that the literal meaning of the clause in the insurance policy must necessarily yield to business sense so that an ambiguity in the wording can be resolved.

Where the meaning of the words in the policy is reasonably clear it must be given full effect even though it operates harshly against the assured.[122]

Contract Deletion- Effect of Deleted Words

There is a divergence of authority on whether a court may take into consideration deleted words as an aid in the construction of a contract. In the headnote to *Mopani Copper Mines plc v Millenium Underwriting* Ltd [2008] EWHC 1331 (Comm) [2008] All ER (D) 192 (June) it was stated:

> The diversity of authority rendered it difficult for a judge of first instance to recognise when recourse to deleted words might properly be made. The tenor of those authorities appeared to be that in general such recourse was illegitimate, save that;

---

[122] MacGillivray on Insurance Law 5th Edition pg. 704.

deleted words in a printed form might resolve the ambiguity of a neighbouring paragraph that remained; and the deletion of words in a contractual document might be taken into account, for what, if anything, it was worth, if the fact of deletion showed what it was the parties agreed that they did not agree and there was ambiguity in the words that remained. That was classically the case in relation to printed forms, or clauses derived from printed forms, but could also apply where no printed form was involved. Even if recourse is had to the deleted words, care must be taken as to what inferences, if any, can properly be drawn from them.

The parties may have deleted the words because they thought they added nothing to, or were inconsistent with, what was already contained in the document; or because the words that were left were the only common denominator of agreement, or for unfathomable reasons or by mistake. They may have had different ideas as to what the words meant and whether or not the words that remained achieved their respective purposes. Further, even in the cases where the fact of deletion was admissible as an aid to interpretation, there was a great difference between a case where a self-contained provision was simply deleted and another case where the draft was amended and effectively re-cast. Where the first provision contained a number of ingredients, some assisting one party and some assisting the other, and that provision was removed, it by no means followed that the parties intended to agree the converse of each of the ingredients in the earlier provision.

Unambiguous Words

In *Putra Perdana Construction Sdn Bhd v AMI Insurance Bhd & Ors* [2005] 2 MLJ 123, Ramly Ali J was satisfied that there was no ambiguity in relation to the condition of the insurance policy under scrutiny. It was stated therefore that 'the rule of *contra proferentum* as alleged by the plaintiff was inapplicable'. It was reiterated that the *contra proferentum* rule should not be used to create an ambiguity where none exists. The court held:

The basic presumption is that the words should receive their ordinary and natural meaning, and this is displaced only when there is a real ambiguity either appearing on the face of the policy or revealed by extrinsic evidence. (See: (i) *Condogianis v Guardian Assurance & Co* (1921) 2 AC 125; (ii) *Yorke v Yorkshire Insurance Company* (1918) 1 KB 662).

If the meaning of the words is reasonably clear it must be given full effect even if it operates harshly against the assured. (See: *Woolford v Liverpool CC* [1968] 2 Lloyd's Rep 256).

...One should not strain the language to find an ambiguity when none exists. The words used in conditions 29 are plain and simple. No technical words or complex phrases are used. There is no ambiguity. Therefore, the plaintiff's allegation that condition 29 is vague and ambiguous cannot stand and must be rejected.

Strict Compliance with Unambiguous Notice Provisions in Insurance Policies

The principle of strict compliance with the notice provisions in insurance policies was recognised in the Singapore context by Judith Prakash J in *Tan Thuan Seng v UMBC Insurans Sdn Bhd*, (1997) 3 SLR (R) 725(18) (High Court, Singapore). Prakash J followed the principles enunciated in *Farrell's case* [1970] 1 WLR 498 and in *Motor and General Insurance Co Ltd v Pavy* [1994] 1 WLR 462 but distinguished them and applied *Barratt Bros' case* [1966] 1 WLR 1334, on the facts. The words used in the notice provision were 'immediately give notice in writing', 'immediately forward to [the defendant] upon receipt every letter claim writ summons or process', 'immediately notify [the defendant] when the [plaintiff] has knowledge of any impending prosecution inquest or inquiry'. The wording was unambiguous and clearly called for strict compliance.[123]

---

[123] *Stork Technology Services Asia Pte Ltd (Formerly Known As Eastburn Stork Pte Ltd v First Capital Insurance Ltd* [2006] SGHC 101; [2006] 3 SLR 652.

AMBIGUITY

The policy must be construed against the insurers and in favour of the assured where there is a doubt as to its meaning. That also applies to a proposal form which is filled in by an assured when the proposal form has been prepared by the insurer. [124]

In *United India Insurance Co Ltd v Pushpalaya Printers* [(2004) 3 SCC 694], the court held, "Where the words of a document are ambiguous, they shall be construed against the party who prepared the document. This rule applies to contracts of insurance and clause 5 of the insurance policy even after reading the entire policy in the present case, should be construed against the insurer."

Further, in *Maye v. Colonial Mutual Life Assurance Society Limited* [1924] HCA 26; (1924) 35 CLR 14 at 22, the court said: "If by reason of its own language in relation to the matter, or by reason of the context or of conflicting or differing provisions elsewhere, a term when fairly read is doubtful or ambiguous and reasonably susceptible of two constructions, that construction should be adopted which is the more favourable to the assured, because that is of the two the more reasonable in the circumstances ...".

There is a principle of construction that if a document *inter partes* contains an ambiguity which cannot otherwise be satisfactorily resolved, it is to be construed adversely against the party who proffered it for execution.[125]

Where, however, the question is ambiguous, in that, the meaning intended by the insurer would not be readily apparent to a reasonable

---

[124] *Galloway v Guardian Royal Exchange (UK) Ltd* [1999] Lloyd's Rep IR 209 (CA).

[125] Lord Brightman in the Privy Council case of *Kandasami v Mohamed Mustafa* [1983] 2 MLJ 85 at p 88. See also *Kandasami v Mohamed Mustafa* [1983] 2 MLJ 85 referred to in *Sim Ah Hee @ Lim Ah Hee & Anor v Affin Bank Bhd and another appeal* [2010] 5 MLJ 1 (CA); *Perembun Consortium (a joint venture between Perembun (M) Sdn Bhd and Road Builder (M) Sdn Bhd) & Anor v AXA Affin General Insurance Bhd (formerly known as AXA Affin Assurance Bhd)* [2011] 6 MLJ 719 (HC)

man, the fact that the assured has misunderstood or misinterpreted the question in giving what he believed to be a truthful answer will, in general, exonerate him.[126]

The more serious proposition arises on the construction of the question and answer. In a contract of insurance, it is a weighty fact that the questions are framed by the insurer, and that if an answer is obtained to such a question, which upon a fair construction is a true answer, it is not open to the insuring company to maintain that the question was put in the sense different from or more comprehensive than the proponent's answer concerned. Where an ambiguity exists, the contract must stand, if an answer has been made to the question, on a fair and reasonable construction of a question. Otherwise the ambiguity would be a trap against which the assured would be protected by courts of law. [127]

If the question is ambiguous, and a person *bona fide* understands it in a particular sense and that sense is a reasonable sense, he cannot be said to be giving an untrue answer if he understands it truly in the sense in which he understands it. In the case of *Taylor v. Eagle Star Insurance Co. Limited* (1940) 67 Lloyd's List L.R. 136, MacNaghten J rejected that first ground on which the insurance company contested the liability under this policy, and held "... I think rightly... that the ground alleged was not well founded and that the answer was not an untrue answer".

If there is an ambiguity or a doubt as to the extent of the Policy, we should have to construe it in favour of the assured, that is to say, if the question arose as to the liability of the insurers, we should have to put on the Policy the construction most favourable to the assured and the less favourable construction to the insurers.[128]

---

[126] Colinvaux and Merkin on Insurance Contract Law April 2009 issue at §A-0665.

[127] *Condogianis v Guardian Assurance Company Limited* [1921] 1 A.C. 125.

[128] *Edwards v Griffiths* [1953] 1 WLR 1199, 1203. See also *Tan Kwang Chin v Public Prosecutor* [1959] MLJ 253 and *Cheong Bee v China Insurance Co Ltd* [1974] 1 MLJ 203.

IMPLIED TERMS

No term, which would conflict with an express term, can ever be implied just because, in the light of subsequent events, it may seem reasonable and desirable. A term will only be implied where it is essential, that is, where without it, the agreement would be without 'business efficacy' or where the court holds that both parties must have intended it.[129] The implication of any terms into a contract is only permissible if it is both necessary and reasonable to work the contract.[130]

There is another rule summarised in the case of *Hamlyn & Co v Wood & Co*, [1891] 2 Q.B. 488, from Lord Esher's judgment at p. 49:

> I have for a long time understood that rule to be that the Court has no right to imply in a written contract any such stipulation, unless, on considering the terms of the contract in a reasonable and business manner, an implication necessarily arises that the parties must have intended that the suggested stipulation should exist. It is not enough to say that it would be a reasonable thing to make such an implication. It must be a necessary implication in the sense that I have mentioned. Another rule of construction is that as a policy is prepared by the underwriters, any ambiguity therein must be taken most strongly against the underwriters by whom it has been prepared. If a policy is reasonably susceptible of two constructions, that one will be adopted which is more favourable to the insured. *Pacific Carriers Ltd v BNP Paribas* [2004] HCA 35, (2004) 218 CLR 451, at 461-462 [22].

---

[129] *Trollope & Colls Ltd v NW Metropolitan Regional Hospital Board* [1973] 1 WLR 601 at pp 606D-610D per Lord Pearson, at p 613 bottom to page 614F per Lord Cross.

[130] *Kin Yuen Co Pte Ltd v Lombard Insurance Co Ltd & Ors* [1994] 2 SLR 887.

CONTRA PROFERENTUM - General

If there is any ambiguity in the language used in a policy, it is to be construed more strongly against the party who prepared it, that is, in the majority of cases, against the insurer.[131]

Policies of insurance are to be construed largely, for the benefit of the trade and in favour of the assured.[132] The rule was stated with approval by Lord Mansfied CJ in *Pelly v Royal Exchange Assurance Co.* (1757) 97 ER 342. The basis of the rule is the long-established principle that a grantor may not derogate from his grant.

Any ambiguous clause in the policy must be construed against, rather than in favour of, the insurance company.[133]

In *Re Bradley and Essex and Suffolk Accident Indemnity Society* [1912] 1 KB 415, Farwell LJ (at 430) regarded the requirement of good faith from both the insurer and the assured as providing the rationale for construing policies of insurance *contra proferentum*. Because the insurer invariably prepares the policies and chooses the wording and because it must act in good faith towards its assured, it is obliged to make the meaning of its policies plain. If it does not, any ambiguity is resolved in favour of the assured.

Contra Proferentum Rule

In *S & M Hotels Ltd v Legal and General Assurance Society Ltd* [1972] 1 Lloyd's Rep 157, 221 EG 1331, Thesiger J had occasion to consider some principles of construction of insurance policies. There it was said:

---

[131] MacGillivray paragraph 703.

[132] Lee CJ in *Tierney v Etherington* (1743) 97 ER 347.

[133] *Re Etherington and the Lancashire and Yorkshire Insurance* Co. [1909] 1 KB 591; *Leong Luen Kiew & Anor v The New Zealand Insurance Co Ltd* [1939] 1 LNS 50.

First as to the law. There is clear authority as to the way in which a Court should interpret a policy of insurance. In 1840 in *Mayor v. Issac* (1840) 6 M. & W. 605, at p. 610, one finds Baron Parke referring to . . . the general rule of the common law, that the words of an instrument are to be taken most strongly against the party using them. He left the Court during the argument but before doing so expressed his entire concurrence with the opinion that was to be delivered and Baron Alderson in delivering his opinion said, at p. 612:

> Undoubtedly, the generally received principle of law is, that the party who makes any instrument should take care so to express the amount of his own liability, as that he may not be bound beyond what it was his intention that he should be; and, on the other hand, that the party who receives the instrument and parts with his goods on the faith of it, should rather have a construction put upon it in his favour, because the words of the instrument are not his, but those of the other party.

In 1858 Chief Justice Cockburn, then in the Common Pleas, said in *Notman v The Anchor Assurance Co* (1858) C.B.N.S. 466, at p. 481:

> This instrument being the language of the company, must, if there be any ambiguity in it, be taken most strongly against them.

In 1861 Mr. Justice Blackburn in *Braunstein v Accidental Death Insurance Co.* (1861) 1 B. & S. 782, at p. 799, said:

> . . . Here the stipulation is the language of one party, the company, and *verba fortius accipiuntur contra proferentem.*

In 1863 the same Judge in *Fowkes v Manchester and London Life Assurance and Loan Association* (1863) 3 B. & S. p. 917, at p. 929, after citing once again the Latin maxim that he had used before, had said:

> .. one of those rules is, that in all deeds and instruments the language used by one party is to be construed in the sense in which it would be reasonably understood by the other.

And then:

> ... And if the party who proffers an instrument uses ambiguous words in the hope that the other side will understand them in a particular sense, and that the Court which has to construe the instrument will give them a different sense, the above rules apply, and they ought to be construed in that sense in which a prudent and reasonable man on the other side would understand them.

Then, in 1864, Mr. Justice Wiles said, in *Fitton v Accidental Death Insurance Company* (1864) 17 C.B.N.S. 122, at pp. 134 to 135

> It is extremely important with reference to insurance, that there should be a tendency rather to hold for the assured than for the company, where any ambiguity arises upon the face of the policy.

Where there is an ambiguity between the indemnity clause and an exception clause, the courts will apply the *contra proferentum* rule as propounded by the Federal Court in the case of *Malaysia National Insurance Sdn Bhd v Abdul Aziz bin Mohamed Daud* [1979] 2 MLJ 29, where the insurance policy was construed in favour of the appellant assured. The Federal Court in that case pointed out that the general rules of interpretation apply to insurance policies as in any other written document and proceeded to lay down a well-trodden principle (at p 32) that:

> ... as between the assured and the insurers, the exception clause in the proviso, on the ordinary principles of construction has, as far as possible, to be read against the insurance company, that is to say, if there is a doubt as to its extent and the question were

to arise as to the liability of the insurers, the construction most favourable to the assured must be given to him.

Thus, from all that has been stated above, it can be summarized that in construing insurance policies, the *contra proferentum* rule should apply if there is ambiguity or doubt as to the extent of the policy. Since the policy is prepared by the insurance company, the doubt and ambiguity should be construed in favour of the assured.[134]

If there is a latent ambiguity in the policy, extrinsic evidence is admissible to identify the persons and things referred to in it.[135]

It is to be noted however that the *contra proferentem* rule, is an aid to the construction of ambiguous documents. It does not permit the artificial creation of an ambiguity in order to reach a particular result.[136] Even where a clause, taken alone, is ambiguous, the *contra proferentem* rule does not apply if its meaning becomes clear in the context of the overall policy.[137]

The *contra proferentum* rule in construing an insurance policy was applied by Mohamed Azmi J in the case of *Central Lorry Service Co Sdn Bhd v The American Insurance Co* [1981] 2 MLJ 40 where it was said[138]:

> In my view, there is only doubt and ambiguity in the clause as to whether the policy covers any accident to the vehicle or is merely confined to accidents caused by the vehicle involuntarily leaving the road or by breakdown of bridges. In construing insurance policies, the *contra proferentum* rule should apply if there is ambiguity or doubt as to the extent of the policy. Since the policy

---

[134] *Central Lorry Service Co Sdn Bhd v The American Insurance Co* [1981] 2 MLJ 40.

[135] *Pacific & Orient Underwriters (M) Sdn Bhd v Choo Lye Hock* [1977] 1 MLJ 131.

[136] Colinvaux ([44] supra) at para 3-10, n 67.

[137] Colinvaux at para 3-10, n 69.

[138] See *Central Lorry Service Co Sdn Bhd v The American Insurance Co* [1981] 2 MLJ 40 referred to in *Mary Colete John v South East Asia Insurance Bhd* [2010] 2 MLJ 222 (CA).

is prepared by the insurance company, the doubt and ambiguity should be construed in favour of the assured, namely, the plaintiff in this case. In the event, I hold that the policy covers all accidents to the vehicle and that the two events described in the clause are mere examples and not exhaustive. The plaintiff's claim is, therefore, covered by the inland transport clause in the policy.

The Federal Court in *Malaysia National Insurance Sdn Bhd v Abdul Aziz bin Mohamed Daud* [1979] 2 MLJ 29 per Raja Azlan Shah FCJ said:

> It is of course established law that in the case of a motor insurance policy which is a contractual document, it is subject to the same general rules of interpretation as any other written document... Only if there is a clause in the policy which is open to two constructions, the court will construe it *contra proferentum*, that is, against the insurers.

> ...if the question were to arise as to the liability of the insurers, the construction most favourable to the assured must be given to him. It would of course be unnecessary to resort to these rules if the contract addresses itself in explicit language to the event or problem in question. See also *TKM (Singapore) Pte Ltd v Export Credit Insurance Corporation of Singapore Ltd* [1993] 1 SLR 1041.

In *Tan Guat Lan & Anor v AETNA Universal Sdn* Bhd [2003] 5 CLJ 384 the court said:

> The insurance companies have massive resources including lawyers to advise them and help them draft documents and the burden ought to be placed on them, to ensure that there can be no ambiguity or doubt in the documents. It is common knowledge that the ordinary person who applies for a policy or a reinstatement of a policy has no say in the wordings of the standard documents that he is asked to sign. These documents are prepared by the insurers and only they decide what words to use and what conditions to be put down in writing. Therefore, given those situations if what was put down in writing is ambiguous, it is only right that the other party (the assured) be given the

benefit of the doubt. Thus, in the present case, if there is a doubt or ambiguity in the policy or in the Declaration of Health Form, it should be resolved in favour of the plaintiffs.

A good rule of construction which has bound underwriters for many years, is that if the language is chosen by them, i.e., that it is their language, then the document must be construed *contra proferentum*, i.e., against the person who determined the language reflected in the document, upon which the parties are relying on[139]

Policies should be construed strictly against the insurers and the *contra proferentum* rule should be applied. In *Stoneham v The Ocean, Railway, and General Accident Insurance Company* (1887) 19 QBD 237 at 239, the court said:

> The Policy did not use the words 'Terms, Conditions and Exclusions' together. 'Exclusions' and 'Conditions' were in separate categories. Therefore, the word 'terms' would not include 'Conditions' and 'Exclusions'. Consequently, the word 'terms' under Condition 10 would not refer to the notice provision. The observance of Condition 10 was not a condition precedent to the defendant's liability. Therefore, any breach of the notice provision would only sound in damages which could be set off against the insured sum payable to the plaintiff. Such a strict reading of the Policy was in accordance with the law. The fact that a policy stated that certain clauses (of which the notice clause was one) were conditions precedent was not necessarily conclusive: see MacGillivray on Insurance Law (Sweet & Maxwell, 10th Ed, 2003) at para 19-35: *Stork Technology Services Asia Pte Ltd (Formerly Known As Eastburn Stork Pte Ltd v First Capital Insurance Ltd* [2006] SGHC 101; [2006] 3 SLR 652.

---

[139] Croom-Johnson J in *Metal Scrap & By Products Limited v Federated Conveyors Limited and Tribble (Third Party)* [1953] 1 Ll LR 221.

Interpretation of Insurance Contracts – Ambiguity - *Contra Proferentum* Rule

In *Condogianis v Guardian Assurance Co* (1923) 29 CLR 341, the Privy Council expressed the view that the rule of fair and reasonable construction was also to be applied to answers given in response to questions. A literal interpretation will not be applied if answers given in relation to a question relating to past or existing fact, as distinct from future intention or events, are in substance false.[140]

Motor Insurance Policy – *Contra Proferentum* Rule

It is of course established law that a motor insurance policy which is a contractual document, is subject to the same general rules of interpretation as any other written document.[141] In any written document the words are *prima facie* to be construed "in their plain, ordinary, popular meaning, rather than their strictly precise, etymological, philosophic, or scientific meaning".[142] Only if there is a clause in the policy which is open to two constructions, will the court construe it *contra proferentem*, that is, against the insurers.

The issue in *Malaysia National Insurance Sdn Bhd v Abdul Aziz Bin Mohamed Daud* [1979] 2 MLJ 29 (FC) was whether the plaintiff was entitled to be indemnified by the defendant insurance company. That issue turned on the construction that was put on the proviso imposed for "authorised driver". It was common ground that that proviso consisted of two limbs as follows:

---

[140] Contrast also *Holt's Motors Ltd v South East Lancashire Insurance* (1930) 35 Com Cas 281 with *Re Sweeney & Kennedy's Arbitration* [1950] IR 85.
[141] *Smith v Accident Insurance Co* (1870) LR 5 Exch 302, 307; *Malaysia National Insurance Sdn Bhd v Abdul Aziz bin Mohamed Daud* [1979] 2 MLJ 29.
[142] 22 Halsbury's Laws of England 3rd Ed. page 212 para. 402.

"Provided that the person driving -

(i) is permitted in accordance with the licensing or other laws or regulations to drive the motor vehicle; or

(ii) has been so permitted and is not disqualified by order of a Court of Law or by reason of any enactment or regulation in that behalf from driving the motor vehicle."

Applying the principles of interpretation stated above, it was held that the exception clause in the proviso was on the ordinary principles of construction, to be read against the insurance company. The court held that the construction most favourable to the assured had to be given to the clause.

INTENTION OF THE PARTIES

In interpreting and construing the terms of a policy in order to determine the intention of the parties, the court must always look to the whole policy. In the case of *Malaysia National Insurance Sdn Bhd*, it was held that the insurance policy in that case was a contract of insurance and that it was subject to the same "general rules of interpretation as any other written document". It was further held that the words used must "*prima facie*...be construed" in their plain, ordinary, popular meaning, rather than their strictly precise, etymological, philosophical, or scientific meaning" and that only if there is a clause in the policy which is open to two constructions, will the court construe it *contra proferentum*.[143]

The cardinal rule of construction has always been that the intention of the parties must prevail.[144] The parties must be bound by the terms and conditions of cl 14 of the policies which is a separate insurance against

---

[143] *Malaysia National Insurance Sdn Bhd v Abdul Aziz bin Mohamed Daud* [1978] 1 LNS 117; [1979] 2 MLJ 29, 31.

[144] *Drinkwater v Corp of London Assurance* [1767] 2 Wils K.B. 363 (fire insurance) per Wilmot CJ, at p 364; *Tarleton v Staniforth* [1794] 5 Term Rep 695 (fire insurance) per Lord Kenyon CJ, at p 699; and *Braunstein v Accidental Death Insurance Co* (1861) 1 B & S 782 (accident insurance) per Blackburn J, at p 799.

total loss (see the Nordic Marine Insurance Plan 2013). The appellant cannot resile from it. As Lord Sumner said in *Yorkshire Insurance Co Ltd v Campbell* [1917] AC 218, at p 224 PC:

> Prima facie all the words which the policy contains ... are words of contract to which effect must be given.

In gathering the intention of the parties from the words in the policy and incorporated documents, the wording is not to be construed in isolation. Evidence may be adduced on the background to the contract, so that the court can appreciate its genesis and purpose, and the facts to which the parties were both aware of when making it.[145]

Plain Ordinary Meaning

The plain ordinary meaning of the words are to be adopted in construing a document. The subject matter may show, however, that the words have a meaning different from their plain, ordinary or popular meaning, if they are used in connection with a particular trade or profession and thus have some special, technical meaning. They may even be used in a special or peculiar sense on a particular occasion, if this construction would affect the intention of the parties, as collected from the documents.[146]

Construction of Insurance Contracts – Intention of the Parties – Duty of Court

In construing a policy and ascertaining the intention of the parties, the court must look at the whole policy and the terms used in it for its plain, ordinary and popular meaning. The court must examine all the

---

[145] MacGillivray on Insurance Law (Sweet & Maxwell, 10th Ed, 2003) at Para 11-27. See also Singapore Court of Appeal decisions of *Pacific Century Regional Development Ltd v Canadian Imperial Investment Pte Ltd* [2001] 2 SLR 443 and *MAE Engineering Ltd v Fire-Stop Marketing Services Pte Ltd* [2005] 1 SLR 379.

[146] Odger's Interpretation of Deeds and Other Instruments, at p. 36.

surrounding circumstances known to the parties at the time the contract of insurance was made. [147]

Wilberforce L in *Reardon Smith Line Ltd v Yngvar Hansen-Tangen* [1976] 1 W.L.R. 989, at pp. 995-996 said:

> The surrounding circumstances ... can be illustrated but hardly defined. In a commercial contract ... the court should know the commercial purpose of the contract and this in turn presupposes knowledge of the genesis of the transaction, the background, the context, the market in which the parties are operating.

The duty of the court is to ascertain objectively what the parties had intended. It has been held that the subjective understandings and intentions of either party which are entertained or locked in the inner recesses of their minds, are not the tests. In *Paal Wilson & Co v Partenreederei Hannah Blumenthal* [1983] 1 AC 854 Lord Diplock examined that particular duty at pp 915-6:

> To the formation of the contract of abandonment, the ordinary principles of the English law of contract apply. To create a contract by exchange of promises between two parties where the promise of each party constitutes the consideration for the promise of the other, *what is necessary is that the intention of each as it has been communicated to and understood by the other* (even though that which has been communicated does not represent the actual state of mind of the communication) *should coincide*. That is what English lawyers mean when they resort to the Latin phrase *consensus ad idem* and the words that I have italicised are essential to the concept of *consensus ad idem*, the lack of which prevents the formation of a binding contract in English law.
>
> Thus if A (the offeror) makes a communication to B (the offeree) whether in writing, orally or by conduct, which, in the circumstances at the time the communication was received, (1)

---

[147] Halsbury's Laws of England (4th Ed) Paras 43 and 45; *Kin Yuen Co Pte Ltd v Lombard Insurance Co Ltd & Ors* [1994] 2 SLR 887.

B, if he were a reasonable man, would understand as stating A's intention to act or refrain from acting in some specified manner if B will promise on his part to act or refrain from acting in some manner also specified in the offer, and (2) B does in fact understand A's communication to mean this, and in his turn makes to A a communication conveying his willingness so to act or to refrain from acting which *mutatis mutandis* satisfies the same two conditions as respects A, the *consensus ad idem* essential to the formation of a contract in English law is complete.

Clause or Phrase – Doubts – Intention of the Parties

Where there is doubt as to the meaning of a clause or phrase, the whole of the policy should be examined in order to see what intention the parties appear to have had concerning the matters governed by the words in question.[148] In *Putra Perdana Construction Sdn Bhd v AMI Insurance Bhd & Ors* [2005] 2 MLJ 123, Ramly Ali J stated that where a clause appearing in one part of the policy is to be read with another clause in a different part of the policy, this should be done to give effect to the intention of the parties.

Negotiations

Negotiations which have not matured into an agreement are inadmissible since they are nothing more than negotiations. However, prior agreements are admissible.[149]

Although the grammatical sense is not the sole or primary method of construing a policy, it gives a useful guide as to the intention of the parties.[150]

---

[148] MacGillivray & Parkington On Insurance Law (8th Ed) at p 448 Para 1091.

[149] *HIH Casualty and General Insurance Ltd v New Hampshire Insurance Co* [2001] 2 Lloyd's Rep 161; *KPMG Llp v Network Rail Infrastructure Ltd* [2007] EWCA Civ 363.

[150] *Provincial Insurance Co Ltd v Yee Chee Swee* [1984] 1 CLJ (Rep) 314 [1984] 2 CLJ 12 (FC).

CLAUSES

In interpreting a contractual provision, the entire clause, including the heading, should be read together. Besides that, the court has to look at the individual clause and distinguish it with other clauses. The court even has to distinguish between the meaning of individual words and the meaning of a document as a whole. The headings of a clause are normally used as a catchword, or a form of identification, or inserted for convenience of reference. Sometimes the heading can be used as guidance to ascertain the meaning of the clause. The weight to be given to the heading of a clause depends on the construction of the provision in that particular clause.[151] In construing the various clauses, the court "may have reference to the whole of the contract and the context in which it was created".[152]

Clause - Commercial Object

In interpreting any clause of an insurance policy, one must bear in mind the commercial object or function of the clause and its apparent relation to the contract as a whole. In adopting this approach, it becomes apparent that the literal meaning of the clause in the insurance policy must necessarily yield to the business sense, so that any ambiguity in the wording can be resolved.[153]

Clause Excluding Liability

The clauses in the policy may entitle the insurer to decline liability. In *Tang Bee Hong v American International Assurance Berhad* [2012] MLJU 1386,

---

[151] *Gurdeep Singh a/l Melkha Singh v Malaysian Airline System Bhd* [2015] 8 MLJ 24 (HC).

[152] Feehan J in *Opron Construction Co Ltd v Her Majesty The Queen in Right of Alberta* 151 1994 A.R. 241.

[153] *Kearney v General Accident Fire and Life Assurance Corp Ltd* [1968] 2 Lloyd's Rep 240, *L Schuler AG v Wickman Machine Tool Sales Ltd* [1974] AC 235: *Poh Siew Cheng v American International Assurance Co Ltd* [2006] 6 MLJ 57.

in interpreting the insurance policy, it was found that the clauses in the policy had excluded liability if the accident was wholly, or partly or directly or indirectly due to drug usage. The post-mortem report clearly pointed to prolonged drug usage being the cause of the eventual drowning that had caused the death, and it was held that liability had been excluded by the policy.

Clause Exempting Liability for Negligence

There are numerous cases in which it has been held that a clause in the contract of carriage, exempting liability for loss or damage but not referring to negligence, does not exempt the assured from liability for negligence.[154] Steve Shim J in *Syarikat Cheap Hin Toy Mfe Sdn Bhd v Syarikat Perkapalan Kris Sdn Bhd & Anor* [1995] 4 CLJ 84 stated:

> In the instant case, the plaintiff has also claimed against the 1st defendant for the negligence of its agent the 2nd defendant. In denying negligence, the 1st defendant appeared to rely on the exemption cl. 2(c) in the bill of lading (Exh. Pl). To appreciate this proposition more fully, I think it appropriate to cite the whole of cl. 2 therein. It stipulates as follows:
>
>> 2. During the period before the goods are loaded on or after they are discharged from the ship on which they are carried by sea.
>>
>> The following terms and conditions shall apply to the exclusion of any other provision in this bill of lading that may be inconsistent therewith, viz.
>>
>> (a) so long as the goods remain in the actual custody of the carrier or his servant (otherwise than as mentioned in sub-clause (b) hereof) the carrier shall not be liable for loss, damage or detention arising or resulting from the act, neglect or default of the servants or agents of

---

[154] Charlesworth on Negligence (6th Edn.) on p. 1286.

the carrier nor from any other cause whatsoever arising without the actual fault or privity of the carrier...

(b) whilst the goods are being transported to or from the ship...such transport or loading or unloading...it shall be done at the sole risk of the owners of the goods ....

(c) in all other cases the responsibility of the carrier whether as carrier or as custodian or bailee of the goods shall be deemed to commence only when the goods are loaded on the ship and to cease absolutely on discharge when they are free of the ship's tackle.

It seems clear that the said clause makes no mention of exempting the carrier from liability for negligence. If exemption for negligence were to apply it would have been expressly stated. As Charlesworth on Negligence (6th Edn.) said on p. 1286:

> ... there are numerous cases in which it has been held that a clause in the contract of carriage exempting liability for loss or damage but not referring to negligence, does not exempt them from liability for negligence.
>
> Thus, in my view, cl. 2(c) relied upon by the 1st defendant could not be construed as exempting it from liability for negligence. Here, I have held the 2nd defendant to be negligent in having lost the delivery order (Exh. P10) which precipitated the release of the goods to person or persons who were not the consignees. The 2nd defendant was at all material times, the shipping agent of the 1st defendant. The act of the 2nd defendant was one which was done in the course of its employment as shipping agent. Such an act must be imputed to the 1st defendant as principal. The 1st defendant was therefore vicariously liable for the negligence of its agent, the 2nd defendant in this case. This I so hold.

I come now to the plaintiff's claim against the 1st defendant for damages for breach of contract, to wit, the failure to deliver the goods, subject-matter of this action, to the consignee under the relevant bill of lading (Exh. Pl). It is the plaintiff's case that the contract as reflected in the bill of lading (Exh. Pl) was fundamentally to deliver the goods stated therein to the consignee Hua Ho (1981) Co. In this respect, it has relied in particular on the clause appearing on the front of the bill of lading (Exh. Pl) which stipulates this:

> This bill of lading shall be construed and governed by Malaysian law and shall apply from the time the goods are received for shipment until delivery, but always subject to the conditions and exceptions of the carrying conveyance; it shall be given up, duly endorsed, in exchange for delivery order if required.

Mr. Kho for the plaintiff has relied on the Privy Council case of *Sze Hai Tong Bank v. Rambler Cycle Co. Ltd.* [1959] AC 576 where it was held that the exemption clause (which is *pari materia* to cl. 2 in our case) did not apply because the non-delivery or misdelivery of the goods, had the effect of defeating a fundamental term of the contract, to wit, the proper delivery of the goods by the shipping company to the consignees or their assigns. Lord Denning in Sze Hai Tong was of the view that the shipping company in that case had deliberately disregarded the fundamental term aforesaid. Citing a number of cases in support, his Lordship went on to say:

> In each case it was held that the principal could not take advantage of the exemption clause. It might have been different if the servant or agent had been merely negligent or inadvertent: see *Smackman v. General Steam Navigation Co.*; *Ashby v. Tolhurst* by Sir Wilfred Green MR and *Swan, Hunter & Wigham Richardson Ltd. v. France Fenwide Tyre & Wear Co. Lt*d.

It may be argued from the part underscored above that negligence would be excluded. I think that the use of the word "might" tends to suggest that it would not operate in all cases of negligence. I would take it that the statement was made in the context of the cases he referred to, where there were specific clauses in the contract exempting the shipping company or its agents from liability for negligence. I think this made sense because unless it was expressly covered by the exemption clause, it would neither be reasonable nor proper to absolve the negligence of the shipping company or its agents in performing a fundamental term of the contract of carriage, namely, the proper delivery of the goods to the designated consignee or consignees.

The exemption in cl. 2 cited above is rather comprehensive and the 1st defendant has construed cl. 2(c) thereof as absolving it from responsibility or liability in this case. Under the contract as reflected in the bill of lading (Exh. Pl) it seems clear that one of the main objects is the proper delivery of the goods stated therein by the 1st defendant to the consignee Hua Ho (1981) Co. It would defeat this object entirely if the 1st defendant or its agent acting negligently had caused the goods to be delivered to some unauthorised person or persons thereby resulting in loss to the plaintiff, without being liable for the consequences.

In my view, cl. 2(c) must therefore be limited and modified to the extent necessary to enable effect to be given to the main object and intent of the contract. It must at least be modified so as not to permit the 1st defendant as the shipping company and/or its agent, in the circumstances of this case, to disregard its obligations as to delivery.

Exception Clause in Proviso – Motor Insurance Policy

If there is a doubt as to the extent of the exception clause and if a question were to arise as to the liability of the insurers, the construction most favourable to the assured must be given. In *Malaysia National Insurance Sdn Bhd v Abdul Aziz Mohamed Daud* [1979] 2 MLJ 29 (FC), Raja Azlan Shah FJ stated:

It also seems to me that as between the assured and the insurers, the exception clause in the proviso, on the ordinary principles of construction has, as far as possible, to be read against the insurance company, that is to say, if there is a doubt as to its extent, and the question were to arise as to the liability of the insurers, the construction most favourable to the assured must be given to him, but I have come to the conclusion that the learned judge was right in the interpretation he put on it.

Clauses – Inapplicability

Where ambiguity is created by certain clauses in an insurance policy, the courts may deem such clauses to be inapplicable. In *Carlingford Australia General Insurance Ltd v EZ Industries Ltd* [1988] VR 349, the court found that the exclusion clause under scrutiny was irrational and unjust in the context of the policy and the ambiguity created would render the exclusion clause inapplicable or inoperable. Gobbo J explained the stance of the Supreme Court thus:

> It was said that it was not to the point that the effect of the clause might be so wide as to entirely deprive an insured handling a whole range of substances capable of causing pollution discharges of any meaningful cover under its indemnity policy. It was said that if the clause was not ambiguous then its apparently very wide meaning had to be given effect to, no matter that this was unexpected and would be capable of leaving very little covered in respect of a major part of the insured's activities. In my view this is not a legitimate approach to construction of an insurance policy exclusion clause. Where the effect given to the language used is such as to do violence to the policy as a whole and produce a both unexpected and irrational result, then there is in fact uncertainty and some ambiguity created. In such a situation, ordinary principles as to resolution of ambiguities come into play. ... In these circumstances it is, in my view, proper to treat the clause as being ambiguous in its language. It is not necessary that an exhaustive definition be attempted that overcomes possible irrational and unjust effects, any more than

one should set the outer limits of the clause on the basis of giving it the widest possible operation.

Another instance in which a provision in a policy might be ignored for inapplicability arises where a standard printed clause in a contract runs counter to the object or subject matter of the insurance policy. In *B-Gold Interior Design & Construction Pte Ltd v Zurich Insurance (Singapore) Pte Ltd* [2007] SGHC 126; [2007] 4 SLR 82 Andrew Ang J explained:

> In *Home Insurance Company of New York v Victoria Montreal Fire Insurance Company* [1907] AC 59, a decision of the Privy Council on appeal from the Supreme Court of Canada, a contract of reinsurance was effected by pasting a printed slip providing for such reinsurance on to a form of a policy applicable to an original insurance. Save for one condition in the form of policy, it was undisputed between the parties that the remaining conditions in the form of the policy were totally inapplicable to a reinsurance contract. That exception was a condition providing that the right to bring an action on the policy was limited to 12 months after the date of the loss.
>
> Apart from its context, that condition would have been applicable, but the Privy Council held that having regard to the true construction of the contract, which carelessly purported to include many conditions inapplicable to reinsurance, that condition had also to be regarded as inapplicable. Whereas such a clause was reasonable in the original policy, it could not apply where the insured was unable to sue until the direct loss was ascertained between parties over whom he had no control.

Yet another instance in which a clause in an insurance policy was held to be inapplicable is found in a decision of the English Court of Appeal in *Hydarnes Steamship Company v Indemnity Mutual Marine Assurance Company* [1895] 1 QB 500. I gratefully adopt the headnotes in the law report as follows:

> By a policy of marine insurance, partly in writing and partly in print, it was declared, in a part of the policy which was in writing,

that the insurance was upon "freight of meat at and from Monte Video" to any ports in the River Plate, including the Boca, and thence to the United Kingdom, and that the underwriters should be liable for any loss occasioned by breaking down of machinery until final sailing of the vessel. By a subsequent clause of the policy it was declared that the assurance should commence "upon the freight and goods or merchandize on board from the loading of the said goods or merchandize on board the said ship or vessel at Monte Video." The name "Monte Video" in this clause was in writing, the rest of the clause being in print. After the arrival of the ship at Monte Video on her outward voyage, she proceeded to the Boca, where a cargo of meat was ready for shipment; but her refrigerating machinery then broke down so completely as to render it necessary to abandon the design of loading the meat. At the date of the policy it was known to both underwriters and assured that meat never was and could not be loaded at Monte Video in consequence of the absence of appliances for freezing the meat at that port:

Held (reversing the decision of Wills J.), that, the words in the clause defining the commencement of the risk with regard to the loading of the goods being absolutely inapplicable under the circumstances of the case, they must be rejected, and therefore the policy attached, although no meat was ever loaded on board the ship. It would be useful to refer to the judgment of Lopes LJ at 507 for its succinct reasoning:

The question is whether the risk had attached. It was said, on the one hand, that it had never attached, because no meat ever was loaded on board the ship. It was said, on the other hand, that it had attached, because the refrigerating machinery broke down after the vessel had left Monte Video, and before she finally sailed from Buenos Ayres. The question depends on the construction of the policy, which like any other document must be construed as far as possible according to the ordinary meaning of the words used, having regard to the circumstances which existed at the time when the contract was made. In this case it was well known to both parties to the contract that no frozen meat ever was loaded at Monte Video. It was also clear that, as soon as the vessel finally sailed with the meat on board, the freight would no longer be at risk, except in the event of the ship's not arriving, because by the terms of the contract the freight was to be earned on the arrival of the ship, even though the meat should have had to be jettisoned.

Therefore, what the assured especially required to be protected against was the loss of the freight, not by a peril of the sea, but by the breaking down of the refrigerating machinery during the period which elapsed between the ship's arrival at Monte Video and her final sailing on her voyage to England. The very object of the insurance was to cover that period. That being so, the insurance is expressed to be upon "freight of meat valued at [3000l], warranted free from all claims (except general average and salvage charges) unless caused by stranding, sinking, burning, or collision, but to be liable for any loss occasioned by breaking down of machinery until final sailing of the vessel ... at and from Monte Video ... to any port or ports in the United Kingdom." If it had stopped there I should imagine there would have been no difficulty in construing the words.

The difficulty arises from a subsequent part of the policy, which is mainly in print, and which states that "the assurance aforesaid shall commence upon the freight and goods or merchandize on board thereof from the loading of the said goods or merchandize on board the said ship or vessel at Monte Video." It is argued that the meaning of that clause is that the risk was not to attach until the frozen meat had been loaded. But it appears to be impossible to give it that meaning, because it is admitted that all parties knew that frozen meat could not be loaded at Monte Video, which is the place mentioned in the clause.

This clause, as it stands, is clearly inconsistent with the previous part of the policy. The question is which portion of the policy is to take effect. It appears to me that we must give effect to the earlier part, and reject so much of the subsequent printed clause as refers to the loading of the said goods or merchandize on board the said ship or vessel, as being inapplicable to the state of things which existed.

Rejecting those words, the effect is that the insurance is on freight, and is to commence at and from Monte Video. Upon this construction of the policy all difficulty disappears.

Bailee Clause – Marine Insurance - Costs of Proceedings against Third Parties

The bailee clause cannot be construed as entitling the assured to recover from the insurers the costs of proceedings against third parties.[155] The learned editors of the 7th Edition of MacGillivray & Parkington on Insurance Law however suggested (at paragraph 1185) that it was arguable that such costs were recoverable. The judges of the Privy Council in *Netherlands Insurance Co Est 1845 Ltd v Karl Ljungberg & Co* [1986] 2 MLJ 321 however, preferred the more tentative opinion expressed in MacGillivray & Parkington on Insurance Law.

Entire Agreement Clause

Gavin Lightman J explained the purpose of an entire agreement clause in *Pub Co v East Crown Ltd* [2000] 2 Lloyd's Rep 611 (at 614):

> The purpose of an entire agreement clause is to preclude a party to a written agreement from threshing through the undergrowth, and finding, in the course of negotiations, some (chance) remark or statement (often long-forgotten or difficult to recall or explain) upon which to found a claim, such as the present, to the existence of a collateral warranty. The entire agreement clause obviates the occasion for any such search and the peril to the contracting parties posed by the need which may arise in its absence to conduct such a search. For such a clause constitutes a binding agreement between the parties that the

---

[155] Paragraph 1320 of the current (16th) Edition of Arnould on Marine Insurance.

full contractual terms are to be found in the document containing the clause and not elsewhere, and that, accordingly, any promises or assurances made in the course of the negotiations (which in the absence of such a clause, might have effect as a collateral warranty) shall have no contractual force, save in so far as they are reflected and given effect in that document. ...[T]he formula used is abbreviated to an acknowledgment by the parties that the agreement constitutes the entire agreement between them. That formula is, in my judgment, amply sufficient to constitute an agreement that the full contractual terms to which the parties agreed to bind themselves are to be found in the agreement and nowhere else. That can be the only purpose of the provision.

In *Sere Holdings Limited v Volkswagen Group United Kingdom Limited* [2004] EWHC 1551 (Ch), Mr Christopher Nugee QC considered Lightman J's observations on the purpose and effect of an entire agreement clause, and perceptively concluded (at [22]):

I can see no flaw in the reasoning. It is elementary that whether an agreement has legal effect is a matter of the intentions of the parties.... I can see no reason why parties who have in fact reached an agreement in pre-contractual negotiations that would otherwise constitute a collateral contract should not subsequently agree in their formal contract that any such collateral agreement should have no legal effect, or in other words should be treated as if the parties had not intended to create legal relations; and for the reasons given by Lightman J this is precisely what an entire agreement clause on its face does.

In *IBM Singapore Pte Ltd v UNIG Pte Ltd* [2003] SGHC 71, Tay Yong Kwang J held that such clauses effectively "erased any legal consequences that might have ensued from prior discussions or negotiations and that the contractual relationship between the parties was now circumscribed by the signed agreements and those alone". This decision was subsequently upheld on appeal. Much earlier in *Chuan Hup Marine Ltd v Sembawang Engineering Pte Ltd* [1995] 2 SLR 629, Selvam J determined that "a similarly worded clause excluded any implied term, collateral warranty and misrepresentation".

Indemnity Clause and Exemption Clause Ambiguity

Where there appears to be an ambiguity between the indemnity clause and the exemption clause, then applying the *contra proferentum* rule, the insurance policy should be construed in favour of the appellant insured.[156]

NATURE OF COVER & RISK

What the policy covers must be gathered from the terms of the policy.[157] Where there is a doubt as to whether a particular use is covered by the policy owing to an ambiguous exceptions clause or other term, it appears that the court may accept evidence from the insurers, that they regard themselves at risk, as establishing that cover was in force. However, such evidence will be of no account if the construction of the relevant clause is clear, or if the question is whether or not an enforceable contract of insurance has been concluded, or if the relevant user is forbidden by law.[158] What the policy covers must be gathered from the terms of the policy and if it insures third party goods, the insurance money cannot be kept by the assured who suffered no loss but must be paid to the third party who suffered the loss. In *London and North Western Railway Co v Glyn* [1859] 1 EL & EL 652, Maurice and Hepburn, the third parties were not named in the policies. All the same, the courts ruled that the assured must pay the insurance monies to them. This further strengthens the fundamental principle of insurance that it is an indemnity.

Risk Insured Against – Interpretation of the Policy

In a policy of insurance, the words expressing the risks covered are not always used in the strict technical sense which they bear in relation to a

---

[156] *Malaysia National Insurance Sdn Bhd v Abdul Aziz bin Mohamed Daud* [1979] 2 MLJ 29; *Poh Siew Cheng v American International Assurance Co Ltd* [2006] 6 MLJ 57.

[157] *Standard Chartered Bank v KTS Sdn Bhd* [2006] 4 MLJ 617 (FC).

[158] MacGillivray on Insurance Law (10th Ed, 2003) at p 875, Para 29-8.

criminal offence.[159] In interpreting an insurance policy and in determining what the policy "covered", it is purely a construction of the words of the policy that are paramount; it is irrelevant to discuss the unilateral intention of the assured. In *William Waters and Barnabas Steel v the Monarch Fire and Life Assurance Company* [1856] 5EL & BL 870, Lord Pearce in Waters stated:

> My Lords, it is a question of construction whether the policy in this case covered the whole proprietary interest in the goods or only the plaintiffs' liability to the owners in respect of them. That question must be answered by construing the words of the policy and, in the case of ambiguity, by considering any surrounding circumstances that may properly be called in aid. Here the matters that are expressed or implied in the document are clear, and there is nothing in the surrounding circumstances that can, or should, throw light on it. Certainly, the unilateral intention of the assured cannot be used in deciding the mutual intention of the parties as disclosed in the document.

The same principle of law enunciated in *Waters* was confirmed by the House of Lords in *Hepburn v A Tomlinson (Hauliers) Ltd* [1966] AC 451, where it was stated that there was "no rule which would make it relevant in this case to go behind the words of the policy and investigate the respondents' intention when they took out this policy."

The High Court in *Sawarn Singh a/l Mehar Singh (named as a nominee) v RHB Insurance Bhd* [2014] 7 MLJ 416 (HC), was called upon to interpret the words "arising from accidental, violent, external and visible means". It was tasked with finding out whether the death had been caused by bodily injury sustained by accidental, violent, external and visible means. Further it had to determine whether the bodily injury sustained had been the sole and direct cause of death. In other words, it had to be the *causa causans* or *causa proxima* and not merely *causa sine qua non*.

Thus, the exercise in interpreting the policy would determine whether the insurer defendant's decision of declining the claim, amounted to a

---

[159] MacGillivray on Insurance Law (5th Ed.), 2026.

breach of the terms and conditions of the policy as alleged by the insured plaintiff.

The insurer defendant relying on the contents of the post-mortem report and the death certificate, contended that the insured plaintiff's claim was not payable because "the circumstances of the death of the insured is not covered by this policy". The post-mortem recorded that the "deceased suffered from a massive heart attack which resulted in left ventricular failure" and that "no external injuries were noted". Further, the medical history of the insured deceased, as recorded in the post-mortem report showed that the deceased insured was "a heart patient".

The insured plaintiff asked the court to invoke the *contra proferentum* rule in his favour for the following reasons. First, because the terms of the brochure or proposal differed from the terms of the insurance policy that was finally sold to him and second, because PW1 for the insurer, was not able to explain the benefits of the said policy; or answer the plaintiff's questions.

Her Ladyship Mary Lim J ruled that the *contra proferentum* rule did not apply. Her Ladyship reasoned:

> ...that having examined both documents very carefully, I do not find any disparity, material or otherwise between these two documents. Both documents provide the cover of insurance for persons from the ages of 50–75 years in the event of death or injury arising from accidental, violent, external and visible means. Obviously, the cover would be subject to terms and conditions, the extent of which can be found in the said policy or Policy Jacket.

It was also the contention of the insured plaintiff that the *contra proferentum* rule should be invoked because there was ambiguity in the terms used. Under the terms of the policy, the benefits became payable "in the event of death or injury". It was his contention that because of the deployment of the article "or", the word "death" must be "read in singular identity and not in the alternative identity (or)". In other words, the event of death was not qualified by the ensuing words "arising from accidental, violent, external and visible means". Those words only served to qualify the event of "injury". In short, the insurer defendant contracted to pay in the event of death, period.

In disagreeing with that contention, the court was of the view that the proper and reasonable reading of the words, "arising from accidental, violent, external and visible means" qualified both the event of death as well as the event of injury. It was concluded that "both" must be occasioned by means which are "accidental, violent, external and visible".

The court then moved on to examine the crux of the case, i.e., the cause of death. It was critical to determine the cause of death and the means that caused it, as it determined whether the insurer defendant's decision of declining the claim had amounted to a breach of the terms and conditions of the said policy, as alleged by the insured plaintiff.

It was concluded that there was an absence of evidence to establish the means which caused the death of the deceased; let alone a means which was "violent, accidental, external and visible".

The court found that the insured plaintiff's claim had not been proved on a balance of probabilities. In dismissing the claim, Her Ladyship stated:

> [42] In this regard, for the sake of completeness, and this is assuming for a moment that the cover is available in the first place under the general provision of cover; one must examine s I of the said policy, the provision for 'Special Exclusions to I', specifically exclusion 4. That clause provides that the policy does not cover death or disablement directly or indirectly caused by 'Any pre-existing physical defect or infirmity, Fits of any kind, Disease or Sickness of any kind'.
>
> [43] The question here is whether Madam Sant Kaur had any 'pre-existing physical defect or infirmity, Fits of any kind, Disease or Sickness of any kind'? If the answer is in the negative, then that would be the end of the matter. The slip in the bathroom (on the assumption that that is proved, which it is not here) which would be reasonable to regard as the 'accidental violent external and

visible means' by which her bodily injury was sustained must be the sole and direct cause of her death.

[44] However, if the answer is in the affirmative, the ensuing question is whether that 'pre-existing physical defect or infirmity, Fits of any kind, Disease or Sickness of any kind' directly or indirectly caused her demise. In other words, is it a proximate cause of her death? If the answer to this question is in the affirmative, then the cover is not available in which case the defendant would not be in breach of the terms and conditions of the said policy when it declined the plaintiff's claim. If the answer is in the negative, leaving then the fall to be the cause of death, then the defendant would be in breach of the said policy in rejecting the claim.

[45] DW2 gave an account of the deceased's medical history. According to his evidence, the deceased was '… a known case of hypertension and bronchial asthma'. It was his evidence that 'the hypertension … is a precursor to heart disease'. From his examination of the deceased's heart, he found that it was grossly enlarged (huge cardiomegaly) with blockages or occlusions in the right and left coronaries. These occlusions at the origins were extensive, '95 to 9-100%'. While he had agreed with the plaintiff that a fall 'probably can' trigger a heart attack, he testified that he 'found no external injuries probably a fall would not have triggered a heart attack'.

[46] It can be safely gathered from the evidence of DW2 that the deceased indeed had 'pre-existing physical defect or infirmity, Fits of any kind, Disease or Sickness of any kind'. Unfortunately, this 'pre-existing physical defect or infirmity, Fits of any kind, Disease or Sickness of any kind' indirectly caused Madam Sant Kaur's death. This existing condition 'cooperated' with the slip/fall resulting in the death of Madam Sant Kaur in which case the slip is not the sole or independent cause of the death.

Policy and the Proposal Form -Inconsistency

Even if there is any inconsistency between the policy and the proposal form, such inconsistency is of no consequence as the policy takes precedence, because it is the primary document which is prepared later in time than the proposal form and thus, represents the formal reduction of the contract, in writing, between the insurer and the assured.

Insurance Claim - Accident Policy – Cause of Death

In determining whether a claim is covered by an insurance policy, say in relation to an accident policy, it may be found that there may be more than one cause of death. Where there are two or more causes, acting together to cause an accident, it may be necessary to determine which was the more dominant of the two causes. The common-sense test must be applied i.e., which is the effective or dominant cause for the accident.[160]

See also the case of *Tang Bee Hong (supra)*.

Accident Insurance

The issue in *Sawarn Singh a/l Mehar Singh (named as a nominee) v RHB Insurance Bhd* [2014] 7 MLJ 416 (HC) was whether the cause of the deceased's death entitled the insurers to decline the claim under the terms and conditions of the Golden Care Plan Insurance Policy. The issue of whether the insurers were entitled to decline the claim or whether in declining the claim the insurers were in breach of the terms of the policy rested on the interpretation of the 'arising from accidental, violent, external and visible means'. The court was of the view that the words qualify both the event of death as well as the event of injury. There it was stated:

> The said policy requires that the deceased to sustain 'bodily injury caused solely and directly by violent accidental external and

---
[160] See *Gray v Burr* [1971] 2 All ER 949.

> visible means and being the sole and direct cause of the Insured Person's death'. It is therefore apparent that what needs to be determined is the cause of death; and the means that caused that death. In that respect, the language in the said policy requires the cause of death to be bodily injury sustained by accidental violent external and visible means.
>
> ...Not only must the means responsible for Madam Sant's death be due to bodily injury sustained by accidental violent external and visible means, but the bodily injury so sustained must be the sole and direct cause of her death. In other words, it must be the *causa causans* or *causa proxima* and not merely *causa sine qua non*.

It was found that the means which caused the death of the deceased had not been established; let alone a means which is 'violent accidental external and visible'. The court concluded that the insured plaintiff's claim had not been proved on a balance of probabilities.

This is a matter of construction of the terms of the said policy based on the evidence presented.

INTERPRETATION OF INSURANCE CONTRACTS

- The Court's Role in Contractual Interpretation
- Interpretation of Contracts as a Whole
- Intention of the Parties
- Interpretation of Contracts - Principle of Objectivity

- The Interpretation of Insurance Contracts
  - Insurance Policy in Mandatory Statutory Form
- Words

- Policy of Insurance - Rules of Construction

    o Meaning of the Words Used

    o (a) Businesslike Interpretation

    o (b) Commercial Objective

    o (c) Construction to Avoid Unreasonable Results

- Insurance Words – Interpretation - Prior Judicial Pronouncements

- Words - Plain Meaning

- Literal Meaning of Words

- Contract Deletion- Effect of Deleted Words

- Unambiguous Words

- Strict Compliance with Unambiguous Notice Provisions in Insurance Policies

- Ambiguity

- Implied Terms

- Contra Proferentum - General

    o Contra Proferentum Rule

- Interpretation of Insurance Contracts – Ambiguity - Contra Proferentum Rule

- Motor Insurance Policy – Contra Proferentum Rule

- Intention of the Parties

- o Plain Ordinary Meaning
- o Construction of Insurance Contracts – Intention of the Parties – Duty of Court
- o Clause or Phrase – Doubts – Intention of the Parties
- o Negotiations

- Clauses
  - o Clause - Commercial Object
  - o Clause Excluding Liability
  - o Clause Exempting Liability for Negligence
  - o Exception Clause in Proviso – Motor Insurance Policy
  - o Clauses – Inapplicability
  - o Bailee Clause – Marine Insurance - Costs of Proceedings against Third Parties
  - o Entire Agreement Clause
  - o Indemnity Clause and Exemption Clause Ambiguity

- Nature of Cover & Risk
  - o Risk Insured Against – Interpretation of the Policy
  - o Policy and the Proposal Form - Inconsistency
  - o Insurance Claim - Accident Policy – Cause of Death
  - o Accident Insurance

CHAPTER 3
GOOD FAITH

INTRODUCTION

Prof T B Smith in "A Short Commentary on the Law of Scotland" (1962), p 836, quoting MA Millner "Fraudulent Non-Disclosure" (1957) 76 SALJ 177 at pp 188-9 stated: "The expression 'utmost good faith' appears to derive from the idea of *uberrimae fidei*, words which indeed appear in the side note, but whose origin I have not been able to trace. The concept of *uberrima fides* does not appear to have derived from civil law and it has been regarded as unnecessary in civilian systems".[161]

Insurance law in Malaysia is based on the law relating to insurance as it developed in the United Kingdom. The law in the UK is based on statute, i.e., the Marine Insurance Act 1906. Lord Justice Rix in *R (on the application of Heather Moor & Edgecomb Ltd) v Financial Ombudsman Service* [2008] EWCA Civ 642, [2008] All ER (D) (CA) had occasion to trace the development of the English law of insurance where His Lordship stated:

> Our insurance law, for instance, has been based on a statute, the Marine Insurance Act 1906, designed for marine insurance but given a dominant status over insurance contracts in general, which encapsulates the common law of over a century ago. For some years the insurance ombudsman (now within the FOS scheme) has been developing a new common law of insurance

---

[161] Lord Clyde in *Manifest Shipping Co Ltd v Uni-Polaris Shipping Co Ltd & Others (The 'Star Sea')* [2001] UKHL 1, [2003] 1 AC 469.

for consumer contracts, without which the courts would have been constrained to find, or alternatively to reject, solutions to problems from which they have been in the main shielded. This new ombudsman developed law is in turn being considered by the Law Commission as part of its current review of certain areas of our insurance law: see Insurance Contract Law, Issues Paper 1, Misrepresentation and Non-Disclosure, September 2006 and Insurance Contract Law, Issue Paper 2, Warranties, November 2006. We await to see what emerges from the Law Commission's consultations. Ultimately, of course, it will be for Parliament to decide on changes, if any, to our law. However, it is possible to see in the "fair and reasonable" jurisdiction of the ombudsman the source not merely of an alternative dispute resolution service but of an important new source of law.

Malaysian marine insurance law is subject to the UK Marine Insurance Act 1906 ('MIA'), by virtue of ss 5(1) and 5(2) of the Malaysian Civil Law Act 1956 ('CLA'). The MIA is an Act which codifies the common law relating to marine insurance.[162]

The chapter examines the implications of mercantile law as the first source of the principles applicable to insurance law. The MIA initially applied to marine insurance policies and then became the applicable law to all insurance contracts. The common law then developed in interpreting the MIA, as that was the law which applied at the pre-contractual stage. As will become evident, mercantile law and common law principles continue to apply even at the post-contract stage.

Section 30 of the MIA provides as follows:

> (1) A policy may be in the form in the First Schedule of the Act.
>
> (2) Subject to the provisions of this Act, and unless the context of the policy otherwise requires, the terms and expressions

---

[162] See Halsbury's Laws of England, 5th edn. para. 238: *Loh Shiiun Hing v Kurnia Insurans (Malaysia) Bhd* [2014] 7 CLJ 490 (CA).

mentioned in the First Schedule to this Act shall be construed as having the scope and meaning in that schedule assigned to them.

The modern practice of insurance, and therefore the modern rules of law, grew out of the inescapable risks that existed by sending and bringing goods across the sea. Because of England's early modern ascendancy with the Netherlands, in the trade of goods by sea, it was not surprising that the common law of insurance in England developed from decisions made by English courts on what we would now call marine insurance.[163]

The MIA contains provisions dealing with, among other things, the parties to a contract of marine insurance, how the contract is formed, the form that it takes, which perils are insured against and which are not, the concept of proximate cause, determination of loss and how it is to be valued, the extent of the indemnity that the insured receives, and the subrogation of the insurer to the rights and remedies of the insured.[164]

While the MIA is a code and regulates all aspects of marine insurance, it does not replace the common law. Section 4 of the MIA provides that:

> 4. The rules of the common law, including the law merchant, save in so far as they are inconsistent with the express provisions of this Act, shall apply to contracts of marine insurance.

In Malaysia, the Financial Services Act 2013, which came into force on the 30 June 2013, repealed the Insurance Act 1996 and it did not provide for retrospective application.

Lord Hobhouse of Woodborough in *Manifest Shipping Co Ltd v Uni-Polaris Shipping Co Ltd & Others (The 'Star Sea')* [2001] UKHL 1, [2003] 1 AC 469 examined the concept of good faith. It was reiterated there that Lord Mansfield who introduced the principle of good faith in *Carter v*

---

[163] M Kirby Foreword to D Kelly and M Ball Principles of insurance law in Australia and New Zealand Butterworths 1991 referring to W Holdsworth's History of English law 2nd ed vol 8, 294.

[164] M Davies and A Dickey Shipping law The Law Book Company Limited Sydney 1990, 311.

Boehm (1766) 3 Burr 1905, did not use the terms utmost good faith or *uberrimae fidei* which only begun to be used in the nineteenth century. Lord Hobhouse went on to state in his judgment:

> The history of the concept of good faith in relation to the law of insurance is reviewed in the speech of Lord Mustill in *Pan Atlantic Ins Co v Pine Top Ins Co* [1995] 1 AC 501 and in a valuable and well researched article (also containing a penetrating discussion of the conceptual difficulties) by Mr Howard Bennett in 1999 LMCLQ 165. The acknowledged origin is Lord Mansfield's judgment in *Carter v Boehm* (1766) 3 Burr 1905. As Lord Mustill points out, Lord Mansfield was at the time attempting to introduce into English commercial law a general principle of good faith, an attempt which was ultimately unsuccessful and only survived for limited classes of transactions, one of which was insurance. His judgment in *Carter v Boehm* was an application of his general principle to the making of a contract of insurance. It was based upon the inequality of information as between the proposer and the underwriter and the character of insurance as a contract upon a "speculation".
>
> 44. It was probably the need to distinguish those transactions to which Lord Mansfield's principle still applied which led to the coining of the phrases "utmost" good faith and "uberrimae fidei", phrases not used by Lord Mansfield and which only seem to have become current in the 19th Century. Storey used the expression "greatest good faith", Wharton "the most abundant good faith"; a Scottish law dictionary (Traynor) used "the most full and copious" good faith; some English judges referred to "perfect" good faith (Willes J, *Britton v Royal Ins Co*, (1866) 4 F&F 905) and Lord Cockburn CJ to "full and perfect faith" (*Bates v Hewitt*, sup at p 607). But 'utmost' became the most commonly used epithet and its place was assured by its use in the 1906 Act. The connotation appears to be the most extensive, rather than the greatest, good faith. The Latin phrase was likewise a later introduction. It has been suggested that its use may have been inspired by the use of similar language in Book IV of the Codex of Justinian (4.37.3) in relation to the contract of partnership. The

best view seems to be that it had been unknown to Roman law and had no equivalent in Roman law: *Mutual and Federal Ins Co v Oudtshoorn Municipality* 1985 (1) SA 419, per Joubert JA at p 432. The first recorded use of the phrase in the law reports was by Lord Commissioner Rolfe (later Lord Cranworth LC) in *Dalglish v Jarvie* (1850) 2 Mac & G 231 at 243 in connection with the duty of disclosure to the court which arises when an *ex parte* application is made for an injunction; the phrase was however already current by that date as the judgment shows.

Although the concept of good faith has its origin in mercantile law and was developed in relation to marine insurance, the principle of utmost good faith is however, not confined to marine insurance; it is applicable to all forms of insurance[165] and is mutual as S.17 of the MIA itself affirms by using the phrase "if the utmost good faith be not observed by either party" and as was expressly stated by Lord Mansfield in *Carter v Boehm* 3 Burr1905.[166]

Sections 17 to 20 of the MIA, codified the common law in an area where there was no difference between marine and other insurance and which therefore had been accepted as having general application.[167]

A contract of marine insurance is a contract based upon the utmost good faith, and, if the utmost good faith is not observed by either party, the contract may be avoided by the other party.[168]

The legal and practical implications of this familiar but far-reaching rule are spelled out in the succeeding sections of the MIA. Thus, subject to some limited and obvious exceptions, the insurer may avoid the contract of insurance if the insured fails, before the contract is concluded, to

---

[165] *London Assurance v Mansel* (1879) 11 Ch D 363, *Cantiere Meccanico Brindisino v Janson* [1912] 3 KB 452.

[166] *Manifest Shipping Co Ltd v Uni-Polaris Insurance Co Ltd & Others* (The 'Star Sea') [2001] UKHL 1, [2003] 1 AC 469.

[167] See *PCW Syndicates v PCW Reinsurers* [1996] 1 WLR 1136, 1140.

[168] Section 17 of the English Marine Insurance Act 1906, which is accepted as expressing generally applicable insurance principles.

disclose to the insurer every material circumstance known to the insured, who is deemed to know every circumstance which, in the ordinary course of business ought to be known by him; and every circumstance is material which would influence the judgment of a prudent insurer in fixing the premium or determining whether he will take the risk.[169]

The confusion pertaining to the ambit of the doctrine of good faith can sometimes be attributed to the multitude of varying definitions and judicial formulations which try to capture its meaning. As was aptly stated by Chesterman J in *Re Zurich Australian Insurance Ltd* [1998] QSC 209:

> I do not find these formulations of any assistance in determining with any degree of clarity or specificity what is the nature and extent of the duty to act in good faith imposed upon an insurer (and an insured) after the contract has been made. A multiplicity of synonyms and rhetorical appeals to 'honesty', 'fairness', 'decency' or lack of caprice merely cause confusion.

In relation to insurance fraud, the requirement of utmost good faith is two pronged, in that, it involves a duty to disclose all material facts to the insurer as well as a duty on the insured to act in good faith when dealing with the insured, which essentially involves not making false claims or exaggerating a claim when it arises under the policy of insurance.

GOOD FAITH AND CONTRACTS

There is no general doctrine of good faith in English contract law and such a term is unlikely to arise by way of necessary implication in a contract

---

[169] Section 18(1), (2): See *HIH Casualty and General Insurance Limited and others (Respondents) v Chase Manhattan Bank (Appellants) and others HIH Casualty and General Insurance Limited and others (Appellants) v Chase Manhattan Bank (Respondents) and others (First Appeal) HIH Casualty and General Insurance Limited and others (Appellants) v Chase Manhattan Bank (Respondents) and others (Second Appeal) (Conjoined appeals)* [2001] 2 Lloyd's Rep 483) (CA).

between two sophisticated commercial parties negotiating at arms' length.[170]

In *Yam Seng Pte Ltd v International Trade Corporation Ltd* [2011] EWHC 111, Leggatt J examined the position in England as well as the experience in other jurisdictions and stated:

> The subject of whether English law does or should recognise a general duty to perform contracts in good faith is one on which a large body of academic literature exists. However, I am not aware of any decision of an English court, and none was cited to me, in which the question has been considered in any depth.
>
> In this regard the following observations of Bingham LJ (as he then was) in *Interfoto Picture Library Ltd v Stiletto Visual Programmes Ltd* [1989] QB 433 at 439, [1988] 1 All ER 348, [1988] 2 WLR 615 are often quoted:
>
>> "In many civil law systems, and perhaps in most legal systems outside the common law world, the law of obligations recognises and enforces an overriding principle that in making and carrying out contracts, parties should act in good faith. This does not simply mean that they should not deceive each other, a principle which any legal system must recognise; its effect is perhaps most aptly conveyed by such metaphorical colloquialisms as 'playing fair', 'coming clean' or 'putting one's cards face upwards on the table.' It is in essence a principle of fair open dealing . . . English law has, characteristically, committed itself to no such overriding principle but has developed piecemeal solutions in response to demonstrated problems of unfairness".

[122] Another case sometimes cited for the proposition that English contract law does not recognise a duty of good faith is *Walford v Miles* [1992] 2 AC 128, [1992] 1 All ER 453, [1992] 2 WLR

---

[170] *Greenclose Ltd v National Westminster Bank Plc* [2014] EWHC 1156 (Ch).

174, where the House of Lords considered that a duty to negotiate in good faith is "inherently repugnant to the adversarial position of the parties when involved in negotiations" and "unworkable in practice" (per Lord Ackner at p 138). That case was concerned, however, with the position of negotiating parties and not with the duties of parties who have entered into a contract and thereby undertaken obligations to each other.

[123] Three main reasons have been given for what Professor McKendrick has called the "traditional English hostility" towards a doctrine of good faith: see McKendrick, Contract Law (9th ed) pp 221-2. The first is the one referred to by Bingham LJ in the passage quoted above: that the preferred method of English law is to proceed incrementally by fashioning particular solutions in response to particular problems rather than by enforcing broad overarching principles. A second reason is that English law is said to embody an ethos of individualism, whereby the parties are free to pursue their own self-interest not only in negotiating but also in performing contracts provided they do not act in breach of a term of the contract. The third main reason given is a fear that recognising a general requirement of good faith in the performance of contracts would create too much uncertainty. There is concern that the content of the obligation would be vague and subjective and that its adoption would undermine the goal of contractual certainty to which English law has always attached great weight.

[124] In refusing, however, if indeed it does refuse, to recognise any such general obligation of good faith, this jurisdiction would appear to be swimming against the tide. As noted by Bingham LJ in the *Interfoto* case, a general principle of good faith (derived from Roman law) is recognised by most civil law systems – including those of Germany, France and Italy. From that source, references to good faith have already entered into English law via EU legislation. For example, the Unfair Terms in Consumer Contracts Regulations 1999, which give effect to a European directive, contains a requirement of good faith. Several other examples of legislation implementing EU directives which use

this concept are mentioned in Chitty on Contract Law (31st ed), Vol 1 at para 1-043. Attempts to harmonise the contract law of EU member states, such as the Principles of European Contract Law proposed by the Lando Commission and the European Commission's proposed Regulation for a Common European Sales Law on which consultation is currently taking place, also embody a general duty to act in accordance with good faith and fair dealing. There can be little doubt that the penetration of this principle into English law and the pressures towards a more unified European law of contract in which the principle plays a significant role will continue to increase.

[125] It would be a mistake, moreover, to suppose that willingness to recognise a doctrine of good faith in the performance of contracts reflects a divide between civil law and common law systems or between continental paternalism and Anglo-Saxon individualism. Any such notion is gainsaid by that fact that such a doctrine has long been recognised in the United States. The New York Court of Appeals said in 1918: "Every contract implies good faith and fair dealing between the parties to it": *Wigand v Bachmann-Bechtel Brewing Co*, 222 NY 272 at 277. The Uniform Commercial Code, first promulgated in 1951 and which has been adopted by many States, provides in s 1-203 that "every contract or duty within this Act imposes an obligation of good faith in its performance or enforcement". Similarly, the Restatement (Second) of Contracts states in s 205 that "every contract imposes upon each party a duty of good faith and fair dealing in its performance and enforcement".

[126] In recent years the concept has been gaining ground in other common law jurisdictions. Canadian courts have proceeded cautiously in recognising duties of good faith in the performance of commercial contracts but have, at least in some situations, been willing to imply such duties with a view to securing the performance and enforcement of the contract or, as it is sometimes put, to ensure that parties do not act in a way that eviscerates or defeats the objectives of the agreement that they

have entered into: see eg *Transamerica Life Inc v ING Canada Inc* (2003) 68 OR (3d) 457, 468.

[127] In Australia the existence of a contractual duty of good faith is now well established, although the limits and precise juridical basis of the doctrine remain unsettled. The springboard for this development has been the decision of the New South Wales Court of Appeal in *Renard Constructions (ME) Pty v Minister for Public Works* (1992) 44 NSWLR 349, where Priestley JA said (at 95) that:

> "... people generally, including judges and other lawyers, from all strands of the community, have grown used to the courts applying standards of fairness to contracts which are wholly consistent with the existence in all contracts, of a duty upon the parties of good faith and fair dealing in its performance. In my view this is in these days the expected standard, and anything less is contrary to prevailing community expectations".

[128] Although the High Court has not yet considered the question (and declined to do so in *Royal Botanic Gardens and Domain Trust v Sydney City Council* (2002) 186 ALR 289) there has been clear recognition of the duty of good faith in a substantial body of Australian case law, including further significant decisions of the New South Wales Court of Appeal in *Alcatel Australia Ltd v Scarcella* (1998) 44 NSWLR 349, *Burger King Corp v Hungry Jack's Pty Ltd* [2001] NWSCA 187 and *Vodafone Pacific Ltd v Mobile Innovations Ltd* [2004] NSWCA 15.

[129] In New Zealand a doctrine of good faith is not yet established law but it has its advocates: see in particular the dissenting judgment of Thomas J in *Bobux Marketing Ltd v Raynor Marketing Ltd* [2002] 1 NZLR 506 at 517.

[130] Closer to home, there is strong authority for the view that Scottish law recognises a broad principle of good faith and fair

dealing: see the decision of the House of Lords in *Smith v Bank of Scotland* [1997] SC (HL) 111 esp at p 121 (per Lord Clyde).

[131] Under English law a duty of good faith is implied by law as an incident of certain categories of contract, for example contracts of employment and contracts between partners or others whose relationship is characterised as a fiduciary one. I doubt that English law has reached the stage, however, where it is ready to recognise a requirement of good faith as a duty implied by law, even as a default rule, into all commercial contracts. Nevertheless, there seems to me to be no difficulty, following the established methodology of English law for the implication of terms in fact, in implying such a duty in any ordinary commercial contract based on the presumed intention of the parties.

[132] Traditionally, the two principal criteria used to identify terms implied in fact are that the term is so obvious that it goes without saying and that the term is necessary to give business efficacy to the contract. More recently, in *Attorney General for Belize v Belize Telecom Ltd* [2009] UKPC 10, [2009] 2 All ER 1127, [2009] 1 WLR 1988 at 1993-5, the process of implication has been analysed as an exercise in the construction of the contract as a whole. In giving the judgment of the Privy Council in that case, Lord Hoffmann characterised the traditional criteria, not as a series of independent tests, but rather as different ways of approaching what is ultimately always a question of construction: what would the contract, read as a whole against the relevant background, reasonably be understood to mean?

[133] The modern case law on the construction of contracts has emphasised that contracts, like all human communications, are made against a background of unstated shared understandings which inform their meaning. The breadth of the relevant background and the fact that it has no conceptual limits have also been stressed, particularly in the famous speech of Lord Hoffmann in *Investors Compensation Scheme Ltd v West Bromwich Building Society* [1998] 1 All ER 98, [1998] 1 BCLC 493, [1998] 1

WLR 896 at pp 912-3, as further explained in *BCCI v Ali* [2001] UKHL 8, [2002] 1 AC 251 at p 269, [2001] 1 All ER 961.

[134] Importantly for present purposes, the relevant background against which contracts are made includes not only matters of fact known to the parties but also shared values and norms of behaviour. Some of these are norms that command general social acceptance; others may be specific to a particular trade or commercial activity; others may be more specific still, arising from features of the particular contractual relationship. Many such norms are naturally taken for granted by the parties when making any contract without being spelt out in the document recording their agreement.

[135] A paradigm example of a general norm which underlies almost all contractual relationships is an expectation of honesty. That expectation is essential to commerce, which depends critically on trust. Yet it is seldom, if ever, made the subject of an express contractual obligation. Indeed, if a party in negotiating the terms of a contract were to seek to include a provision which expressly required the other party to act honestly, the very fact of doing so might well damage the parties' relationship by the lack of trust which this would signify.

[136] The fact that commerce takes place against a background expectation of honesty has been recognised by the House of Lords in *HIH Casualty v Chase Manhattan Bank* [2003] UKHL 6, [2003] 1 All ER (Comm) 349, [2003] 2 Lloyd's Rep 61. In that case a contract of insurance contained a clause which stated that the insured should have "no liability of any nature to the insurers for any information provided". A question arose as to whether these words meant that the insured had no liability even for deceit where the insured's agent had dishonestly provided information known to be false. The House of Lords affirmed the decision of the courts below that, even though the clause read literally would cover liability for deceit, it was not reasonably to be understood as having that meaning. As Lord Bingham put it at 15 "Parties entering into a commercial contract . . . will assume the honesty

and good faith of the other; absent such an assumption they would not deal". To similar effect Lord Hoffmann observed at 68 that parties "contract with one another in the expectation of honest dealing", and that:

> ". . . in the absence of words which expressly refer to dishonesty, it goes without saying that underlying the contractual arrangements of the parties there will be a common assumption that the persons involved will behave honestly".

[137] As a matter of construction, it is hard to envisage any contract which would not reasonably be understood as requiring honesty in its performance. The same conclusion is reached if the traditional tests for the implication of a term are used. In particular the requirement that parties will behave honestly is so obvious that it goes without saying. Such a requirement is also necessary to give business efficacy to commercial transactions.

[138] In addition to honesty, there are other standards of commercial dealing which are so generally accepted that the contracting parties would reasonably be understood to take them as read without explicitly stating them in their contractual document. A key aspect of good faith, as I see it, is the observance of such standards. Put the other way around, not all bad faith conduct would necessarily be described as dishonest. Other epithets which might be used to describe such conduct include "improper", "commercially unacceptable" or "unconscionable".

[139] Another aspect of good faith which overlaps with the first is what may be described as fidelity to the parties' bargain. The central idea here is that contracts can never be complete in the sense of expressly providing for every event that may happen. To apply a contract to circumstances not specifically provided for, the language must accordingly be given a reasonable construction which promotes the values and purposes expressed or implicit in the contract. That principle is well established in the modern English case law on the interpretation of contracts:

see eg *Rainy Sky SA v Kookmin Bank* [2011] UKSC 50, [2012] 1 All ER 1137, [2012] 1 All ER (Comm) 1; *Lloyds* TSB *Foundation for Scotland v Lloyds Banking Group plc* [2013] UKSC 3 at 23, 45 and 54. It also underlies and explains, for example, the body of cases in which terms requiring cooperation in the performance of the contract have been implied: see *Mackay v Dick* (1881) 6 App Cas 251, 263, 8 R 37, 29 WR 541; and the cases referred to in Chitty on Contracts (31st ed), Vol 1 at paras 13-012 – 13-014.

[140] The two aspects of good faith which I have identified are consistent with the way in which express contractual duties of good faith have been interpreted in several recent cases: see *Berkeley Community Villages Ltd v Pullen* [2007] EWHC 1330 (Ch) at 95 – 97, [2007] 3 EGLR 101; *CPC Group Ltd v Qatari Diar Real Estate Investment Co* [2010] EWHC 1535 (Ch) at 246.

[141] What good faith requires is sensitive to context. That includes the core value of honesty. In any situation it is dishonest to deceive another person by making a statement of fact intending that other person to rely on it while knowing the statement to be untrue. Frequently, however, the requirements of honesty go further. For example, if A gives information to B knowing that B is likely to rely on the information and A believes the information to be true at the time it is given but afterwards discovers that the information was, or has since become, false, it may be dishonest for A to keep silent and not to disclose the true position to B. Another example of conduct falling short of a lie which may, depending on the context, be dishonest is deliberately avoiding giving an answer, or giving an answer which is evasive, in response to a request for information.

[142] In some contractual contexts the relevant background expectations may extend further to an expectation that the parties will share information relevant to the performance of the contract such that a deliberate omission to disclose such information may amount to bad faith. English law has traditionally drawn a sharp distinction between certain relationships – such as partnership, trusteeship and other fiduciary relationships – on

the one hand, in which the parties owe onerous obligations of disclosure to each other, and other contractual relationships in which no duty of disclosure is supposed to operate. Arguably at least, that dichotomy is too simplistic. While it seems unlikely that any duty to disclose information in performance of the contract would be implied where the contract involves a simple exchange, many contracts do not fit this model and involve a longer-term relationship between the parties in which they make a substantial commitment. Such "relational" contracts, as they are sometimes called, may require a high degree of communication, cooperation and predictable performance based on mutual trust and confidence and involve expectations of loyalty which are not legislated for in the express terms of the contract but are implicit in the parties' understanding and are necessary to give business efficacy to the arrangements. Examples of such relational contracts might include some joint venture agreements, franchise agreements and long-term distributorship agreements.

[143] The Agreement in this case was a distributorship agreement which required the parties to communicate effectively and cooperate with each other in its performance. In particular, ITC needed to plan production and take account of the expected future demand from Yam Seng for Manchester United products. For its part Yam Seng, which was incurring expense in marketing the products and was trying to obtain orders, was arguably entitled to expect that it would be kept informed of ITC's best estimates of when products would be available to sell and would be told of any material change in this information without having to ask. Yam Seng's case was not advanced in this way, however, and it is therefore unnecessary for me to decide whether the requirements of good faith in this case extended to any such positive obligations of disclosure.

[144] Although its requirements are sensitive to context, the test of good faith is objective in the sense that it depends not on either party's perception of whether particular conduct is improper but on whether in the particular context the conduct

would be regarded as commercially unacceptable by reasonable and honest people. The standard is thus similar to that described by Lord Nicholls in a different context in his seminal speech in *Royal Brunei Airlines v Tan* [1995] 2 AC 378 at pp 389-390, [1995] 3 All ER 97, [1995] 3 WLR 64. This follows from the fact that the content of the duty of good faith is established by a process of construction which in English law is based on an objective principle. The court is concerned not with the subjective intentions of the parties but with their presumed intention, which is ascertained by attributing to them the purposes and values which reasonable people in their situation would have had.

[145] Understood in the way I have described, there is in my view nothing novel or foreign to English law in recognising an implied duty of good faith in the performance of contracts. It is consonant with the theme identified by Lord Steyn as running through our law of contract that reasonable expectations must be protected: see *First Energy (UK) Ltd v Hungarian International Bank Ltd* [1993] BCLC 1409, [1993] 2 Lloyd's Rep 194, 196; and (1997) 113 LQR 433. Moreover, such a concept is, I believe, already reflected in several lines of authority that are well established. One example is the body of cases already mentioned in which duties of cooperation in the performance of the contract have been implied. Another consists of the authorities which show that a power conferred by a contract on one party to make decisions which affect them both must be exercised honestly and in good faith for the purpose for which it was conferred, and must not be exercised arbitrarily, capriciously or unreasonably (in the sense of irrationally): see eg *Abu Dhabi National Tanker Co v Product Star Shipping Ltd (The "Product Star")* [1993] 1 Lloyd's Rep 397, 404; *Socimer International Bank Ltd v Standard Bank London Ltd* [2008] EWCA Civ 116, [2008] Bus LR 1304, [2008] 1 Lloyd's Rep 558, 575-7. A further example concerns the situation where the consent of one party is needed to an action of the other and a term is implied that such consent is not to be withheld unreasonably (in a similar sense): see eg *Gan v Tai Ping (Nos 2 & 3)* [2001] Lloyd's Rep IR 667; *Eastleigh BC v Town Quay Developments Ltd* [2009] EWCA Civ 1391, [2010] 2 P & CR 19. Yet another example, I would suggest,

is the line of authorities of which the *Interfoto* case is one, which hold that an onerous or unusual contract term on which a party seeks to rely on must be fairly brought to the notice of the other party, if it is to be enforced.

[146] There are some further observations that I would make about the reasons I mentioned earlier for the reluctance of English law to recognise an implied duty on contracting parties to deal with each other in good faith.

[147] First, because the content of the duty is heavily dependent on context and is established through a process of construction of the contract, its recognition is entirely consistent with the case by case approach favoured by the common law. There is therefore no need for common lawyers to abandon their characteristic methods and adopt those of civil law systems in order to accommodate the principle.

[148] Second, as the basis of the duty of good faith is the presumed intention of the parties and meaning of their contract, its recognition is not an illegitimate restriction on the freedom of the parties to pursue their own interests. The essence of contracting is that the parties bind themselves in order to co-operate to their mutual benefit. The obligations which they undertake include those which are implicit in their agreement as well as those which they have made explicit.

[149] Third, a further consequence of the fact that the duty is based on the parties' presumed intention is that it is open to the parties to modify the scope of the duty by the express terms of their contract and, in principle at least, to exclude it altogether. I say "in principle at least" because in practice it is hardly conceivable that contracting parties would attempt expressly to exclude the core requirement to act honestly.

[150] Fourth, I see no objection, and some advantage, in describing the duty as one of good faith "and fair dealing". I see no objection, as the duty does not involve the court in imposing its view of what

is substantively fair on the parties. What constitutes fair dealing is defined by the contract and by those standards of conduct to which, objectively, the parties must reasonably have assumed compliance without the need to state them. The advantage of including reference to fair dealing is that it draws attention to the fact that the standard is objective and distinguishes the relevant concept of good faith from other senses in which the expression "good faith" is used.

[151] Fifth, in so far as English law may be less willing than some other legal systems to interpret the duty of good faith as requiring openness of the kind described by Bingham LJ in the *Interfoto* case as "playing fair", "coming clean" or "putting one's cards face upwards on the table", this should be seen as a difference of opinion, which may reflect different cultural norms, about what constitutes good faith and fair dealing in some contractual contexts rather than a refusal to recognise that good faith and fair dealing are required.

[152] Sixth, the fear that recognising a duty of good faith would generate excessive uncertainty is unjustified. There is nothing unduly vague or unworkable about the concept. Its application involves no more uncertainty than is inherent in the process of contractual interpretation.

[153] In the light of these points, I respectfully suggest that the traditional English hostility towards a doctrine of good faith in the performance of contracts, to the extent that it still persists, is misplaced.

[154] I have emphasised in this discussion the extent to which the content of the duty to perform a contract in good faith is dependent on context. It was Mr Salter's submission that the relevant content of the duty in this case was captured by two more specific terms which Yam Seng contends are to be implied into the Agreement. I therefore turn to consider these.

In *TSG Building Services v South Anglia Housing Ltd* [2013] EWHC 1151 (TCC), 148 Con LR 228, Akenhead J refused to imply a term that an unqualified right to serve notice to terminate the contract should be exercised in good faith, even though in that case there was an express clause in that contract requiring the parties to work together in a spirit of trust, fairness and mutual co-operation. He said, at 51:

> Even if there was some implied term of good faith, it would not and could not circumscribe or restrict what the parties had expressly agreed in Clause 12.3, which was in effect that either of them for no, good or bad reason could terminate at any time before the term of four years was completed. That is the risk that each voluntarily undertook when it entered into the Contract. . . .

Recently in Singapore, it was noted that 'the doctrine of good faith remains a fledgling doctrine in both English and Singapore contract law.' In *KS Energy Services Ltd v BR Energy (M) Sdn Bhd* [2014] SGCA 16, V K Rajah JA delivering the judgment of the Singapore Court of Appeal said:

> Until and unless the theoretical foundations and architecture of the doctrine are settled, our courts cannot imprecisely endorse an implied duty of good faith in the local context (at [47] [60]). Parties to a contract governed by Singapore law therefore do not ordinarily have either the burden or the benefit of a general obligation to conduct themselves in accordance with an ascertainable standard of commercial behaviour. To address this lacuna, express endeavours clauses are often introduced into written contracts to regulate the parties' obligations. However, as will be seen, notwithstanding the relative prevalence of such clauses, there remains a degree of uncertainty as to what legal responsibilities they might entail. As our discussion in this judgment will illustrate, the wealth of case law from across the various common law jurisdictions provides some degree of insight, but ultimately, each case will have to be resolved on its own facts. The same endeavours formulation, when used in different factual matrices, does not necessarily have the same or a similar meaning or implication.

In Malaysia, the Court of Appeal in *Aseambankers Malaysia Bhd & Ors v Shencourt Sdn Bhd & Anor* [2014] 4 MLJ 619 had occasion to delve into the same issue. Abdul Malik Ishak JCA, delivering the judgment of the court reiterated that a breach of duty of good faith was not a cause of action and there was no general duty of good faith in common law. He stated:

> Chitty on Contracts (29th Ed), London Sweet & Maxwell 2004, at Vol 1, at p 1-020 carried this caption:
>
>> Nevertheless, the modern view is that, in keeping with the principles of freedom of contract and the binding force of contracts, in English contract there is no principle of good faith of general application
>
> [74] Continuing at p 1-024, the authors of Chitty on Contracts aptly said:
>
>> Given the remarkably open-textured nature of good faith, this would lead to a very considerable degree of legal uncertainty, and could be seen as trespassing too far into the legislative domain.
>
> [75] Lord Ackner writing for the House of Lords in *Walford v Miles* [1992] 2 AC 128, at p 138 laid down the law in these erudite terms:
>
>> However, the concept of a duty to carry on negotiations in good faith is inherently repugnant to the adverserial position of the parties when involved in negotiations. Each party to the negotiations is entitled to pursue his (or her) own interest, so long as he avoids making misrepresentations. To advance that interest he must be entitled, if he thinks it appropriate, to threaten to withdraw from further negotiations or to withdraw in fact, in the hope that the opposite party may seek to reopen the negotiations by offering him improved terms. Mr Naughton, of course, accepts that the agreement upon which he relies does not contain a duty to complete the negotiations. But that still leaves the vital question

— how is a vendor ever to know that he is entitled to withdraw from further negotiations? How is the court to police such an agreement? A duty to negotiate in good faith is unworkable in practice as it is inherently inconsistent with the position of a negotiating party. It is here that the uncertainty lies.

[76] Andrew Phang Boon Leong JA writing for the Court of Appeal of Singapore in *Ng Giap Hon v Westcomb Securities Pte Ltd and others* [2009] 3 SLR 518 extensively discussed the issue of good faith in various countries and came to the conclusion that there is no general duty of good faith in common law. At p 544 of the judgment, His Lordship had this to say:

> 47. The doctrine of good faith is very much a fledgling doctrine in English and (most certainly) Singapore contract law. Indeed, a cursory survey of the relevant law in other Commonwealth jurisdictions appears to suggest a similar situation.

[77] Continuing at p 546 of the judgment, His Lordship remarked:

> 51. Indeed, the copiousness as well as the variety of (and, perhaps more importantly, the debates in) the academic literature (coupled with the relative dearth of case law) suggest that the doctrine of good faith is far from settled. The case law itself appears to be in a state of flux: ....

[78] Proceeding ahead at p 548 of the judgment, His Lordship remarked:

> 54. Prof Furmston confirms the observation which we have just made in the preceding paragraph, ie, that the doctrine of good faith, although not lacking in supporters, particularly from theoretical as well as aspirational perspectives (see, for example, Roger Brownsword, 'Good Faith in Contracts' Revisited' (1996) 4 CLP 111 and, by the same author, 'Two Concepts of Good Faith'

> (1994) 7 JCL 197), is nevertheless still far from being an established doctrine under English law ...

[79] Finally, at p 550 of the judgment, His Lordship rounded it up by saying:

>> 60. In the circumstances, it is not surprising that the doctrine of good faith continues (as mentioned at (47) above) to be a fledgling one in the Commonwealth. Much clarification is required, even on a theoretical level. Needless to say, until the theoretical foundations as well as the structure of this doctrine are settled, it would be inadvisable (to say the least) to even attempt to apply it in the practical sphere (see also Service Station Association (51), especially at 406-407 (per Gummow J); cf Peden's 2001 article (51) at 228–230). In the context of the present appeal, this is, in our view, the strongest reason as to why we cannot accede to the appellant's argument that this court should endorse an implied duty of good faith in the Singapore context.

However, in Canada it has been said that "it is implied in every agreement that one party owes good faith to the other, both in the manner of stating the agreement and in its performance", with all the consequences which equity may demand.[171] The ruling that good faith is an implicit, necessary obligation in all contractual relationships was confirmed in *Houle v Banque Nationale du Canada* [1990] 3 S.C.R. 122; 114 N.R. 161; 35 Q.A.C. 161.

It is to be noted however that "recently there have been steps toward judicial recognition of an independent doctrine of good faith existing in the common law".[172]

---

[171] *Banque Nationale du Canada v Soucisse, Groulx and Robitaille*, [1981] 2 S.C.R. 339; 43 N.R. 283.

[172] For example, *International Corona Resources Ltd. v. Lac Minerals Ltd.* (1989), 101 N.R. 239; 36 O.A.C. 57; 61 D.L.R.(4th) 14 (S.C.C.); *LeMesurier v. Andrus* (1986), 12 O.A.C. 299; 54 O.R.(2d) 1 (C.A.); *Gateway Realty Ltd v Arton Holdings Ltd. and LaHave Developments Ltd.* (No. 3) (1991), 106 N.S.R.(2d)

In *Gateway Realty Ltd v Arton Holdings Ltd. and LaHave Developments Ltd.* (No. 3) (1991), 106 N.S.R.(2d) 180; 288 A.P.R. 180 (T.D.), Kelly, J., of the Supreme Court held that the good faith requirement was applicable to the entire contractual process. His Lordship said:

> The law requires that parties to a contract exercise their rights under that agreement honestly, fairly and in good faith. This standard is breached when a party acts in a bad faith manner in the performance of its rights and obligations under the contract. 'Good faith' conduct is the guide to the manner in which the parties should pursue their mutual contractual objectives. Such conduct is breached when a party acts in 'bad faith' - a conduct that is contrary to community standards of honesty, reasonableness or fairness. The insistence on a good faith requirement in discretionary conduct in contractual formation, performance and enforcement is only the fulfilment of the obligation of the courts to do justice in the resolution of disputes between contending parties.
>
> His Lordship was of the view that 'what will constitute bad faith or breach of the conduct described above will depend on the terms of contract and the circumstances of each case. In most cases, bad faith can be said to occur when one party, without reasonable justification, acts in relation to the contract in a manner where the result would be to substantially nullify the bargained objective or benefit contracted for by the other, or to cause significant harm to the other, contrary to the original purpose and expectation of the parties.'

Gateway Realty was extensively reviewed and adopted by Shannon, J., of the Court of Queen's Bench of Alberta in *Mesa Operating Ltd. Partnership v. Amoco Canada Resources Ltd.* (1992), 129 A.R. 177 (Q.B.).

Feehan J in *Opron Construction Co Ltd v Her Majesty The Queen in Right of Alberta 1994* 151 A.R. 241 went on to say:

180; 288 A.P.R. 180 (T.D.): *Opron Construction Co Ltd v Her Majesty The Queen in Right of Alberta* 1994 151 A.R. 241.

In Canada, the test for deciding whether or not the parties have fulfilled the terms of the contract in a good faith manner does not include the need for the plaintiff to show that the defendant intentionally acted in bad faith. The Canadian test is laid out by the Nova Scotia Supreme Court in *Gateway Realty Ltd v Arton Holdings Ltd. et al.* (1991), 106 N.S.R.(2d) 180; 288 A.P.R. 180 (T.D.).

> 'There the court enunciated the principal that there was an obligation on parties to a contract to act in good faith and that duty limits the exercise of discretion conferred on parties by an agreement. In that case it was held that the common law duty to perform in good faith is breached when a party acts in bad faith, that is, when a party acts in a manner that substantially nullifies the contractual objectives or causes significant harm to the other, contrary to the original purposes or expectations of the parties.'

The court concluded on p. 221 that:

> 'the knowledge that [Dome] possessed at the time of pooling should have alerted them to their good faith obligation to consult with Mesa. Only then would Mesa have had a reasonable opportunity to reach an equitable agreement with Dome, or alternatively, urge that an application be made ... to resolve the matter. The failure to proceed in that manner constituted a breach of the implied term of the contract obliging Dome to act in good faith.'

Thus, Dome's liability rested on the good faith doctrine.

These cases suggest that the control mechanism defining the content of the doctrine of good faith in contractual relations appears to be the reasonable expectations of the parties.

It is clear that the obligation of good faith does not spring solely from a fiduciary or quasi-fiduciary relationship. In *LAC Minerals*, *Gateway Realty* and *Mesa*, the defendant could have unilaterally deprived the plaintiff of the benefits of the contract which the parties had contemplated would enure. Taking advantage of such a position without reasonable justification, and in defiance of the normal expectations of the particular commercial sector in such circumstances, constituted bad faith.

I have already noted that in the construction industry, tenderers reasonably expect that the owner will not, having provided some information, withhold information which could materially affect the prospective tenderers' bids. It is not in the ultimate interests of either party for such information to be withheld, for the consequent delays and cost overruns in the completion of contracts where the other party labours in ignorance, can be disastrous.

I conclude that in the circumstances of this case there is a covenant implied by law that the parties will deal fairly and in good faith with one another in the exchange of information. It is reasonable, where the owner or its agents impart critical information in the tender documents which form part of the contract, that there is an implied covenant that such information has been furnished in good faith, in the honest and reasonable belief that it is complete and accurate, with all material information provided, in the sense that there is no inconsistent information within the owner's knowledge, bearing upon the tender or the performance of the contract.

In this respect, I find that the law does reflect the reasonable expectations of the parties to the tendering process. Thus, I find that Alberta Environment owed an obligation of good faith and fair dealing to the plaintiff to disclose that it possessed material geotechnical information which was inconsistent with or which contradicted the information which had been provided to the plaintiff in the tender documents.

The requirement of good faith is therefore anchored on principles of law and are not contractual. It may however be provided for in the contract of insurance by the parties, upon the conclusion of the contract.

Having a contractual obligation of good faith in the performance of the contract presents no conceptual difficulty in itself. Such an obligation can arise from an implied or inferred contractual term. It is commonly the subject of an express term in certain types of contract such as partnership contracts. Once parties are in a contractual relationship, the source of their obligations, the one to the other, is the contract (although the contract is not necessarily exclusive and the relationship which comes into existence may of itself give rise to other liabilities, for example liabilities in tort).[173]

GOOD FAITH AND INSURANCE CONTRACTS

Unlike contracts in general, insurance contracts have already been recognised as being governed by the doctrine of *uberrima fides* or utmost good faith.

Uberrima fides is a Latin terminology which literally means most abundant faith. The duty of utmost good faith has a uniquely distinguished pedigree. The essential role of good faith in law was embraced by the Athenians (as "epieikeia") and later by the Romans (as "aequitas") and those concepts were later developed into a concept that has become known as 'equity' under the English general common law and subsequently they had given rise to the specific reciprocal obligation owed between insurers and the insureds known as *uberrima fides*.[174] Of course, the earliest records of insurance contracts have been found in the archives of Genoa and Florence in the year 1523 where they were identified with risks in sale or loan contracts, particularly as regards carriage by sea.[175]

---

[173] *Manifest Shipping Co Ltd v Uni-Polaris Shipping Co Ltd & Others (The 'Star Sea')* [2001] UKHL 1, [2003] 1 AC 469.

[174] See generally JF O'Connor, Good Faith in English Law 2 (1990).

[175] Peter Eggers & Patrick Foss, Good Faith and Insurance Contracts, 71 & n 22 (1998).

In *Tan Jing Jeong v Allianz Life Insurance Malaysia Bhd & Anor* [2012] 7 MLJ 179 (HC), His Lordship Abang Iskandar J went on discuss the duty of good faith in relation to insurance contracts and said:

> [21] So, it is now commonly accepted as the basis for the legal doctrine which governs the insurance contracts. This means that all parties to an insurance contract must deal in good faith, making a full declaration of all material facts in the insurance proposal. Thus, the insured must reveal the exact nature and potential of the risks that he transfers to the insurer, while at the same time the insurer must make sure that the potential contract fits the needs of, and benefits, the assured.
>
> [22] A higher duty is exacted from parties to an insurance contract than from parties to most other contracts in order to ensure the disclosure of all material facts so that the contract may accurately reflect the actual risk being undertaken. The principles underlying this rule were stated by Lord Mansfield in the leading and often quoted case of *Carter v Boehm* (1766) 97 ER 1162, at p 1164, as follows:
>
>> Insurance is a contract of speculation .... The special facts, upon which the contingent chance is to be computed, lie most commonly in the knowledge of the insured only: the under-writer trusts to his representation, and proceeds upon confidence that he does not keep back any circumstances in his knowledge, to mislead the under-writer into a belief that the circumstance does not exist .... Good faith forbids either party by concealing what he privately knows, to draw the other into a bargain from his ignorance of that fact, and his believing the contrary.

The doctrine of good faith is one of the principal distinctions between insurance law and general contract law. There is a requirement to be *bona fide*. *Bona fide* is defined to mean "in good faith, honestly, without fraud, collusion or participation in wrongdoing".[176]

The doctrine commences before the policy is made, manifests as the duty of disclosure, and continues as long as the parties remain in a contractual or continuing relationship and applies equally to the insurer and the insured.[177]

It is established beyond doubt that the *uberrima fides* principle, as it is sometimes called, imposes reciprocal duties on the insured and insurer. In *Banque Keyser Ullmann SA v Skandia (UK) Insurance Co Ltd and others and related actions* [1987] 2 All ER 923, Steyn J stated:

> Indeed, the principle was settled by the celebrated judgment of Lord Mansfield CJ in *Carter v Boehm* (1766) 3 Burr 1905, [1558–1774] All ER Rep 183. The contingency insured against by the Governor of Fort Marlborough in Sumatra was whether the fort would be taken by a European enemy between October 1759 and October 1760. In April 1760 a French man-of-war captured the fort. The governor claimed on the policy. The underwriters put forward a defence of non-disclosure, *viz* that the weakness of the fort, and the probability of it being attacked, was not disclosed. It was established that the fort was not designed to resist European enemies but only 'for defence against the natives of Sumatra'. The defence failed for reasons which are perhaps summarised in the following observation of Lord Mansfield CJ (3 Burr 1905 at 1918, [1558–1774] All ER Rep 183 at 189):
>
>> 'The underwriter, here, knowing the governor to be acquainted with the state of the place; knowing that he apprehended danger, and must have some ground for his apprehension; being told nothing of either; signed this policy, without asking a question.'

---

[176] Osborn's Concise Law Dictionary (8th Ed), Sweet and Maxwell). See also *Fauziah Khanom bt Irshad Ali Khan v Pegawai Pejabat Pelajaran Daerah Johor Bahru & Ors* [2013] 7 MLJ 737.

[177] *Boulton v Holder Bros* (1904) 1 KB 784, 791.

The requirement of utmost good faith gives rise to a range of duties, some of which apply before formation of the contract and others which apply post-formation. For these reasons some legal commentators prefer to refer to the 'doctrine' of utmost good faith.

The mutual obligation of utmost good faith, under a contract of insurance, exists both before the making of the contract and after the contract is made throughout the performance of the contract with reference to "relevant facts which are relevant to later stages of the contract". [178]

Owen J in *Kelly v New Zealand Insurance Company Ltd* (1996) 9 ANZ Insurance Cases 61-317 had accepted that "at common law, contracts of insurance are described as contracts *uberrimae fidei* or contracts of good faith, the precise definition of which was said to depend on the legal context in which it is used but includes notions of fairness, reasonableness, honesty, community standards of decency and fair dealing".

It can be said that Owen J considered that the element of honesty was the gravamen of the duty. It was concluded that there was no dishonest, capricious or unreasonable conduct by the insured respondent but added that it was not necessary for a party to point to conduct of any particular degree of seriousness in order to establish a breach of the duty.

There is no doubt, however, that the duty of good faith, standing alone, does not give rise to a cause of action in damages. The only remedy for its breach is the remedy of avoidance, i.e., the right to avoid. That is the effect of section 17 of the MIA ("A contract of marine insurance is a contract based upon the utmost good faith, and, if the utmost good faith be not observed by either party, the contract may be avoided by the other party").[179] By itself, the duty of good faith gives rise to neither contractual nor tortious obligations but exists *sui generis* as a matter of law.

---

[178] *Black King Shipping Corp v Massie, The 'Litsion Pride'* [1985] 1 Lloyd's Rep 437.

[179] This was also the decision in *Banque Keyser Ullmann SA v. Skandia (UK) Insurance Co Ltd* [1990] 1 QB 665 at 773/781 ("Issue 5") and *Banque Financière de la Cité SA (formerly Banque Keyser Ullmann SA) v. Westgate*

In *Chariot Inns Ltd v Assicurazione Generali Spa* [1981] IR 199 at 225, Kenny J said:

> A contract of insurance requires the highest standard of accuracy, good faith, candour and disclosure by the insured when making a proposal for insurance...[a]ny misstatement in the answers given, when they relate to a material matter affecting the insurance, entitles the insurance company to avoid the policy and repudiate liability if the event insured against happens.

A contract of insurance is a contract which is *uberrimae fidei*. In plain English this means that it is a contract where the parties are under a duty to exercise the utmost good faith. This duty exists throughout the tenure of the contract and must be complied with by both the insurer and the insured.[180]

There are certain contracts expressed by the law to be contracts of the utmost good faith, where material facts must be disclosed; if not, the contract is voidable. Apart from special fiduciary relationships, contracts for partnership and contracts of insurance are the leading instances. In such cases the duty does not arise out of the contract; the duty of a person proposing an insurance for instance, arises before a contract is made.[181]

Lord Clyde in *Manifest Shipping Co Ltd v Uni-Polaris Co Ltd & Others (The 'Star Sea')* [2001] UKHL 1, [2003] 1 AC 469 said:

> In a contract of insurance, and indeed in certain other contracts, an element of good faith is to be observed, and that element may impose certain duties, particularly of disclosure between one party and the other, which may vary in their content and

---

Insurance Co Ltd (formerly Hodge General & Mercantile Co Ltd) [1991] 2 AC 249.

[180] Excerpt from Principles of Insurance Law by Poh Choo Chai (5th Ed) p 159): *Pacific & Orient Insurance Co Bhd v Vigneswaran a/l Rajarethinam & Ors* [2014] 8 MLJ 423 (HC).

[181] Per Lord Atkin, *Bell v Lever Bros* [1932] AC 161 at 227.

substance according to the circumstances, then a question may arise as to the utility of the concept of utmost good faith or an *uberrima fides*. In my view, the idea of good faith in the context of insurance contracts reflects the degrees of openness required of the parties in the various stages of their relationship. It is not an absolute. The substance of the obligation which is entailed can vary according to the context in which the matter comes to be judged. It is reasonable to expect a very high degree of openness at the stage of the formation of the contract, but there is no justification for requiring that degree necessarily to continue once the contract has been made.

Being a contract of good faith, there are many duties that are owed by the insured, and in some instances by the insurer.

The general principle requiring the utmost good faith applies to claims as well as to matters preceding the contract.[182]

Since a contract of insurance is a contract which is *uberrimae fidei*, it follows that when a party to a contract of insurance acts in bad faith, the innocent party is entitled to be discharged from his obligations under the contract. The exercise of good faith is fundamental to the relationship between the insurer and the insured.[183]

In relation to the insurer, it has been held that in every contract of insurance, an insurer has an implied obligation to deal with the claims of its insured in good faith. It was held that a breach of the implied duty of good faith meets the requirement of an independent actionable wrong.[184]

One of the consequences of the principles that a contract of insurance is one of the utmost good faith[185] is that fraudulent claims made under it

---

[182] *Black King Shipping Corp v Massie, The 'Litsion Pride'* [1985] 1 Lloyd's Rep 437.

[183] Law of Insurance by Poh Chu Chai 6th Edition at page 910-911.

[184] *Katotikidis v Mr Submarine Ltd* [2002] ACWSJ 10135.

[185] See *Heyman v Darwins Limited* [1942] AC 356 at p 365.

give the insurers the right to avoid the whole policy.[186] Thus, if the assured makes a fraudulent claim, he cannot recover at all[187], and conditions in the policy to this effect[188] are declaratory of the legal position without them.[189]

Requirement of Utmost Good Faith

The principle that a contract of insurance is a contract based on the utmost good faith, and that if the utmost good faith is not observed by either party the contract may be avoided by the other party, is of universal application to all types of insurance contracts. The utmost good faith imposes a positive obligation of disclosure. In its practical application, the principle permits either party to avoid the contract altogether if it is established against the other party that: (1) there has been a failure by the other party to disclose a material fact; or (2) the other party has made an innocent misrepresentation of a material fact, since statements made in a contract must be true in fact. "Now, nothing can be clearer than that in stating the essence of an insurance contract. Both parties bear the same duty to be frank and truthful upfront. If by reason either of non-disclosure of a material fact or a misrepresentation of a material fact, although an innocent one, such contract becomes voidable at the instance of the party who had suffered by reason of the failure of the other party to observe its attendant duty to be faithfully truthful".[190]

"Good faith forbids either party concealing what it privately knows, to draw the other into a bargain, from his ignorance of that fact, and his believing the contrary".[191]

---

[186] See *Stebbing's case* [1917] 2 KB 433 at p 438.

[187] See *Norton v The Royal Fire and Life Assurance C* [1885] 1 TLR 460.

[188] See *Jureidini v National British and Irish Millers Insurance Co Ltd* [1915] AC 499.

[189] *Wong Cheong Kong Sdn Bhd v Prudential Assurance Sdn Bhd* [1998] 1 CLJ 916.

[190] Halsbury's Laws of England, (4th Ed) 2003 Reissue Vol 25 at p 36.

[191] *Asia Insurance Co Ltd v Tat Hong Plant Leasing Pte Ltd* [1992] 4 CLJ (Rep) 324.

This duty to exercise the utmost good faith exists throughout the tenure of the contract and must be complied with by both parties: Principles of Insurance Law by Poh Choo Chai (5th Ed) p 159.

In *Leong Kum Whay v QBE Insurance (M) Sdn Bhd & Ors* [2006] 1 MLJ 710; [2006] 1 CLJ 1 (CA), Gopal Sri Ram JCA (as he then was) said at p 719 (MLJ); p 19 (CLJ):

> It is settled beyond dispute that a contract of insurance is one that imposes a mutual duty on the parties to it to act *uberrimae fides* towards each other. Whether a particular fact is a material act is a question of fact ... But the duty to make full disclosure of all material facts is not an implied term of a contract of insurance. There is in fact no contract at the point at which the duty arises; the parties being still at the stage of negotiations. It is therefore a pre-contractual duty imposed by the common law. I take these propositions to be settled by authority.

Generally, the remedy for breach of contract is damages, however the breach of good faith in an insurance contract has far-reaching consequences. Where there is a breach of the duty of utmost good faith, Section 17 of the MIA provides for the remedy of avoidance. Lord Hobhouse in *Manifest Shipping Co Ltd v Uni-Polaris Co Ltd & Others (The 'Star Sea')* [2001] UKHL 1, [2003] 1 AC 469 in his judgment said:

> The right to avoid referred to in s.17 is different. It applies retrospectively. It enables the aggrieved party to rescind the contract *ab initio*. Thus, he totally nullifies the contract. Everything done under the contract is liable to be undone. If any adjustment of the parties' financial positions is to take place, it is done under the law of restitution not under the law of contract. This is appropriate where the cause, the want of good faith, has preceded and been material to the making of the contract. But, where the want of good faith first occurs later, it becomes anomalous and disproportionate that it should be so categorised and entitle the aggrieved party to such an outcome.

Good Faith – The Australian Context

The duty of utmost good faith in Australia is a statutory duty as provided by Sections 13 and 14 of its Insurance Contract Act 1984 ('IC Act'). Section 13 implies into every contract of insurance to which the Act applies, a term requiring each party to act towards the other in respect of any matter arising under or in relation to the contract, with the utmost good faith. Section 14 provides that a party to a contract of insurance may not rely upon one of its terms, if to do so would be to fail to act with the utmost good faith.

Section 13 entitled "The duty of the utmost good faith" provides that:

> (1) a contract of insurance is a contract based on the utmost good faith and there is implied in such a contract a provision requiring each party to it to act towards the other party, in respect of any matter arising under or in relation to it, with the utmost good faith.

Section 14 entitled "Parties not to rely on provisions except in the utmost good faith" states:

> (1) If reliance by a party to a contract of insurance on a provision of the contract would be to fail to act with the utmost good faith, the party may not rely on the provision.

> (2) Sub-section (1) does not limit the operation of section 13,

> (3) In deciding whether reliance by an insurer on a provision of the contract of insurance would be to fail to act with the utmost good faith, the court shall have regard to any notification of the provision that was given to the insured, whether a notification of a kind mentioned in section 37 or otherwise.

Hunter J in *Wyllie v National Mutual Life Association of Australasia Ltd* (1997) 217 ALR 324 observed that where s 13 of the IC Act imports a duty into a contract of insurance upon parties to the contract to act with the utmost good faith towards each other "in respect of any matter arising under or in relation" to the contract, it is extremely difficult to see how such a duty is not extended as an "incident of the relationship" in respect of a third party in the position of the plaintiff. He also concluded that the insurer was under a duty to the plaintiff to act with utmost good faith in the assessment of his claim. It was also held that the insurer was under an implied obligation to the plaintiff, in forming an opinion as to the plaintiff's disability, to act fairly, in good faith and reasonably, having due regard for the interests of the plaintiff.

Owen J in *Kelly v New Zealand Insurance Company Ltd* (1996) 9 ANZ Insurance Cases 61-317 observed that by Section 13 of the IC Act the common law duty of good faith was now an implied term in every contract of insurance.

In Australia, it has been said that the question of utmost good faith must depend on the context in which it is used. Owen J in *Kelly v New Zealand Insurance Company Ltd* (1996) 9 ANZ Insurance Cases 61-317 referred to the duty to act in utmost good faith in these terms:

> The duty of parties to an insurance contract to act towards one another with utmost good faith has long been a fundamental principle of Insurance Law. It is also recognised in s 13 of the Act: see Sutton: 'Insurance Law in Australia' (2nd ed).

This can also be gleaned from various judgments which were reviewed by Chesterman J in *Re Zurich Australian Insurance Ltd* (1999) 10 ANZ Ins Cas 61-429. It was noted that the "nature of the duty apart from contracts covered by the Act is obscure". Reference was made to Report No. 20 of the Australian Law Reform Commission (1982) where it was said:

> 328. The Duty of Utmost Good Faith. The common law requirement that insurer and insured act in the utmost good faith towards each other forms the basis of their relationship. This requirement has usually been recognised in connection with the duty of disclosure. In principle, it should apply equally to other aspects of the insurance relationship. That view was adopted by Mr Justice Stephen in *Distillers Bio-Chemicals (Australia) Pty Ltd v. Ajax Insurance Co. Ltd.* However, there is no reported decision

in Australia applying the duty to the payment of claims. The position must, therefore, remain in some doubt. That doubt should be resolved ...

Chesterman J in *Re Zurich Australian Insurance Ltd (supra)*, concluded that there is not a separately existing independent general duty to act in good faith which would circumscribe Zurich's exercise of the choice given it by Condition 3. Consistent with the principles of the law of insurance and the nature of the relationship between an insurer and an insured/assured, that it requires good faith from each to the other, there is an implied limitation in any term of a policy which confers rights or powers on the insurer that they be exercised with due regard for the interests of the insured/assured where those interests conflict with the insurer's.

The dispute in *Re Zurich Australian Insurance Ltd* [1998] QSC 209 was between the insurers and the hospital where the insured sought medical treatment and incurred costs. Policy Condition 3 provided that "(Zurich) may at any time pay to (the hospital) in respect of all claims against (the hospital) ... the amount of the Limit of Indemnity ... or any lesser sum for which the claim ... can be settled and upon such payment (Zurich) shall relinquish conduct or control of and be under no further liability under the Policy in connection with such claim or claims except for costs charges and expenses recoverable from (the hospital) or incurred by (Zurich) or by (the hospital) with the written consent of (Zurich) prior to the date of such payment".

In the words of Chesterman J "the nub of the contest is whether the temporal qualification, 'prior to the date of such payment', qualifies only the costs of the hospital's defence or whether it applies to all costs for which Zurich might have been liable under the policy".

The hospital submitted that it was a breach of the duty of good faith which an insurer and an insured, owe to each other respectively, for Zurich to rely upon Condition 3 so as to decline indemnity for costs which the hospital may have had to pay the insured and for defending the insured plaintiff's claim.

Chesterman J found that on its true construction, Condition 3 did not exonerate Zurich the insurers from the obligation to indemnify the hospital in respect of the insured's costs.

> In relation to the question whether there had been a breach of the duty, Chesterman J as found that it was necessary first to consider what the content and scope of the duty of good faith was, as it affects the present circumstances. It was noted that as the policy of insurance was effected in 1972, Sections 13 and 14 of the Insurance Contracts Act 1984 did not apply.

> In *Wiltrading (WA) Pty Ltd v Lumley General Insurance Ltd* [2005] WASCA 106; (2005) 30 WAR 290, the Court of Appeal in Western Australia again considered the issue of the duty of good faith in the context of insurance contracts and also in the particular context of the conduct of an action.

> It is also to be noted that the duty of an insured to take reasonable steps to reduce or to minimise its loss and therefore the liability of the insurer is "a manifestation of the principle of utmost good faith".[192]

GOOD FAITH

- Introduction

    o Good Faith and Contracts

    o Good Faith and Insurance Contracts

    - Requirement of Utmost Good Faith

    - Good Faith – The Australian Context

---

[192] *Newnham v Baker* [1989] 1 Qd R 393 at 399.

CHAPTER 4
DUTY OF DISCLOSURE

DUTY OF GOOD FAITH

The law imposes a duty of utmost good faith on the insured in his dealings with the insurer. One part of this duty is the duty of disclosure, which is mandated by both the common law and the UK Marine Insurance Act 1906 ('MIA'), as being applicable to all insurance contracts.

The duty of disclosure is codified in Section 24 of the MIA as follows:

> 24(1) Subject to the provisions of this section, the assured must disclose to the insurer, before the contract is concluded, every material circumstance which is known to the assured, and the assured is deemed to know every circumstance which, in the ordinary course of business, ought to be known by him. If the assured fails to make such disclosure, the insurer may avoid the contract.
>
> (2) Every circumstance is material which would influence the judgment of a prudent insurer in fixing the premium, or determining whether he will take the risk.

The MIA was a codification of the common law, and it is inconceivable that the common law regarded only marine insurers and not other insurers, as bound by a duty of the utmost good faith.[193] The rationale of the rule imposing a duty of utmost good faith on the insured is that matters material to the risk are, generally speaking, peculiar to matters in his knowledge. In so far as matters are peculiar to the insurer's knowledge, as in Lord Mansfield CJ's example of the arrived ship (i.e., that it is a ship owner's duty to a charterer to maintain the ship in a 'seaworthy' state), a breach of that term encompasses anything from a sinking vessel to the lack of a medicine chest or second anchor or even a nail. Because of this inherent variability, it is unthinkable that seaworthiness is a condition. This principle and fairness require the imposition of a similar duty on the insurer. Indeed, it is difficult to imagine a more retrograde step, subversive of the standing of our insurance law and our insurance markets, than a ruling today that the great judge erred in *Carter v Boehm* 3 Burr 1905, a landmark English case, in stating that the principle of good faith rests on both parties. In *Banque Keyser Ullmann SA v Skandia (UK) Insurance Co Ltd and others and related actions* [1987] 2 All ER 923, Steyn J observed:

> ..the judgment of Lord Mansfield CJ (in *Carter v Boehm* (1766) 3 Burr 1905, [1558–1774] All ER Rep 183) is important for his lucid statement of the principles governing non-disclosure in insurance transactions. The following passage in his judgment is relevant to the issues in this case (3 Burr 1905 at 1909–1910, [1558–1774] All ER Rep 183 at 184–185):
>
>> 'Insurance is a contract upon speculation. The special facts, upon which the contingent chance is to be computed, lie most commonly in the knowledge of the insured only: the under-writer trusts to his representation, and proceeds upon confidence that he does not keep back any circumstance in his knowledge, to mislead the under-writer into a belief that the circumstance does not exist, and to induce him to estimate the *risque*, as if it did not exist. The keeping back such circumstance is a fraud, and therefore the policy is void. Although the

---

[193] See *Container Transport International Inc v Oceanus Mutual Underwriting Association (Bermuda) Ltd* [1984] 1 Lloyds Rep 476 at 496, 525 per Kerr and Stephenson LJJ.

suppression should happen through mistake, without any fraudulent intention; yet still the under-writer is deceived, and the policy is void; because the *risque* run is really different from the *risque* understood and intended to be run, at the time of the agreement. The policy would equally be void, against the under-writer, if he concealed; as, if he insured a ship on her voyage, which he privately knew to be arrived: and an action would lie to recover the premium. The governing principle is applicable to all contracts and dealings. Good faith forbids either party by concealing what he privately knows, to draw the other into a bargain, from his ignorance of that fact, and his believing the contrary. But either party may be innocently silent, as to grounds open to both, to exercise their judgment upon. *Aliud est celare; aliud, tacere; neque enim id est celare quicquid reticeas; sed cum quod tuscias, id ignorare emolumenti tui causa velis eos, quorum intersit id scire.* This definition of concealment, restrained to the efficient motives and precise subject of any contract, will generally hold to make it void, in favour of the party misled by his ignorance of the thing concealed.'

The law may also place upon a party an obligation to speak from the outset, originating in the nature of the relationship between the parties. If that duty of care is breached, the positive misstatement or non-disclosure may be actionable in deceit or negligence. Such relationships are a fiduciary relationship and contracts *uberrimae fidei*: *Hedley Byrne & Co v Heller & Partners Ltd* [1963] 2 All E.R. 575 (HL).

In other words, reciprocal duties rest on both parties to an insurance contract not only to abstain from bad faith but to observe in a positive sense the utmost good faith by disclosing all material circumstances. That principle, Lord Mansfield CJ said, is applicable to all contracts. To that extent Lord Mansfield CJ's generalised statement has not prevailed. Admittedly, there are other contracts which are sometimes described as contracts of the utmost good faith, such as contracts of suretyship, partnership and salvage, but the principles of disclosure applicable to those contracts cannot be equated with those applicable to contracts of insurance. Generally speaking, in the subsequent developments of the common law the idea that parties when negotiating a contract are dealing at arms length won the day: the philosophy of *caveat emptor* prevailed. This does not detract from the validity of Lord Mansfield CJ's observation in relation to contracts of insurance, namely that reciprocal duties of the utmost good faith are owed to one another by an insured and an insurer. There has been a considerable controversy about the ambit of an insured's duty of disclosure: see *Container Transport International Inc v Oceanus Mutual Underwriting Association (Bermuda) Ltd* [1984] 1 Lloyd's Rep 476. But the proposition that the duties of utmost good faith rests on both parties has been repeated on many occasions in judgments, and appears in leading textbooks. It has, to date, never been questioned. Section 17 of the Marine Insurance Act 1906 enacted it in the following terms:

'A contract of maritime insurance is a contract based upon the utmost good faith, and, if the utmost good faith be not observed by either party, the contract may be avoided by the other party.'

The pre-contractual breach of the duty of utmost good faith owed by the insured to the insurer, encompasses the duty of disclosure. In respect of a pre-contractual breach of the duty of utmost good faith, the remedy available would be the remedy of avoidance, whereby the insurers would be entitled to avoid the policy with retrospective effect.

FIDUCIARY DUTIES

As noted, the concept of good faith on which the requirement of disclosure is based, is founded on principles of mercantile law which are embodied in Sections 17 and 18 of the MIA. Section 17 which is accepted as expressing the generally applicable principles of insurance states that "A contract of marine insurance is a contract based upon the utmost good faith, and, if the utmost good faith be not observed by either party, the contract may be avoided by the other party". The section has been held to have an effect on both the pre-contractual and post-contractual conduct of the insured. Pre-contractually, it has been interpreted to mean that a consumer insured is under a duty to volunteer material information, and that the penalty for failing to do so is avoidance,[194] whereas post-contractually, it is an agreement between two or more parties for the doing or not doing of something specified.

The duty of disclosure as defined by sections 18 to 20 of the MIA only applies until the contract is made. Sections 18, 19 and 20 of the MIA spells out in some detail the content of the duty of disclosure owed by the insured to the insurer, before the contract is concluded and stipulates the yardstick for assessing whether a representation made by the insured to the insurer is material and is true.[195]

The utmost good faith principle, and the duty of disclosure are in most instances, linked together. However, there are cases where judges have stressed that non-disclosure may occur even though the proposer did not act mala fide.[196]

More traditional jurisprudence however, is inclined towards placing the emphasis on the duty of disclosure as a means of protecting the insurer and decoupling the duty from the wider implications of the (mutual) duty of utmost good faith[197]

At common law, a person who enters into a contract with another, is under no legal obligation to make a voluntary disclosure of information relating

---

[194] See *Manifest Shipping Co Ltd v Uni-Polaris Insurance Co Ltd (The Star Sea)* (supra)

[195] *Ibid*

[196] *Curran v Norwich Union Life Insurance Society* [1987] IEHC 5.

[197] MacDonald Eggers, Picken and Foss, Good Faith and Insurance Contracts (3rd ed) (2010) (Eggers, et al): Bennet, 'Mapping the Doctrine of Utmost Good Faith in Insurance Law' [1999] LMCLQ 165; Bennett Reflections on Values in Soyer, Reforming Marine and Commercial Insurance Law (Informa Law 2008); Bridge, 'Does Anglo-American Contract Law Need a Doctrine of Good Faith' (1984) 9 Can Bus LJ 385. Butcher, in 'Good Faith in Insurance Law: A Redundant Concept?' [2008] JBL 375.

to it. A duty to disclose material information only arises in contracts which are *uberrimae fides* and a contract of insurance is one such contract.[198]

In *Reynolds and Anderson v Phoenix Assurance Co Ltd* [1978] 2 Lloyd's Rep 440 the court said:

> The object of requiring disclosure of circumstances which affect the moral risk is to discover whether the proposer is a person likely to be an additional risk from the point of view of insurance. The most relevant circumstance for disclosure is therefore that he has actually committed an offence of a character which would in fact influence the insurer's judgment. The proposer is bound to disclose the commission of that offence even though he has been acquitted or even if no one other than he has the slightest idea that he committed it: the material circumstance is the commission of the offence.

The imposition of the duty of disclosure, is to ensure that a person seeking insurance accurately provides to the insurer all relevant information that will enable the insurer to assess the risk to be covered and set an appropriate premium. Breach of the rules can have drastic results for the person seeking the insurance. The insurance contract can be avoided by the insurer retrospectively from the commencement of the insurance cover, not just from the moment of avoidance. Non-compliance with the rules can therefore lead to a claim being defeated even when the breach of common law duty is only discovered after a loss has occurred and a claim has been made. There will have been a total failure of consideration, the insurer never having been 'at risk'. Premiums paid will normally be repayable by the insurer, but after a loss has been suffered this is likely to provide small comfort to the insured.

In relation to *uberrimae fides*, the main area of contention would be the question of non-disclosure of facts by the insured to the insurance

---

[198] *March Cabaret Club & Casino Ltd v London Assurance Ltd* [1975] 1 Lloyd's Rep 169; *Manifest Shipping Co Ltd v Uni-Polaris Insurance Co Ltd (The Star Sea)* (supra)

company. The requirement in relation to the duty of disclosure is one of honesty.[199]

In *David Robert Zeller v British Caymanian Insurance Company Ltd* [2008] UKPC 4 (PC), Lord Bingham of Cornhill, delivering the judgment had this to say:

> Thus, the applicant is expected to exercise his judgment on what appears to him to be worth disclosing. He does not lose his cover if he fails to disclose a complaint which he thought to be trivial but which turns out later to be a symptom of some much more serious underlying condition.

Kennedy LJ in *London General Omnibus Co Ltd v Holloway* [1911-13] All ER Rep 518 at p 524 said:

> No class of case occurs, to my mind, in which our law regards mere non-disclosure as a ground for invalidating the contract, except in the case of insurance. That is an exception which the law has wisely made in deference to the plain exigencies of this particular and most important class of transaction. The person seeking to insure may fairly be presumed to know all the circumstances which materially affect the risk, and generally is, as to some of them, the only person who has the knowledge. The underwriter, whom he asks to take the risk, cannot as a rule know, and rarely has either the time or the opportunity to learn by inquiry, circumstances which are or may be most material to the formation of his judgment as to the acceptance or rejection of the risk and as to the premium which he ought to require:
>
>> The basic assumption the law makes in relation to an insurance contract is that an insured entering into such a contract is in possession of facts which may influence the decision of a prudent insurer in computing the risk the insurer is requested to undertake. Such information must be disclosed by an insured to enable the insurer to

---

[199] See *Economides v Commercial Assurance Co Plc* [1998] QB 587, 598, and 599.

assess the risk to be undertaken. A duty is placed on an insured as a basis of the contract to disclose all material information relating to the risk to be insured: *Banque Financiere vs Skandia (UK) Insurance Co Ltd* [1990] 2 Lloyd's Rep 377(HL).

Duties of disclosure may arise in the course of negotiations, from special facts in the particular case, irrespective of the kind of contract contemplated.[200]

The duty to make a full disclosure attaches at the commencement of the negotiations and continues right down to the completion of a binding contract. The insured does not therefore discharge this duty merely by disclosing such facts as are within his knowledge at the time when he makes his proposal for insurance; he must equally disclose every material fact which may come to his knowledge at any stage of the negotiations, whether or not his proposal has been forwarded to the insurers. Since it is the duty of the insured to observe the utmost good faith in his dealings with the insurers throughout, the claim which he puts forward must be honestly made; and, if it is fraudulent, he will forfeit all benefit under the policy whether there is a condition to that effect or not.[201]

Thus, any facts which would increase the risk, should be disclosed by the insured and any facts known to the insurer but not to the insured, which would reduce the risk, should be disclosed by the insurer.[202]

The duty of disclosure extends to circumstances that affect the 'physical hazard', for example, physical characteristics of a building proposed for fire insurance which might make it more vulnerable or more likely to catch fire. It also extends to facts affecting the 'moral hazard'; that is, any matter going to the honesty and personal characteristics of the insured person that might increase the risk of loss.

---

[200] Spencer-Bower, Turner and Sutton, The Law Relating to Actionable Non-Disclosure (2nd Ed. 1990), at pp. 205-206.

[201] Welford & Otter-Barry's Fire Insurance (4 Ed).

[202] Poh Chu Chai, Principles of Insurance Law, 6th Edition, p 114.

In relation to motor insurance, Halsbury's Laws of England (4th ed. 1978), vol. 25, para. 369 provides that "it is important to know that the proposer has had convictions for motoring offences recorded against him and it is irrelevant to show that in other cases policies have been issued by the same insurers even with knowledge of such convictions. The age of the person who is to drive may also be material. It is material to disclose that the insured under a burglary policy, a trade combined insurance policy, an all risks insurance policy or a fire policy has a criminal record".

It can be said that there are various stages in which the duty of utmost good faith can be evaluated. There is the pre-contract stage, the post-contract stage, the claim stage and the litigation stage. This is particularly evident in relation to the duty of disclosure. The extent of the obligation to observe good faith has a different application and requirement in different situations.

An insured is under a duty of disclosure and that duty is the same whether he is applying for a renewal or whether he is applying for the original policy.[203]

Whether the renewal of a policy is a continuation of the original contract or the making of a new contract is a question of importance, in view of its effect on the duty of disclosure and the operation of conditions subsequent.[204]

Renewal of Policy and Material Non-Disclosure

It is important to distinguish between a renewal of a policy and its mere extension. This vital distinction was adverted to by Deane J in *CE Heath Underwriting & Insurance (Australia) Pty Ltd v. Edwards Dunlop & Co Ltd* [1992] 112 ALR 161 as follows:

---

[203] *Lambert v Co-operative Insurance Society Ltd* [1975] 2 Lloyd's Rep 485.

[204] See Ivamy, General Principles of Insurance Law (5th Ed) at p 247.

The distinction between the renewal of a policy and the extension of a policy was expressed in the following terms by Mayo J in *Re Kerr* [1943] SASR 8, at 16:

> Strictly, a "renewal" is descriptive of a repetition of the whole arrangement by substituting the like agreement in place of that previously subsisting, to be operative over a new period, whereas an "extension" betokens a prolongation of the subsisting contract by the exercise of a power reserved thereby to vary one of its provisions, that is, by enlarging the period. Upon a renewal similar rights revest.... A contract reserving continuous rights of renewal will, if these be exercised, lead to succeeding contracts in a series, the identity of each contract (being) separate and distinct. On the other hand, the exercise of the right of extension augments the length of time over which the contract operates, without changing its identity.

Whether there is a renewal or an extension of an insurance policy is a question of construction,[205] the term 'renewal' often being used to refer to both 'renewal' and 'extension', in the sense that those words are used above. It is, however, well established that, where a policy is renewable only by mutual consent (i.e., not as of right), the renewal results in a fresh contract rather than the extension of an existing contract.[206]

Of course, a policy may expressly stipulate that it is not to continue in force beyond the period of insurance, unless renewed by mutual consent.[207] Where a policy, such as the ordinary form of life policy, expressly provides for continuation beyond the specified period of insurance unless a particular event, such as the non-payment of the premium, takes place,

---

[205] *GIO (NSW) v. Kimmedy* [1988] 5 ANZ Insurance Cases 60-880, at 75,541.

[206] See *Re Kerr* [1943] SASR, at 15; Halsbury's Laws of England, 4th ed, vol 25, para 494.

[207] See, eg, *Stokell v. Heywood* [1897] 1 Ch 459.

the renewal is an extension of the original contract.[208] However, where a policy is silent on the question of renewal, renewal of it will generally constitute a new contract.[209]

In *Leong Kum Whay v QBE Insurance (M) Sdn Bhd & Ors* [2006] 1 CLJ 1; [2006] 1 MLJ 710, Gopal Sri Ram JCA stated:

> when, a policy of insurance for a fixed period is renewed by mutual consent, the original proposal form becomes incorporated into the renewed policy and continues to form the basis of the contract. And more so in the present case where the renewal certificate expressly states that the renewal is 'subject to all terms, conditions and endorsements in your original policy'. One of the terms in the original policy was cl. 6.3 which reads as follows:
>
>> Before renewing this policy, the Insured shall give written notice to QBE of any material fact affecting this Insurance which has come to the Insured's notice during the preceding Period of Insurance including notice of any disease, physical or mental defect or Infirmity affecting the Insured Person.

On the facts of that case, the insured when questioned on whether he had been insured against life, accident or sickness, had replied in the negative in the proposal form. That was correct at that time.

He subsequently purchased such protection. He did not inform his insurers upon renewal of his policy. It was held to be a material non-disclosure. Gopal Sri Ram in so holding stated thus:

> Clause 6.3 says "material fact". Now, were the life policies a "material fact" in this case? I think they were. When the renewal certificate said "subject to all terms, conditions and endorsements in your original policy", it includes the declarations in the original

---

[208] See *Re Anchor Assurance Co* [1870] LR 5 Ch App 632, at 638.

[209] See Ivamy General Principles of Insurance Law, (5th ed, 1986), pp. 249-50.

proposal form which formed the basis of the contract. They too became part of the renewed policy. And so you have the appellant saying to QBE in the renewed policy that he did not have any life insurance. That is a material fact because of the basis clause. But it was untrue. Hence QBE was clearly within its contractual rights to refuse payment.

There could also exist a duty on the insured to cooperate with the insurers and to come forward to give information and evidence, for example, in relation to the property lost or damaged as required by the insurers. In *Capital Insurance Bhd v Cheong Heng Loong Goldsmiths (KL) Sdn Bhd* [2005] 4 CLJ 1, a condition in the policy provided that "The Assured shall in case of loss or damage and as a condition precedent to any right of indemnification in respect thereof give to the company such information and evidence as to the property lost or damaged and the circumstances of the loss or damage as the company may reasonably require and as may be in the Assureds power".

It was found that the insured did not comply strictly with the condition precedent and held that the insurer defendant was not liable under the policy.[210]

In *Bank of Nova Scotia v Hellenic Mutual War Risks Association (Bermuda) Ltd; The Good Luck* [1989] 3 All ER 628 (CA), May LJ stated that the "Continuance of an obligation to speak after the making of the contract can be illustrated by reference to other contracts, in which a duty to speak may arise, although the contracts are not within the category of contracts of utmost good faith".[211]

A fortiori, those considerations can apply to contracts of insurance and a duty of disclosure can exist under the continuing obligation. At the time of performance of the contract, the obligation arises from an implied

---

[210] See also *London Guarantee Company v Benjamin Lister Fearley* (Vol. V - the Law Reports, House of Lords 911) and *Chong Kok Hwa v Taisho Marine & Fire Insurance Co. Ltd.* [1975] 1 LNS 14; [1977] 1 MLJ 244.

[211] See *Phillips v Foxall* (1872) LR 7 QB 666 and *Stag Line Ltd v Tyne Shiprepair Group Ltd, The Zinnia* [1984] 2 Lloyd's Rep 211.

term in it, where it is in accordance with the presumed intention of the parties.[212]

MUTUAL DUTY

The fact that insurance contracts are in the nature of *ubberrima fides* has placed the duty of utmost good faith on both parties, with equal force. All parties to an insurance contract must deal in good faith and make a full declaration of all material facts in the insurance proposal. Thus, the insured must reveal the exact nature and potential of the risks that he transfers to the insurer, while at the same time the insurer must make sure that the potential contract fits the needs of, and benefits, the insured.[213]

Good faith forbids either party, by concealing what he privately knows, to draw the other into a bargain from his ignorance of that fact, and from his believing the contrary.[214]

There is a mutual duty owed by an insured and his insurer. In *Banque Financiere vs Skandia (UK) Insurance Co Ltd*,[215] Lord Jauncey, in the House of Lords, stated:

> The duty of disclosure arises because the facts relevant to the estimation of the risk are most likely to be within the knowledge of the insured and the insurer therefore has to rely upon him to disclose matters material to that risk. The duty extends to the insurer as well as to the insured… The duty is, however, limited to facts which are material to the risk insured, that is to say, facts which would influence a prudent insurer in deciding whether to accept the risk and, if so, upon what terms … Thus, any facts which would increase the risk should be disclosed by the insured

---

[212] *Myers and another v Kestrel Acquistions Ltd and others* [2015] EWHC 916 (Ch).
[213] *Tan Jing Jeong v Allianz Life Assurance Malaysia* [2011] 4 CLJ 710 (HC).
[214] *Carter v Boehm* (1766) 3 Burr 1905.
[215] [1990] 2 All ER 947.

and any facts known to the insurer but not to the insured, which would reduce the risk, should be disclosed by the insurer.

As can be seen from the above statement, the duty of disclosure is not confined to the insured. The insurers are also bound by this common law. It is a reciprocal duty.[216]

While the duty of good faith is most readily identified with an insured proposer's duty to make full disclosure, the duty is a mutual duty that can be invoked by the insured proposer. In *Banque Financiere de la Cite v Westgate Insurance Co* [1990] 2 All ER 947, in relation to non-disclosure by an insurer to an insured, it was held that liability in contract, tort and the UK Misrepresentation Act 1967 cannot be established *vis-a-vis* damages: the sole remedy that is available following on from breach of the mutual duty of good faith is limited to avoidance. Damages are not available for breach of the mutual duty, which, in a post contractual setting is wholly one sided as a remedy, of value to the insurer only, and affording the insurer a disproportionate benefit by allowing the insurer to retrospectively avoid the liability to indemnify the insured.

The duty of good faith is now commonly accepted as the basis for the legal doctrine which governs insurance contracts. This means that all parties to an insurance contract must deal in good faith, making a full declaration of all material facts in the insurance proposal. Thus, the insured must reveal the exact nature and potential of the risks that he transfers to the insurer. It is settled beyond dispute that a contact of insurance is one that imposes a mutual duty on the parties to it to act *uberrimae fides* towards each other. On the part of the insured, he or she must make full disclosure of all material facts. It does not matter whether the insurer asks any questions of the insured. The duty is on the insured to make full disclosure of material facts within his knowledge. Whether a particular fact is material is a question of fact.[217] But the duty to make full disclosure of all material facts is not an implied term of insurance

---

[216] *Carter v Boehm* (1766) 3 Burr 1905*(supra)*, *Brownlie v Campbell* (1880) 5 App Cas 925.

[217] See, *Mann Macneal & Steeves Ltd v Capital & Counties Insurance Co. Ltd* [1921] 2 KB 300.

contracts. There is in fact no contract at the point at which the duty arises; the parties being still at the stage of negotiations. It is therefore a pre-contractual duty imposed by the common law[218]. At the same time the insurer must make sure that the potential contract fits the needs of, and benefits, the insured.[219]

The pre-contractual duty imposed by the common law was alluded to by Scrutton LJ in *Rozanes v Bowen* [1928], 32 Ll.L Rep 98, at p. 102 where His Lordship said:

> As the underwriter knows nothing and the man who comes to him to ask him to insure knows everything, it is the duty of the assured, the man who desires to have a policy, to make a full disclosure to the underwriters without being asked of all the material circumstances, because the underwriter knows nothing and the assured knows everything. That is expressed by saying that it is a contract of the utmost good faith - *uberrima fides*.

The insured's duty is balanced by a reciprocal duty on the insurer to make its own reasonable inquiries, to carry out all prudent investigations and to act at all times in a professional manner. In fact, the onus to do this, because of its experience and expertise, lies primarily on the insurer. The law is willing to assist this process by obliging the insured to volunteer information not easily available to the insurer which is material to the risk. The *uberrimae fidei* principle applies with the greatest force to situations where the relevant facts are peculiarly within the knowledge of the insured and are not easily available to the insurer. Where, however, the full extent of the risk can readily be defined without the insured's participation, the law does not insist on full disclosure.[220]

---

[218] *Leong Kum Whay v QBE Insurance (M) Sdn Bhd & Ors* [2006] 1 CLJ at page 19 *(supra)*.

[219] *Tan Jing Jeong v Allianz Life Insurance Malaysia Bhd & Anor* [2012] 7 MLJ 179 at 192 (HC).

[220] *Manor Park Homebuilders Ltd v AIG Europe (Ireland) Ltd* [2009] 1 ILRM 190.

In relation to this mutual duty, it is incumbent upon the insurer to follow up on facts that are disclosed, for example, to carry out an examination of the property, the medical condition of the insured, and so on.

In relation to the insurer's mutual duty of disclosure, the Court of Appeal in Singapore in *Tay Eng Chuan v Ace Insurance Ltd* [2008] 4 SLR 95 (2008) S 6CA 26 stated that "just as the insured is under a legal obligation to disclose fully to the insurer, on an *uberrima fides* basis, all material facts relating to his personal conditions and circumstances, the insurer must also inform the insured of any unusual clause(s) in an insurance policy that may deprive the latter of his right to make a claim". Reference was made to the *dicta* of Woo Bih Li J stated in *NTUC Co-operative Insurance Commonwealth Enterprise Ltd v Chiang Soong Chee* [2008] 2 SLR 373 ("NTUC Co-operative Insurance") (at [50]):

> Besides highlighting what the cover of each policy extends to, insurers should also highlight the more obvious areas which the cover does not extend to, although this may be counter-intuitive to them ...

Further, the English Court of Appeal in *In Re Bradley and Essex and Suffolk Accident Indemnity Society* [1912] 1 KB 415 ("Bradley") at 430–431 (per Farwell LJ) commented as follows:

> Contracts of insurance are contracts in which *uberrima fides* is required, not only from the assured, but also from the company assuring. ... It is especially incumbent on insurance companies to make clear, both in their proposal forms and in their policies, the conditions which are precedent to their liability to pay, for such conditions have the same effect as forfeiture clauses, and may inflict loss and injury to the assured and those claiming under him out of all proportion to any damage that could possibly accrue to the company from non-observance or non-performance of the conditions. Accordingly, it has been established that the doctrine that policies are to be construed *"contra proferentes"* applies strongly against the company: [*In the matter of an arbitration between Etherington and The Lancashire and Yorkshire Accident Insurance Company* [1909] 1 KB 591]. ... It is, in my opinion,

incumbent on the company to put clearly on the proposal form the acts which the assured is by the policy to covenant to perform and to make clear in the policy the conditions, non-performance of which will entail the loss of all benefits of the insurance

Extent of Duty

The limits of the duty of disclosure owed by the insured to the insurer was commented upon by Lord Buckmaster in *Niger Co Ltd v Guardian Assurance Co Ltd* (1922) 13 Ll L Rep 75 82 where it was said:

> The object of disclosure being to inform the underwriter's mind on matters immediately under his consideration, with reference to the taking or refusing of a risk then offered to him, I think it would be going beyond the principle to say that each and every change in an insurance contract creates an occasion on which a general disclosure becomes obligatory, merely because the altered contract is not the unaltered contract, and therefore the alteration is a transaction as the result of which a new contract of insurance comes into existence. This would turn what is an indispensable shield for the underwriter into an engine of oppression against the assured. The authority of *Lishman's case, sup*, is against such a contention and I think it ought to be followed.

The House of Lords in *Manifest Shipping Co Ltd v Uni-Polaris Insurance Co Ltd (The Star Sea)* [2001] UKHL 1, [2003] 1 AC 469 held that once a claim had been filed and litigation was in process, the obligation of good faith and disclosure was inapplicable.

In this case, in relation to the duty of utmost good faith, the insurer defendants had alleged that there had been a failure to observe the utmost good faith, in that, there had been a failure to disclose material information and misleading statements had been made. They argued that this duty continued notwithstanding that litigation had started and had been broken by the insured's (and their lawyer's) failure to disclose certain facts material to the defence under Section 39(5) of the MIA.

It was therefore contended that they were entitled to avoid the whole contract *ab initio*, with retrospective effect, and therefore had a complete defence to the whole of the claim.

The House of Lords held that the duty of good faith in relation to the duty of disclosure, did not apply at the litigation stage and made a distinction of that duty which was applicable at the pre-contract stage and at the litigation stage. The court refused to accept the insurer's contention that they were entitled to avoid the contract *ab initio* and their argument that "the obligation as stated in Section 17 continues throughout the relationship with the same content and consequences."

It was argued that "any non-disclosure at any stage should be treated as a breach of the duty of good faith: it has the same essential content and gives rise to the same remedy - the right to avoid".

Lord Hobhouse went on to state the view of the courts:

> But this will be the effect of accepting the defendants' argument. The result is effectively penal. Where a fully enforceable contract has been entered into insuring the assured, say, for a period of a year, the premium has been paid, a claim for a loss covered by the insurance has arisen and been paid, but later, towards the end of the period, the assured fails in some respect fully to discharge his duty of complete good faith, the insurer is able not only to treat himself as discharged from further liability but can also undo all that has perfectly properly gone before. This cannot be reconciled with principle. No principle of this breadth is supported by any authority whether before or after the Act. It would be possible to draft a contractual term which would have such an effect but it would be an improbable term for the parties to agree to and difficult if not impossible to justify as an implied term. The failure may well be wholly immaterial to anything that has gone before or will happen subsequently.
>
> 52. A coherent scheme can be achieved by distinguishing a lack of good faith which is material to the making of the contract itself (or some variation of it) and a lack of good faith during

the performance of the contract which may prejudice the other party or cause him loss or destroy the continuing contractual relationship. The former derives from requirements of the law which pre-exist the contract and are not created by it although they only become material because a contract has been entered into. The remedy is the right to elect to avoid the contract. The latter can derive from express or implied terms of the contract; it would be a contractual obligation arising from the contract and the remedies are the contractual remedies provided by the law of contract. This is no doubt why judges have on a number of occasions been led to attribute the post-contract application of the principle of good faith to an implied term.

53. The principle relied on by the defendants is a duty of good faith requiring the disclosure of information to the insurer. They submit that the obligation as stated in s.17 continues throughout the relationship with the same content and consequences. Thus, they argue that any non-disclosure at any stage should be treated as a breach of the duty of good faith: it has the same essential content and gives rise to the same remedy - the right to avoid.

54. In the pre-contract situation it is possible to provide criteria for deciding what information should be disclosed and what need not be. The criterion is material to the acceptance of the risk proposed and the assessment of the premium. This is spelled out in the 1906 Act and was the subject of the *Pine Top* case. But when it comes to post-contract disclosure the criterion becomes more elusive: to what does the information have to be material? Some instructive responses have been given. Where the contract is being varied, facts must be disclosed which are material to the additional risk being accepted by the variation. It is not necessary to disclose facts occurring, or discovered, since the original risk was accepted material to the acceptance and rating of that risk. Logic would suggest that such new information might be valuable to the underwriter. It might affect how hard a bargain he would drive in exchange for agreeing to the variation; it might be relevant to his reinsurance decisions. But it need not be disclosed.

In *Lishman v Northern Maritime Insurance Co* (1875) LR 10 CP 179, at 182 Blackburn J said:

> 'concealment of material facts known to the assured before effecting the insurance will avoid the policy, the principle being that with regard to insurance the utmost good faith must be observed. Suppose the policy were actually executed, and the parties agreed to add a memorandum afterwards, altering the terms: if the alteration were such as to make the contract more burdensome to the underwriters, and a fact known at that time to the assured were concealed which was material to the alteration, I should say the policy would be vitiated. But if the fact were quite immaterial to the alteration, and only material to the underwriter as being a fact which showed that he had made a bad bargain originally, and such as might tempt him, if it were possible, to get out of it, I should say that there would be no obligation to disclose it.'

55. Blackburn J is adopting a similar approach to that which he adopted in the leading case *Cory v Patton* (1872) LR 7 QB 304 which concerned whether there was a duty to disclose adverse facts discovered between the time that the underwriter had accepted the risk by initialling the slip binding in honour only, and the issue of the legally binding policy. Blackburn J said at pp 308-9 that the underwriter cannot depart 'from terms thus agreed on [in the slip] without a breach of faith'; and the assured need not disclose to the underwriter 'information which ought to have no effect on him, but would expose him to a temptation to break his contract. ..... he is not bound to lead his neighbour into temptation.' The duty of good faith is even-handed and is not to be used by the opposite party as an opportunity for himself acting in bad faith.

56. The decision in *Cory v Patton* was endorsed by the 1906 Act. What Blackburn J said in *Lishman* was followed

in many subsequent cases, for example, *Niger Co v Guardian Ass Co* (1922) 13 LlLR 75, particularly per Lord Buckmaster at p 76-7, *Iron Trades Mutual Insurance Co Ltd v Compania De Seguros Imperio* 31/7/90 Commercial Court (unreported); *Bank of Nova Scotia v Hellenic Mutual War Risks Association (Bermuda Ltd)* [1988] 1 Lloyd's Rep 514. In the *Niger* case an additional argument was advanced. The policy in that case was one which covered the assured for a number of years but it included a cancellation clause which allowed the insurance company to cancel the policy. The risk turned out to be more onerous than had been expected because there was a tendency for considerable quantities of goods to accumulate in the up-river warehouse from which they were to be dispatched. The insurance company sought to avoid the policy or resist a claim because this post-contract development of which the assured was aware had not then been disclosed by the assured to the insurance company. Obviously the development was of interest to the insurance company and might have led it to exercise its right of cancellation. But the Court of Appeal ((1921) 6 LlLR 239, particularly per Bankes LJ at p 245) and the House of Lords held that such facts need not be disclosed. (See also *New Hampshire Ins Co v MGN* [1997] LRLR 24.) A similar decision has been reached in Australia, *NSW Medical Defence Union v Transport Industries Ins Co* (1985) 4 NSWLR 107.

57. These authorities show that there is a clear distinction to be made between the pre-contract duty of disclosure and any duty of disclosure which may exist after the contract has been made. It is not right to reason, as the defendants submitted that your Lordships should, from the existence of an extensive duty pre-contract positively to disclose all material facts to the conclusion that post-contract there is a similarly extensive obligation to disclose all facts which the insurer has an interest in knowing and which might affect his conduct. The courts have consistently set their face against allowing the

> assured's duty of good faith to be used by the insurer as an instrument for enabling the insurer himself to act in bad faith. An inevitable consequence in the post-contract situation is that the remedy of avoidance of the contract is in practical terms wholly one-sided. It is a remedy of value to the insurer and, if the defendants' argument is accepted, of disproportionate benefit to him; it enables him to escape retrospectively the liability to indemnify which he has previously and (on this hypothesis) validly undertaken. Save possibly for some types of reinsurance treaty, it is hard to think of circumstances where an assured will stand to benefit from the avoidance of the policy for something that has occurred after the contract has been entered into; the hypothesis of continuing dealings with each other will normally postulate some claim having been made by the assured under the policy.

Lord Clyde was further of the view that:

> there was no duty upon the insured to make a full disclosure of his own case to the other side in a litigation. I see no practical justification for such an obligation at that stage. Unlike the initial stage when the insurer may rely very substantially upon the openness of the insured in order to decide whether or not to agree to provide insurance cover, and if so at what level of premium, the insurer has open to him means of discovery of any facts which he requires to know for his defence to the claim..... The idea of a requirement for full disclosure superseding the procedural controls for discovery in litigation is curious and unattractive, and one which would require to be soundly based in authority or principle.

Lord Hobhouse concluded that "when a writ is issued the rights of the parties are crystallised. The function of the litigation is to ascertain what those rights are and grant the appropriate remedy". It was said:

> ....77. I am therefore strongly of the view that once the parties are in litigation it is the procedural rules which govern the extent of

the disclosure which should be given in the litigation, not s.17 as such, though s.17 may influence the court in the exercise of its discretion. The cases upon ship's papers, far from supporting the continuing application of the duty of good faith in truth support the opposite conclusion. As previously discussed, the fact that orders for ship's papers were only made in marine insurance despite the fact that the principle of good faith applies to all insurance and the fact that the order was a matter of discretion not of right shows that it is a procedural remedy not a matter of contract although the principle of good faith clearly influenced the attitude of the court to making such an order. But, most conclusively, the fact that the remedy was to obtain an order from the court and not to avoid the contract shows both the limits of the principle and the change of relationship which comes about when the parties are in hostile litigation.

Lord Scott of Foscote went on to state that:

> I would, however, limit the duty owed by an insured in relation to a claim to a duty of honesty. If the duty derives from section 17, nonetheless this limitation does not, in my opinion involve a judicial re-writing of section 17. On the contrary, it would be the creation out of section 17 of a duty that could be broken notwithstanding that the assured had acted throughout in good faith that would constitute a re-writing of the section. Unless the assured has acted in bad faith he cannot, in my opinion, be in breach of a duty of good faith, utmost or otherwise. For these reasons, I agree with Tuckey J and the Court of Appeal in concluding that the insurers' section 17 claim cannot succeed.

Statutory Requirement

Other than the common law, there is a statutory requirement to disclose material facts. Paragraph 4(1), Schedule 9 of Section 129 of the Malaysian Financial Services Act 2013 ('FSA 2013') [formerly Section 150 of the Malaysian Insurance Act 1996 ('IA 1996')], provides that before a contract of insurance is entered into, varied or renewed, a proposer shall disclose to the licensed insurer a matter that (a) he knows to be relevant to the decision of the licensed insurer on whether to accept the risk or not and the rates and terms to be applied; or (b) a reasonable person in the circumstances could be expected to know to be relevant.

The Financial Services Act 2013 repealed the IA 1996, which in turn had repealed the Insurance Act 1963 and the Life Assurance Companies (Compulsory Liquidation) Act 1962 . The preamble to the FSA 2013 provides that it is an Act to provide for the regulation and supervision of financial institutions, payment systems and other relevant entities and the oversight of the money market and foreign exchange market to promote financial stability and for related, consequential or incidental matters. Under Paragraph 4(2) and (3), Schedule 9 of Section 129 of the FSA 2013, there were no amendments or modifications for the common law requirement of strict compliance of a duty to disclose material facts. The two subsections are intended to protect the interests of an insured or a consumer in respect of insurance matters.

It has been held that the insured has to disclose all facts within his knowledge which would affect the mind of a prudent and experienced insurer, in determining whether he will take the risk and, if so, at what premium and on what conditions. The test is what a reasonable man, in the shoes of the insured, would have considered material.[221]

In addition, Paragraph 4(2), Schedule 9 of Section 129 of the FSA 2013 (previously Section 150(2) of the IA 1996) provides that the duty of disclosure does not require the disclosure of a matter that (a) diminishes the risk to the licensed insurer; (b) is of common knowledge; (c) the licensed insurer knows or in the ordinary course of his business ought to know; or (d) in respect of which the licensed insurer has waived any requirement of disclosure.[222]

---

[221] *Asia Insurance Co Ltd v Tat Hong Plant Leasing Pte Ltd* [1992] 1 CLJ 330: *Lau King Kieng v AXA Affin General Insurance Bhd and another suit* [2014] 8 MLJ 883 (HC) *(supra)*.

[222] *Lau King Kieng v AXA Affin General Insurance Bhd and another suit* [2014] 8 MLJ 883 (HC) *(supra)*.

In *Lau King Kieng v AXA Affin General Insurance Bhd and another suit* [2014] 8 MLJ 883, the proposal form was dated 11 June 2008 and the insurance policy was issued on 17 June 2008. Similarly, in respect of the Pacific insurance, the proposal form was dated 12 May 2009 and the insurance policy was issued effective 12 May 2009. The insurer defendants did not ask or seek clarification to the answers given by the insured plaintiff in the proposal forms. The defendants did not send any such letter to the plaintiff. The defendants did not pursue the matter further before the insurance policies were issued to the plaintiff. Section 150(3) of the IA 1996 [now Paragraph 4(3), Schedule 9 of Section 129 of the FSA 2013] deemed that the compliance with the duty of disclosure had been waived by the defendants. It was found that the insurer defendants did not plead that the failure to disclose all the insurance policies, which the insurer plaintiff had, would affect or diminish the risk or the premium or the terms or conditions of the two policies under AXA and or Pacific. None of the defendants' witnesses had testified as such. There was no evidence that the non-disclosure of the several insurance policies which the plaintiff had bought or were insured under, would in any way affect or diminish the risk or the premium or the terms or conditions of the two policies issued to them.[223]

Where there is a waiver by the insurance company, there is no duty to disclose. Further, Section 150(3) of the IA 1996 [now Paragraph 4(3), Schedule 9 of Section 129 of the FSA 2013] provides that where a proposer fails to answer or gives an incomplete or irrelevant answer to a question contained in the proposal form or asked by the licensed insurer and the matter was not pursued further by the licensed insurer, compliance with the duty of disclosure in respect of the matter shall be deemed to have been waived by the licensed insurer.

In *Hew Soon Tai dan lain-lain (plaintif-plaintif kedua dan ketiga adalah budak-budak di bawah umur yang menuntut melalui ibu yang sah Hew Soon Tai) lwn Hong Leong Assurance Bhd* Vol 7 (part 4 & 8)(2016) 1 MLRA 295-376, it was held that the insurer's failure to reveal his past criminal records was not in contravention with Section 150(1) of the IA 1996 [now Paragraph 4(1), Schedule 9 of Section 129 of the FSA 2013] which only

---

[223] See *Abu Bakar v Oriental Fire & General Insurance Co Ltd* [1974] 1 MLJ 149.

requires disclosure of matters known to be relevant to the insurer, for the insurer to determine whether to take the risk or not, based on the disclosure. Whether the matter that must be revealed was relevant, could only be seen based on the questions asked by the insurance agent to the proposer. Even though the insured had a past criminal record, that did not mean that the fact relating to the criminal record was relevant to the insurer if he was not asked by the insurer through the questions in the proposal form. The responsibility under s 150(1) of the IA 1996 [now Paragraph 4(1), Schedule 9 of Section 129 of the FSA 2013] was in relation to disclosure of material matters. The insured's criminal records were held not to be material to the insurer when the proposal for the purchase of policies were made.

Waiver

Even assuming that there was a non-disclosure and misrepresentation, it was held by the Federal Court in *Tan Kang Hua v Safety Insurance Co* [1973] 1 MLJ 6 that if "the insurers were aware of the facts which were alleged to have been concealed by the defendants at the time of the issue of the policy, they were not entitled to the declaration they asked for", i.e., a declaration to avoid the contract.[224]

In *HIH Casualty and General Insurance Limited and others (Respondents) v Chase Manhattan Bank (Appellants), HIH Casualty and General Insurance Limited and others (Appellants) v Chase Manhattan Bank (Respondents) and others (First Appeal) and HIH Casualty and General Insurance Limited and others (Appellants) v Chase Manhattan Bank (Respondents) and others (Second Appeal) (Conjoined appeals)* [2003] UKHL 6 (HL), it was stated:

> 51. Section 18(3)(c) provides that the insured need not disclose 'any circumstances as to which information is waived by the insurer'. Phrase 6, said Lord Grabiner, was a waiver of disclosure by Chase of any information whatever. It followed that the agent need not disclose any information either. And if the agent had no

---

[224] *Pacific & Orient Insurance Sdn Bhd v Lim Sew Chong & Anor* [1985] 2 MLJ 60 (HC).

obligation to disclose anything, his failure to do so could not be characterised as fraudulent or negligent, whatever his motives may have been: *National Westminster Bank v Utrecht-America Finance* [2001] 3 All ER 733, 750, para 51, per Clarke LJ.

52. Aikens J. rejected this argument (see [2001] 1 Lloyd's Rep 30, 50) but Rix LJ, who gave the judgment of the Court of Appeal, accepted it. He said, at [2001] Lloyd's Rep 483, 509, para 137:

> If...the principal assured is excused the duty of disclosure, because of waiver, the waiver negatives materiality and the waiver applies to the agent too.

53. I respectfully think that Aikens J. was right. The insurers may have waived disclosure of information on the ground that it was not material or that they were prepared to treat the information as not being material. In that case, I agree that the reasoning of Rix LJ would be pertinent and, for the reasons given by Saville LJ in the SAIL case, it would be illogical to say that good faith required the agent to disclose circumstances which the insured would not have had to disclose. In the SAIL case the circumstance which it was claimed that the broker should have disclosed was that the insurer (for whom he also happened to be acting as broker for the purpose of obtaining reinsurance by way of retrocession) had not actually obtained it. Saville LJ said that the insured had no obligation to disclose this fact under section 18 because it was a matter which the insurer, in the ordinary course of his business, ought to have known: 'in the ordinary course of his business an insurer ought to know the state of his retrocession'. It followed that the duty of disclosure by the insured was excluded by section 18(3)(b). It was in this context that Saville LJ said that the broker could not be under an obligation to disclose circumstances which his principal would not have had to disclose.

54. The reasoning of Saville LJ seems to me to depend upon being able to identify the circumstances which the principal insured is not obliged to disclose. It is those circumstances which need not be disclosed by the agent either. But I do not think that phrase

6 can be construed as constituting a waiver of any particular circumstances or all circumstances whatever. In my opinion the more natural construction is that it is a waiver personal to the principal insured. He is relieved of the obligation of disclosure without prejudice to the question of whether the circumstances would otherwise have had to be disclosed or not. The structure of phrases 6 to 8 suggests that the draftsman was well acquainted with sections 17-20 of the 1906 Act and its distinction between the obligations of the principal insured and the agent. Phrase 6 deals with the principal insured by excluding his disclosure obligations altogether. The disclosure obligations of other parties are the subject of phrases 7 and 8, which does not exclude them but limits their effect by saying that they shall not be a ground for the avoidance or cancellation of the policy. Phrases 7 and 8 contemplate that the disclosure obligations of the agent exist despite the exclusion of the principal's obligations by phrase 6.

55. Phrase 6 does not therefore in my opinion impinge upon Heaths' duty of disclosure. Any limitation upon the effect of nondisclosure must be found in phrases 7 and 8.

Parties entering into a commercial contract will no doubt recognise and accept the risk of errors and omissions in the preceding negotiations, even negligent errors and omissions, but each party will assume the honesty and good faith of the other; in the absence of such an assumption they will not deal. What is true of the principal is true of the agent, not least in a situation where, as here, the agent, if not the sire of the transaction, plays the role of a very active midwife. As Bramwell LJ observed in *Weir v Bell* (1878) 3 Exch D 238 at 245:

> I think that every person who authorizes another to act for him in the making of any contract, undertakes for the absence of fraud in that person in the execution of the authority given, as much as he undertakes for its absence in himself when he makes the contract.

16. It is clear that the law, on public policy grounds, does not permit a contracting party to exclude liability for his own fraud

in inducing the making of the contract. The insurers have throughout contended for a similar rule in relation to the fraud of agents acting as such. After a very detailed examination of such authority as there is, both the judge ([2001] 1 Lloyd's Rep 30 at 45, paragraph 35) and the Court of Appeal ([2001] 2 Lloyd's Rep 483 at 504, paragraph 109) decided against the existence of such a rule. It is true that the ratio of the leading authority on the point, *S Pearson & Son Ltd v Dublin Corporation* [1907] AC 351, despite the distinction and numerical strength of the House which decided it, is not easy to discern. I do not however think that the question need be finally resolved in this case. For it is in my opinion plain beyond argument that if a party to a written contract seeks to exclude the ordinary consequences of fraudulent or dishonest misrepresentation or deceit by his agent, acting as such, inducing the making of the contract, such intention must be expressed in clear and unmistakable terms on the face of the contract. The decision of the House in *Pearson v Dublin Corporation* does at least make plain that general language will not be construed to relieve a principal of liability for the fraud of an agent: see in particular the speeches of Lord Loreburn LC at page 354, Lord Ashbourne at page 360 and Lord Atkinson at page 365. General words, however comprehensive the legal analyst might find them to be, will not serve: the language used must be such as will alert a commercial party to the extraordinary bargain he is invited to make. It is no doubt unattractive for a contracting party to propose a term clearly having such effect, because of its predictable effect on the mind of the other contracting party, and this may explain why the point of principle left open in *Pearson v Dublin Corporation* has remained unresolved for so long. But I think it clear that, judged by this exacting standard, the language of phrase [7] falls well short of what is required to meet Chase's objective, as both the judge (paragraph 81(3)) and the Court of Appeal (paragraphs 159, 160) held.

Truth of Statement Clause

An insured's duty of disclosure may be impacted by the "Truth of Statement Clause" contained in the insurance contract. In assessing the extent to which the draftsman of that clause intended to modify the respective rights and obligations of the parties, it is helpful to recall what, in the absence of such a clause, the rights and obligations of the parties would have been, a matter that the draftsman must have had in mind.[225]

Since an agent is subject to an independent duty of disclosure, the deliberate withholding from the insurer of information which the agent knows or believes to be material to the risk, if done dishonestly or recklessly, may well amount to a fraudulent misrepresentation. In *HIH Casualty and General Insurance Limited and others (Respondents) v Chase Manhattan Bank (Appellants) and others HIH Casualty and General Insurance Limited and others (Appellants) v Chase Manhattan Bank (Respondents) and others (First Appeal) and HIH Casualty and General Insurance Limited and others (Appellants) v Chase Manhattan Bank (Respondents) and others (Second Appeal) (Conjoined appeals)* (supra), it was held that if the insurers established non-disclosure by Heaths (the agent), nothing in the truth of statement clause would deprive them of their ordinary right to avoid the policy and recover damages from Chase and Heaths.

DISCLOSURE OF MATERIAL FACTS

As stated earlier, a contract of insurance is a contract *uberrimae fidei*. There must be an honest disclosure of material facts and the contract requires the utmost good faith; the insurer knows nothing; whilst the

---

[225] *HIH Casualty and General Insurance Limited and others (Respondents) v Chase Manhattan Bank (Appellants) and others, HIH Casualty and General Insurance Limited and others (Appellants) v Chase Manhattan Bank (Respondents) and others (First Appeal) and HIH Casualty and General Insurance Limited and others (Appellants) v Chase Manhattan Bank (Respondents) and others (Second Appeal) (Conjoined appeals)* [2003] UKHL 6 (HL).

insured knows everything about the risk he wants to insure and he must disclose to the insurer every fact material to the risk.[226]

A higher duty is exacted from parties to an insurance contract compared to from parties to most other contracts, in order to ensure the disclosure of all material facts, so that the contract may accurately reflect the actual risk being undertaken.[227]

Viscount Haldane in *Dawsons Ltd v Bonnin & Ors* [1922] All ER Rep 88 at page 94 said:

> It is established law that in cases of insurance a party is required not only to state all matters within his knowledge which he believes to be material to the question of the insurance, but all which in point of fact are so. If he conceals anything that he knows to be material, it is fraud; but besides that, if he conceals anything that may influence the rate of premium which the underwriter may require, although he does not know that it would have that effect, such concealment entirely vitiates the policy.

It is a general principle in insurance law that an insured is under a duty to disclose material facts and the absence of a proposal form does not modify this duty.

It is to be noted however, that such a breach of duty to disclose is distinct and separate from the duty to disclose material facts. There is no duty to disclose facts which the insured did not know, and which he could not reasonably have been expected to know at any material time.[228]

---

[226] *Newsholme Brothers v Road Transport and General Insurance Co Ltd* [1929] 2 KB 356 at p 362.

[227] *Carter v Boehm* (1766) 97 ER 1162, at p 1164: *Tan Jing Jeong v Allianz Life Assurance Malaysia (supra)*.

[228] *Toh Kim Lian v Asia Insurance Co Ltd* [1996] 1 MLJ 149. See also *The 'Melanie' United Oriental Assurance Sdn Bhd Kuantan v WM Mazzarol* [1984] 1 MLJ 260.

The first part of the duty placed on the insured as the basis of the contract, is to disclose all material information relating to the risk to be insured.[229]

The duty of disclosure of material facts (the rule of *uberrima fides* or utmost good faith) applies to all classes of insurance, and the question in every case is whether the fact not disclosed was material to the risk, and not whether the insured, reasonably or otherwise, believed it to be so.[230]

The law imposes a duty on prospective policyholders to disclose all material facts. This duty is set out in Section 18 of the MIA, which states that a person who is seeking to obtain insurance "must disclose to the insurer, before the contract is concluded, every material circumstance which is known to the assured, and the assured is deemed to know every circumstance, in the ordinary course of business, ought to be known by him. If the assured fails to make such disclosure, the insurer may avoid the contract".

The court in *Joel v Law Union & Crown Insurance Co* [1908] 2 KB 863 said:

> The duty is a duty to disclose, and you cannot disclose what you do not know. The obligation to disclose, therefore, necessarily depends on the knowledge you possess. I must not be misunderstood. Your opinion of the materiality of that knowledge is of no moment. If a reasonable man would have recognized that it was material to disclose the knowledge in question, it is no excuse that you did not recognize it to be so. But the question always is, was the knowledge you possessed such that you ought to have disclosed it?

It is now well-established law that it is the duty of the insured to disclose information, which a prudent insurer would regard as material.[231]

---

[229] *Carter v Boehm* (supra).

[230] *Brownlie v Campbell* (1880) 5 App Cas 925, 954, *Bates v Hewitt* (1867) LR 2 QB 595, 607; *Zurich General Accident and Liability Insurance Company Limited v Morrison* [1942] 2 KB 53, 64-65. See also *David Robert Zeller v British Caymanian Insurance Company Ltd* (supra).

[231] *Loh Shiiun Hing v Kurnia Insurans (Malaysia) Bhd* [2014] 7 CLJ 490 (CA). See also *Lambert v Co-operative Insurance Society Ltd* (supra).

The duty of disclosure of material facts is a continuing duty so long as the insurer is at risk, at the material time.[232] It follows that when a party to a contract of insurance acts in bad faith, the innocent party is entitled to be discharged from his obligations under the contract.[233]

Now, it is generally recognised that the duty to exercise the utmost good faith and to make disclosure of material information, applies equally to both an insured and his insurer.

A "material circumstance" is defined as one which would influence the judgment of a prudent insurer in fixing the premium, or determining whether he will take the risk.[234]

The general principle in insurance law is that a fair and reasonable construction must be placed on the questions in the proposal form.[235]

In interpreting the questions in the proposal form in order to determine whether the fact not disclosed is a material fact, it is to be remembered that a fair and reasonable construction should be placed on any question therein.[236]

In relation to a life policy, three conditions have to be established before that policy can be challenged by the insurer. The conditions are as follows:

(1) That the statement must relate to a material matter or must suppress facts which are material to disclose;

---

[232] See *Black King Shipping Corporation And Wayang (Panama) S.A. v Mark Ranald Massie (the 'Litsion Pride')* (1985) Vol. 1 Q.B. (Com. Ct.) 437(1985); *Galloway v Guardian Royal Exchange (UK) Ltd* [1999] Lloyd's Rep. IR 209.

[233] See *Anali Marketing Sdn Bhd v Allianz General Insurance Malaysia Berhad* [2012] MLJU 38 (HC).

[234] Marine Insurance Act 1906 UK, s 18(2).

[235] See *Pacific and Orient Insurance Co Sdn Bhd v Kathirevelu* [1992] 1 MLJ 249; *Toh Kim Lian & Anor v Asia Insurance Co Ltd* [1996] 1 MLJ 149 (HC).

[236] *Pacific and Orient Insurance Co Sdn Bhd v Kathirevelu (supra)*, SC: *Azizah Bte Abdullah v Arab Malaysian Eagles Sdn Bhd* [1996] 5 MLJ 569.

(2) That the suppression or misstatement must have been fraudulently made by the policyholder; and

(3) That the policyholder must have known at that time, that the statement was false or that the facts suppressed were material to disclose.[237]

A failure on the part of the insured to disclose a material fact within his actual or imputed knowledge, renders the policy voidable at the option of the insurers.[238]

Material Facts are "facts which show that, in the circumstances, the liability of the insurers may be greater than would naturally be expected under an insurance of the property in question.[239] A fact is material if it would have reasonably affected the mind of a prudent insurer in determining whether he will accept the insurance, and if so, at what premium and on what conditions".[240]

It is not for the insured to decide what is material, in his or her own mind. Whether a particular fact is material is a question of fact.[241]

The proposer is under a duty to disclose material facts, even if the insurer or a broker fails to ask questions or the insurance is negotiated without the use of a proposal form.[242]

As stated above, an insured is under a duty to disclose material facts. Any misrepresentation or non-disclosure of material facts by the insured will

---

[237] See *New India Insurance Company v Raghava Reddi* AIR [1961] AP 295 (SC).

[238] Hardy Ivamy, General Principles of Insurance Law, 6 Edition, p 174.

[239] Ivamy (5th Edn).

[240] *Mayne Nickless Ltd. v Pegler & Anor.* (1974) 1 N.S.W.L.R. 228; *Mutual Life Insurance Co of New York v Ontario Metal Products Company Ltd.* [1925] A.C. 344 at 350-1; *Southern Cross Assurance Company Ltd v Australian Provincial Assurance Association Ltd*, (1939) 39 S.R. (NSW) 174 at 187 and *Western Australian Insurance Co Ltd v Dayton*, (1924) 35 C.L.R. 355 at 378-9.

[241] *Mann Macneal & Steeves Ltd v Capital & Counties Insurance Co Ltd* [1921] 2 KB 300).

[242] MacGillivray, paras 17-017 to 17-021.

entitle the insurance company to avoid the contract. A fact is material if it would influence the judgment of a prudent or reasonable insurer in fixing the premium or determining the risk.[243]

A duty is placed on the insured as the basis of the contract to disclose all material information relating to the risk to be insured[244] The duty of disclosure of material facts is a continuing duty so long as the insurer is at risk at the material time[245]

On the facts in *Lee Bee Soon & Ors v Malaysia National Insurance Sdn Bhd* [1980] 2 MLJ 252, Yusoff J went on to state that the duty of the insured to disclose all material facts to the insurers must be done before the contract is concluded. Hence, if everything material is communicated up to the time of the initialling of the 'slip' (or proposal) by the insurer, but something material that arises between that time and the time of executing the policy is not communicated, there is no non-disclosure so as to vitiate the policy.[246]

In the case of *Cory v Patton* (1874) LR 9 QB 577, it was held that if there is a duty to disclose material facts concerning the health of the deceased for a personal accident policy, then this duty should be confined to disclosure of a serious illness or disease which would prevent the insured from leading a normal working life.

Elizabeth Chapman JC in *Toh Kim Lian & Anor v Asia Insurance Co Ltd* [1996] 1 MLJ 149 (HC) said:

---

[243] *Goh Chooi Leong v Public Life Assurance Co Ltd* [1964] 1 MLJ 5, *National Insurance Co Ltd v S Joseph* [1973] 2 MLJ 195. See also *Lau King Kieng v AXA Affin General Insurance Bhd and another suit* (supra).

[244] *Carter v Boehm* (supra).

[245] See *Black King Shipping Corporation and Wayang (Panama) S.A. v Mark Ranald Massie (the 'Litsion Pride')* (supra); *Galloway v Guardian Royal Exchange (UK) Ltd* (supra): *Anali Marketing Sdn Bhd v Allianz General Insurance Malaysia Berhad* (supra).

[246] See *Cory v Patton* (1874) LR 9 QB 577; Ivamy Marine Insurance 2nd Ed. page 67.

A breach of duty to disclose is distinct and separate from the duty to disclose material facts. There is no duty to disclose facts which the assured did not know, and which he could not be reasonably expected to know at any material time.

Thus, Fletcher Moulton LJ stated the principle concerning life insurance in the following words:

> But the question always is: was the knowledge that you possess such that you ought to have disclosed it? Let me take an example. I will suppose that a man, as in the case with most of us, occasionally had a headache. It may be that a particular one of these headaches would have told a brain specialist of hidden mischief. But to the man it was an ordinary headache indistinguishable from the rest. Now, no reasonable man would deem it material to tell an insurance company of all the casual headaches he had in his life, or if he knew no more as to this particular headache than that it was an ordinary casual headache, there would be no breach of his duty towards the insurance company in not disclosing it. He possessed no knowledge that it was incumbent on him to disclose, because he knew of nothing which a reasonable man would deem material, or of a character to influence the insurers in their action. It was what he did not know which would have been of that character, but he cannot be held liable for non-disclosure in respect of facts which he did not know.

In law, once a positive duty is imposed on a party to be truthful, including a duty to disclose a material fact, that duty is not discharged simply on account of the fact that the other party has failed to inquire about some material fact that has not been disclosed, but which fact was within the knowledge of the party having such knowledge. As Halsbury had said, the duty is a positive obligation to disclose a material fact.[247]

---

[247] *Tan Jing Jeong v Allianz Life Assurance Malaysia* (supra).

Insurers are entitled to avoid the insurance policy on the ground of material non-disclosure.[248] An insurance contract can be avoided for non-disclosure of material facts. This is a well-established principle.[249] In *Tang Tung Thian & Anor v United Oriental Assurance Sdn Bhd* [2000] 5 MLJ 696 (HC), it was held that although the insurers did not plead in their defence that theft is not covered by the policy, the said contract of insurance was vitiated by the non-disclosure of material facts.

There is also an obligation on an insured to give the insurer reasonable notice of facts that take the insured's interest out of the scope of the insurance cover. That obligation is implied into each contract of insurance.[250] This obligation exists so that the insurer has time to consider what additional conditions he should impose and what additional premium he should charge for the covered clause.

NON-DISCLOSURE

When there is non-disclosure, the insurers will contend that due to the non-disclosure they will not be bound by the contract. In *Goh Chooi Leong v Public Life Assurance Co Ltd* [1964] 1 MLJ 5, Gill J at p 7 said that "It is trite law that the contract of insurance is a contract *uberrimae fidei* which can be avoided for non-disclosure of material facts".

In *Tan Kang Hua v Safety Insurance Co* (supra), the insured falsely stated in the proposal form that he had not made a previous claim for damage to the insured vehicle under any motor policy. The Federal Court held that "the learned trial judge was correct in holding that there had been non-disclosure and misrepresentation in the proposal form relating to material particulars".

---

[248] *Cornhill Insurance Co Ltd v L & B Assenheim* [1937] 59 Ll L Rep 27: *Tan Kang Hua v Safety Insurance Co* [1973] 1 MLJ 6 (FC).

[249] *Asia Insurance Co Ltd v Tat Hong Plant Leasing Pte Ltd* (supra); *Chang Kuo Ping v Malaysian Assurance Alliance Bhd* [2008] 3 CLJ 752.

[250] See *Thames and Mersey Marine Insurance Co Ltd v HT Van Laun & Co* [1917] 2 KB 48.

Examples of cases which illustrate where the non-disclosure of material facts will affect or diminish or increase the risks to a licensed insurer are (1) *Asia Insurance Co Ltd v Tat Hong Plant Leasing Pte Ltd (supra)*, where the insured failed to disclose that he had released a third party from the obligation to repair the insured property. The court decided that the fact was material and ought to have been disclosed, (2) *Goh Chooi Leong v Public Life Assurance Co Ltd (supra)*, where the insured did not disclose that he had been treated for pulmonary tuberculosis not long before the date of the declaration. He instead answered 'No' and it was held that it was a deliberate lie and (3) *National Insurance Co Ltd v S Joseph (supra)*, where the insured did not disclose that he had a policy of insurance which had been cancelled or that he had been involved in a motor accident.

In *Tang Bee Hong v American International Assurance Berhad* [2012] MLJU 1386 (HC), it was held that the insured Plaintiff had failed to disclose drug usage when filling up the questions and answers that had become part of the contract of insurance and the Defendant insurer was entitled to repudiate the said policy on that basis.

In the following cases, it has been held that there was non-disclosure by the insured:-

Locker & Woolf Ltd v Western Australian Insurance Co [1936] 1 KB 408 failure to disclose the fact that the proposer had been refused motor insurance allowed the insurer company to avoid a policy of fire insurance.

Schoolman v Hall [1951] 1 Lloyd's Rep 139, *Quinby Enterprises v General Accident* [1995] 1 NZR 736, the insured responded negatively to a claim on a domestic contents policy arising out of a burglary, by invoking the proposer's failure to disclose a criminal record, the most recent conviction being some 15 years prior to taking out the policy.

Regina Fur Co v Bossom [1958] 2 Lloyd's Rep 425, where the non-disclosure related to a conviction for receiving stolen goods some 20 years previously, material non-disclosure was made out in a claim brought for theft on an "all risks" policy.

The duty of disclosure also attaches to criminal convictions recorded against family members, notwithstanding that a considerable period of time has elapsed since the conviction and the fact that embarrassing matters such as a criminal past are likely to be shunted into a remote part of a person's consciousness.[251]

In *Joel v Law Union Insurance Co* [1908] 2 KB 863, it was held that in the area of life insurance, failure to disclose that the insured was exhibiting symptoms of consumption some four years previously,[252] or had habits or addictions that could be prejudicial to him, did not absolve the insurer from being under a duty to indemnify the insured, in circumstances where the insured did not know of the material facts and where he did not turn a wilful blind eye to the matters at hand.

NON-DISCLOSURE AND MISREPRESENTATION

In practice the line between misrepresentation and non-disclosure is often imperceptible.[253]

The general rule is that mere non-disclosure does not constitute misrepresentation, and that in the absence of a duty to speak there can be no liability in fraud, however dishonest the silence.

However, in certain circumstances a combination of silence together with a positive representation may itself create a misrepresentation. Such a situation may be called partial non-disclosure, and such cases may be explained as either, instances of actual misrepresentation or as cases where a duty to speak arises because of matters already stated. An exception to the general rule relating to non-disclosure, however, arises in the insurance context, because of the duty of good faith, more particularly the duty of utmost good faith (*uberrimae fidei*). That creates what may be called a duty to speak, defined in the terms of sections 17

---

[251] *Lambert v Cooperative Insurance Co* [1975] 2 Lloyd's Rep 485.

[252] *Geach v Ingall* (1845) 14 M & W 95; *Morrison v Muspratt* (1827) 4 Bing 60.

[253] *Pan Atlantic Insurance Co Ltd v Pine Top Insurance Co Ltd* [1995] 1 AC 501 at 549, per Lord Mustill.

and 19 of the MIA. The Marine Insurance Act 1906 or MIA is a UK Act and it applies to both "ship & cargo" marine insurance.

Where there is non-disclosure in an absence of the truth of statement clause, the insurers might avoid the policy and deprive an insured of its intended security if either the insured or its agent however innocently, fail to disclose any circumstance found as a fact to be material (see s.18(4) of the MIA), or were to make any representation found as a fact to be material (see s. 20(7) of the MIA) and to be untrue.

Where however the non-disclosure or misrepresentation were other than innocent, the insurer might have rights additional to that of avoidance, i.e., the right to damages given by section 2(1) of the UK Misrepresentation Act 1967 to the victim of a negligent misrepresentation; and the right to recover damages for deceit given by the common law to the victim of a fraudulent misrepresentation.[254]

Rix LJ stated:

> In sum, I do not think that, in the absence of express language, any line is to be drawn between the various possible causes of or motives for non-disclosure. It is not in this way that the distinction is to be drawn. The question to my mind is whether a non-disclosure can support a claim in fraud, with its remedies in damages and/or rescission: either because [on] analysis it amounts or gives rise to a fraudulent misrepresentation or perchance for any other reason.

---

[254] *HIH Casualty and General Insurance Limited and others (Respondents) v Chase Manhattan Bank (Appellants) and others, HIH Casualty and General Insurance Limited and others (Appellants) v Chase Manhattan Bank (Respondents) and others (First Appeal) and HIH Casualty and General Insurance Limited and others (Appellants) v Chase Manhattan Bank (Respondents) and others (Second Appeal) (Conjoined appeals) (supra).*

Fraudulent Misrepresentation

Derry v Peek (1889) UKHL 1 in English Contract Law, summarised the elements of actionable fraudulent misrepresentation as requiring any person alleging deceit to show that "a false representation has been made (1) knowingly, or (2) without belief if its truth, or (3) recklessly, careless whether it be true or false", while MacGillivray summarised the position within insurance law thus:

> In order to constitute an actionable fraudulent misrepresentation the statement of which complaint is made must be (1) false, (2) made dishonestly, and (3) acted upon by the recipient in the sense that it induced him to make the proposed contract: MacGillivray Paragraph 16-001.

Both Lord Hershell's speech and the extract from MacGillivray were applied in *McAleenan v AIG (Europe) Ltd* [2010] IEHC 128 where the plaintiff was employed as a solicitor in the practice of Michael Lynn & Co. Mr Lynn was the principal and in preparing an application for professional indemnity cover Mr Lynn stated on the proposal form that the plaintiff was a partner in the firm. After holding that this was both untrue and a material misstatement, Finlay Geoghegan J went on to consider whether the misstatement was fraudulent in the light of two further findings, (1) that the plaintiff did not know of Mr Lynn's misstatement, and (2) she signed the form on behalf of the practice, in Mr Lynn's absence from his office. Finlay Geoghegan J continued:

> Neither of the above findings precluded a finding of fraud in the making of the false statement if the untrue statement was made 'recklessly', in the sense that the term was used in *Derry v Peek*, i.e. careless as to whether the statement be true of false. It is clear that 'careless' for this purpose is not the same as when used in relation to the tort of negligence. The carelessness must be something greater, if it is to constitute recklessness for the purposes of fraud. As pointed out by Lord Herschell, in the extract from his speech referred to above, a statement may be considered as made recklessly where the circumstances are such that the Court considers that the maker can have no real belief

in the truth of what he states. It appears to require an objective consideration by the Court as to whether the circumstances in which the plaintiff signed the Proposal Form (and, by doing so, made the representations or statements contained therein) were so careless as to whether the statements were true or false that the Court must conclude that she could have had no real belief in the truth of the statements contained in the Proposal Form.... On her own evidence, notwithstanding that the Form, when presented to her for signature, had been completed, she did not read the answers given in relation to her status in the practice and was unaware of the type of person by whom the Form was required to be completed and signed, notwithstanding the express statement at the start of the Form and the description immediately under which she signed. As already stated her actions must be considered in the context of the obligations of 'utmost good faith' in relation to the completion of a proposal form for insurance of which she was or ought to have been aware. Considering the matter from the plaintiff's potential belief in the truth of the statements made in the completed Proposal Form, as on her own evidence, she was unaware of what statements she was making by signing the Form, and was unaware of the person expressly required to sign the Form. It is not possible for me to conclude that she had any belief in the truth of the statements made.

See also *Goldsmith Williams v Travellers Insurance* [2010] Lloyd's Law Reports IR 309.

INDUCEMENT

The UK Marine Insurance Act 1906 ('MIA') does not contain any inducement test. It has been said that prior to the *Pan Atlantic* case, there was no clear view in England on the issue of inducement. In *Pan Atlantic Insurance Co Ltd v Pine Top Insurance Co Ltd* [1994] 3 All ER 581 the House of Lords adopted an inducement test that sits alongside the traditional prudent insurer test for materiality.

In *Pan Atlantic*, Lord Mustill stated that[255]:

> there is to be implied in the [Marine Insurance Act 1906] a qualification that a material misrepresentation will not entitle the underwriter to avoid the policy unless the misrepresentation induced the making of the contract, using 'induced' in the sense in which it is used in the general law of contract.

There has been a divergence of judicial opinion as to the inducement brought about by a misrepresentation. In *St Paul Fire and Marine Insurance Co Ltd v McConnell Dowell Constructors Ltd* [1995] 2 Lloyd's Rep 116, the Court of Appeal applied a presumption that if a misrepresentation is material, it induced the contract.

On the other hand, in *Assicurazioni Generali v Arab Insurance Group* [2002] EWCA Civ 1642, [2002] All ER (D) 177, it was stated that inducement cannot be presumed. The insurer must prove inducement on the balance of probabilities, though it may sometimes be possible to infer inducement from the facts, in the absence of direct evidence.[256]

Under current law, an insurer is entitled to bring a claim for misrepresentation only if it can show that it has been "induced" to enter into the contract. This test was first set out in *Pan Atlantic Insurance Co Ltd v Pine Top Insurance Co (supra)*. It meant that the insurer must show that without the misrepresentation, it would not have entered into the policy, either at all or on the same terms. In other words, had the insurer known the truth, at least one term of the policy would have been different; it would have done something different, either by refusing the cover, increasing the premium or changing the terms of the policy.

---

[255] See also *St Paul Fire and Marine Insurance Co (UK) v McConnell Dowell Constructors Ltd* [1996] 1 All ER 96 and *Drake Insurance plc v Provident Insurance plc* [2004] QB 601.

[256] See also *Laker Vent Engineering Ltd v Templeton Insurance Ltd* [2009] EWCA Civ 62.

Clarke LJ in *Assicurazioni Generali Spa v Arab Insurance Group* summarised the English law on inducement as follows:[257]

> (i) In order to be entitled to avoid a contract of insurance or reinsurance, an insurer or reinsurer must prove on the balance of probabilities that he was induced to enter into the contract by a material non-disclosure or by a material misrepresentation.
>
> (ii) There is no presumption of law that an insurer or reinsurer is induced to enter in the contract by a material non-disclosure or misrepresentation.
>
> (iii) The facts may, however, be such that it is to be inferred that the particular insurer or reinsurer was so induced even in the absence of evidence from him.
>
> (iv) In order to prove inducement, the insurer or reinsurer must show that the non-disclosure or misrepresentation was an effective cause of his entering into the contract on the terms on which he did. He must therefore show at least that, but for the relevant non-disclosure or misrepresentation, he would not have entered into the contract on those terms. On the other hand, he does not have to show that it was the sole effective cause of his doing so.

Silence, where there is a duty to speak, may amount to misrepresentation.[258] In cases where the proposal form is not completed, some questions being ignored or the space for insertion of an answer is left blank, it may be that the inference to be drawn is that a negative answer was intended. In *Roberts v Avon Insurance Co* [1956] 2 Lloyd's Rep 240, a question asking about previous losses was not answered; the policy was avoided for

---

[257] [2003] 1 WLR 577; followed in *Laker Vent Engineering v Templeton Insurance Ltd* [2009] 2 All ER (Comm) 755

[258] See *Brownlie v Campbell* (1880) 5 App Cas 925 at 950, per Lord Blackburn; *Banque Keyser Ullmann SA v Skandia (UK) Insurance Co Ltd* [1990] 1 QB 665 at 773-774, 782-783, per Slade LJ; Spencer Bower, Turner & Sutton, Actionable Non-Disclosure (2nd ed 1990) at 249-250.

fraudulent concealment, on the basis that the proposer had effectively answered that there were no previous losses.

ONUS

The onus of proof of non-disclosure is on the insurers, i.e., that there has been non-disclosure of a material fact, on a balance of probabilities. This, in a typical case, will be done by proving that material information existed at the time of contract, that it was known to the insured, and that this information was not disclosed. As the onus is on the insurer, it is the insured who receives the benefit of any doubt.[259]

An insurer may contend that it is not liable to pay the sum claimed by a claimant insured due to non-disclosure by the insured.[260]

The position of the law is that, where insurers allege non-disclosure, they must adduce evidence in support of their plea. In *Williams v Atlantic Association Co Ltd* [1933] 1 KB 81, Scrutton L.J. said:[261]

> The underwriters have not taken the course, which in my view should always be pursued, of going to the box and saying what they knew and what was the material fact which they did not know. In my view an underwriter pleading concealment must come and say what he was or was not told.

As already stated above, it is trite law that the burden of proof is on the insurer to prove non-disclosure of material facts.[262] In *Tan Guat Lan & Anor v Aetna Universal Insurance Sdn Bhd* [2003] 1 MLJ 430; [2003] 5 CLJ 384 it, was held that the burden was on the insurers to prove that

---

[259] Author Malcom (2006) in the book titled 'The Law of Insurance Contracts' at page 670.

[260] *Amanah Raya Berhad v Jerneh Insurance Berhad* [2005] 2 CLJ 393.

[261] See *Lee Bee Soon & Ors v Malaysia National Insurance Sdn Bhd* (supra).

[262] See *Goh Chooi Leong v Public Life Assurance Co Ltd* (supra); *Azizah bt Abdullah v Arab Malaysian Eagles Sdn. Bhd* (supra). See also *Tan Mooi Sim and Anor v United Overseas Bank (Malaysia) Berhad and Anor* [2010] MLJU 945 (HC).

the insured "knew" that he was suffering from "hypertension/ischaemic heart disease" at the time he signed the relevant document. It was stated that "one cannot fail to disclose something that one was unaware of". It was found that there was no evidence to show that the insured ever knew he had "ischaemic heart disease". His Lordship Ramly Ali J said:

> These is no evidence to show that LHH ever knew he had 'Ischaemic heart disease'. It is also unclear whether he got that disease (if at all) before or after 14 February 1993. Both the medical doctors who gave evidence (DW1 and DW2) did not mention any 'Ischaemic heart disease' nor was there any attempt to explain what 'Ischaemic heart disease' is, let alone linking 'hypertension' to 'Ischaemic heart disease'. In the premises, the allegations in the defendant' pleadings are not proven. Parties are bound by their pleadings. (See: *State Government of Perak v Muniandy* [1985] 1 LNS 11; [1986] 1 MLJ 490).

EFFECT OF NON-DISCLOSURE

At common law innocent non-disclosure gives rise to the right of avoidance, the duty of disclosure of material facts being absolute.[263]

Under the general law of insurance, an insurer can avoid a policy if he proves that there has been misrepresentation or concealment of a material fact by the insured. What is material is that which would influence the mind of a prudent insurer in deciding whether to accept the risk or fix the premium, and if this is proven, it is not necessary to further prove that the mind of the actual insurer was so affected. In other words, the insured cannot rebut the claim to avoid the policy because of a material representation, by a plea that the particular insurer concerned was so stupid, ignorant, or reckless that he could not exercise the judgment of a prudent insurer and was in fact unaffected by anything the insured had represented or concealed. In such a case as this, therefore, I think the plaintiffs must establish two propositions: (1) that the matter relied on was "material" in the sense that the mind of a prudent insurer would be

---

[263] *Rego v Fai General Insurance Company Ltd* [2001] WADC 98 (Australia).

affected by it, and (2) that in fact their insurer's mind was so affected, and the policy was thereby obtained.[264]

In *Soh Keng Hian v American International Assurance Co Ltd* [1995] MLJU 234, it was held that the insurers had rightfully avoided the contract of insurance for non-disclosure of material facts namely, the father's illnesses in relation to gout and diabetes and in as much as the action was based on that contract, it had to fail.

As stated above, the effect of non-disclosure or misrepresentation is that the insurers have the right to repudiate the contract. The remedy is not normally available where there has been a mere non-disclosure; there must be a misrepresentation, and innocent misrepresentation will suffice.[265]

INCONTESTABILITY CLAUSE

In *Tan Mooi Sim and Anor v United Overseas Bank (Malaysia) Berhad and Anor* [2010] MLJU 945, it was the view of the court that as the policy had been in force for more than two (2) years, section 147 (4) of the IA 1996[now under Paragraph 13(2) Schedule 9 of Section 129 of Financial Services Act 2013] that applied to the case. It was held that therefore, the insurer defendants should be precluded from contesting the validity of the policy on the ground of non-disclosure of material facts, unless fraud was proven under the second limb of Paragraph 13 Schedule 9 Section 129 of Financial Services Act 2013.[266]

---

[264] *Zurich General Accident and Liability Insurance Co v Morrison & Ors* [1942] 2 KB 53 at p 60.
[265] Halsbury's Laws of England (4th Ed, Reissue) at p 215.
[266] See also *Tan Guat Lan & Anor v Aetna Universal Insurance Sdn Bhd* (supra); *Malaysia Assurance Alliance Bhd v Chong Nyuk Lan* [2003] 5 CLJ 245.

Incontestability Provisions under Section 129 Financial Services Act 2013 (FSA 2013) Malaysia

The incontestability provisions embodied in Section 15C of the repealed Malaysian Insurance Act 1963 and Section 147 of the repealed Insurance Act 1996 are now provided in Paragraph 13 Schedule 9 of Section 129 (FSA 2013).

Paragraph 13(2) Schedule 9 of Section 129 FSA 2013 states that "Where a contract of life insurance has been in effect for a period of more than two years during the lifetime of the insured, such a contract shall not be avoided by a licensed life insurer on the ground that a statement made or omitted to be made in the proposal for insurance or in a report of a doctor, referee, or any other person, or in a document leading to the issue of the life policy, was inaccurate or false or misleading unless the insurer shows that the statement was on a material matter or suppressed a material fact and that it was fraudulently made or omitted to be made by the policy owner or the insured".

This statutory restriction can only be defeated by proof of fraudulent suppression or omission of material facts. Fraud must be specifically pleaded and proved.[267]

On the facts in *Tan Guat Lan & Anor v Aetna Universal Insurance Sdn Bhd* (*supra*), it was held that the incontestability provisions under Section 15C(4) of the 1963 Act [now Paragraph 13(2) Schedule 9 of Section 129 FSA 2013] were not applicable and that the policy could be contested by the insurer defendant on the ground of non-disclosure, without having to prove any element of fraud. In allowing the insured plaintiff's claim, His Lordship Ramly Ali J stated:

> Having perused all the materials before me and having considered the respective contentions by both parties as well as all the relevant authorities cited, I am of the view that the

---

[267] See *LEC Contractors (M) Sdn Bhd (formerly known as Lotterworld Engineering & Construction Sdn Bhd) v Castle Inn Sdn Bhd & Anor* [2000] 3 MLJ 339 at p 359.

computation of the two years period as stipulate in s 15C(4) of the 1963 Act [as well as s 147(4) of the 1996 Act] should start from the original date the policy was first issued and affected, ie 2 May 1990 in the present case, and not from the date of the last reinstatement on 14 February 1993. The decision of the Indian Supreme Court in *Mithoolal v Life Insurance Corporation of India* AIR (1962) SC 814 and the decision of our High Court in *Leong Kum Whay & Anor v American International Assurance Ltd* [1999] 1 MLJ 24 and *Malaysian Assurance Alliance Bhd v Chong Nyuk Lan (Administrator of the Estate of Liew Kin On, deceased)* [2002] 6 MLJ 648, clearly support my view.

In the case of *Mithoolal*, the Indian Supreme Court was considering s 45 of the Indian Insurance Act 1938 (which is *in pari materia* with s 15C(4) of our 1963 Act) and stated:

> Whether the revival of a lapsed policy a new contract or not for other purposes, it is clear from the wording of the operative part of s 45 that the period of two years for the purpose of the section has to be calculated from the date on which the policy was originally effected...

Similarly, in the case of *Leong Kum Whay* it was held by Mohd Noor Ahmad J (as he then was) that for the first insurance policy the computation of the two years period for the purpose of the re-amended s 15C(4) of the 1963 Act [now Paragraph 13(2) Schedule 9 of Section 129 FSA 2013] should be from the original date it was first effected.

His Lordship held there at p 28 that:

> The first policy was effected on 9 August 1989 and the accident happened on 26 June 1993, that is to say, the two-year requirement under the section had expired. Hence, it is caught by the section. Under the section, the first policy cannot be called in question by the defendant on the ground that the statement made in the proposal for insurance was inaccurate or false unless the defendant

shows that such statement was on a material matter or suppressed a material fact and that it was fraudulently made by the first plaintiff with the knowledge that the statement was false or that it suppressed a material fact. To my mind the defendant failed to prove the required ingredients as I have stated in para 4 above, the first policy is valid and therefore, the defendant cannot avoid its liabilities under it.

In the case of *Chong Nyuk Lan*, Richard Malanjum J (as he then was), in interpreting Section 147(4) of the 1996 Act [now Paragraph 13(2) Schedule 9 of Section 129 FSA 2013] in relation to the two years period) followed the earlier decisions and stated:

> Having given serious consideration to the opposing contentions of learned counsel for the parties, I am inclined to accept the position of the law as regards s 147(4) of the Act as interpreted in *Mithoolal* and that is to say that the computation of the two years period should start from the time the policy was originally effected regardless of lapse or renewal of the said policy.

In the present case, the policy was first affected on 2 May 1990 and LHH died on 28 August 1993 and the claim was filed after that date. The two years period has definitely expired and the defendant should be precluded from contesting the validity of the policy on the ground of false and non-disclosure of material facts unless fraud is alleged. There is no evidence of fraud adduced in the present case. Therefore, the defendant is not entitled to have the benefit of the second limb of the said Section 15C(4) [now Paragraph 13(2) Schedule 9 of Section 129 FSA 2013].

For the foregoing reason alone, the plaintiffs' claim should be allowed with costs.

The defendant is saying that the two years period as provided under cl 1 of the general provisions of the said policy, should start from the date of the last reinstatement, ie 14 February 1993. The incontestability clause under cl 1 provides:

> Incontestability: This policy (excluding all supplementary rider contracts attached to the Policy) shall be incontestable except for non-payment of premium, after it had been in force during the life time of the Insured for a period of two years from the date of issue or reinstatement of this policy, whichever is later.

The defendant also relied on the 'Declaration of Good Health' (D6 and D7) submitted by the LHH for the purpose of reinstatement of the policy which say:

> I further agree that if the policy be reinstated or issued the Incontestability and Suicide Provisions thereof shall be deemed and held and so modified as to have effect from the date of this certificate instead of the original issue date of the policy.

These contractual incontestability provisions do not contain the proviso or exception as provided under Section 15C(4) of the 1963 Act [now Paragraph 13(2) Schedule 9 of Section 129 FSA 2013] . However, it contained a part stating that the period of two years will run from the date of reinstatement of the policy (if there is a reinstatement).

The words used in those documents as well as the policy, clearly show that it affects only the contractual incontestability provisions. It does not affect the statutory incontestability provisions provided under Section 15C(4) of the 1963 Act (which was applicable to the present case) [now Paragraph 13(2) Schedule 9 of Section 129 FSA 2013] . Section 15C(4) or any other relevant provisions of the Insurance Act was not even mentioned in the said documents. The insured need not rely on the contractual incontestability provisions as he is adequately protected by the statutory incontestability provisions under the Act. In any event, one cannot contract out of an Act of Parliament. The relevant

Section 15C(4) [now Section 129 FSA 2013] was not worded so as to be 'subject to any contrary agreement or modification by the parties.' Therefore the defendant cannot agree with the insured (LHH) to override Section 15C(4). Any such agreement would be void and unenforceable as being contrary to public policy. In the case of *Hotel Ambassador (M) Sdn Bhd v Seapower (M) Sdn Bhd* [1991] 1 MLJ 221, Edgar Joseph Jr J (as he then was) held the following:

> In any event, any attempt to contract out of clear statutory provisions would be void and wholly ineffective as being contrary to public policy. Condition 12 must be read in the same light.

PROPOSAL FORM

The issue of whether there is a non-disclosure or incorrect disclosure or misrepresentation in an answer in the proposal form, is firstly, a question of fact to be determined by the court and secondly, given the decision in *China Insurance Co Ltd v Ngau Ah Kau* [1972] 1[MLJ at page 52, it is not the court's function to inquire into the materiality of the answer. In *American International Assurance Company Ltd v Nadarajan Subramaniam* [2013] 5 CLJ 697 (CA), His Lordship Nordin Abu Samah JCA said:

> The answer to the question in the proposal form will be deemed material as the truth of the answer has been made a condition of the policy. It will be noted that *China Insurance* was not considered by the Supreme Court in *Pacific & Orient*. It will be further noted that in *Pacific & Orient* it was a finding of the court made on the facts of that case that the non-disclosure was not material. In any event, in *Pacific & Orient* the court was not concerned with the 'basis clause' when concluding that the non-disclosure was not material whereas in the present case, the 'basis clause' was applicable to the contract of insurance entered into between the insured and the appellant. Accordingly, the ratio in *China Insurance* will still be applicable. In short, the court with respect cannot agree with counsel for the respondent that *Pacific & Orient*

has set aside the decision in *China Insurance* and that what is only material is the nature of employment of the insured and not the amount of his annual income.

[29] It is observed that the learned trial judge did not consider the decision in *China Insurance* in his grounds of judgment although the same had been referred to by counsel for the appellant in his submission. If he had so considered, perhaps he would have arrived at a different conclusion.

[30] The court was satisfied that the appellant had in the circumstances discharged its burden of proving the allegation of non-disclosure or incorrect disclosure of a material fact in the proposal form (see *Azizah Abdullah 'v Arab-Malaysian Eagles Sdn Bhd* [1996] 3 CLJ 426; [1996] 5 MLJ 569).

In determining whether there was full disclosure, it has been held that a fair and reasonable construction is to be placed on any question in the proposal form.[268]

In Malaysia, the insurer is required to provide a clear warning to the proposed insureds, in proposal forms, of the consequences of pre-contractual non-disclosure on the insurance contract. This appears in Section 149(4) of the IA 1996 [now Paragraph 5, Schedule 9 of Section 129 of the FSA 2013] and it only requires disclosure of matters known and provides that 'A proposal form and, where no proposal form is used, a request for particulars by the licensed insurer shall prominently display a warning that if a proposer does not fully and faithfully give the facts as he knows them or ought to know them, the policy may be invalidated.'

In fire insurance claims, it has been stated that there is no need to impute a need for reliance on information from the proposer. See the American case of *Hartford Protection Insurance Co v Harmes* 2 Ohio St. 452 (1853) where it was said that:

---

[268] *Pacific & Orient Insurance Co Sdn Bhd v Kathirevelu* [1992] 1 MLJ 249, SC; *Azizah Bte Abdullah v Arab Malaysian Eagles Sdn Bhd (supra)*.

...in fire insurance no such necessity for reliance exists, and, if the underwriter assumes the risk without taking the trouble to either examine, or inquire, he cannot very well, in the absence of all fraud, complain that it turns out to be greater than he anticipated.

The question in relation to whether there is non-disclosure in the proposal form turns on the question as to the "materiality" of the non-disclosure. Pursuant to Section 149(4) of the IA 1996 [now Paragraph 5, Schedule 9 to Section 129 of the FSA 2013], the insured is obliged to disclose in the proposal form, all the facts which he knew or ought to have known fully and faithfully, otherwise the policy issued may be invalidated and further under Section 150 of the IA 1996 [now Paragraph 4(1), Schedule 9 of Section 129 of the FSA 2013], the insured must disclose to the insurer before the contract of insurance is entered into, any matter which the insured knew would be relevant to the decision of the insurer on whether to accept the risk or not and the rates and terms to be applied or any matter a reasonable person in the circumstances could be expected to know to be relevant.[269]

In *American International Assurance Company Ltd v Nadarajan Subramaniam (supra)*, it was held that the insured was not acting in the utmost good faith (*uberrimae fide*) when he informed the insurer appellant that he was earning an estimated annual income of RM150, 000 when in fact, according to PW1, he was only earning an annual income of about RM50, 000. There it was said:

> The big difference in the estimated income of about RM100, 000 per annum is a material fact as it may have a bearing on the true occupation of the insured and this in turn may affect the decision of the appellant on whether or not to accept the risk and consequently to determine the rates/premiums and terms to be applied in the policies issued by the appellant.
>
> [23] The insured was bound by the warranty in each of the three proposal forms that the answers given were true and that the

---

[269] See *American International Assurance Company Ltd v Nadarajan Subramaniam (supra)*.

answers would form the basis of the contract between the insured and the appellant. In part IV of the insurance policies, it was clearly stated that the proposal forms shall be the basis of the insurance policies.

It is settled law that insurers are entitled to full disclosure of all knowledge possessed by the insured that is material to the risks.[270]

The rule we find established is this; that the person who proposes an insurance should communicate every fact which he is not entitled to assume to be in the knowledge of the other party; the insured is bound to communicate every fact to enable the insurer to ascertain the extent of the risk against which he undertakes to protect the former and it is also well established law that it is immaterial whether the omission to communicate a material fact arises from intention, or indifference, or a mistake, or from it not being present to the mind of the insured that the fact was one which it was material to make known because as Mellor J said "the risk run is really different from the risk understood and intended to be run at the time of the agreement".[271]

The disclosure must be made voluntarily, in the sense that even if the insurer does not ask an appropriate question either in the proposal form or otherwise, the insured is bound to disclose any information which is material or relevant to the risk. He must not wait to be asked. An insured's duty to disclose material information to the insurer is a duty which exists independently of any proposal form.[272]

It is also incumbent on the insurers to make the information sought plain and clear. On the facts in *Azizah Bte Abdullah v Arab Malaysian Eagles Sdn Bhd* [1996] 5 MLJ 569, it was found that the information regarding prolonged illnesses was vague and doubtful. If the words are obscure or

---

[270] *Joel v Law Union and Crown Insurance Company* (*supra*).

[271] Cockburn CJ in *Bates v Hewitt* [1866-67], LR 2 QB 595, 607.

[272] *Tan Mooi Sim and Anor v United Overseas Bank (Malaysia) Berhad and Anor* (*supra*).

doubtful in their meaning, the court should so construe them in order to avoid injustice.[273]

In this case, it was held that the insurers had not discharged their burden and had failed to prove non-disclosure, fraud and knowledge on the part of the insured deceased to avoid their liability to pay under the policy. His Lordship Nik Hashim JC in rejecting the contention of the insurers in his judgment said:

> Based on this evidence, it can be inferred that the deceased did not even know that he was suffering from diabetes. Though SP5 agreed that diabetes is a prolonged illness, his testimony has created some doubts whether the diabetes that the deceased was alleged to be suffering from could be classified as a prolonged illness. Surely if he was suffering from diabetes, it would have been detected when SP5 examined him on 10 December 1990. It follows therefore that the duty to disclose material facts cannot extend to disclose facts which the deceased did not know or which he could not reasonably be expected to have known at the time when he signed the declaration in exh D6 (see *Toh Kim Lian & Anor v The Asia Insurance Co Ltd* [1995] 3 AMR 2304). Indeed, the deceased died on 13 December 1990 not due to diabetes but due to high fever.

Where the answers to the questions in the proposal form had become terms of the contract of insurance, Sections 91 and 92 of the Malaysian Evidence Act 1950 prevented the insured from adducing oral evidence to contradict, vary or add to or subtract from them. The truth of the answers had been made a condition of the policy and it was not open to the trial judge to consider the question whether the answers to these questions had been material or not.[274]

The insurers in *Ngu Siew Kong v ING Insurance Bhd* [2011] MLJU 719, failed and refused to pay the sum insured on a life insurance policy. It

---

[273] Per Gunn Chit Tuan SCJ in *Dirkje Peiternella Halma v Mohd Noor bin Baharom* [1990] 3 MLJ 103 at p 107.

[274] *China Insurance Co. Ltd v Ngau Ah Kau* (*supra*).

was provided under the policy that the insurer defendant would pay the sum insured if while the said policy remained in force, the plaintiff was diagnosed to be suffering from prostate cancer. Some two and a half months after the policy was issued the plaintiff was diagnosed with prostate cancer in respect of which the insurers failed and refused to pay the sum insured, contending that there was non-disclosure by the insured plaintiff.

It was not disputed that in the statement to the Medical Examiner which was an integral part of the proposal form, the plaintiff had answered in the negative to two questions, namely whether he had ever been treated for prostate cancer and whether in the past 5 years he had any blood or urine studies carried out. The plaintiff had himself admitted that he had blood and urine tests carried out at Normah Medical Specialist Centre and this was confirmed by the evidence of Dr. Ching Hing Sa (PW7). It was also established that the plaintiff had ordered 50 tablets of Androcur (50mg) on 17.4.2003 and another 300 tablets on 26.4.2003. Dr Tan Hui Meng (PW4) the consultant urologist consulted by the plaintiff testified that Androcur was primarily used to treat prostate cancer.

It was the view of the court that those were unarguably material facts because naturally they could influence the insurer defendant's decision on whether to accept the risk. It was found that the insured plaintiff was already suffering from prostate cancer when the Policy was issued which therefore rendered the insurers not liable.

AGENT

The duty of disclosure must also be examined in relation to agents. The duty of an agent to disclose circumstances within his own knowledge is independent of the duty of the insured.[275]

Section 19 of the UK Marine Insurance Act 1906 ('MIA') imposes upon an agent a separate obligation to "disclose to the insurer every material circumstance which is known to himself, and an agent to insure is deemed

---

[275] *Blackburn, Low & Co. v Vigors* (1887) 12 App. Cas. 531, 542-543.

to know every circumstance which in the ordinary course of business ought to be known by, or to have been communicated to, him".

Where facts need not have been disclosed by the insured under section 18, they need not be disclosed by the agent under section 19.

As stated by Saville LJ in *Société Anonyme d'Intermediaries Luxembourgeois v Farex Gie* [1995] LRLR 116, 157:

> Why should it be a breach of good faith sufficient to deprive the assured of his contract if the agent fails to disclose something which, had the assured known of it, would not have had to have been disclosed by the latter?
>
> Where, as in the ordinary case and as in the present case, insurance is effected for the assured by an agent, the agent is subject to a very similar and independent duty of disclosure: section 19. The insurer may also avoid the contract of insurance if any material representation made by the assured or his agent to the insurer during the negotiations for the contract is untrue, the test of materiality being the same as that already noted: section 20(1), (2).
>
> If a party to a written contract seeks to exclude the ordinary consequences of fraudulent or dishonest misrepresentation or deceit by his agent, acting as such, inducing the making of the contract, such intention must be expressed in clear and unmistakable terms on the face of the contract.

The relations existing between an insured and his insurer are such that a full disclosure of all the facts concerning the risk must be made. In the words of Lord Mansfield, in the case of *Carter v Boehm (supra)*:

> The special facts upon which the contingent chance is to be computed lie most commonly in the knowledge of the insured only; the underwriter trusts to his representation and proceeds upon confidence that he does not keep back any circumstance in his knowledge to mislead the underwriter into a belief that the

circumstance does not exist, and to induce him to estimate the risk as if it did not exist. The keeping back such circumstance is a fraud, and therefore the policy is void. Although the suppression should happen through mistake without any fraudulent intention, yet still the underwriter has been deceived, and the policy is void because the risk run is really different from the risk understood and intended to be run at the time of the agreement. The policy would equally be void against the underwriter if he concealed anything within his own knowledge as, for example, if he insured a ship on a voyage, and he privately knew that she had already arrived, and in such circumstances he would be liable to return the premium paid. Good faiths forbids either party, by concealing what he privately knows, to draw the other party into a bargain owing to his ignorance of that fact, and his believing the contrary: Templemann on Marine Insurance, 6th edition at page 21, in relation to section 17 of M.I.A.

An agent may make a contract for his principal which has the same consequences as if the principal has made it himself. In respect of the acts which the principal expressly or impliedly consents that the agent shall do on his behalf, the agent is said to have the authority to act and it is this authority that constitutes the power to affect the principal's legal relations with third parties. This means that the fundamental rule that a person cannot be affected, either beneficially or adversely, by a contract to which he is not a party, is considerably diminished in its effect. In short, an agency agreement is an agreement by which the agent is authorised to establish privity of contract between the agent's employer known as the principal, and the third party. The essential characteristic of an agent is that he is invested with a legal power to alter his principal's legal relations with third parties; the principal is under a correlative liability to have his legal relations altered.[276]

It is settled law that where an agent is authorized to negotiate and settle terms of a proposal or is delegated with a duty to investigate certain

---

[276] Dowrick (1954) 17 MLR 36, Reynolds 94 LQR 225.

matters, the agent's knowledge is also the knowledge of the insurance company.[277]

In the Court of Appeal case of *O'Connor v BDB Kirby Co* [1971] 2 All ER 1415, it was held by Megaw LJ that a broker who takes it upon himself to fill in a proposal form for a client, owes the client a duty to use such care, as is reasonable, in all the circumstances, towards ensuring that the answers recorded to the questions in the proposal form accurately represents the answers given to the broker by the client. He does not owe a duty to ensure that every answer is correct.

It has to be noted that there has been a divergence of legal opinion as to whether the insurance agent is the agent of the insurer or the insured. The position used to be that the insurance agent was the agent of the insured. This meant that the insurers could avoid liability where it had been determined that there was non-disclosure and that the non-disclosure was a material non-disclosure.

The position now is that the insurance agent is an agent of the insurers. The legal transition can be traced to the position existing at the time when the decision in *Newsholme Brothers v Road Transport and General Insurance Company Limited* [1929] 2 KB was the prevalent view.

The offer to enter into a contract of insurance is generally submitted to the insurance agent of the insurer. The offer is in the form of a proposal form which is prepared by the insurers and the insured will answer questions therein, which the insurers may accept or decline.

In determining various issues, most pertinently as to the formation of the insurance contract and the duty of utmost good faith in relation to the duty of disclosure, it is important to determine whether the agent is the agent of the insured or the insurers.

---

[277] *Bawden v The London, Edinburgh and Glasgow Assurance Co* [1892] 2 QB 534; *Ayrey v British Legal and United Provident Assurance Co Ltd* [1918] 1 KB 136 and *Evans v Employers Mutual Insurance Association Ltd* [1936] 1 KB 505.

As stated earlier, there was a conflict of judicial opinion in relation to the question as to whether the agent was the agent of the insured or the insurers.

In relation to the question of evidence, this was impounded by the inadmissibility of extrinsic evidence as evidence could not be introduced on explanations from an insurance agent explaining how answers to certain questions in the proposal form were put in. Sections 91 and 92 of the Malaysian Evidence Act 1950 were an obstacle.

The question of whether the agent was the agent of the insured or the insurers was relevant in relation to the liability of the parties in two areas. One was in relation to the formation of the insurance contract and the other was in relation to the duty of good faith, which could cause the insurer to deny liability under the policy on the ground of non-disclosure.

The duty of disclosure requires the insured to disclose material facts when answering questions in the proposal form. Whether or not a matter must be revealed can only be determined based on the questions asked by the insurance agent to the proposer.

The determination of whether the insured had in fact disclosed all material facts, is impinged upon by whether the agent may or may not have passed on or conveyed all the answers given by the insured.

The agent may, in some instances, be guilty of fraud by fraudulent misrepresentation or deceit, thereby inducing the making of the contract between the insured and the insurers. The deliberate withholding from the insurer of information which the agent knows or believes to be material to the risk, if done dishonestly or recklessly, may well amount to a fraudulent misrepresentation.

The consequence of such conduct of the agent may cause the insurers to avoid the policy and deprive an insured of its intended security.

The practicalities of the situation in Malaysia is that it is a well-known practice that in this country insurance agents do assist proposers to answer questions in an insurance proposal form.[278]

The inequity of the decision in *Newsholme (supra)*, was that it allowed insurers to avoid their liability by imputing that the insurance agent or broker was the agent of the insured, thereby imputing that any non-disclosure in the proposal form was within the knowledge of the insured and not the insurers. This was even when the insurance agent was employed by the insurers.

The common law position in Malaysia was as was decided in *Newsholme*, where it was held that where the agent helped the insured to complete the proposal form, the agent acted as an agent for the insured. This meant that the insured would be liable for misrepresentation or non-disclosure in a situation where the insured had told the agent the truth but the agent had recorded the insured's statement inaccurately in the proposal form.

That is no longer the case. The common law and the legislative amendments to the Malaysian Insurance Act 1996[now Financial Services Act 2013], provide that the current state of the law is that the insurance agent is the agent of the insurers.

There has been a move away from the judicial pronouncement in *Newsholme*. As was aptly stated by F. M. B. Reynolds in the Law Quarterly Review (1972) starting at page 462; "Though unexceptional from the point of view of legal reasoning, the decision (*Newsholme*) undoubtedly does not accord with the expectations of many proposers: indeed the contrary result had already at the time been prescribed for certain forms of insurance by the Industrial Assurance Act 1923, section 20(4)".

As was stated by Harminder Singh JC in *Nadarajan A/l Subramaniam v American International Assurance Co Ltd* [2010] MLJU 1775 "thankfully, this position no longer prevails as it was inclined to produce unjust consequences".

---

[278] See *Abu Bakar v Oriental Fire & General Insurance Co Ltd* (*supra*).

Newsholme has been held to be inequitable. As was pointed out by Abdul Malik Ishak in *Poh Siew Cheng v American International Assurance Co Ltd* [2006] 6 MLJ 57; "the decision in *Newsholme Brothers v Road Transport and General Insurance Company Limited* has caused a great deal of heartache. It was rejected outright in Ghana as reflected in the case of *Mohamed Hijazi v New India Assurance Co Ltd* (1969) 1 African L Rev Comm. 7. It was reversed by way of a legislation in Jamaica — to be precise by Insurance Act 1971 s 74(1) of the…Even England proceeded to distinguish *Newsholme* restrictively as reflected in the case of *Stone v Reliance Mutual Insurance Society Ltd* [1972] 1 Lloyd's Rep 469. Canada too followed suit as seen in the case of *Blanchette v CIS Ltd* (1973) 36 DLR (3d) 561".

His Lordship went on to state that "In Malaysia too legislative intervention brought an end to the rigours of *Newsholme* and that was in the form of s 44A of the Insurance Act 1963".

Harminder Singh Dhaliwal JC in *Nadarajan A/l Subramaniam v American International Assurance Co Ltd (supra)* re-clarified the current position in relation to whether the insurance agent was an agent of the insurance company or the insured. His Lordship said:

> Thankfully, this position no longer prevails as it was inclined to produce unjust consequences (as observed by Gopal Sri Ram JCA (as he then was) in *Leong Kum Whay v QBE Insurance (M) Sdn Bhd & Ors* [2006] 1 CLJ 1 at 23). The way in which the legal position in this regard has evolved is well documented in the judgment of Abdul Malik Ishak J (as he then was) in *Poh Siew Cheng v American International Assurance Co. Ltd* [2006] 6 MLJ 57.

In fact, reliance can be placed on the decision of the Federal Court in *The 'Melanie' United Oriental Assurance Sdn Bhd Kuantan v WM Mazzarol* [1984] 1 MLJ 260, where at page 262 it was clearly pronounced that "It is settled law that where an agent is authorized to negotiate and settle terms of a proposal or delegated with a duty to investigate certain matters, the agent's knowledge is also the knowledge of the insurance company. *Bawden v The London, Edinburgh and Glasgow Assurance Co* [1892] 2 QB 534; *Ayrey v British Legal and United Provident Assurance Co.*

Ltd [1918] 1KB 136 and *Evans v Employers Mutual Insurance Association Ltd* [1936] 1 KB 505)".

Now legislation has also come to the aid of the insured "consumer". Reference can be made to Sections 44A IA 1963;Sections 150 (in particular sub-ss (2) and (3)) and 151 (1) of the IA 1996 [now Paragraphs 4(2) and (3), 12 Schedule 9 of Section 129 of the FSA 2013].

Ian Chin J in *Syarikat Tai Yuen Supermarket (Tawau) Sdn Bhd v Mercantile Insurance Sdn Bhd & Anor* [1994] 1 CLJ 228, rightly interpreted Section 44A of the Malaysian Insurance Act 1963 in this way:

> I take it that s. 44A of the Insurance Act 1963, has the effect of putting it out of reach of an insurer to set up as a defence the false answers in a proposal form when such answers were inserted by its authorised agent and when such answers were to the knowledge of its authorised agent false save where there was collusion or connivance and save where the person has ceased to be an agent of the insurer and the insurer has taken all reasonable steps to inform or bring to the knowledge of potential policy owners and the public in general of such cessation. What then is the meaning of the words 'authorised agent' appearing in s 44A of the Insurance Act 1963? The words 'authorised agent' have not been defined in either the Insurance Act 1963 or the Interpretation Act 1967. I am of the opinion that the words 'authorised agent' refer to an agent who has the actual, as distinct from apparent or ostensible, authority of the insurer because the section also speaks of the cessation of authority of the agent and there is no question of cessation of authority if there was no actual authority in the first place.

The preamble to the Insurance Act 1996 ('IA 1996') [now repealed by the Financial Services Act 2013 ('FSA 2013')], provides that this is an Act to provide new laws for the licensing and regulation of insurance business, insurance broking business and adjusting business and for other related purposes. The provisions of sub-ss (2) and (3) of Section 150 of the IA 1996 [now Paragraph 4(2) and (3), Schedule 9 of Section 129 of the FSA 2013], amended or modified the common law requirements of strict compliance of a duty of disclosure of material facts. The two subsections are intended to protect the interests of an insured or a consumer in respect of insurance matters.[279]

Section 151(1) of the IA 1996 [now Paragraph 12, Schedule 9 of Section 129 of the FSA 2013] provides that "a person who is authorized by a licensed insurer to be its insurance agent and who solicits or negotiates a contract of insurance in that capacity shall be deemed, for the purpose of the formation of the contract of insurance, to be the agent of the licensed insurer and the knowledge of that insurance agent shall be deemed to be the knowledge of the licensed insurer".[280]

BASIS CLAUSE

Where it was provided in the insurance policy that the proposal forms shall be the basis of the insurance policy, the insured was bound by the warranty in the proposal form that the answers given were true and that the answers would form the basis of the contract between the insured and the insurer.

When a proposal for an insurance policy contains such a warranty and the policy expressly states that the proposal form is to be the basis for the policy, the truth of the answers to the questions in the proposal form are deemed to be material. In the Federal Court in *China Insurance Co Ltd v Ngau Ah Kau* (supra), the court held that the truth of the answers to the questions had been made a condition of the contract of insurance and it was not open to the trial judge to consider the question of whether the answers to these questions were material or not.

The Court of Appeal in *American International Assurance Co, Ltd v Nadarajan a/l Subramaniam* (supra), was of the view that whether there was a non-disclosure or incorrect disclosure or misrepresentation in an answer in the proposal form is firstly, a question of fact, to be determined by the court and secondly, given the decision in *China Insurance*, it is not

---

[279] *Lau King Kieng v AXA Affin General Insurance Bhd and another suit* (supra).
[280] See also *Abu Bakar v Oriental Fire & General Insurance Co Ltd* (supra).

the court's function to inquire into the materiality of the answer. The answer to the question in the proposal form will be deemed material as the truth of the answer has been made a condition of the policy. There it was said:

> The insured was bound by the warranty in each of the three proposal forms that the answers given were true and that the answers would form the basis of the contract between the insured and the appellant. In part IV of the insurance policies, it was clearly stated that the proposal forms shall be the basis of the insurance policies.

> [24] In *China Insurance Co Ltd v Ngau Ah Kau* [1971] 1 LNS 20; [1972] 1 MLJ 52, the Federal Court held that when a proposal for an insurance policy contains such a warranty and the policy expressly states that the proposal form is to be the basis for the policy, the truth of the answers to the questions in the proposal form are deemed to be material. The court held that the truth of the answers to the questions had been made a condition of the contract of insurance and it was not open to the trial judge to consider the question of whether the answers to these questions were material or not.

On the evidence, the Court of Appeal was satisfied that the appellant insurer had, in the circumstances, discharged its burden of proving the allegation of non-disclosure or incorrect disclosure of a material fact in the proposal form.[281]

It was found that the insured was not of utmost good faith (*uberrimae fide*) when he informed the insurer appellant that he was earning an estimated annual income of RM150,000 when in fact, according to PW1, he was only earning an annual income of about RM50,000. The big difference in the estimated income of about RM100,000 per annum was a material fact, as it may have had a bearing on the true occupation of the insured and this in turn may have affected the decision of the appellant on whether or

---

[281] *89 American International Assurance Co, Ltd v Nadarajan a/l Subramaniam* (*supra*),

not to accept the risk and consequently to determine the rates/premiums and terms to be applied in the policies issued by it.

It is possible for persons to stipulate that answers to certain questions shall be the basis of the insurance, and if that is done, then there is no question as to materiality left, because the persons have contracted that there should be materiality in those questions; but quite apart from that and alongside of that, there is a duty of no concealment of any consideration which would affect the mind of the ordinary prudent man in accepting the risk.[282]

LJ Cohen in *Schoolman v Hall* [1951] Lloyd's Rep 139 at p 143 said:[283]

> So, I think, applying those observations here, while the insurers have stipulated that the answers to the fifteen questions 'shall be the basis of the contract', that only has the effect of preventing any argument as to the materiality of those questions should dispute arise, but it does not relieve the proposer of his general obligation at common law to disclose any material which might affect the risk which was being run, or which might affect the mind of the insurer as to whether or not he issue a policy.

Viscount Haldane in *Dawsons Ltd v Bonnin & Ors* [1922] All ER Rep 88 at p 94 said at page 94:

> The proposal – in other words – the answers to the questions specifically put in it is made basic to the contract. ... Both on principle and in the light of authorities such as those which I have already cited, it appears to me that, when answers, including that in question, are declared to be the basis of the contract, this can only mean that their truth is made a condition exact fulfilment of which is rendered by stipulation foundational to its enforceability: Of course, there is no presumption in insurance law that matters

---

[282] *Glicksman v Lancashire & General Assurance Co Ltd* [1926] Lloyd LR 69; [1926] All ER 161; [1927] AC 139.
[283] See also *Asia Hotel Sdn Bhd v Malayan Insurance (M) Sdn Bhd* [1992] 2 MLJ 615.

not dealt with in a proposal form are not material. *Schoolman v Hall* [1951] 1 Lloyd's Rep 139 142.

The legal position of the insurance agent was set out in Halsbury's Laws of England Vol. 22 (3rd Edition) at page 204:

> In filling in the answers in a proposal form an insurance agent, is normally regarded as the agent for the proposer, at the request, express or implied, of the latter. Even if the agent knows the truth, his knowledge is not in that case imputed to the insurers. If he is careless in filling up the form, it is the proposer, not the insurers, who may maintain an action in negligence against him. Furthermore, where the proposer himself signs the proposal form, as is usually insisted upon by insurers, by signing he adopts whatever answers the agent has inserted and makes them his own. This is clearly the case where he reads and approves the answers before signing: but the position is the same if he chooses to sign the proposal without reading them, or if he signs the form when it is blank, leaving it to the agent to insert the answers later. It is irrelevant to inquire how the inaccuracy arose; or whether the agent acted honestly or dishonestly; or whether the agent had forgotten or misunderstood the correct information he had been given; or whether the answers were a mere invention on the part of the agent; if the result is that inaccurate or inadequate information is given on material matters, or that a contractual stipulation as to accuracy or adequacy of any information given is broken, it is the proposer who has to suffer.

A broker or agent who takes it upon himself to fill in a proposal form for a client, owes the client a duty to use such care as is reasonable in all the circumstances, towards ensuring that the answers recorded to the questions in the proposal form, accurately represents the answers given by the client to the broker. He does not owe a duty to ensure that every answer is correct.[284]

---

[284] *O'Connor v BDB Kirby Co* [1971] 2 All ER 1415 (CA).

It is the duty of the proposer for insurance to see and make sure that the information contained in the proposal form is accurate and not to sign it if it is inaccurate. In *O'Connor v BDB Kirby & Co* [1972] 1 QB 90, the plaintiff wished to take out insurance on his car and consulted an insurance broker. The latter filled in the proposal form for the plaintiff and in answer to a question as to where the car was normally kept at night inadvertently stated that it was in 'a private garage'. That was not correct. The proposal form was approved by the plaintiff who failed to notice this incorrect information. After the policy had been issued and while it was in force, the car which was parked outside the plaintiff's house was damaged. On a claim against the insurance company, liability was repudiated on the ground that the proposal contained an inaccurate answer as to where the car was garaged at night. The plaintiff therefore claimed against the insurance broker for breach of contract and negligence. It was held by the Court of Appeal that it was the duty of the plaintiff to ensure that the information given to the insurance company was correct and since the plaintiff had failed to rectify the incorrect information given, he was solely to blame. Davis LJ in his judgment said, at p 99:

> It is argued by Mr Norris that the failure of the assured properly to read the form was the cause of this loss, the cause of putting the insurance company in a position to repudiate liability. I think that Mr Norris is right in that regard ... And in each of those cases it was emphasized that it is the duty of the proposer for insurance to see and make sure that the information contained in the proposal form is accurate and not to sign it if it is inaccurate, and that he cannot be heard to say that he did not read it properly or was not fully appraised of its contents ... I think that the principle applies with equal force in this case. It would be different if the assured was unable to read or was in some degree illiterate. But there is no suggestion of that in this case. He was fully able to read this proposal form, although perhaps he could not have been able to read the copy we have, and there had been this discussion about the garaging of the car and its relevance to the amount of the premium, and it was there staring him in the face. If he did not read it properly, I think that he has only himself to blame ... it was the duty of the assured to have read that form; it was his application; he signed it and, if he was so careless as not to have

read it properly, then in my opinion he has only himself to blame for his loss.

Megaw LJ said, at p 101:

> When the broker took it on himself to fill in the proposal form, the duty upon him was to use such care as was reasonable in all the circumstances towards ensuring that the answers recorded to the questions in the proposal form accurately represented the answers given to the broker by the assured. But the duty was not a duty to ensure that every answer was correct.

In *Globe Trawlers Pte Ltd v National Employers' Mutual General Insurance Association Ltd v Anor* [1989] 1 MLJ 463 (HC Singapore), the owners of the vessels damaged in a fire treated the damage to each of the vessels as a total loss and made a claim under the fire insurance policy. The first defendant's insurers did not settle or meet any part of the claim and, in consequence, the plaintiffs instituted proceedings against the first defendants claiming for an indemnity under the fire insurance policy. Liability was disputed.

The first defendants raised three defences: (i) there was a material misdescription of the property to be insured in the proposal forms submitted for insurance; (ii) the claim by the plaintiffs was fraudulent, and (iii) the damage was caused by the plaintiffs' wilful act or with their connivance. Initially, only the first defendants were sued in this action, but in view of the defence of a material misdescription in the proposal forms, the plaintiffs joined the second defendants, the insurance brokers in the action. Thean J dismissed the claim of the plaintiffs.

On appeal to the Court of Appeal; *National Employers' Mutual General Insurance Association Ltd v Globe Trawlers Pte Ltd* [1991] 2 MLJ 92, the plaintiffs' appeal was allowed. The Court of Appeal found that "there was a material misdescription in the proposal form on 'Super Trawl' and that the appellants are entitled to avoid the policy". Chao Hick Tin J delivering the judgment of the court stated thus:

It was held that the general rule is that a broker who completes the proposal form is not acting as an agent for the insurer but for the insured. The courts have departed from the general rule only when there have been some unusual circumstances. In this case, as the respondents read and signed the proposal form the respondents should not be allowed to hide behind the broker.

The general rule is that a broker who completes the proposal form is not acting as an agent for the insurer but for the insured. This is laid down in the leading case *Newsholme Bros v Road Transport & General Insurance Co Ltd* [1929] 2 KB 356. We will cite only two passages from the case — first of Scrutton LJ (at p 369):

> I find considerable difficulty in seeing how a person who fills up the proposal can be the agent of the person to whom the proposal is made. A man cannot contract with himself. A makes a proposal to B by signing it, and communicating it to B. If A gets someone — C — to fill up the form for him before he signs it, it seems to me that C in doing so must be the agent of A who has to make the proposal, not of B who has to consider whether he will accept it. If C is also the agent of B to procure proposals, and induces A to make a proposal by representing that a certain form of proposal contains the particulars that B wants to know, when it does not the remedy seems to be to rescind the written contract procured by misrepresentation, not to alter the written contract and claim the benefit of it as altered.

and second of Greer LJ (at p 382):

> ... I also take the view that notice to the agent whose duty was to obtain a signed proposal form and send it to the company, was not notice to the company of anything inconsistent with the signed proposal form, and that in filling up the form, whether he mistook the instructions of the insured, or whether he intentionally filled in something different from what he was told, he was not

acting as the agent of the company, but as the agent of the insured.

In an earlier case *Biggar v Rock Life Assurance Co* [1902] 1 KB 516 Wright J decided that an insured who signed a proposal form was bound by what he stated therein even though the inaccurate answers were written in by the agent.

The law is summarized in 25 Halsbury's Laws of England (4th Ed) at para 396 as follows:

> Except in the case of industrial assurance, in filling in the answers in a proposal form an insurance agent is normally regarded as the agent for the proposer at the proposer's request, express or implied. Even if the agent knows the truth, his knowledge is not in that case imputed to the insurers. If he is careless in filling up the form, it is the proposer, not the insurers, who may maintain an action in negligence against him. Further, where the proposer himself signs the proposal form, as is usually insisted upon by insurers, by signing he adopts whatever answers the agent has inserted and makes them his own. This is clearly the case where he reads and approves the answers before signing, but the position is the same if he chooses to sign the proposal without reading them or if he signs the form when it is blank, leaving it to the agent to insert the answers later. It is irrelevant to inquire how the inaccuracy arose, whether the agent acted honestly or dishonestly, whether the agent had forgotten or misunderstood the correct information he had been given or whether the answers were a mere invention on the part of the agent. If the result is that inaccurate or inadequate information is given on material matters or that a contractual stipulation as to accuracy or adequacy of any information given is broken, it is the proposer who has to suffer.

The courts have departed from the general rule only where there have been some unusual circumstances in the case, eg the insured was blind or illiterate. *Bawden v London, Edinburgh & Glasgow Assurance Co* [1892] 2 QB 534 was effectively concerned with an illiterate insured. To the extent that *Bawden's case* [1892] 2 QB 534 sought to lay down any general rule, Scrutton LJ in *Newsholme* [1929] 2 KB 356 seriously doubted its validity.

In our opinion, where an insurance broker filled up a proposal form on behalf of an insured of full capacity, the insured should not be allowed to hide behind the broker. The reasons given by Scrutton LJ in *Newsholme* [1929] 2 KB 356 are convincing (at pp 375–376):

> If the answers are untrue and he knows it, he is committing a fraud which prevents his knowledge being the knowledge of the insurance company. If the answers are untrue, but he does not know it, I do not understand how he has any knowledge which can be imputed to the insurance company. In any case, I have great difficulty in understanding how a man who has signed, without reading it, a document which he knows to be a proposal for insurance, and which contains statements in fact untrue, and a promise that they are true, and the basis of the contract, can escape from the consequences of his negligence by saying that the person he asked to fill up for him is the agent of the person to whom the proposal is addressed.

A fortiori, in the case of an insured who had approved and signed a proposal form which contained material misdescriptions.

We note that Robert Tan in cross-examination said that in filling the form, he was acting as the agent of the insurance company. This might be Robert Tan's impression, but it certainly was not the position in law. The proposal was from the respondents and if it was filled up by Robert Tan with information furnished to him by Fritz Schneppe, Robert Tan was acting as the agent of the respondents. We would stress that the respondents, through Fritz Schneppe, had declared that the statements and particulars set out in the proposal had been 'read over and checked are true'.

The case *Woolcott v Excess Insurance Co Ltd* [1979] 1 Lloyd's Rep 231 does not appear to us to establish any general rule that an insurance broker's knowledge is automatically imputed to the insurers. That case was more concerned with a question of fact as to whether the agent knew about the previous criminal record of the insured. It also dealt with the principles upon which an appellate court should disturb a finding of fact of the court below. In that case, it was accepted that if there were such knowledge, the knowledge would be imputed to the insurers. Most importantly we note that in *Woolcott* [1979] 1 Lloyd's Rep 231 the agent was given the authority to issue a cover right away to the insured as appears from the judgment of Megaw LJ at p 233:

> Mr Smith, acting on behalf of the third party (the insurance agents) arranged on 28 January 1974 for insurance cover to be given forthwith by Excess Insurance Co Ltd, the defendants in the action. This was within the authority which the third party had as agents for the defendants.

That was a different sort of situation altogether. Obviously in that case, the agent stood in the shoes of the insurers and his knowledge would be the knowledge of the insurers.

In the light of the foregoing we respectfully have to differ from the learned judge. We find that there was a material misdescription in the proposal form on 'Super Trawl' and that the appellants are entitled to avoid the policy. Further, while the learned judge found that Robert Tan knew that the trawlers were still under construction, we hold that in the circumstances of the case, such knowledge could not be imputed to the appellants.

As the first ground is sufficient to dispose of the entire appeal, there is no need for us to proceed to deal with the second ground raised in the appeal. Accordingly, the judgment entered against the appellants is set aside. The action of the respondents against the appellants is dismissed with costs, here and below.

Where there is non-disclosure of material facts, it would not absolve an insured who contends that an agent was responsible for filing up the proposal form. In *Ngu Siew Kong v ING Insurance Bhd* (*supra*), the court held that it was of no assistance to the Plaintiff that the statement to the Medical Examiner was not filled by him but by one Su Tien Oh, the Defendant's agent. The court then went on to examine the principle to be applied in such circumstances and referred to *Chung Kuo Ping v Malaysian Assurance Alliance Bhd* [2008] 3 CLJ 752 where at page 790 it was stated:

> The principle which was applied in *Dawson's case* supra, in my respectful opinion, must likewise apply to the present case. In *Newsholme Brothers v Road Transport and General Insurance Company, Limited* Scrutton, L.J had the same principle in mind when he said on page 376 this:
>
>> ...In any case, I have great difficulty in understanding how a man has signed without reading it, a document which he knows to be a proposal for insurance, and which contains statements in fact untrue, and a promise that they are true, and the basis of the contract, can escape from the consequences of his negligence by saying that the person he asked to fill it up for him is the agent of the person to whom the proposal is addressed.
>
> Applying the principle to this case as I do, I cannot escape the conclusion that this appeal must be allowed...

AVOIDANCE

Under the general law of insurance, an insurer can avoid a policy if he proves that there has been misrepresentation or concealment of a material fact by the insured.

Avoidance is the appropriate remedy for material misrepresentation in relation to marine and non-marine contracts of insurance.[285]

It may be said that a deliberate concealment of facts may amount to fraudulent non-disclosure. However the court in *HIH Casualty and General Insurance Limited and others (Respondents) v Chase Manhattan Bank (Appellants) and others, HIH Casualty and General Insurance Limited and others (Appellants) v Chase Manhattan Bank (Respondents) and others (First Appeal) HIH Casualty and General Insurance Limited and others (Appellants) v Chase Manhattan Bank (Respondents) and others (Second Appeal) (Conjoined appeals) (supra)* recognised the difficulty of ascertaining the causes or motives to determine whether a non-disclosure was a fraudulent non-disclosure:

> The term has never been defined. Sometimes it is referred to as a deliberate concealment: but I am by no means sure that the two can be equated. A matter may be deliberately concealed in the honest but mistaken belief that it is not relevant or material or that enquiry of it has been waived. There may be nothing dishonest in that, but *ex hypothesi* the remedy of avoidance remains. In other circumstances, outside the insurance context a deliberate concealment might be described as dishonest, or at any rate extremely unattractive, and yet, in the absence of any duty to speak, cannot be additionally castigated and remedied as fraudulent. No authority has been cited for a definition of fraudulent non-disclosure: and the absence of such authority in my judgment is not a merely collateral matter but intimately connected with the current problem of asking whether it makes sense to distinguish between fraudulent and non-fraudulent non-disclosure. I am doubtful that it is. No case has been cited in which the distinction has been material to any remedy or absence of remedy under an insurance contract.
>
> 166. On the other hand a distinction is sometimes drawn by the policy itself. Thus in *Arab Bank Plc 'v Zurich Insurance Co* [1999] 1 Lloyd's Rep 262 there was an 'Innocent Non-disclosure' clause

---

[285] Arnould, Law of Marine Insurance and Average, 16th edition, Vol. 2 p.62.

which excluded the insurer's right to avoid for non-disclosure or misrepresentation where the assured could establish that 'such alleged non-disclosure, misrepresentation or untrue statement was innocent and free of any fraudulent conduct or intent to deceive'. So there the clause itself distinguished on the basis of 'fraudulent conduct or intent to deceive'. It would seem that dishonesty rather than deliberateness was the test. In the absence of express language, however, I know of no authority which requires a distinction between the possible causes of non-disclosure.

167. In saying that I am conscious that in *Carter v Boehm* itself Lord Mansfield does seem to have considered that there was a difference between that concealment which the duty of good faith prohibited and mere silence ('*Aliud est celare; aliud tacere...*'). As a result non-disclosure in the insurance context in the early years was referred to as 'concealment', and the doctrine has sometimes been viewed and explained as constructive fraud. However, Lord Mansfield was seeking to propound a doctrine of good faith which would extend throughout the law of contract, and in that respect his view did not bear fruit. Where, however, in the insurance context it put down firm roots, it came to be seen as a doctrine which went much further than the antithesis of fraud, and, as it has come to be developed, 'non-disclosure will in a substantial proportion of cases be the result of an innocent mistake' (*Pan Atlantic Insurance Co Ltd 'v Pine Top Insurance Co Ltd* [1995] 1 AC 501 at 549D (per Lord Mustill).

168. In sum, I do not think that, in the absence of express language, any line is to be drawn between the various possible causes of or motives for non-disclosure. It is not in this way that the distinction is to be drawn. The question to my mind is whether a non-disclosure can support a claim in fraud, with its remedies in damages and/or rescission: either because on analysis it amounts or gives rise to a fraudulent misrepresentation or perchance for any other reason. Aikens J has held in effect, for the purposes of preliminary issue two, that only misrepresentation, and not non-disclosure, can give a remedy in damages for fraud, and there

has been no appeal from that conclusion. In any event I would respectfully disagree with him about the need to distinguish between the causes of non-disclosure for the purposes of preliminary issue one. If a distinction is drawn by contract, then effect will have to be given to that distinction according to its terms (cf *Arab Bank v Zurich Insurance*). In the absence of such contractual provision, however, I do not think that the law has so far equipped itself to mark out the fine lines which would have to be drawn between the various degrees of culpable non-disclosure.

169. If that is right, does it affect the attitude to be taken to misrepresentation? Having paused to consider the question, my conclusion is, No. Where misrepresentation is concerned, it is not merely a question of seeking to distinguish between various ways in which the duty of good faith can be broken. If a misrepresentation is fraudulent, the common law always gave a right of rescission and the tort of deceit remains with its remedy in damages. In my judgment, the exclusion of liability for breach of the duty of good faith is one thing; the exclusion of liability to pay damages for breach of any applicable common law duty of care or of the statutory duty under section 2(1) of the Misrepresentation Act is another thing; but apart from all of that, the exclusion of the common law remedies for fraud is yet something else. Fraud remains a thing apart. In my judgment, in the absence of express language covering fraud, those remedies for fraud have not been excluded. It follows that to the extent that fraud would have given a remedy under the common law it has not been excluded, either from phrase 7, or from phrase 8. In such a case, the insurers can rescind and/or claim damages in tort under the common law, even though any remedy pursuant to the duty of good faith may have been excluded: see Pan Atlantic at 543F/545B and section 91(2) of the MIA 1906.

170. It follows that on points (2) and (3) above in relation to phrase 7, and in relation to the judge's limitation of phrase 8 to an exclusion of innocent non-disclosure alone, Chase's appeal succeeds in large part. It fails only to the extent that anything in Schedules 2 or 3 can support a remedy at common law in fraud.

The remedy of avoidance for non-disclosure has its critics. In *Kausar v Eagle Star Insurance Co* [2000] Lloyd's IR 154, Mr Justice Colman stated that "avoidance for non-disclosure is a drastic remedy. It enables the insurer to disclaim liability after, and not before, he has discovered that the risk turns out to be a bad one; it leaves the insured without the protection which he thought he had contracted and paid for. Of course, there are occasions where a dishonest insured meets his just desserts if his insurance is avoided; and the insurer is justly relieved of liability. I do not say that non-disclosure operates only in cases of dishonesty. But I do consider that there should be some restraint in the operation of the doctrine. Avoidance for honest non-disclosure should be confined to plain cases".

DUTY OF DISCLOSURE

Duty of Good Faith

Fiduciary Duties

Renewal of Policy and Material Non-Disclosure

Mutual Duty

- Extent of Duty

- Statutory Requirement

- Waiver

- Truth of Statement Clause

Disclosure of Material Facts

Non-Disclosure

Non-Disclosure and Misrepresentation

- Fraudulent Misrepresentation

Inducement

Onus

Effect of Non-Disclosure

Incontestability Clause

Proposal Form

Agent

Basis Clause

Avoidance

CHAPTER 5

FRAUD

Fraud unravels all: *fraus omnia corrumpit*. It also reflects the practical basis of commercial intercourse. Once fraud is proven, "it vitiates judgments, contracts and all transactions whatsoever".[286]

Lord Sumption SCJ in *Prest v Prest and others* [2013] 4 ALL ER 673, SC, had occasion to refer to *Lazarus Estates Ltd v Beasley* in relation to the basis of legal relationships. His Lordship stated:

> The law defines the incidents of most legal relationships between persons (natural or artificial) on the fundamental assumption that their dealings are honest. The same legal incidents will not necessarily apply if they are not. The principle was stated in its most absolute form by Denning LJ in a famous *dictum* in *Lazarus Estates Ltd v Beasley* [1956] 1 All ER 341 at 345, [1956] 1 QB 702 at 712:
>
>> No court in this land will allow a person to keep an advantage which he has obtained by fraud. No judgment of a court, no order of a Minister, can be allowed to stand if it has been obtained by fraud. Fraud unravels everything. The court is careful not to find fraud unless it is distinctly pleaded and proved; but once it is proved, it vitiates judgments, contracts and all transactions whatsoever.

---

[286] *Lazarus Estates Ltd v Beasley* [1956] 1 QB 702 at 712.

The principle is mainly familiar in the context of contracts and other consensual arrangements, in which the effect of fraud is to vitiate consent so that the transaction becomes voidable *ab initio*. But it has been applied altogether more generally, in cases which can be rationalised only on grounds of public policy, for example to justify setting aside a public act such as a judgment, which is in no sense consensual, a jurisdiction which has existed since at least 1775: *Duchess of Kingston's Case* [1776] 2 Smith LC 644 at 646, 651, or to abrogate a right derived from a legal status, such as marriage: *R v Secretary of State for the Home Dept, ex p Puttick* [1981] 1 All ER 776, [1981] QB 767, or to disapply a statutory time bar which on the face of the statute applies: *Welwyn Hatfield BC v Secretary of State for Communities and Local Government* [2011] UKSC 15; [2011] 4 All ER 851; [2011] 2 AC 304. These decisions (and there are others) illustrate a broader principle governing cases in which the benefit of some apparently absolute legal principle has been obtained by dishonesty. The authorities show that there are limited circumstances in which the law treats the use of a company as a means of evading the law as dishonest for this purpose.

(19) The question is heavily burdened by authority, much of it characterised by incautious *dicta* and inadequate reasoning. I propose, first, to examine those cases which seek to rationalise the case law in terms of general principle, and then to look at a number of cases in which the court has been thought, rightly or wrongly, to have pierced the corporate veil in order to identify the critical features of these cases which enabled them to do so.

Lord Bingham also reiterated the view of the courts in *HIH Casualty and General Insurance Ltd v Chase Manhattan Bank* [2003] UKHL 6 where it was said:

> Parties entering into a commercial contract will no doubt recognize and accept the risk of errors and omissions in the preceding negotiations, even negligent errors and omissions. But each party will assume the honesty and

>good faith of the other; absent such an assumption they would not deal.

The law relating to fraud in insurance claims must begin with the examination of the concept of fraud. In essence, fraud involves a wilful misrepresentation. It is an intentional act by way of documents or words, a course of conduct positively intended to induce reliance on such misrepresentation. The state of mind of the representor is crucial to the determination of the tort of deceit.

There must be intentional fraud for liability to be incurred. There must be proof of such course of conduct in executing that intent, i.e., the intent to deceive. There must be convincing evidence of a specific intent to deceive.

The false misrepresentation must cause harm or loss to the representee. There must be a causal link between the misrepresentation and the harm.

The ambit of fraud is wide and "the range of fraud is infinite" and this is one of the reasons why there has been considerable debate about what constitutes "fraud" as a matter of English law. In *Cavell USA, Inc and another v Seaton Insurance Co and another* [2009] EWCA Civ 1363, Longmore LJ traced the early part of the legal debate pertaining to what is "fraud" and stated:

>Thirdly, as I have already observed, the concept of fraud is notoriously difficult to define. In his letter to Lord Kames of 30 June 1759 (which the editors, if not the original author, of Snell on Equity, have done well to preserve, see 25th edition 1960 ed Megarry and Baker p 496 and 31st edition ed McGhee para 8-01) Lord Hardwicke said:
>
>>Fraud is infinite, and were a Court of Equity once to lay down rules, how far they would go, and no further, in extending their relief against it, or to define strictly the species or evidence of it, the jurisdiction would be cramped and perpetually eluded by new schemes which the fertility of man's invention would continue.

Twenty-three years after the fusion of law and equity Lord Macnaghten agreed:

> Fraud is infinite in variety: sometimes it is audacious and unblushing; sometimes it pays a sort of homage to virtue, and then it is modest and retiring; it would be honesty itself if it could only afford it, see *Reddaway v Banham* [1886] AC 199, 221.

One can only reflect how brave it was of Gross J to volunteer to define the phrase "claims in fraud" and track a path which Lord Hardwicke and Lord Macnaghten feared to tread. It is perhaps not surprising that he felt that the common law of the tort of deceit was the only rock to which he could safely cling.

[16] Other great judges have had similar difficulties in defining fraud. In *Welham v DPP* [1961] AC 103, 133, [1960] 1 All ER 805, [1960] 2 WLR 669, Lord Denning drew a distinction between "intent to deceive" and "intent to defraud" by saying that the former conveyed the element of deceit which induced a state of mind "without the element of fraud which induces a course of action or inaction". When he came to consider a person's entitlement to trial by jury on the ground that "a charge of fraud against that party was in issue" pursuant to s 6(1) (a) of the UK Administrative of Justice (Miscellaneous Provisions) Act 1933, he said:

> 'Fraud' in ordinary speech means the using of false representations to obtain an unjust advantage . . . Likewise in law 'fraud' is proved when it is shown that a false representation has been made knowingly or without belief in its truth, or recklessly, careless whether it be true or false, see *Derry v Peek* per Lord Herschell.

> He concluded in *Barclays Bank v Cole* [1967] 2 QB 738, [1966] 3 All ER 948, [1967] 2 WLR 166, that a Claimant alleging robbery did not make a "charge of fraud" because robbery did not "involve a false representation".

This equation of fraud and the tort of deceit was much relied on by Mr Hofmeyr in his submissions in support of the judge.

[17] Diplock LJ thought that the phrase "a charge of fraud" as used in the 1933 Act had had a special meaning as a term of art for over a hundred years. He cited the 3rd edition of Bullen & Leake and said:

> 'fraud' in civil actions at common law, whether as a cause of action or as a defence, has meant an intentional representation (or, in some cases, concealment) of fact made by one party with the intention of inducing another party to act on it which does induce the other party to act on it to his detriment.

This is, of course, the language of the common law tort of deceit, although the reference to concealment shows that silence can sometimes be enough. When, however, the House of Lords had to consider whether deceit was a necessary ingredient of the criminal offence of conspiracy to defraud, it was held in *Scott v Commissioner of Police for the Metropolis* [1975] AC 819, [1974] 3 All ER 1032, [1974] 3 WLR 741, that the criminal offence did not necessarily involve deceit. Lord Diplock (as he had by then become) said at p 841:

> The intended means by which the purpose [of the conspiracy to defraud] is to be achieved must be dishonest. They need not constitute the civil tort of deceit. Dishonesty of any kind is enough.

Fraud is defined in Osborne Concise Law Dictionary (8th Ed), at p 152 as "the obtaining of a material advantage by unfair or wrongful means; it involves obliquity. It involves the making of a false representation knowingly, or without belief in its truth, or recklessly. If the fraud causes injury, the deceived party may claim damages for the tort of deceit. A contract obtained by fraud is voidable at the option of the injured party. Conspiracy to defraud remains a common law offence, the *mens rea* of which has been defined as to cause the victim economic loss by depriving him of some property or right corporeal or incorporeal, to which he is or would or might become entitled to, per Lord Diplock in *R v Scott* [1975] AC 814. Certain other frauds are likewise criminal offences, e.g., under the Prevention of Fraud (Investments) Act 1958".

What is fraud? As the range of fraud is infinite, it is impossible to lay down a complete and comprehensive definition of it. Examples of actual fraud may be found in decided cases. Actual fraud is where one person causes pecuniary injury to another by intentionally misrepresenting or concealing a material fact which from their mutual position he was bound to explain or disclose. If a person by intentional misrepresentation or concealment of a material fact, peculiarly within his knowledge, induces another person to enter into a contract, conveyance or similar transaction with him, which he would not have entered into had he known the truth, the contract or other transaction is fraudulent.[287]

Section 17 of the Contracts Act 1950 (Malaysia) recognises the various shades of fraud by defining it as follows:

> Fraud includes any of the following acts committed by a party to a contract, or with his connivance, or by his agent, with intent to deceive another party thereto or his agent, or to induce him to enter into the contract:
>
> (a) the suggestion, as to a fact, of that which is not true by one who does not believe it to be true;
>
> (b) the active concealment of a fact by one having knowledge of belief of the fact;
>
> (c) a promise made without any intention of performing it;
>
> (d) any other act fitted to deceive; and

---

[287] Jowitt's Dictionary of English Law 2nd Edn.

(e) any such act or omission as the law specially declares to be fraudulent.

Explanation - Mere silence as to facts likely to affect the willingness of a person to enter into a contract is not fraud, unless the circumstances of the case are such that, regard being had to them, it is the duty of the person keeping silence to speak, or unless his silence is, in itself, equivalent to speech.

Fraud is conduct either by letter or words, which induces the other person or authority to take a definite determinative stand as a response to the conduct of the former, either by word or letter. It vitiates every solemn act. Fraud and justice never dwell together. A collusion or conspiracy with a view to deprive the rights of others in relation to a property would render the transaction *void ab initio*. Fraud and deception are synonymous. Although in a given case a deception may not amount to fraud, fraud is anathema to all equitable principles and any affair tainted with fraud cannot be perpetuated or saved by the application of any equitable doctrine including *res judicata*.[288]

Ian HC Chin J held in the case of *BP (Sabah) Sdn Bhd v Syarikat Jubrin Enterprise & Anor* [1996] MLJU 449; [1997] 1 LNS 354 that:

> Fraud implies some base conduct and moral turpitude and a person is taken to have acted fraudulently or with intent to defraud if he acts with the intention that some person be deceived and by means of such deception that either an advantage should accrue to him or injury, loss or detriment should befall some other person. That is known as 'fraud' or 'fraudulently'.

Fraud is 'a serious allegation which must be clearly substantiated and must not be confused with carelessness, however gross that may be'.[289]

Fraud is generally subjective and requires an intention to defraud, as well as an intention to withhold information or mislead. If relevant facts are

---

[288] Per Sinha J in *Ram Chandra Singh v Savitri Devi & Ors* (2003) 8 SCC 319.

[289] MacGillvray on Insurance Law at 16-002.

withheld or misrepresented without that fraudulent intent e.g., on the grounds that the insured does not believe that the information would be relevant to the insured's decision, then fraud is not established.[290]

A sham is not fraud. The High Court in *Kawasaki Kisen Kaisha Ltd v Owners of the Ship or Vessel 'Able Lieutenant'* [2002] 6 MLJ 433 noted that the insured defendant's attempt to equate sham with fraud was a baseless attempt to raise the standard of proof. There Zulkefli J stated:

> A sham transaction in the context of the present case means not a genuine sale and not an arm's length transaction but a commercial arrangement. It may even be called a sale of convenience. All cases involving sham transactions such as *The 'Tjaskemolen'*, *The 'Saudi Prince'*, *The 'Aventicum'* and the Malaysian case of *The 'Loon Chong'*, sham was proven on a balance of probabilities. In another Malaysian case, *The 'Sino Glory'* [1997] 4 AMR 3694, sham was also proved on a balance of probabilities.

TORT OF DECEIT

The term common law fraud is often used to describe the tort of deceit, or the making of fraudulent misrepresentations. The tort of deceit is said to encompass cases where the defendant knowingly or recklessly makes a false statement, with the intention that another will rely on it to his or her detriment.[291]

In order to sustain an action in deceit, firstly, there must be proof of fraud and nothing short of that will suffice. Secondly, fraud is proven when it is shown that a false representation has been made (1) knowingly, (2) without belief in its truth, or (3) recklessly, careless whether it be true or false.[292]

---

[290] See Insurance Law in Australia, Sutton, 3rd edition, par 3.138 and fn 617. See also *Twenty-First Maylux Pty Ltd v Mercantile Mutual Insurance (Australia) Ltd* [1990] VR 919 at 925.

[291] *Takako Sakao (f) v Ng Pek Yuen (f) & Anor* [2009] 6 MLJ 751 (FC).

[292] *Derry v Peek* (1889) LR 14 App Cas 337 at 374.

Lord Nicholls in *Royal Brunei Airlines Sdn Bhd v Tan* [1995] 2 AC 378 at p 389 said:

> In most situations there is little difficulty in identifying how an honest person would behave. Honest people do not intentionally deceive others to their detriment. Honest people do not knowingly take others' property. Unless there is a very good and compelling reason, an honest person does not participate in a transaction if he knows it involves a misapplication of trust assets to the detriment of the beneficiaries. Nor does an honest person in such a case deliberately shut his eyes and ears, or deliberately not ask questions, lest he learn something which he would rather not know, and then proceed regardless....The standard of what constitutes honest conduct is not subjective. Honesty is not an optional scale, with higher or lower values according to the moral standards of each individual.

False representation requires a discussion on the concept of dishonesty. Whenever a person causes another to act on a false representation which the maker himself does not believe to be true, the maker is said to have committed a fraud. It is a simple statement of the law.[293] There is an objective standard and a subjective standard test to be applied in determining dishonesty. In *Twinsectra Ltd v Yardley* [2002] 2 AC 164, Lord Hutton described it as the "combined test". Having referred to the purely subjective standard (the "Robin Hood test") and the purely objective standard, Lord Hutton stated at p172C-D:

> Thirdly, there is a standard which combines an objective test and a subjective test and which requires that before there can be a finding of dishonesty, it must be established that the defendant's conduct was dishonest by the ordinary standards of reasonable and honest people and that he himself realised that by those standards his conduct was dishonest. I will term this the "combined test".

---

[293] *Double Acres Sdn Bhd v Tiarasetia Sdn Bhd* [2000] 7 CLJ 550.

The test has two distinct limbs, each of which must be satisfied before there can be any finding of dishonesty. The combined test is the relevant test for determining if there is a fraudulent claim or the use of fraudulent means or devices but it is however subject to two main points.

Firstly, motive is irrelevant, i.e., a person who acts fraudulently cannot say by way of defence that he thought he was justified in acting fraudulently because, for example, he had been treated badly by the other party, and secondly, if the relevant misrepresentation was made "recklessly, careless whether it be true or false". A person who makes a false statement recklessly, careless of whether it is true or false can have no honest belief in the truth of what he states.

Mr Justice Elder in *Aviva Insurance Limited v Roger George Brown* [2011] EWHC 362 (QB) went on to state:

> 257. In effect, recklessness is a species of dishonest knowledge, for in both cases there is an absence of belief in truth. It is for that reason that there is "proof of fraud" in the cases of both knowledge and recklessness. This was stressed by Bowen LJ in *Angus v Clifford* [1891] 2 Ch 449 where he said (at 471):
>
>> Not caring, in that context, did not mean not taking care, it meant indifference to the truth, the moral obliquity of which consists in a wilful disregard of the importance of truth, and unless you keep it clear that that is the true meaning of the term, you are constantly in danger of confusing the evidence from which the inference of dishonesty in the mind is to be drawn - evidence which consists in a great many cases of gross want of caution - with the inference of fraud, or of dishonesty itself, which has to be drawn after you have weighed all the evidence.
>
> 258. And in *Armstong v Strain* [1951] 1 TLR 856 at 871 Devlin J, after a full citation of passages in earlier authorities which stress the need for dishonesty (also called actual fraud, *mens rea*, or moral delinquency), said this about the necessary knowledge:

> A man may be said to know a fact when once he has been told it and pigeon-holed it somewhere in his brain where it is more or less accessible in case of need. In another sense of the word, a man knows a fact only when he is fully conscious of it. For an action of deceit there must be knowledge in the narrower sense; and conscious knowledge of falsity must always amount to wickedness and dishonesty. When Judges say, therefore, that wickedness and dishonesty must be present, they are not requiring a new ingredient for the tort of deceit so much as describing the sort of knowledge which is necessary.

259. Moreover, whether it is in the matter of identifying the relevant misstatement or in the finding of a dishonest mind, it is necessary to bear in mind the heightened burden of proof which bears on the claimant, as discussed in cases from *Hornal v Neuberger Products Ltd* [1957] 1 QB 247 to *In re H (Minors)* [1996] AC 563. In the latter case Lord Nicholls of Birkenhead said this (at 586):

> Built into the preponderance of probability standard is a generous degree of flexibility in respect of the seriousness of the allegation. Although the result is much the same, this does not mean that where a serious allegation is in issue the standard of proof required is higher. It means only that the inherent probability or improbability of an event is itself a matter to be taken into account when weighing the probabilities and deciding whether, on balance, the event occurred. The more improbable the event, the stronger must be the evidence that it did occur before, on the balance of probability, its occurrence will be established. Ungoed-Thomas J. expressed this neatly in *In re Dellow's Trusts* [1964] 1 WLR 451, 455: 'The more serious the allegation the more cogent is the evidence required to overcome the unlikelihood of what is alleged and thus to prove it.'

70. In considering an issue as to what constituted a fraudulent misrepresentation in a claim for deceit, those passages were cited by Flaux J in *Grosvenor Casinos Ltd v National Bank of Abu Dhabi* [2008] 2 Lloyd's Rep 1 at para 106 and, as stated there by Flaux J, the Kriti Palm is a salutary reminder to any judge as to the importance of not confusing fraud with incompetence, even if it amounts to gross negligence and as to the importance of being satisfied to the necessary heightened standard of proof that what is involved is dishonesty. I agree.

There must be conscious and deliberate dishonesty.[294] Where the author of a document has through carelessness or ignorance failed to appreciate the meaning which others are likely to take from the document and in consequence, the facts alleged in the document prove to be false, it seems inappropriate to describe the author as "dishonest".[295]

Deceit – Proof of Fraud

In an action for deceit, the plaintiff must prove actual fraud. Fraud is proven when it is shown that a false representation has been made knowingly, or without belief in its truth, or recklessly, without caring whether it be true or false.[296] A false statement, made through carelessness and without reasonable ground for believing it to be true, may be evidence of fraud but does not necessarily amount to fraud. Such a statement, if made in the honest belief that it is true, is not fraudulent and does not render the person making it liable to an action for deceit.[297] In *King v Victor Parsons & Co* [1973] 1 WLR 29, it was held that fraud was not confined to the common law sense of fraud or deceit. Lord Denning MR said at p 33:

---

[294] *Ampthill Peerage, The* [1977] AC 547; [1976] 2 All ER 411 (HL) per Lord Wilberforce.

[295] *Martin v Ryan* [1990] 2 NZLR 209.

[296] *Derry v Peek (supra).*

[297] *Ibid*

The word 'fraud' here is not used in the common law sense. It is used in the equitable sense to denote conduct by the defendant or his agent such that it would be 'against conscience' for him to avail himself of the lapse of time. The cases show that, if a man knowingly commits a wrong (such as digging underground another man's coal); or a breach of contract (such as putting in bad foundations to a house), in such circumstances that it is unlikely to be found out for many a long day, he cannot rely on the Statute of Limitations as a bar to the claim: see *Bulli Coal Mining Co v Osborne* [1899] AC 351 and *Applegate v Moss* [1971] 1 QB 406. In order to show that he 'concealed' the right of action 'by fraud', it is not necessary to show that he took active steps to conceal his wrong-doing or breach of contract. It is sufficient that he knowingly committed it and did not tell the owner anything about it. He did the wrong or committed the breach secretly. By saying nothing he keeps it secret. He conceals the right of action. He conceals it by 'fraud' as those words have been interpreted in the cases.

Megaw LJ at p 36 said:

The defendants say that 'ought to know' [in our s 29 of the Limitation Act] is not enough. I agree. I do not think that the cases go so far; or that, at least as a general principle and in the absence of very special circumstances, the meaning of 'concealed by fraud' should be extended to cover a case where the defendant, whether himself or by persons whose knowledge should be treated as his knowledge, did not know the fact or facts which constituted the cause of action against him.

Test for Fraud

The test for fraud is "whether the representor had or had not an honest belief in the truth of the representation as he understood it".[298] In *Martin v Ryan* [1990] 2 NZLR 209, Fisher J went on to state:

---

[298] Spencer Bower and Turner, The Law of Actionable Misrepresentation (3rd ed, 1974) p 117.

Secondly, I think that before a misrepresentation attributable to recklessness could amount to fraud, the representor would have to have specifically adverted to the subject of truth or falsity and made the deliberate decision to allow the misrepresentation to be made, notwithstanding his knowledge that it might be incorrect. Counsel referred me to a number of authorities, on the point, most of which are discussed in Spencer Bower and Turner at pp 115-117. ...For myself I am not sure that it is sufficient to stop at that point. For example, in the present case, Ms X did not have any honest belief in the truth of the statement in her letter as to the proposed settlement date – rather, she says that she simply overlooked the fact that the statement was contained in the letter at all. In that regard I find more helpful the statement in Salmond on Torts (17th ed, 1977) at p 390:

> It is sometimes said that it is sufficient for liability that the statement should be made recklessly. The term recklessly, however, must here be taken to be used to indicate the absence of any genuine belief – the presence of conscious ignorance of the truth of the matter. Recklessness, in the sense of gross negligence, is no ground of liability.

Similarly, Fleming in The Law of Torts (7th ed, 1987) at pp 601-602 states:

> Even recklessness in the sense of gross negligence will not suffice, unless the defendant is consciously indifferent to the truth and thus lacks an honest belief... So, where the representor deliberately shuts his eyes to the fact, purposely abstains from investigation, or consciously lacks sufficient information to support an assertion couched in positive and unqualified form, the conclusion is open that his belief is not really honest.

Those statements seem to me to more usefully reflect dicta such as that of Bowen LJ in *Angus v Clifford* [1891] 2 Ch 449 (CA) at p 471 that for present purposes fraud means 'a wilful disregard of the importance of truth' and that of Lord Herschell in *Derry v Peek* at p 376 when he said:

> '.. if I thought that a person making a false statement had shut his eyes to the facts, or purposely abstained from inquiring into them, I should hold that honest belief was absent, and that he was just as fraudulent as if he had knowingly stated that which was false'.

The essential element seems to lie in the words "conscious", "deliberately", "purposely" and "wilful" in the above statements. These indicate that the representor must have turned his mind to the subject of the truth or falsity of the representation and then made the deliberate decision to allow the representation to be made, in the knowledge that it might not necessarily be correct. I do not think that it is a question of starting with the false representation and then going immediately to the question whether or not the representor had an honest belief in its truth. Rather, one needs to begin with the mind of the representor and then ask whether he or she had adverted to the subject of truth or falsity or risk of falsity at all. Only if that subject had been addressed by the representor could the question of honest belief, or lack of it, arise.

REPRESENTATIONS

Some definitions that have been given to the word representation and misrepresentation, are set out below: -

- A representation may be as to a fact, in which case it must be substantially correct, or as to a matter of expectation or belief, in which case it must be made in good faith, but a representation may be withdrawn or corrected before the contract is concluded.[299]

---

[299] Section 20(3), (4), (5), (6): *HIH Casualty and General Insurance Limited and others (Respondents) v Chase Manhattan Bank (Appellants) and others, HIH Casualty and General Insurance Limited and others (Appellants) v Chase Manhattan Bank (Respondents) and others (First Appeal) HIH Casualty and General Insurance Limited and others (Appellants) v Chase Manhattan Bank*

- A representation is a statement of fact, whilst a misrepresentation is simply a representation that is untrue. A fraudulent misrepresentation is a false statement which, when made, the representor did not honestly believe it to be true.[300]

- The traditional rule is that a representation must be a statement of fact, past or present, as distinct from a statement of opinion, or of intention, or of law. A mere statement of opinion, which proves to be unfounded, will not be treated as a misrepresentation, nor will a simple statement of intention which is not put into effect; for as a general rule, these cannot be regarded as representations of fact.[301]

- A representation is a statement of fact made by one party to the contract (the representor) to the other (the representee) which, while not forming a term of the contract, is one of the reasons that induces the representee to enter into the contract. A misrepresentation is simply a representation that is untrue. The representor's state of mind and degree of carefulness are not relevant to classifying a representation as a misrepresentation but only to determining the type of misrepresentation, if any.[302]

- A representation is a statement which relates to a matter of fact, which may be a past or present fact. But a statement as to a man's intention, or as to his own state of mind, is no less a statement of fact and a misstatement of the state of a man's mind is a misrepresentation of fact.[303]

(Respondents) and others (Second Appeal) (Conjoined appeals) [2001] 2 Lloyd's Rep 483) (CA).

[300] Mohd Ghazali J in *Tay Tho Bok & Anor v Segar Oil Palm Estate Sdn Bhd* [1996] 3 MLJ 181; [1996] 1 LNS 60; [1997] 4 AMR 3541; [1996] 4 MLRH 452.

[301] Chitty on Contracts (27th Ed) Vol 1 (Para 6-004).

[302] Cheshire, Fifoot and Furmston's Law of Contract, Singapore and Malaysian Ed (at p 407).

[303] Per Bowen LJ in *Edgington v Fitzmaurice* (1885) 29 Ch D 459 at 483.

- A representation is a statement made by, or on behalf of, one person to, or with the intention that it shall come to the notice of, another person which relates, by way of affirmation, denial, description, or otherwise, to a matter of fact. A "matter of fact" means either an existing fact or thing, or a past event.[304]

- To be actionable in law, a "representation" must generally be in respect of an ascertainable "fact" rather than a mere matter of "opinion" because the representee is not justified in placing reliance upon an opinion.[305]

- A representation made by the insured is fraudulent if he knows it to be false and makes it in order that the insurers may act upon it.[306]

Pre-contractual statements or representations are divided into either: (a) representations that do not induce the making of a contract which are called "'mere representations'"; or (b) representations that induce the making of a contract. The former are not ordinarily actionable because the law treats them as purely harmless. The latter type may however give rise to liability. Gopal Sri Ram JCA in *Abdul Razak Datuk Abu Samah v Shah Alam Properties Sdn Bhd and Anor Appeal* [1999] 2 MLJ 500; [1999] 3 CLJ 231 (CA) said:

> Whether a particular statement made in the course of negotiations leading to the making of a contract is a representation or a term depends upon the intention of the parties and is to be deduced from the totality of the evidence.

---

[304] Spencer-Bower and Turner, in The Law of Actionable Misrepresentation (3rd Ed. 1974), at p. 3.

[305] *Hinchey v Gonda* [1955] OWN 125 at 128 (H.C.J.).

[306] Raoul Colinvaux in 'The Law of Insurance' (5th encl at p. 167).

False Representation

A representation is false when there is a substantial discrepancy between it and any material fact which it expressly or impliedly purports to state. A discrepancy is substantial when it would be deemed material by any normal representee in the circumstances of the individual case.[307]

In an action for deceit, it is not enough to establish a false representation. It must also be proven that the representation was made with knowledge that it was false or without belief in its truth.[308]

The tort of deceit is complete only when the representation is acted upon. Where there is an interval between the time when the representation is made and the time when it is acted on, and the representation relates to an existing state of things, the representation is deemed to be repeated throughout the interval. Hence if it is false to the maker's knowledge at the time when it is relied on, there will be a deceit at that time. Thus if, during the time between the making of the representation and the insured claimant acting upon it, the insurer defendant discovers it to be false or circumstances change to his knowledge so that it is now untrue, liability may be incurred.[309]

MISREPRESENTATIONS

It is also well settled that misrepresentation itself amounts to fraud. Indeed, innocent misrepresentation may also give rise to a claim or relief against fraud. A fraudulent misrepresentation is called deceit and consists of leading a man into damage, by wilfully or recklessly causing him to believe and act on a falsehood. It is a fraud in law if a party makes representations which he knows to be false, and injury ensues therefrom,

---

[307] Spencer Bower & Turner, The Law of Actionable Misrepresentation (3rd Ed) p 5.

[308] *Raiffeisen Zentralbank Osterreich AG v Archer Daniels Midland Co and Ors* [2006] SGHC 182; [2007] 1 SLR 196.

[309] Clerk & Lindsell on Torts (Anthony M Dugdale & Michael A Jones Gen Eds) (Sweet & Maxwell, 19th Ed, 2006) at para 18-16.

although the motive from which the representations originated may not have been bad. An act of fraud is always viewed seriously by the courts.[310]

A misrepresentation is a representation that is untrue. It is a false statement made by one contracting party to the other, either before or at the time of contracting, on which that other party has relied on, in entering into the contract. If the representor falsely states his intention, then he has falsely misrepresented the fact.[311]

The Concise Oxford Dictionary, 9th ed. (Oxford: Clarendon Press, 1995) at p.482 defines the noun "fact" as: (1) a thing that is known to have occurred, to exist, or to be true, (2) a datum of experience, (3) (usu. in pl.) an item of verified information, a piece of evidence, (4) truth, reality or (5) a thing assumed as the basis for argument or inference.

Any behaviour, by words or conduct, is sufficient to be a misrepresentation if it is such as to mislead the other party about the existence or extent of any exemption relating to it. If it conveys a false impression, that is enough. If the false impression is created knowingly, it is a fraudulent misrepresentation; if it is created unwittingly, it is innocent misrepresentation; but either is sufficient to disentitle the creator of it to the benefit of the exemption.[312]

A misrepresentation may be defined as an unambiguous, false statement of fact which is addressed to the party misled and which materially induces the contract to be entered into.

---

[310] *Ram Chandra Singh v Savitri Devi & Ors* (2003) 8 SCC 319.(See also the case of *Muhammad Zaihasri Hassan v Pacific & Orient Insurance Co Bhd* [2019] 3 CLJ p 530.)

[311] *Travelsight (M) Sdn Bhd & Anor v Atlas Corp Sdn Bhd* [2003] 6 MLJ 658; [2003] 6 CLJ 344.

[312] *Curtis v Chemical Cleaning and Dyeing Co* [1951] 1 KB 805, 807 per Lord Denning LJ.

Misrepresentation means a false representation of a statement or assertion, made by one party to the other.[313]

A representation is deemed to have been false and therefore a misrepresentation, if it was at the material date false in substance and in fact. For the purpose of determining whether there has or has not been a misrepresentation at all, the knowledge, belief, or other state of mind of the representor is immaterial, save in cases where the representation relates to the representor's state of mind; though his state of mind is of the utmost importance for the purpose of considering whether the misrepresentation was fraudulent.[314]

Where there is a misrepresentation, the nature of the misrepresentation has to be determined. On the facts in *Lie Kee Pong v Chin Chow Yoon & Anor* [1998] 3 SLR 92 for instance, Chao Hick Tin J was of the view that the misrepresentation in question was an innocent misrepresentation. It was held that the misrepresentation in that case was not fraudulent:

> I do not think in all the circumstances that the misrepresentation could be considered to be fraudulent, in the sense that it was made recklessly, without caring whether it was true or false. There may well be a degree of negligence. But there is nothing to suggest that he did not care what the truth was in giving the answer. In my view he gave what he honestly thought was the correct answer.

Where it has been found that there is a misrepresentation, the court must then go on to determine whether the misrepresentations and non-disclosures were fraudulent or negligent, or constituted a breach of contract. Another issue that must also be examined is whether the contract has effectively excluded the insurer defendant's liability to the insured plaintiff.[315]

---

[313] Pullock & Mulia, 'Indian Contract, and Specific Relief Acts' 10th Edition at page 187.

[314] Halsbury's Laws of England, Third Ed., vol. 26. Para 1556

[315] *Opron Construction Co Ltd (plaintiff) v Her Majesty the Queen in Right of Alberta (1994)* 151 A.R. 241.

Opinion

A mere statement of opinion that is proven to be unfounded, is not a misrepresentation. Statements of opinion or intention may not amount to representations, where the maker of the statement has no real knowledge or was simply passing on information.[316]

In *Ravichanthiran Ganesan v Percetakan Wawasan Maju Sdn Bhd & Ors* [2008] MLJU 0488, it was held that as the defendant was merely passing on information he had obtained from another party to the plaintiff, that in itself did not amount to misrepresentation.

Materiality of Representation

The "misrepresentation" is merely descriptive of a false pre-contractual statement that induces a contract or other transaction. A misrepresentation is innocent "where the representor believes his assertion to be true and consequently has no intention of deceiving the representee".[317] It is the state of mind of the representor that determines whether a "misrepresentation" is innocent or fraudulent. If the misrepresentation is made fraudulently, then the representee is entitled to rescission of the contract and to damages which directly flow from the fraudulent inducement.[318]

If the discrepancy between the facts as represented, and the facts as they exist, is such as would have reasonably influenced the mind of a normal representee in considering whether or not to alter his position as he did, the representation is false; otherwise, it is true. This is one way of stating the rule. Another more common form of stating it is to say that falsity in substance is, on the one hand, necessary, and, on the other, adequate, to establish misrepresentation; for "substance" is applied to those features

---

[316] Pullock & Mulla, 'Indian Contract, and Specific Relief Acts' 10th Edition at page 187.
[317] Cheshire & Fifoot, Law of Contract (6th Ed).
[318] Gopal Sri Ram JCA in *Sim Thong Realty Sdn Bhd v Teh Kim Dar Tee Kim* [2003] 3 MLJ 460.

in the statement which were intended to have, and did in fact have, an effect on the representee, or, in other words, which to the representee reasonably appeared to be material. [319]

In testing materiality, a court may consider the degree of interest which a plaintiff has shown on the subject of the representation. See *Seaton v Burnand* [1900] AC135.[320]

Falsification of Material Facts

Once the nature of the misrepresentation has been determined, then the next point to consider is, was it a material misrepresentation, and if so, was it relied upon. A representation is material when its tendency, or its natural and probable result, is to induce the representee to enter into the contract or transaction, which in fact he did enter into, or to otherwise alter his position in the manner in which he did.[321]

Cautionary language may negate the materiality of an alleged misrepresentation or omission, but it must be specific.[322]

"Operative Misrepresentation"

An operative misrepresentation is a false statement of existing or past fact, made by one party (the 'misrepresentor'), before or at the time of making the contract, addressed to the other party (the 'misrepresentee'), which induces the other party to enter into the contract.[323]

---

[319] Spencer Bower & Turner, The Law of Actionable Misrepresentation (3rd Ed) p 82.

[320] *Weiss et al v Schad et al* [1999] OTC 228.

[321] Spencer Bower and Turner, The Law of Actionable Misrepresentation (3rd Ed) at p 144.

[322] See *In Re Donald J. Trump Casino Securities Litigation ('Trump')* 7 F.3d 357 at 371 (3rd Cir.1993). See also *Douglas Kerr v Danier Leather Inc., Irving Wortsman, Jeffrey Wortsman and Bryan Tatoff* [2001] O.T.C. 181.

[323] Anson's Law of Contract (28th Ed, 2002) states at p 237.

Entire Agreement Clause and Misrepresentation

In Singapore, in the case of *Chuan Hup Marine Ltd v Sembawang Engineering Pte Ltd* [1995] 2 SLR 629, Selvam J determined that an entire agreement clause excluded any implied term, collateral warranty and misrepresentation.

One of the issues before V K Rajah JA in the Singapore Court of Appeal case of *Lee Chee Wei v Tan Hor Peow Victor and Others and Another Appeal* [2007] SGCA 22 [2007] 3 SLR 537, was whether or not an entire agreement clause can purport to exclude a claim in misrepresentation. There were differing judicial opinions on the subject.

In yet another Singapore case, *Exklusiv Auto Services Pte Ltd v Chan Yong Chua Eric* [1996] 1 SLR 433, Rajendran J considered (at 439, [21]) the status of an entire agreement clause (which in that case provided that "[t]his agreement when made shall supersede all terms and conditions previously agreed upon, whether in writing or otherwise, and the terms of this agreement shall not be varied or changed except by agreement in writing") and arrived at the following conclusion:

> In my view, the presence of exemption, limitation of liability or exclusion clauses (such as condition 5) do not have any special significance in considering the admissibility of oral evidence under the provisos to s 94. This is so for the simple reason that s 94 does not give any hallowed position to such clauses. So long as the requirements of the provisos to s 94 are complied with, oral evidence would be admissible whatever the written contract might provide.

The Singapore Court of Appeal did not agree with the above view of Rajendran J in *Exklusiv Auto Services*. In delivering the judgment of the court it was stated:

> With respect, we are unable to agree with these observations. There is certainly sometimes an inherent tension between the apparently uncomfortable co-existence of the statutorily encapsulated parol evidence rule and an entire agreement clause,

which is primarily a creature of contract incorporated with the consent of the parties. Rajendran J's dictum therefore, appears to stem from what he perceived as an unresolved conflict as to whether an entire agreement clause contractually operates 'to denude what would otherwise constitute a collateral warranty of legal effect' (*Intrepreneur Pub Co v East Crown Ltd*) or whether it 'renders inadmissible extrinsic evidence to prove terms other than those in the written contract, since the parties have by the clause expressed their intention that the document is to contain all the terms of the agreement' (Chitty on Contracts vol 1 (Sweet & Maxwell, 29th Ed, 2004) at para 12-104).

If one opts for the latter interpretation, then the entire agreement clause serves only to replicate the extrinsic (parol) evidence rule in a contractual form; such a formula would not preclude reliance on exceptions to the rule. Extrapolating from this, a collateral agreement which runs alongside the agreement neither contradicting nor varying it could be admissible in evidence. This possibly is what Rajendran J was alluding to.

The decision of the British Columbia Court of Appeal in *MacMillan v Kaiser Equipment Ltd* [2004] BCJ 969 (at [37]) provides considerable assistance in addressing and assessing the intricate relationship between such clauses and the parol evidence rule:

> Given the rule of construction that a court should strive to give effect to all the terms of an agreement, however, it is at least arguable that a provision such as [the entire agreement clause] must be intended to have a broader effect than the parol evidence rule would have by itself - otherwise, the clause would be redundant. Certainly, the wording used here was not limited to 'any agreement, representation or warranty that contradicts or varies' the terms of the written agreement - the clause stated that there were no collateral agreements between the parties, whether at variance with the written document or not. In practical terms, the obvious purpose of such a clause is to ensure that parties who have conducted

oral negotiations, from which (as this case illustrates) misunderstandings might easily arise, will finally review and by execution, confirm in writing the terms they have agreed upon. It is a normal, and in my view, legitimate expectation in the commercial world that, absent fraud or some other vitiating element, provisions such as [the entire agreement clause] will generally be given effect to, so that prior discussions concerning the contract may not prevail over what has been acknowledged in writing to constitute the parties' 'entire agreement'.

33 Significantly, the court concluded that whether one applies the wording of the entire agreement clause (an acknowledgment that no collateral agreements exist) or whether one applies the parol evidence rule (thereby disallowing proof of a collateral contract because such a result would contradict the clause), the collateral oral contract would not prevail, for to rule otherwise would 'render entire agreement clauses meaningless and remove an important safeguard used in countless agreements'. We fully support such a conclusion. Much in the same vein, McLachlin CJSC in *Power Consolidated (China) Pulp Inc v British Columbia Resources Investment Corp* (1988) 14 ACWS (3d) 11 when she referred to the intention of parties in formulating an entire evidence clause, incisively declared:

> That intention, as in all matters relating to contractual construction, must be determined objectively. Here the parties expressly agreed that the contract documents constituted the whole of their agreement. While in most cases such an agreement is only a presumption based on the parol evidence rule, in this case it has been made an express term of the contract. A presumption can be rebutted; an express term of the contract, barring mistake or fraud, cannot.

34 A similar approach has also been adopted by the Malaysian courts in the context of a statutory evidential scheme analogous to that prevailing in Singapore. In *Master Strike Sdn Bhd v Sterling*

Heights Sdn Bhd [2005] 3 MLJ 585, the Malaysian Court of Appeal endorsed Abdul Aziz J's views in *Macronet Sdn Bhd v RHB Bank Sdn Bhd* [2002] 3 MLJ 11 at 25, where the latter had determined that the entire agreement clause precluded any purported variation by oral agreement in the following terms:

> My opinion is simply this. The entire agreement clause was an agreement between the plaintiffs and the defendants. In agreeing to the clause, the parties must be presumed to have known of the existence of s 92 and of the exceptions in it and to have intended what the clause intended, that is to exclude any attempt to vary the agreement by an oral agreement or statement, which attempt can only be made through the exceptions in s 92. By agreeing, therefore, to the entire agreement clause, the plaintiffs agreed not to resort to any of the exceptions in s 92. They cannot, therefore, be allowed to prove the second pre-contractual representation or the Oral agreement and to rely on them.

35 Although these cases considered the purported effect of differently framed clauses, it can be cogently asserted that an appropriately worded provision would be acknowledged and upheld if it clearly purports to deprive any pre-contractual or collateral agreement of legal effect, whether from the perspective of evidential admissibility or contractual invalidation. Ultimately, whether the agreement in its final form is intended to constitute the entire agreement, thereby superseding and replacing all representations that might have inspired and culminated in such an agreement in the first place, but which were never actually incorporated in the written agreement, is a matter of construction. From a policy perspective, it should be reiterated that the courts will strive to give effect to the parties' expressed intent and their legitimate expectations. The courts seek to honour the legitimate expectations that the parties hold when they enter into a contract.

36 An entire agreement clause can therefore be viewed through a legal prism and construed as denuding a collateral warranty of legal effect ('the legal perspective') and/or by rendering inadmissible extrinsic evidence which reveals terms inconsistent with those in the written contract ('the evidential perspective'). In so far as the legal perspective is concerned, the effectiveness of the clause may potentially be subject to the reasonableness requirements of s 11 of the Unfair Contract Terms Act (Cap 396, 1994 Rev Ed) ('UCTA') (if applicable). For example, in Thomas Witter, Jacob J held that the clause in question failed to satisfy the requirement of reasonableness. It was observed that should parties intend to exclude liability for particular sorts of misrepresentations (see Misrepresentation Act (Cap 390, 1994 Rev Ed), s 3), the draftsman 'cannot be mealy mouthed' but must clearly and explicitly make provision for such.

37 At this juncture, it should be cautioned and emphasised that the intent and purport of the clause, in certain contracts, may find itself subject to the strictures of the reasonableness test as provided for in the UCTA if the contract is embraced by it. Moreover, it is only when the nature of the liability which the clause is seeking to exclude or restrict has been ascertained that it is possible to inquire whether the term was a fair and reasonable one having regard to the circumstances which were or ought reasonably to have been in the contemplation of the parties when the contract was made: *Watford Electronics Limited v Sanderson CFL Limited* [2001] EWCA Civ 317.

38 Without prejudice to the generality of the guidelines contained in the Second Schedule to the UCTA, the degree of reasonableness of the entire agreement clause may then depend on, inter alia, (a) the relative equality of bargaining power between the parties; (b) whether a party received an inducement to agree to the term, or in accepting it has an opportunity of entering into a similar contract with other persons without having to accept a similar term; (c) whether the aggrieved party knew or ought reasonably to have known of the existence of the term (having regard, among other things, to any custom of the trade and any

previous course of dealing between the parties); and (d) whether it was reasonable or practicable at the time of the contract to expect compliance with the clause.

39 In summary, entire agreement clauses perform a useful role as legitimate devices for the allocation of risk between the parties, subject to an overriding judicial right to police clauses which are oppressively employed against consumers or parties of unequal bargaining power. In jurisprudential terms, the objective is to strike a happy medium, ensuring on the one hand that a dominant bargaining position is not abused, while on the other hand preserving freedom of contract and the fair allocation of risk.

40 Returning now to the issue at hand in the present proceedings, counsel for the fourth defendant, Mr Pillai, attempted to ameliorate the effect of the entire agreement clause by relying on the decision of *John v Price Waterhouse* [2002] EWCA Civ 899. In that decision, Robert Walker LJ was of the view that a conventional entire agreement clause could not 'affect the question whether some matter of fact (whether or not in documentary form) is admissible as an aid to the process of construing a contractual document'.

41 Notwithstanding the often-blurred boundaries between extrinsic evidence which 'assists in the construction of a document' (which is permissible), and that which 'adds to, varies or contradicts' the agreement (which is prohibited), we agree with Walker LJ that in so far as contracts are not interpreted in a vacuum, objective facts can potentially assist in the interpretation of ambiguous terms. Entire agreement clauses will usually not prevent a court from justifiably adopting a contextual approach in contract interpretation. Such clauses would have little bearing on textual or interpretative controversies as to the meaning of particular words or terms in contracts. Having said that, unless the contract is embraced by the UCTA, it would be theoretically possible for an entire agreement clause to expressly preclude any reference to the factual matrix as an interpretative tool.

Non-Disclosure of Material Fact and Misrepresentation

The effect of non-disclosure of a material fact in an insurance contract is exactly the same as that of a misrepresentation, in that, it gives justification for the aggrieved party to avoid the contract. See the case of *Asia Insurance Co Ltd v Tat Hong Plant Leasing Pte Ltd* [1992] 4 CLJ (Rep) 324.[324]

Where misrepresentation is found on a proposal for insurance, and where the policy declares that such misrepresentation would render the policy absolutely void, it has been held that the policy was void.[325]

In *Mustapha Ally v The Hand-In-Hand Fire Insurance Co Ltd* (1965) 9 WIR 242, the court was of the view that the law should be no different with respect to claims for compensation in which misrepresentation exists.

It is to be noted that mere negligence in supplying details of a claim cannot constitute a breach of the obligation of good faith. In *McAlpine (Alfred) plc v BAI (Run-Off) Ltd* [2000] 1 All ER (Comm) 545, CA; affirming [1998] 2 Lloyd's Rep 694, it was clarified that dishonesty would have to be established.[326]

On the facts in *Tan Jing Jeong v Allianz Life Assurance Malaysia* [2011] 4 CLJ 710 (HC), His Lordship Abang Iskandar J found that the plaintiff had acted on the misrepresentations made by D2 and was induced into entering the contract to purchase the Investpro policy from D1. It was also found that the misrepresentations and the non-disclosure as referred to in para 1 in "The issues to be tried" were material factors in the plaintiff's

---

[324] *Tan Jing Jeong v Allianz Life Insurance Malaysia Bhd & Anor* [2012] 7 MLJ 179 (HC).

[325] *Glicksman v Lancs & Gen Assce Co* ([1926] All ER Rep 161, [1927] AC 139, 43 TLR 46, 70 Sol Jo 1111, 32 Com Cas 62, HL, 29 Digest (Repl) 495, 3532) ([1926] All ER Rep at p 163].

[326] See also *K/S Merc-Scandia XXXXII v Certain Lloyd's Underwriters and others* [2000] 2 All ER (Comm) 731.

consideration before he finally decided to purchase the Investptro policy from D1. In so holding, His Lordship said:

> [30] From the appreciation of the available evidence, the defendants had deliberately failed to bring to the notice of the plaintiff that the balance 55% of the premium would go towards the alleged administration charges at the very onset of the purchase of the policy. Even from the agreed facts between the litigating parties as contained in bundle B, para 5 therein, it is clear that the use of the 55% of the premium fund was not a term that was expressly disclosed in the policy. The issue on the role of Bank Negara Malaysia was not a pleaded case for the defendants and like any statutory defence, a litigant desirous of availing itself to it must expressly plead it. In this case, there was no such pleading advanced by neither D1 nor D2 in answer to the plaintiff's claim. SD1, a manager in the customer relations department of D1, said in cross-examination that the use of the balance 55% of the premium in respect of the Investpro policy was a trade secret of D1, a disclosure of which would compromise it adversely on its competitive edge vis-a-vis its market rivals. But as rightly argued by learned counsel for the plaintiff, the issue of trade secret was never part of the pleaded case for the defendants as well. The two belated 'defences' advanced by the defendants' witness (es) would smack of an afterthought on their part. Such evidence lacks inherent credibility to be taken seriously by this court. A perusal of D2's witness statement (OTS) when he explained to the plaintiff about the Investpro policy would show that he did not disclose the fact about the use of the 55% of the balance of the premium, to the plaintiff. That would add credence to SD2's telling testimony that D1 had never intended to inform the use of the balance 55% of the premium for the Investpro policy to the investing public. The evidence of the non-disclosure of the material fact concerning the use of the balance 55% of the premium paid for the Investpro policy to the plaintiff by the defendants was therefore overwhelming.
>
> [31] It is my finding too, that in the circumstances of this case, the plaintiff was not estopped from avoiding the said contract.

From the evidence, nothing can be adversely attributed to the plaintiff such that he ought to be estopped from avoiding the Investpro contract. From the moment that he became aware of the true nature of the contract, he had taken positive steps to get clarifications on it and it was only after he failed to get a satisfactory explanation from the defendants that he had instructed his solicitors to write to D1 to terminate the said contract. His legal rights under the circumstances, to avoid the Investpro policy, had not been in any way compromised by his conduct upon him becoming aware of the true nature of the Investpro policy which he had purchased from D1 through D2. There is nothing in the evidence led before this court that would have justified this court to rule otherwise. The plaintiff had done what he ought to do with respect to the policy. He had paid the premium in full. But as borne out by the evidence as led before this court, he was entitled to rescind it by reason of misrepresentation and material non-disclosure by the defendants. No estoppel ought to apply against the plaintiff.

[32] Having observed the demeanour of the two main protagonists in this case, I have found that the plaintiff had shown candour in his testimony before this court. I had found that he had been forthright in his answers during trial. On the other hand, I found that D2 was rather evasive and at crucial times in the course of his evidence, he had been less than frank in his responses. I have not been impressed in a positive manner as a result thereof. As such, I had preferred the evidence of the plaintiff to that of D2.

[33] Under the circumstances, it is my finding as a matter of fact as well as of law, that the plaintiff was entitled to avoid the Investpro policy contract. It is therefore my finding that the Investpro policy had been validly avoided by way of the letter from the plaintiff's solicitor dated 6 June 2006 to D1.

[34] In conclusion, it is my considered view that the plaintiff had proven his case on the balance of probabilities. Both the defendants (D1 and D2), on the other hand, had not succeeded in establishing their case on the same legal threshold. In fact, both

the misrepresentation and non-disclosure by the defendants, as proven above, had breached the *uberrimae fidei* requirements that imposed the attendant duty on them to be frank and truthful to the plaintiff.

[35] As such, I would therefore enter judgment in favour of the plaintiff and I allow the prayers as claimed by the plaintiff in terms, with general damages to be assessed before the deputy registrar. After hearing submissions on costs, I had ordered that the both the defendants pay costs of RM60, 000 to the plaintiff.

Where there is no fiduciary duty or contract requiring *uberrimae fidei* which would compel disclosure, mere silence or non-disclosure of a material fact is not considered misrepresentation, as mere silence cannot, by itself, constitute wilful conduct designed to deceive or mislead. The misrepresentation of statements need to come from a wilful suppression of material and important facts, thereby rendering the statements untrue.[327]

FRAUDULENT MISREPRESENTATION

Fraudulent misrepresentation comes under the tort of deceit. The tort of deceit involves a false representation made by the defendant, who knows it to be untrue, or who has no belief in its truth, or who is reckless as to its truth. If the defendant intends that the plaintiff should act in reliance on such a representation and the plaintiff, in fact, does so act, the defendant will be liable in the tort of deceit for the damage caused.[328]

It is established law that the expression "fraud" means fraud in the technical sense as used in *Derry v Peek* (1889) 14 App Cas 337, i.e., the

---

[327] See *Trans-World (Aluminium) Ltd v Cornelder China (Singapore)* [2003] 3 SLR 501 ('Cornelder China') at 518 per Belinda Ang Saw Ean J; *Yap Boon Keng Sonny v Pacific Prince International Pte Ltd and Another* [2008] SGHC 161; [2009] 1 SLR 385.

[328] Clerk and Lindsell on Torts (17th Ed, para 14–01).

tort of deceit.[329] In the *Barclays Bank case* [1967] 2 QB 738, the Court of Appeal held that robbery was not fraud. Lord Denning MR at p 744 said:[330]

> ... in law 'fraud' is proved when it is shown that a false representation has been made knowingly or without belief in its truth or recklessly, careless whether it be true or false: see *Derry v Peek* (1889) 14 App Cas 337, 374, per Lord Herschell. In any case, 'fraud' involves a false representation.

At common law, deceit requires four things to be established. First, there must be a representation of fact made by words, or, by conduct. This will include a case where the defendant has manifestly approved and adopted a representation made by some third person. Mere silence, on the other hand, however morally wrong, will not support an action in deceit. Secondly, the representation must be made with the knowledge that it is false. It must be wilfully false, or at least made in the absence of any genuine belief that it is true. Thirdly, it must be made with the intention that it should be acted upon by the plaintiff, in a manner which results in damage to him. If however, fraud is established, it is immaterial that there was no intention to cheat or injure the person to whom the false statement was made to and lastly, it must be proven that the plaintiff has acted upon the false statement and has sustained damage by so doing.[331]

Nature of Fraudulent Misrepresentation

A representation is fraudulent when the person who makes it either knows that it is false or makes it recklessly without caring whether it is false or true.[332] Ascertaining the nature of fraudulent misrepresentation

---

[329] See *Barclays Bank Ltd v Cole* [1967] 2 QB 738 and *Newton Chemical Ltd v Arsenis* [1989] 1 WLR 1297.

[330] See also *Loh Bee Tuan v Shing Yin Construction (Kota Kinabalu) Sdn Bhd & Ors* [2002] 2 MLJ 532.

[331] *Bradford Third Equitable Benefit Building Society v Borders* [1941] 2 All ER 205 (HL) per Viscount Maugham at page 211.

[332] *Exklusiv Auto Services Pte Ltd v Chan Yong Chua Eric* [1996] 1 SLR 433.

or deceit is, in fact, a matter of importance, as a number of consequences flow from it.[333]

Dishonesty and Fraudulent Misrepresentation

Dishonesty is the touchstone which distinguishes fraudulent misrepresentation from other forms of misrepresentation. This turns on the intention and belief of the representor. A party complaining of having been misled by a representation to his injury, has no remedy in damages under the general law unless the representation was not only false, but fraudulent[334]. In *Raiffeisen Zentralbank Osterreich AG v Archer Daniels Midland Co and Ors* [2006] SGHC 182; [2007] 1 SLR 196, Andrew Ang J explained:

> In deciding whether the representation was fraudulent, the question is not whether the representor honestly believed it to be true in the sense assigned to it by the court, or on an objective consideration of its truth and falsity, but whether he honestly believed it to be true in the sense in which he understood it when it was made. See Spencer Bower at para 101. Belief, not knowledge, is the test. Good faith need not be rational, it may indeed be opposed to reason and good sense, but it must be good faith, ie, it must be sincere. See Spencer Bower at para 107. Thus, negligence, however gross, is not fraud. Irrational or ill-founded belief is also not fraud. The plaintiff has to show that the belief was as incredible or unreasonable as to infer an absence of honest belief. See Spencer Bower at paras 109-110.

> In the Australian case of *Rego v Fai General Insurance Company Ltd* [2001] WADC 98 one of the issues inter alia before the court was whether the misrepresentations made by the insured in relation to questions on the proposal form was made fraudulently. In Australia, in examining this question the court had to consider

---

[333] *Wishing Star Ltd v Jurong Town Corp* [2008] SGCA 17; [2008] 2 SLR 909.

[334] Spencer Bower, Turner & Handley, Actionable Misrepresentation (Butterworths, 4th Ed, 2000) at Para 98.

Sections 28 and 21 of its Insurance Contracts Act 1984 which provided as follows:

Section 28 of the Insurance Contracts Act 1984 provides:

General insurance

(1) This section applies where the person who became the insured under a contract of general insurance upon the contract being entered into:

> (a) failed to comply with the duty of disclosure; or
>
> (b) made a misrepresentation to the insurer before the contract was entered into;

but does not apply where the insurer would have entered into the contract, for the same premium and on the same terms and conditions, even if the insured had not failed to comply with the duty of disclosure or had not made the misrepresentation before the contract was entered into.

(2) If the failure was fraudulent or the misrepresentation was made fraudulently, the insurer may avoid the contract.

(3) If the insurer is not entitled to avoid the contract or, being entitled to avoid the contract (whether under subsection (2) or otherwise) has not done so, the liability of the insurer in respect of a claim is reduced to the amount that would place the insurer in a position in which the insurer would have been if the failure had not occurred or the misrepresentation had not been made.

Section 21 - The insured's duty of disclosure

(1) Subject to this Act, an insured has a duty to disclose to the insurer, before the relevant contract of insurance is entered into, every matter that is known to the insured, being a matter that:

(a) the insured knows to be a matter relevant to the decision of the insurer whether to accept the risk and, if so, on what terms; or

(b) a reasonable person in the circumstances could be expected to know to be a matter so relevant.

(2) The duty of disclosure does not require the disclosure of a matter:

(a) that diminishes the risk;

(b) that is of common knowledge;

(c) that the insurer knows or in the ordinary course of the insurer's business as an insurer ought to know; or

(d) as to which compliance with the duty of disclosure is waived by the insurer.

(3) Where a person:

(a) failed to answer; or (b) gave an obviously incomplete or irrelevant answer to;

a question included in a proposal form about a matter, the insurer shall be deemed to have waived compliance with the duty of disclosure in relation to the matter.

On the facts in *Rego v Fai General Insurance Company Ltd*, the insured said that he misrepresented the absence of the assault convictions because he found the convictions embarrassing and personal and did not think that they had any relevance to his insurance claim. Martino DCJ of the District Court of Western Australia accepted that evidence and concluded therefore that the misrepresentation of the insured plaintiff's assault convictions was not fraudulent.

Further if was found that the insured was mistaken when he completed the proposal and that he thought his answer addressed a two-year period. It was concluded therefore that his misrepresentation in failing to disclose the RAC claim was not fraudulent. It was found on the facts that the misrepresentations in issue were not fraudulent.

Fraudulent Recklessness v Negligence

It has been stated that ever since *Derry v Peek*, the courts have distinguished between fraudulent recklessness and negligence. In *K.R.M. Construction Ltd v British Columbia Railway Co* (1982), 18 C.L.R. 277 (B.C.C.A.), Fawcus J said at p. 200 that "neither bungling, ineptitude nor gross negligence establishes fraud".

The requirement to prove the absence of honest belief does not, however, mean that the plaintiff must prove the defendant's knowledge of the falsity of the statement. It is enough to establish that the latter suspected that his statement might be inaccurate, or that he neglected to inquire into its accuracy, without proving that he actually knew that it was false.[335]

False Statement – Whether Fraudulent Misrepresentation

A false statement is not necessarily a fraudulent statement in the context of fraudulent misrepresentation. There are innocuous reasons why a person might have made a statement that turns out to be untrue. As stated above, a fraudulent misrepresentation is a representation made by a person, knowing that it is false or so recklessly uncaring as to whether it is true or not.[336]

---

[335] Chitty on Contracts (25th Ed. 1983), vol. 1, at p. 227.

[336] *Kim Hok Yung & Ors v Cooperatieve Centrale Raiffeisen – Boerenleen bank* [2000] 4 SLR 508.

Fraudulent Misrepresentation – Proof of Fraud – Intention of Representor

A representor is not fraudulent if he believes the statement to be true in the sense in which he understood it, provided that that was a meaning that might reasonably be attached to it.[337] If fraud is proven, the motive of the person guilty of it is immaterial. It does not matter that there was no intention to cheat or injure the person to whom the statement was made to.[338]

The law with regards to fraudulent representation is clear. Since the case of *Pasley v Freeman* (1789) 3 Term Rep 51, it has been settled that a person can be held liable to another in tort, if he knowingly or recklessly makes a false statement to the other with the intent that it would be acted upon, and that other does act upon it and suffers damage. This came to be known as the tort of deceit. In *Derry v Peek* (1889) 14 App Cas 337, the tort was further developed. It was held that in an action for deceit, the plaintiff must prove actual fraud. This fraud is proven only when it is shown that a false representation has been made knowingly, or without belief in its truth, or recklessly, without caring whether it is true or false. Although an essential element in the tort is the representor's intention that the representee should act in the way he did, there is no need to prove any further intention and the representor's motive is irrelevant.[339] In *DBS Bank Ltd v Carrier Singapore (Pte) Ltd*, the plaintiff issuing bank (DBS) sued the defendant beneficiary (Carrier) under a letter of credit for deceit and negligent misrepresentation arising out of a representation in a delivery order. On the facts, it was found that the representation in the delivery order was false and on the applicable principles, as per Andrew Ang J, it was reiterated that it was irrelevant that Carrier might have had no intention of damaging DBS when it made the representation.

---

[337] *Yap Boon Keng Sonny v Pacific Prince International Pte Ltd and Another* (supra).

[338] *Derry v Peek* (1889) 14 App Cas 337 at 374 per Lord Herschell.

[339] *Panatron Pte Ltd v Lee Cheow Lee* [2001] 3 SLR 405 (CA).

Andrew Ang J in this case, further went on to examine the falsity of representation test to be applied and after referring to the dicta of Lord Herschell in *Derry v Peek* at 359, he said:

> Further on in his judgment, at 374, Lord Herschell identified what that 'something more' was:
>
>> To prevent a false statement being fraudulent, there must, I think, always be an honest belief in its truth. The 'something more' therefore is the absence of an honest belief by the representor that his statement was true.
>
> In this regard, the test to be applied is different from that as to the falsity of the statement. Spencer Bower at Para 101 explains it thus:
>
>> [T]he falsity of a representation is to be tested by the meaning which the words reasonably conveyed to the representee. It is no defence to a charge of falsity that the representor intended the words to convey a different meaning which was true. But where the inquiry is whether the representation was fraudulent, another test must be applied. What we are now investigating is not the effect of the words upon the representee, but the state of mind of the representor when he uttered them. In deciding whether the representation was fraudulent, the question is not whether the representor honestly believed it to be true in the sense assigned to it by the court, or on an objective consideration of its truth or falsity, but whether he honestly believed it to be true in the sense in which he understood it when it was made. There are limitations. The meaning professed by the representor may be so unreasonable that the court will find that he did not honestly believe it was true in that sense. But the principle is clear: proof of fraud involves an examination of the representation in the sense in which the representor honestly understood it.

The above passage in Spencer Bower was drawn largely from the Privy Council decision in *Akerhielm v De Mare* [1959] AC 789. In that case, the defendant had signed a circular letter wrongly stating that about a third of the capital of a certain company had 'already been subscribed in Denmark'. The defendant was wrong although, as the trial judge found, he had honestly thought his statement was true. The Court of Appeal for Eastern Africa reversed the trial judge's finding that the defendant honestly believed it to be true, and awarded damages. The Privy Council were firstly of the view that the Court of Appeal was not justified in reversing the trial judge's view formed after seeing and hearing the defendant give his evidence.

Secondly, and more significantly for our purposes, the Privy Council held at 805 that the Court of Appeal had construed the representation:

> as they thought it should be construed according to the ordinary meaning of the words used, and having done so went on to hold that on the facts known to the defendants it was impossible that either of them could ever have believed the representation, as so construed, to be true. Their Lordships regard this as a wrong method of approach. The question is not whether the defendant in any given case honestly believed the representation to be true in the sense assigned to it by the court on an objective consideration of its truth or falsity, but whether he honestly believed the representation to be true in the sense in which he understood it albeit erroneously when it was made. This general proposition is no doubt subject to limitations. For instance, the meaning placed by the defendant on the representation made may be so far removed from the sense in which it would be understood by any reasonable person as to make it impossible to hold that the defendant honestly understood the representation to bear the meaning claimed by him and honestly believed it in that sense to be true.

In reliance on the foregoing, Carrier submitted that:

> (a) DBS's interpretation of the LC was irrelevant; what was in issue was Lim's honesty in believing what the LC meant; and (b) whether Lim's construction of the LC and Fields 46A and 47A was legally correct was equally irrelevant; the relevant question was whether Lim honestly believed 'his own private interpretation' of the LC.

Carrier went on to cite Clerk & Lindsell on Torts (Anthony M Dugdale gen ed) (Sweet & Maxwell, 19th Ed, 2006) ('Clerk & Lindsell') at para 18-17 for the proposition that it did not matter how unreasonable the belief was so long as it was honestly held:

> The state of mind necessary for liability in deceit. Although the decision in *Pasley v Freeman* established the existence of a tort based on fraud, it did not make entirely clear what state of mind was required in the defendant in order to establish it. The leading case on this point is the later decision of the House of Lords in *Derry v Peek*.

There, Lord Herschell laid down the essentials of fraud in the following propositions:

> First, in order to sustain an action of deceit, there must be proof of fraud and nothing short of that will suffice. Secondly, fraud is proved when it is shown that a false representation has been made (i) knowingly, (ii) without belief in its truth, or (iii) recklessly, careless whether it be true or false. Although I have treated the second and third as distinct cases, I think the third is but an instance of the second, for one who makes a statement under such circumstances can have no real belief in the truth of what he states. To prevent a false statement from being fraudulent, there must, I think, always be an honest belief in its truth.

It follows from this that a statement honestly believed to be true, however implausible it may be, is not capable of amounting to fraud.

Thus, in *Niru Battery Manufacturing Co v Milestone Trading Ltd*, a bank presented a letter of credit to a buyer for payment, despite the fact that it was obvious to any reasonable person that no payment was due under it since the goods had never been shipped. But this fact was not in the mind of the relevant bank officer when he arranged the presentation: it followed that, however casual or naive he might have been, no claim lay in deceit.

Had counsel read further on, he would have noted this qualification:

> Nevertheless, although the unreasonableness of the grounds of the belief will not of itself support an action for deceit, it will of course be evidence from which fraud may be inferred. As Lord Herschell has pointed out, there must be many cases 'where the fact that an alleged belief was destitute of all reasonable foundation would suffice of itself to convince the court that it was not really entertained, and that the representation was a fraudulent one.'

Moreover, DBS's submissions on *Niru Battery Manufacturing Co v Milestone Trading Ltd* [2004] 1 Lloyd's Rep 344('Niru Battery') shed further light as to how the statement in Clerk & Lindsell relied upon by Carrier (in [53] above) ought properly to be understood. It appears that the Queen's Bench report of *Niru Battery* ([2004] QB 985) reproduced in Carrier's bundle of authorities does not report the Court of Appeal's judgment on deceit as fully as the Lloyd's Law Reports.

55 In *Niru Battery*, a false bill of lading (representing a fictitious shipment of goods) was presented by a bank (Credit Agricole Indosuez ('CAI')) to the claimant bank (Bank Sepah Iran ('Bank Sepah')) for payment under a letter of credit. Bank Sepah brought a claim in deceit against CAI on the basis (at [96]) that:

> [I]n presenting the documents to Bank Sepah under the letter of credit CAI represented that the bill of lading was genuine, although it knew that it was in fact false, and did so with the intention that Bank Sepah should accept it as genuine and make payment accordingly.

Fraudulent Misrepresentation - Representation must be 'Acted Upon'

The tort of fraudulent misrepresentation is not complete when the representation is made. It becomes complete when the representation, not having been corrected in the meantime, is acted on by the representee. A claim for damages may not follow or result until a later date, but once the misrepresentation is acted upon by the representee, the tortious act is complete, provided that the representation is false at that date. If false when made but true when acted on, there is no misrepresentation.[340]

The law as regards fraudulent representation is clear. Since the case of *Pasley v Freeman (supra)*, the tort has been further developed in the case of *Derry v Peek (supra)*, where it was held that in an action for deceit, the plaintiff must prove actual fraud. This fraud is proven only when it is shown that a false representation has been made knowingly, or without belief in its truth, or recklessly, without caring whether it be true or false.[341] In *Panatron Pte Ltd* it was stated:

> Basically, there are the following essential elements. First, there must be a representation of fact made by words or conduct. Second, the representation must be made with the intention that it should be acted upon by the plaintiff, or by a class of persons which includes the plaintiff. Third, it must be proved that the plaintiff had acted upon the false statement. Fourth, it must be proved that the plaintiff suffered damage by so doing. Fifth, the representation must be made with knowledge that it is false;

---

[340] *Briess v Woolley* [1954] AC. 333 (H.L.) per Lord Tucker at 353.

[341] *Panatron Pte Ltd v Lee Cheow Lee* [2001] 3 SLR 405.

it must be wilfully false or at least made in the absence of any genuine belief that it is true.

In this case, the Court of Appeal held (at [23]) that the misrepresentations need not be the sole inducement to the respondents, so long as they had played a real and substantial part and operated on their minds, no matter how strong or how many were the other factors which played their part in inducing them to act. In addition, the Court of Appeal held (at [24]) that it was no defence that the respondents acted incautiously and failed to take those steps to verify the truth of the representations, which a prudent man would have taken.[342] Acting incautiously and failing to take steps to verify the truth of representations on the part of the representee, is no defence to the tort.[343]

INDUCEMENT

A party is entitled to avoid a contract by showing that he was induced to agree to it, by the fraud of the other party. Generally, in law, a fraudulent misrepresentation must be shown to have induced the entering into of the contract, before the promisor has a right to avoid it, although the task of proof may be made easier by a presumption of inducement.[344]

Representations that do in fact induce the making of a contract fall into three categories, namely: (a) representations that amount to collateral contracts; (b) misrepresentations; and (c) statements that give rise to an estoppel against the maker.[345]

Materiality is a thing distinct from inducement. Each is a question of fact, and each must be separately proven. A representation is material when its tendency, or its natural and probable result, is to induce the

---

[342] *Singapore Tourism Board v Children's Media Ltd and Ors* [2008] SGHC 77; [2008] 3 SLR 981.

[343] *Panatron Pte Ltd v Lee Cheow Lee (supra)*.

[344] *Pine Top Insurance Co Ltd* [1995] 1 AC 501(HL).

[345] *Abdul Razak Bin Datuk Abu Samah v Shah Alam Properties Sdn Bhd and Anor Appeal* [1999] 2 MLJ 500; [1999] 3 CLJ 231 (CA).

representee to enter into the contract or transaction, which he did in fact enter into, or otherwise alter his position in the manner in which he did in fact alter it. For the purpose of determining the question of materiality in any case, as distinct from inducement, the view of either of the parties are of no importance whatever. If in any case, a representation is not material, the fact that the representee thought that it was at the time, or says that it was at the trial, cannot make it so; on the other hand, the fact that the representee, at the time, considered a material representation to be immaterial, does not negative its materiality, though of course it destroys all prospect of establishing actual inducement.[346]

Inducement cannot be inferred in law from materiality that is successfully proven, although there may be cases where the materiality is so obvious as to justify an inference of fact that the representee was actually induced, but, even in such exceptional cases, the inference is only a *prima facie* one and may be rebutted by counter evidence.[347]

The inducement can be in the form of statements, conversations and documents. Where one party induces the other to contract on the faith of representations made to him, any one of which is untrue, the whole contract is, in a Court of Equity, considered as having been obtained fraudulently.[348] As a general rule, the burden is on the representee to show that the misrepresentation induced him to enter into the contract.[349]

It is not necessary that the misrepresentation should be the sole cause which induced the representee to make the contract. It is sufficient if it can be shown to have been one of the inducing causes. In other words, where a person seeks to rescind a contract on the grounds of misrepresentation, it is not necessary for him to prove that if the misrepresentation had not been made, he would not have made the contract; it is sufficient

---

[346] Spencer Bower and Turner, The Law of Actionable Misrepresentation 3rd ed. (London: Butterworths, 1974) at Paras 124-6.

[347] Halsbury's Laws of England vol. 31 par. 1067.

[348] *Pertab Chunder Ghose v Mohendra Purkait* (1888-89) 16 IA 233 per Sir Richard Couch.

[349] *Sim Thong Realty Sdn Bhd v Teh Kim Dar* [2003] 3 MLJ 460; [2003] 4 AMR 460 (CA).

if there is evidence to show that he was materially affected by the misrepresentation.[350] The misrepresentation relied on need not be the sole inducement. It must simply be an operative inducement.[351]

It has been held by the Court of Appeal of New South Wales in *Australian Steel & Mining Corp Pty Ltd v Corben & Ors* [1974] 2 NSWLR 202 that it was not correct to say that the representation must be the very ground upon which the transaction had taken place. It was held that once it was shown that the representation was one of the factors which induced the contract, that was sufficient. The court went on to hold that even if the grantors had decided to sell before the misrepresentations were made, nevertheless, the position was still the same because the misrepresentation had the effect of inducing the grantors to persevere in a decision they had already reached.

To succeed in having a contract avoided on the ground of misrepresentation, the defendant has only to show that the misrepresentation was but one factor which induced the contract.[352] Young J in *Ashfind Pty v McDonald* held that on the facts of the case, there was such inducement.

A purchaser may in equity rescind a contract for the sale of land, on the ground of misrepresentation, where a false statement of fact made by the vendor to the purchaser induced the latter to enter into the contract. [353]

On the facts in *Golden Bond Sdn Bhd v Sabtra Sdn Bhd & Anor* [2004] 7 MLJ 493, Linton Albert JC found that "the Plaintiff has proved beyond reasonable doubt its contention that the fraudulent misrepresentation made by John Nip induced the Plaintiff to enter into what amounted to a useless agreement".

---

[350] Chitty on Contracts (27th Edn, 1994), Para 6-021.

[351] See for example the well-known case of *Edgington v Fitzmaurice* (1885) 29 Ch D 459.

[352] *Ashfind Pty v McDonald* [1990] NSW Conv R 55-509.

[353] Also vice versa: Emmet on Title (19th Ed) states at para 4002.

Inducement – State of Mind of Representee

If a man to whom a representation has been made to, knows, at the time it is made or discovers before entering into a transaction, that the representation is false, or resorts to other means of knowledge open to him, and chooses to judge for himself in the matter, he cannot avail himself of the fact that there has been misrepresentation, or say that he has acted on the faith of the representation. The allegation of misrepresentation may be effectually met by proof that the party complaining was well aware and cognisant of the real facts of the case.[354]

Even where a representation is both false and fraudulent, if the representee did not rely upon it, he has no case. Where a material representation is made, calculated to induce the representee to enter into a contract and that person in fact enters into the contract, there arises a fair inference of fact that he was induced to do so by the representation. The inference that he was induced to do so by the representation may be rebutted, for example, by showing that the representee, before he entered into the contract, was either possessed of actual knowledge of the true facts and knew them to be true or alternatively, made it plain that whether he knew the true facts or not, he did not rely on the representation.[355]

AGENT AND INDUCEMENT

Where an agent represents that he has authority to do a particular act, but he does not have such authority, and another person is misled to his prejudice, the ground upon which the agent is held liable in damages is through an implied contract or warranty that he had the authority which he professed to have had. It would seem to follow from this, in principle, that, where the authority upon which an agent is professing to act is a continuing authority, there is a continuing representation by him that he has authority to do the series of acts, and an implied contract or warranty

---

[354] Kerr on Fraud and Mistake Ed. 1952.
[355] See *Gould v Vaggelas* (1985) 157 CLR 215 at 236.

that he possesses such authority. In *Firbank's Executors v Humphreys* 1887 LR Q.B.D. 54, at p. 60 the law was stated by Lord Esher as follows:

> The principle of *Gotten v Wright* 8 E. & B. 647 extends further than the case of one person inducing another to enter into a contract. The rule to be deduced is, that where a person by asserting that he has the authority of the principal, induces another person to enter into any transaction which he would not have entered into but for that assertion, and the assertion turns out to be untrue, to the injury of the person to whom it is made, it must be taken that the person making it undertook that it was true, and he is liable personally for the damage that has occurred.

And Lindley L.J. said at p. 62:

> Speaking generally, an action for damages will not lie against a person who honestly makes a misrepresentation which misleads another. But to this general rule there is at least one well established exception, namely, where an agent assumes an authority which he does not possess, and induces another to deal with him upon the faith that he has the authority which he assumes.[356]

Under English law, a party seeking to exonerate himself from the consequences of his agent's fraud (assuming that is legally possible), is required to do so expressly and openly.[357] General language will not be construed to relieve a principal of liability for the fraud of an agent.[358]

---

[356] *Yonge v Toynbee* [1910] 1 K.B. 215 per Swinfen Eady J at 231.

[357] *HIH Casualty and General Insurance Limited and others (Respondents) v Chase Manhattan Bank (Appellants) and others, HIH Casualty and General Insurance Limited and others (Appellants) v Chase Manhattan Bank (Respondents) and others (First Appeal) HIH Casualty and General Insurance Limited and others (Appellants) v Chase Manhattan Bank (Respondents) and others (Second Appeal) (Conjoined appeals)* [2003] UKHL 6 (HL).

[358] *S Pearson & Son Ltd v Dublin Corporation* [1907] AC 351 (HL). See in particular the speeches of Lord Loreburn LC at page 354, Lord Ashbourne at page 360 and Lord Atkinson at page 365.

General words, however comprehensive the legal analyst might find them to be, will not serve: the language used must be such as will alert a commercial party to the extraordinary bargain he is invited to make. It is no doubt unattractive for a contracting party to propose a term clearly having such an effect, because of its predictable effect on the mind of the other contracting party, and this may explain why the point of principle left open in *S. Pearson v Dublin Corporation* has remained unresolved for so long.

RELIANCE

In order to succeed in an action in deceit, a claimant must show that he acted in reliance on the defendant's misrepresentation. If he would have acted no differently in the absence of such representation, he will fail. Whenever the representee has failed to discharge the burden of establishing that he was in fact induced to act as he did, he has failed. He may have relied solely on something other than the misrepresentation, his own skill or judgment, his general knowledge of business, faith in the venture, special enquiries, or knowledge of the truth. The representee may not have read the document containing the misrepresentation; it may not have been addressed to, or intended for him, or for a class of which he was a member, he may not have examined the article so that the active concealment of its defects had no effect on his decision; or it may appear that he was determined to take the risk, whatever it was.[359]

Reliance by the plaintiff is crucial. Without such reliance, there can be no legal effect of a fraudulent misrepresentation; it establishes the causal connection between the defendant's fraud and the harm resulting.[360]

Besides an intention to rely on the misrepresentation, the plaintiff must have actually done so. A mere attempt to deceive is not actionable. Hence, if the representee did not allow the falsehood to affect his judgment, as where he either knew the statement to be false or regarded it as so unimportant that he would have acted in the same way without it, he cannot complain even if he acted in the way intended and suffered

---

[359] Spencer Bower at Para 116.

[360] Fridman's Law of Contract, at p. 315.

harm in consequence of it. At the same time, a defendant cannot excuse himself by proving that his misrepresentation was not the sole inducing cause, because it might have been precisely what tipped the scales, as in the case of the plaintiff who had taken up debentures, partly by reason of a falsehood contained in the prospectus and partly in the mistaken belief that they created a charge on the company's property. Nor is it a defence that the plaintiff was negligent or foolish in relying on the misrepresentation or had an opportunity of verifying it.[361]

MISREPRESENTATIONS AND CONTRACTS OF INSURANCE

A valid contract requires *consensus ad idem*, *i.e.*, a meeting of minds, between the contracting parties. The consensus may be vitiated by misrepresentation. Misrepresentation occurs when a contracting party's decision to enter into a specific contract is influenced by a false representation.

Under the general law of insurance, an insurer can avoid a policy if he proves that there has been misrepresentation or concealment of a material fact by the insured. What is material is that which would influence the mind of a prudent insurer in deciding whether to accept the risk or fix the premium, and if this is proven, it is not necessary to further prove that the mind of the actual insurer was so affected. In other words, the insured cannot rebut a claim to avoid the policy because of a material representation, by a plea that the particular insurer concerned was so stupid, ignorant, or reckless, that he could not exercise the judgment of a prudent insurer and was in fact unaffected by anything the insured had represented or concealed. However, under the provisions of the UK Road Traffic Act, 1934, I think this general rule of insurance law is modified. The section requires the insurer to establish that the policy was "obtained" by non-disclosure or misrepresentation.[362]

---

[361] Fleming in The Law of Torts (7th Ed. Sydney: Law Book, 1987) at p. 604.

[362] *Zurich General Accident and Liability Insurance Co v Morrison & Ors* [1942] 2 KB 53 at p 60.

The effect of non-disclosure or misrepresentation is that the insurers have the right to repudiate the contract. The remedy is not normally available where there has been a mere non-disclosure - there must be a misrepresentation, although innocent misrepresentation will suffice.[363]

At common law, an insurer could avoid a policy of insurance, if a misrepresentation made prior to its inception, was either fraudulent or material.[364]

The common law principle dealing with misrepresentation concerns that person's duty to respond accurately to questions put to him by the insurer. The requirement that the matter misrepresented be material to the risk, applies equally to misrepresentation as to disclosure.[365]

However, with misrepresentation, it must be shown that the misrepresentation actually induced the insurer to enter into the contract. An honest but mistaken representation on a matter of opinion will not permit the insurer to avoid the policy on the ground of misrepresentation.

It was held that there had been non-disclosure and misrepresentation in the proposal form relating to material particulars, when false answers had been given to questions in the form. In *Tan Kang Hua v Safety Insurance Co* [1973] 1 MLJ 6, the insured had falsely stated in the proposal form that he had not made a previous claim for damage to the insured vehicle, under any motor policy. The Federal Court held that "the learned trial judge was correct in holding that there had been non-disclosure and misrepresentation in the proposal form relating to material particulars".

A statement made by the insured is fraudulent, if he knows it to be false and makes it in order that the insurers may act upon it. The most common examples are claims made by an insured who has himself destroyed the property insured, or who has made grossly exaggerated claims. Mere

---

[363] Halsbury's Laws of England (4th Ed, Reissue) at p 215.

[364] See *Babatsikos v Car Owners' Mutual Insurance Co Ltd* [1970] VR 297 at 307 per Pape J. See also *The Bedouin* [1894] P 1 at 12 per Lord Esher MR.

[365] MacGillivray and Parkington Para.582.

exaggeration, however, is not conclusive evidence of fraud[366], for value is often a matter of opinion, though such exaggeration will amount to fraud if it is dishonestly made, or so greatly in excess of the true amount as to be incompatible with good faith.[367]

In Australia, Buchanan JA in *TO v Australian Associated Motor Insurers Ltd* (2001) 3 VR 279 (Supreme Court of Victoria), was of the view that a claim is made fraudulently if a false statement is knowingly made in connection with the claim for the purpose of inducing the insurer to meet the claim.

Callaway JA in the same case, however, was of the view that that was not an exhaustive definition. His Lordship said:

> A false statement made recklessly in the sense explained in *Derry v Peek* would suffice and I would leave open for some future occasion a lie that was not told for the purpose of inducing the insurer to meet the claim but was nevertheless material to the question whether, or perhaps when, a payment or other benefit under the policy would be made or conferred. It might be material in the mind of the insurer but not of the insured or it might seriously (and not just in some minor respect) affect the investigation.
>
> [5] If Buchanan JA's formulation is understood with that extension and that qualification, it probably overcomes the problem of a false statement designed to cover up some matter of personal embarrassment to the insured that has no bearing on the claim. At least in most cases, it would not be made for the proscribed purpose or be material to the insurer.

A false statement made in a claim is fraudulent, if it is made to influence the insurer's decision to accept, reject or compromise the claim.[368]

---

[366] See *London Assurance v Clare* (1937) 57 Ll LR 254 at p 268.

[367] *Chapman v Pole* (1870) 22 LT 306.

[368] *Naomi Marble & Granite Pty Ltd v FAI General Insurance Co Ltd* [1999] 1 Qd R 507. See also *Rego v Fai General Insurance Company Ltd (supra)*.

On the facts in *Rego v FAI General Insurance Company Ltd* [2001] WADC 98 (District Court) (Australia), it was held that as the misrepresentation in issue was made to affect the way in which the insurer defendant had handled the claim, the misrepresentation was made fraudulently. It was also held in that case, that an insurer is deprived of its property dishonestly, if it is induced to make payment, due to a dishonest statement.

The question as to whether the remedies made available by the advent of *Hedley Byrne & Co Ltd v Heller & Partners Ltd* [1964] AC 465 and the UK Misrepresentation Act 1967, were also available to cases of insurance for claims in tort for negligent non-disclosure, was examined in *HIH Casualty and General Insurance Limited and others (Respondents) v Chase Manhattan Bank (Appellants) and others, HIH Casualty and General Insurance Limited and others (Appellants) v Chase Manhattan Bank (Respondents) and others (First Appeal) HIH Casualty and General Insurance Limited and others (Appellants) v Chase Manhattan Bank (Respondents) and others (Second Appeal) (Conjoined appeals)* [2001] 2 Lloyd's Rep 483) (CA).

Lord Justice Rix agreed with the view expounded in *Banque Keyser Ullmann SA v Skandia (UK) Insurance Co Ltd* [1990] 1 QB 665 at 773/781 ("Issue 5"), *Banque Financière de la Cité SA (formerly Banque Keyser Ullmann SA) v Westgate Insurance Co Ltd (formerly Hodge General & Mercantile Co Ltd)* [1991] 2 AC 249, that mere non-disclosure, even when underpinned by the duty to speak, that was imposed by the duty of good faith, did not amount to the "making" of a representation within the meaning of section 2(1) of the UK Misrepresentation Act 1967. As for a claim to damages in lieu of rescission under section 2(2) thereof, His Lordship referred to the decision in *Highlands Insurance Co v Continental Insurance Co* [1987] 1 Lloyd's Rep 109, where Steyn J expressed the view that where a contract of insurance had been validly avoided on the grounds of a material misrepresentation, it would be "difficult to conceive of circumstances in which it would be equitable within the meaning of s.2 (2) to grant relief from such avoidance...". Lord Rix further stated thus:

> 52. As for negligent misstatement and the *Hedley Byrne* duty of care, it was established in *Banque Keyser* that at any rate in a case of mere non-disclosure and in the absence of fraud (the circumstances there in issue), there was no remedy in negligence

simply premised on the duty of good faith which existed between insurer and assured: see issue 8 at 790/805. Since I shall have to go further into the reasoning in *Banque Keyser* for the purpose of the insurers' submission that its rationale does not extend to a case of misrepresentation as distinct from non-disclosure but on the contrary runs in favour of promoting a remedy in negligence in the case of misrepresentation, I shall for the present simply state the conclusion there of Slade LJ (giving the judgment of this court) to be found at 801A/D:

> We do not think that the nature of the contract as one of utmost good faith can be used as a platform to establish a common law duty of care. Parliament has provided that in the case of marine insurance, the consequence of a failure to disclose a material fact, and by inference the only consequence, is that the contract may be avoided. It is not suggested that the consequences in non-marine insurance should be different. In those circumstances it is not, we think, open to the court to assist the banks by providing a supplementary remedy in tort...What the banks cannot do in our judgment is to invoke the nature of the contract as one of good faith, with its limited contractual remedy, to bridge the gap so as to give them a cause of action in tort. The error in the submission made for the banks is that it ignores the nature of the special obligation imposed in contracts of the utmost good faith. The obligation does not, if we are right, create a duty to speak for breach of which the law attaches the consequences which flow from an ordinary breach of duty, whether statutory or otherwise. It is a rule of law which provides, and provides only, that certain stated consequences (namely the assured party's right to avoid the contract) will follow if utmost good faith be not observed.

53. Aikens J regarded this rationale as applying not only to negligent non-disclosures but also to negligent misrepresentations (see at para 88): "in each case there is no right at all". He held that special

facts would be needed to create a duty of care as between an insurer and an assured and that none were pleaded.

PROVING FRAUD

Section 101 of the Evidence Act 1950 (Malaysia) provides that the burden of proof rests upon the party who desires any court to give judgment, on any legal right or liability, which are dependent on the existence of facts which he asserts.

The burden of proof in any particular case depends on the circumstances in which the claim arises. In general, the rule which applies is *ei qui affirmat non ei qui negat incumbit probatio*. It is an ancient rule founded on considerations of good sense, and it should not be departed from without strong reasons.[369]

Thus, a legal affirmative is by no means necessarily a grammatical affirmative, nor is a legal negative always a grammatical negative. Allegations essential to the support of a party's case, although negative in form, may be affirmative in reality; and the nature of language is such that the same proposition may in general be expressed at pleasure in an affirmative or negative shape. The rule may therefore more correctly be laid down as such: that the issue must be proven by the party who states the affirmative in substance and not merely the affirmative in form.[370]

References to a shifting burden of proof can be found in many cases. The expression may have more than one significance. In some cases, it signifies that, in order to reach a conclusion on the entire dispute, the court must successively decide two or more issues, in respect of which the burden is not consistently on the same party.[371]

---

[369] *Joseph Constantine Steamship Line Ltd v Imperial Smelting Corporation Ltd, The Kingswood* [1941] 2 All ER 165 179.

[370] Woodroffe & Ameer Ali, 9th Edition at page 704.

[371] *Brady (Inspector of Taxes) v Group Lotus Car Cos plc and another* [1987] 3 All ER 1050.

Under Section 101 of the Evidence Act (Malaysia) 1950, the burden of proving facts rests on the party who substantially asserts the affirmative of the issue. It is not intended to relieve any person of that duty or burden.[372]

The Federal Court in *Nanyang Development (1966) Sdn Bhd v How Swee Poh* [1970] 1 MLJ 145 (FC), was of the view that that rule means that the burden of proving a fact rests on the party who substantially asserts the affirmative of the issue and not upon the party who denies it: for a negative is usually incapable of proof.

In view of Section 101 above, a plaintiff must prove such facts as is necessary, if he desires the court to give judgment on his right to claim against the defendant or the defendant's liability to pay him.[373]

The expression "burden of proof" is self-explanatory. It simply means the obligation to prove. A legal burden is defined as the obligation imposed on a party, by a rule of law, to prove a fact in issue. The standard of proof required to discharge the legal burden depends upon whether the proceedings are civil or criminal. In the former, the standard required is proof "on the balance of probabilities". In the latter, the standard required is proof "beyond reasonable doubt". In a negligence action, for example, where the defendant alleges contributory negligence, the plaintiff bears the legal burden on the issue of negligence while the defendant has to prove contributory negligence.[374]

Where a party on whom the burden of proof lies, has discharged it, then the evidential burden shifts to the other party[375] What shifts is the responsibility of adducing evidence to discharge that burden[376] When the burden shifts to the other party, it can be discharged by the

---

[372] Sarkar on Evidence, on page 916.

[373] *Tenaga Nasional Bhd v Perwaja Steel Sdn Bhd* [1995] 4 MLJ 673 (HC).

[374] *Ong Boon Hua @ Chin Peng & Anor v Menteri Hal Ehwal Dalam Negeri, Malaysia* [2008] 3 MLJ 625 (CA).

[375] See *UN Pandey v Hotel Marco Polo Pte Ltd* [1980] 1 MLJ 4; *Wong Chong Chow v Pan-Malaysian Cement Works Bhd* [1980] 2 MLJ 75 and *Johara Bi bte Abdul Kadir Marican v Lawrence Lam Kwok Fou & Anor* [1981] 1 MLJ 139).

[376] See *International Times & Ors v Leong Ho Yuen* [1980] 2 MLJ 86.

cross-examination of the witnesses to the party on whom the burden of proof lies or by the calling of witnesses or by the giving of evidence by the accused himself or by a combination of all the different methods. No adverse inference can be drawn against a party for his failure to give evidence himself. If he does not adduce any evidence when the burden has shifted to him, he will fail.[377]

In *Capital Corp Securities Sdn Bhd v Abdul Malek Beh Bin Abdullah* [2005] 7 MLJ 35, Abdul Malik Ishak J stated thus:[378]

> [27] The expression 'burden of proof has been bandied around by legal experts the world over. It is an expression which is self-explanatory. It is nothing more than the obligation to prove. The standard of proof required to discharge the legal burden depends largely on whether the proceedings are criminal or civil. In a criminal case, the standard required of the prosecution is proof 'beyond reasonable doubt'. In a civil case, like the present case at hand, the standard required is proof 'on the balance of probabilities'. The phrase 'legal burden' may be defined as the obligation that is imposed on a party to prove a fact in issue. And whether a party has discharged this legal burden and proved a fact in issue, is decided by the tribunal of fact at the end of the case when both parties — referring to the plaintiff and the defendant, have called all their evidence. A party who fails to discharge the legal burden will lose his case.

The burden of proof, such as referred to in section 101 of the Evidence Act 1950 (Malaysia), is the burden of establishing a case and this rests

---

[377] Augustine Paul JC in *Tan Kim Khuan v Tan Kee Kiat (M) Sdn Bhd* [1998] 1 MLJ 697 at p 706.

[378] See also: *Ong Boon Hua @ Chin Peng & Anor v Menteri Hal Ehwal Dalam Negeri, Malaysia (supra)* referred to in *Yew Yin Lai v Teo Meng Hai & Anor* [2013] 8 MLJ 78; *International Times & Ors v Leong Ho Yuen (supra)* referred to in *Keongco Malaysia Sdn Bhd v Ng Seah Hai* [2012] 7 MLJ 288; *John Driscoll v Teleplan Technology Services Sdn Bhd* [2012] 10 MLJ 267; *Kamalul Arifin bin Yusof v Mayban Trustees Bhd & Anor* [2013] 2 MLJ 526; *Kesatuan Kebangsaan Pekerja-Pekerja Bank & Ors v The New Straits Times Press (M) Bhd & Ors and another suit* [2013] 8 MLJ 199.

throughout the trial on the party who asserts the affirmative of the issue. The onus of proof, on the other hand, relates to the responsibility of adducing evidence in order to discharge the burden of proof. The onus as opposed to burden, is not stable and constantly shifts during the trial from one side to the other, according to the scale of evidence and other factors. Such shifting is one continuous process in the evaluation of evidence. According to sections 102 and 103 of the Evidence Act 1950 (Malaysia), if the party with whom this onus lies, whether initially or subsequently as a result of its shifting, does not give any or further evidence or gives evidence which is not sufficient, such party must fail.[379]

The burden of proving fraud is on the party who alleges fraud and in cases of criminal fraud he is required to prove it beyond reasonable doubt.[380]

Where the particulars of fraud in civil proceedings disclose fraud of the criminal kind, such as in a fraudulent insurance claim, it is settled law that the burden of proof is the criminal standard of proof beyond reasonable doubt, and not on the balance of probabilities.[381]

STANDARD OF PROOF

In Malaysia, there is no specific legislation that stipulates the relevant standard of proof required in both criminal and civil proceedings. Accordingly, the principles governing the standard of proof are based on common law principles. The standard of proof has been the subject of various interpretations by the courts from which several differing principles have been propounded in addressing the issue of what is the standard of proof required in civil claims where fraud is raised.

---

[379] *International Times & Ors v Leong Ho Yuen* [1980] 2 MLJ 86 (FC)

[380] See *Saminathan v Pappa* [1981] 1 MLJ 121; *Tai Lee Finance Co Sdn Bhd v Official Assignee & Ors* [1983] 1 MLJ 81 and *Boonsom Boonyanit @ Sun Yok Eng v Adorna Properties Sdn Bhd* [1995] 2 MLJ 863.

[381] *Wong Cheong Kong Sdn Bhd v Prudential Assurance Sdn Bhd* [1998] 1 CLJ 916; [1998] 3 MLJ 724 (HC).

The initial shift away from the civil standard of proof i.e. a balance of probabilities, was in the Federal Court case of *Lau Kee Ko & Anor v Paw Ngi Siu* [1973] 1 LNS 71; [1974] 1 MLJ 21 where the court applied "a very high degree of" the balance of probability standard in civil claims when fraud was alleged. In this case, Raja Azlan Shah J (as His Majesty then was) said at p. 23:[382]

> It is a wholesome rule of our law that where a plaintiff alleges fraud, he must do more than establish the allegation on the basis of probabilities. While the degree of certainty applicable to a criminal case is not required, there must, in order to succeed, be a very high degree of probability in the allegation.

A clear departure from the civil standard of proof was in the case of *Saminathan v Pappa* [1980] 1 LNS 174; [1981] 1 MLJ 121 which adopted the standard applied in criminal cases, that is, beyond reasonable doubt. In this case, the Privy Council upheld the decision of the then Federal Court that adopted the principle enunciated in *Narayanan Chettiar v Official Assignee of the High Court*, Rangoon (28) AIR 1941. Lord Atkin at p. 95 said:

> There are other difficulties in the plaintiffs' way which have been sufficiently considered in the judgments of the High Court. Fraud of this nature, like any other charge of a criminal offence, whether made in civil or criminal proceedings, must be established beyond reasonable doubt.

Following *Saminathan* (supra) a majority of subsequent decisions by the courts in Malaysia applied the criminal standard of proof.[383]

---

[382] See also *Ratna Ammal v Tan Chow Soo* [1967] 1 LNS 137; [1967] 1 MLJ 296.

[383] See also *Lee Cheong Fah v Soo Man Yoh* [1996] 2 MLJ 627; [1996] 2 BLJ 356; *Seri Mukali Sdn Bhd v Kertih Port Sdn Bhd* [2012] 7 MLJ 437; *Metro Gain Sdn Bhd v Commerce Assurance Bhd* [2012] 9 MLJ 682; *Chong Wai Automobile Enterprise (M) Sdn Bhd v Saga Autoparts Industries Sdn Bhd (Long Kwok Seng & Ors, third parties)* [2013] 8 MLJ 850; *Reignmont Estate Sdn Bhd v Jaya Ikatan Plantations Sdn Bhd* [2013] 9 MLJ 1.

Then, in the case of *Lee You Sin v Chong Ngo Khoon* [1981] 1 LNS 116; [1982] 2 MLJ 15, the Federal Court appeared to revert to the earlier position of the civil standard of proof for civil claims, that is, on a balance of probabilities, which was adopted despite the allegation of fraud. However, the court imposed the requirement of a higher degree of probability for the serious allegation of fraud.

Some years later came the case of *Ang Hiok Seng @Ang Yeok Seng v Yim Yut Kiu* [1997] 2 MLJ 45 where the Federal Court held that the standard of proving fraud should be dependent on the nature of the fraud alleged and it appeared to draw a distinction between civil fraud and criminal fraud even in civil proceedings. Mohd Azmi FCJ at pp. 59 – 60 said:

> ... where the allegation of fraud in civil proceedings concerns criminal fraud such as conspiracy to defraud or misappropriation of money or criminal breach of trust, it is settled law that the burden of proof is the criminal standard of proof beyond reasonable doubt, and not on the balance of probabilities.... But where the allegation of fraud (as in the present case) is entirely founded on a civil fraud — and not based on a criminal conduct or offence — the civil burden is applicable.

The confusion was compounded when the Federal Court in the case of *Yong Tim v Hoo Kok Chong & Anor* [2005] 3 CLJ 229 adopted the principle propounded in *Saminathan* (supra), stating:

> ...the standard of proof for fraud in civil proceedings is one of beyond reasonable doubt which has been consistently applied by the courts in Malaysia. We see no reason to disturb that trend."

This position was reinforced in *Asean Securities Paper Mills Sdn Bhd v CGU Insurance Bhd* [2007] 2 CLJ 1 (FC) and thereafter, the lower courts, being bound by the principle of stare decisis, adopted the criminal standard of proof for fraud in civil claims following this decision.[384]

---

[384] See *Chong Song@ Chong Sum & Anor v Uma Devi V Kandiah* [2011] 3 CLJ 1; [2011] 2 MLJ 585; *Shell Malaysia Trading Sdn Bhd v Tan Bee Leh @ Tan Yue Khoen & Ors* [2012] 1 LNS 1071; [2013] 8 MLJ 533.

The position came full circle with the decision in *Sinnayah & Sons Sdn Bhd v Damai Setia Sdn Bhd* [2015] 7 CLJ 584 where Richard Malanjum CJ (Sabah & Sarawak) (as he then was) in delivering the decision of the Federal Court said at p. 597:

> ...at law there are only two standards of proof, namely, beyond reasonable doubt for criminal cases while it is on the balance of probabilities for civil cases. As such even if fraud is the subject in a civil claim the standard of proof is on the balance of probabilities. There is no third standard. And "(N)either the seriousness of the allegation nor the seriousness of the consequences should make any difference to the standard of proof to be applied in determining the facts".

With the decision in *Sinnayah* (supra), the position of the law was thus brought in line with the generally accepted standard as applied in other common law jurisdictions, in particular among the Commonwealth countries such as England, Canada, Australia and Singapore.[385]

Insurance Fraud – Standard of Proof

Insurance claims are based on contract. Where fraud is proved in an insurance claim, it entitles the insurers to void the whole policy, and not merely to repudiate liability under it. Thus, a claim involving insurance fraud should be pursued via civil proceedings as it is founded on civil fraud and not on criminal conduct. Fraud can either be proved by direct evidence or by an inference based on the facts and surrounding circumstances of the case. The fraudulent intent on the part of the insured can be inferred, for example, from the conduct of the insured in deliberately and intentionally inflating the claim to deceive the insurer. The standard

---

[385] See *In re B (Children) (Care Proceedings: Standard of Proof) (CAFCASS intervening)* (2008) UKHL 35; *FH v. McDougall* [2008] SCC 53; *Rejfek v. McElroy* (1965) 39 ALJR 177; *Tang Yoke Kheng v. Lek Benedict* (2005) 3 SLR 263.

of proof in such fraudulent insurance claims, following *Sinnaiyah (supra)*, is on the balance of probabilities.[386]

Notwithstanding that the standard of proof is on a balance of probabilities, but in practice, as Lord Nicholls noted in *Re H and Others (Minors)* [1996] AC 563 at p586, since allegations of fraud are serious, "...hence, the stronger should be the evidence before the court concludes that the allegation is established on the balance of probabilities....". This is because, if an event is inherently improbable, then it takes better evidence to satisfy the court that it has happened – the allegations must be proved to the necessary high standard of proof. [387]

"Proof Beyond Reasonable Doubt"- Meaning of the Phrase

The term "proof beyond reasonable doubt" was briefly elaborated on in the earlier case of *Mohamed Isa v Haji Ibrahim* [1968] 1 MLJ 186, which found that the phrase in civil cases did not mean that proof had to reach certainty, although it had to carry a high degree of probability. What this meant was that the evidence adduced had to be such that the court believed its existence or a prudent man considered its existence probable, in the circumstances of the particular case; that if such proof extended only to a possibility but not in the least to a probability, then it would fall short of the phrase "proving beyond reasonable doubt". The appellate court in that case held that the facts and circumstances had pointed to the probability that there had been fraud.[388]

The phrase does not however mean, proof beyond the shadow of doubt. The degree of proof must carry a high degree of probability so that on the

---

[386] *ALW Car Workshop Sdn Bhd v Axa Affin General Insurance Bhd* [2019] 7 CLJ 667 . *See also* Veheng Global Traders Sdn Bhd v AmGeneral Insurance Bhd & Anor and Another Appeal [2019] 7 CLJ 715.

[387] *Aviva Insurance Limited v Roger George Brown* [2011] EWHC 362 (QB).

[388] *Lim Kim Hua v Ho Chui Lan & Anor* [1995] 3 MLJ 165.

evidence adduced, the court believes its existence or a prudent man considers its existence probable, in the circumstances of the particular case.

PLEADINGS

The party who has the burden of proving the pleadings, should begin. This rationale is in consonance with the provisions of O 35 r 4(6) of the Rules of Court 2012 (Malaysia). Hence, by virtue of logical postulation, the question as to whom the burden of proof of an issue lies with, must depend on the construction of the pleadings. At this juncture, it is useful to refer to the case of *Grunther Industrial Developments Ltd v Federated Employers Insurance Association Ltd* [1973] 1 Lloyd's Report 394 where Roskill LJ after having agreed to the decision of Cairns LJ held that:

> ... the substantial issue in this case is to the question of fraud raised by the defendant. That in the event may well prove to be so; but that, in my judgment, does not in the least determine upon whom is the obligation to open the case. For that, it is necessary to look at the pleadings, and when one looks at the pleadings, one finds that the statement of claim alleges a loss under a consequential loss policy of fire insurance. The defence first of all requires the production of that policy as a condition precedent to its admission; and, secondly, puts in issue the loss. Therefore, it seems to me that before there can be any question of the issue of fraud arising here, the plaintiff must first of all produce the original policy, because otherwise, without its production, the claim fails *in limine*; and, secondly, the plaintiff must prove some loss even though it is agreed that liability is only to be determined at the trial; because without proof of some loss there could be no cause of action in any event.

Fraud must be specifically pleaded and proven.[389]

A party must in any pleading, subsequent to a Statement of Claim, specifically plead matters, for example, performance, release, any relevant statute of limitation, fraud or any fact showing illegality – (a) which he alleges makes any claim or defence of the opposite party not maintainable; or (b) which, if not specifically pleaded, might take the opposite party by surprise; or (c) which raises issues of fact not arising out of the preceding pleading.[390]

Order 18 rule 12 (1) (a) of the Rules of Court 2012 (Malaysia) provides that:

> Particulars of pleading
>
> 12(1) Subject to paragraph (2), every pleading shall contain the necessary particulars of any claim, defence or other matter pleaded including, without prejudice to the generality of the foregoing words -
>
> (a) particulars of any misrepresentation, fraud, breach of trust, wilful default or undue influence on which the party pleading relies;

It is trite law that a general allegation of fraud is not enough; the particulars of the fraudulent misrepresentation must be pleaded in the Plaintiff's Statement of Claim.

Full particulars of any misrepresentation relied on, must be stated in the pleadings. Any charge of fraud or misrepresentation must be pleaded with utmost particularity. The Statement of Claim must show the nature and extent of each alleged misrepresentation and contain particulars

---

[389] *LEC Contractors (M) Sdn Bhd (formerly known as Lotterworld Engineering & Construction Sdn Bhd) v Castle Inn Sdn Bhd & Anor* [2000] 3 MLJ 339 at p 359.

[390] *Malayan Banking Bhd v Ong Kee Chong Motors Sdn Bhd* [1991] 1 CLJ 363 (HC).

showing by whom and to whom it was made, and whether orally or in writing, and if in writing, identifying the relevant document.[391]

Where all the material facts being complained of have not been pleaded, it has to follow that all evidence relevant to the unpleaded facts must be disregarded.[392]

Specific Pleadings

The mere averment of fraud, in general terms, is not sufficient to prove the allegation. There must be a specific averment to point out the specific error and later establish it by evidence, beyond reasonable doubt.[393]

Sufficient Particulars of Fraud

In *Dato' Toh Kian Chuan v Swee Construction and Transport Company (Malaysia) Sdn Bhd* [1996] 1 MLJ 730, a minority shareholder filed a petition alleging that the directors had misled members, including the petitioner, to agree to the sale of the company's asset. It was held that the petitioner had failed to particularise sufficient particulars of the alleged fraud i.e., that there had been a general vagueness in the evidence relating to it. In so deciding Mohd Ghazali J stated:

> [62] Under the circumstances, I cannot see how the contention of the petitioner that the members of the respondent company,

---

[391] Bullen Leake and Jacob's Precedents of Pleading. See also *So Ka Soong v Bank Kerjasama Rakyat (M) Berhad & Lagi* [1996] 1 CLJ 783, *Double Acres Sdn Bhd v Tiarasetia Sdn Bhd* (supra) and *Lee Kim Luang v Lee Shiah Yee* [1988] 1 CLJ Rep 717; [1988] 1 MLJ 193.

[392] *Asia Hotel Sdn Bhd v Malayan Insurance (M) Sdn Bhd* [1992] 2 MLJ 615. See also: *Elizabeth Jeevamalar Ponnampalam & Ors v Karuppanan a/l Ramasamy & Anor (Sundram a/l Marappa Goundan & Anor as Interveners; Raya Realty (sued as a firm) as third party)* [2007] 4 MLJ 214 and *Arasis Sdn Bhd lwn Pacific & Orient Insurance Co Bhd* [2013] 1 MLJ 784 (HC).

[393] *RHB Bank Bhd v Yap Ping Kon & Anor* [2007] 2 MLJ 65.

including himself, had been misled by the directors to agree to the signing of the shareholders agreement and that the circumstances above 'smell of fraud' can stand at all. In his submission, counsel for the respondent company objected to the allegation of fraud on the ground that it was never pleaded. Notwithstanding that it was never pleaded, I have considered this allegation of fraud and find that it contains no merits. The law is that he who alleges fraud must clearly and distinctly prove it and a general allegation of fraud is insufficient. In *Chu Choon Moi v Ngan Sew Tin* [1986] 1 MLJ 34, Syed Agil Barakbah SCJ said (at p 38)[394]:

> We agree that fraud whether made in civil or criminal proceedings must be proved beyond reasonable doubt and cannot be based on suspicion and conjecture (*Narayanan v Official Assignee, Rangoon* AIR (1941) PC 93; *Saminathan v Pappa* [1981] 1 MLJ 121). Proof beyond reasonable doubt does not mean proof beyond the shadow of doubt. The degree of proof need not reach certainty but it must carry a high degree of probability. What it means is that evidence adduced is such that the court believes its existence probable in the circumstances of the particular case. If such proof extends only to a possibility, then it falls short of proving beyond reasonable doubt.

[64] I find that the petitioner has failed to forward any sufficient particulars of fraud or if there were any, there was a general

---

[394] *Chu Choon Moi v Ngan Sew Tin* [1986] 1 MLJ 34 and *PJTV Denson (M) Sdn Bhd & Ors v Roxy (M) Sdn Bhd* [1980] 2 MLJ 136 followed. See also: *Chu Choon Moi v Ngan Sew Tin* [1986] 1 MLJ 34 referred to in *Air Express International(M) Sdn Bhd v MISC Agencies Sdn Bhd* [2012] 4 MLJ 59; *Panchanath a/l Ratnavale (suing as the beneficiary to the estate of Ratnavale s/o Mahalingam @ Mahalingam Ratnavale deceased under will dated 10 February 1971) v Sandra Segara Mahalingam (sued as the executor and trustee of the last will of Ratnavale s/o Mahalingam @ Mahalingam Ratnavale deceased dated 10 February 1971) & Ors* [2012] 5 MLJ 109.

vagueness in the evidence relating to the fraud which actually took place.

The issues of fraud that are to be tried by a judge, are circumscribed by and decided solely upon the particulars of the fraud that is pleaded. In other words, the court is only bound to decide the charge of fraud solely upon the allegations pleaded under "'Particulars of Fraud'".[395]

Whether fraud exists is a question of fact, to be decided upon after considering the circumstances of each particular case. Decided cases are only illustrative of fraud. In *Waimiha Sawmilling Co Ltd v Waione Timber Co Ltd* [1926] AC 101 at p 106, it was held that "if the designed object of a transfer be to cheat a man of a known existing right, that is fraudulent".[396]

> An insurer who alleges that a particular claim is tainted with fraud, is required to prove that allegation. The question whether or not an individual is fraudulent, ultimately depends on the facts of each case, having regard to all relevant circumstances in that particular case.

FRAUD

Tort of Deceit

Deceit – Proof of Fraud

Test for Fraud

Representations

False Representation

Misrepresentations

---

[395] See *M Ratnavale v S Lourdenadin* (supra).

[396] *PJTV Denson (M) Sdn Bhd & Ors v Roxy (Malaysia) Sdn Bhd* [1980] 2 MLJ 136 (FC). See also *Galloway v Guardian Royal Exchange (UK) Ltd* [1999] 2 Lloyd's Rep IR 209 (CA).

- Opinion
- Materiality of Representation
- Falsification of Material Facts
- "Operative" Misrepresentation
- Entire Agreement Clause and Misrepresentation
- Non-Disclosure of Material Fact and Misrepresentation

Fraudulent Misrepresentation
- Nature of Fraudulent Misrepresentation
- Dishonesty and Fraudulent Misrepresentation
- Fraudulent Recklessness v Negligence
- False Statement – Whether Fraudulent Misrepresentation
- Fraudulent Misrepresentation – Proof of Fraud – Intention of Representor
- Fraudulent Misrepresentation - Representation must be 'Acted Upon'

Inducement
- Inducement – State of Mind of Representee

Agent and Inducement

Reliance

Misrepresentations and Contracts of Insurance

Proving Fraud

Standard of proof

    Insurance Fraud – Standard of Proof

    "'Proof Beyond Reasonable Doubt'"- Meaning of the Phrase

Pleadings

    Specific Pleadings

    Sufficient Particulars of Fraud

INDEX

A

abandonment, 105
abrogate, 35, 55, 245
abrogating, 37
abrogation, 36
    judicial, 36–37
absence, 19, 21, 49, 52, 55, 114, 116–17, 191, 193–94, 202–3, 206, 239–41, 253, 256–57, 276
absolute legal principle, 245
absurdity, 73, 85
acceptance, 1, 3–4, 8–10, 19, 170, 182
    general social, 138
    ordinary, 53
accident, 2, 61–62, 99–100, 108, 123, 174, 212
    motor, 201
accident policy, 123, 126
accord, 35, 37, 41–42, 225
    common, 38
accuracy, 53, 156, 231, 235, 280
acknowledgment, 117, 268
act, 56–57, 63–66, 82, 106, 108–9, 128–30, 132–35, 149–50, 160–62, 180–83, 187, 191, 211–14, 222, 247–50, 252–53, 260–62, 275, 281, 290
    intentional, 246
    particular, 290
    public, 245
    solemn, 250
    tortious, 286
act imports, 160
action
    cause of, 62–63, 65, 146, 155, 248, 256, 297, 306
    civil, 248
    direct, 67
activity, 73
    commercial, 138
actual amount, 24
actual custody, 108
actual fraud, 249, 253, 255, 281, 286
actual policy numbers, 23
administration charges, alleged, 273
admissibility, 12, 266
    evidential, 269
admissible background, 40
admission, 13, 306
advertisement, 8, 10
aequitas, 152
affirmation, 260
afterthought, 273
against conscience, 256
agent, 8, 10, 108–11, 189–93, 220–28, 231, 234–38, 243, 249, 256, 290–91
agents impart, 151
agent's knowledge, 223, 226
ages, 26, 120, 172
agree, 6–7, 87, 91, 181, 185–86, 190, 214–15, 255–56, 266, 270–71, 308–9

313

agreement, 1–2, 4, 6–8, 15, 33–35, 37–39, 41–43, 77–81, 86, 117, 143–44, 146–50, 215, 222, 266–69
    agency, 222
    antecedent, 38
    binding, 34, 116
    collateral, 117, 267–69
    common, 42
    complete, 39, 43
    distributorship, 141
    entire, 268
    equitable, 150
    franchise, 141
    new, 61
    oral, 269
    original, 43
    preliminary, 79
    reached, 4
    real, 33–34
    shareholders, 309
    signed, 117
    true, 34, 38, 41
    written, 116, 267, 269
agreement clause, 116–17, 266–71, 311
agreement clause obviates, 116
aid, 7–8, 12, 15, 78, 80, 88, 90–91, 99, 119, 227, 271
aliud, 166, 240
aliud tacere, 240
allegation, 209, 250, 254, 290, 298, 302, 304–5, 308, 310
    plaintiff's, 92
allocation, 271
    fair, 271
allowance, 26–27
    fixed, 27
all risks policy, 201
alteration, 180, 183
alternative interpretations, possible, 80

ambiguity, 13, 15–16, 73, 80, 84–85, 87, 90–102, 107, 112, 118–20, 125
    latent, 13, 16, 80, 99
    real, 92
    resolving, 76
ambiguous documents, 99
ambiguous exceptions clause, 118
ambiguous questions, 16
ambit, 132, 167, 246
amendments, 6, 187
    legislative, 225
amount, 25–26, 37–38, 63, 65, 67, 203, 207, 239–40, 254–55, 257, 261, 264, 295–96
    true, 295
anchor, second, 165
annual income, 216–17, 229
    estimated, 217, 229
annuity, 67
annum, 217, 229
answers, 16–18, 30, 52–53, 94, 102, 120–22, 140, 188, 215, 217–19, 223–24, 227–33, 235–36, 273–74, 279–80
    correct, 263
    false, 227, 294
    inaccurate, 232, 235
    irrelevant, 188, 279
    negative, 207
    obvious, 56
    proponent's, 94
    right, 56
    true, 94
    truthful, 94
    untrue, 94
antecedent, complete, 42
appeal, 23–24, 41, 43, 66–67, 135–36, 145–47, 179, 192, 228–29, 232–33, 237–38, 241, 266–67, 283, 287

present, 63, 90, 148
appeal case, 223, 266
appeal decisions, 104
applicable insurance principles, 131
applicable principles, 167, 281
applicant, 75, 170
application, 3, 36, 63, 83, 127, 130, 144, 150, 158, 172, 204
   continuing, 186
   general, 131, 146
   post-contract, 182
   retrospective, 129
   sensible, 81, 87
   universal, 158
apprehension, 154
approach
   legitimate, 112
   objective, 77–78
   traditional, 73
arbitration, 7, 62, 67, 179
arbitration clauses, 6
architecture, 145
argument, 36, 57, 88, 97, 181, 185, 190, 192, 230, 262
   additional, 184
   appellant's, 148
   bank's, 61
   key, 37
arms length, 167
arrangements, 22, 141, 173
   commercial, 251
   consensual, 245
   contractual, 139
arrival, 31, 114–15
   ship's, 115
asbestos fires, 64
ascertainment, 63, 74
ascribing meaning, 72
aspirational perspectives, 147
assault convictions, 279
   insured plaintiff's, 279
assertion, 257, 263–64, 291
assessment, 161, 182
assurance aforesaid, 115
assurances, 52, 114, 117
   industrial, 235
assured appellant, 47
assured items, 26
assured person, 2
assured proposer, 21
assured respondent, 16
assured's pecuniary interest, 30
attributes, 14, 76, 79, 182
attributing, 142
Australia, 35, 129, 136, 160–62, 172, 184, 209, 251, 277, 295–96, 304
authorised agent, 227
authorised driver, 102
authorities, 28–29, 56, 58–60, 62–65, 90, 142–43, 180–81, 184–85, 191–92, 222, 227, 237, 239–40, 245, 290–91
   actual, 227
   cessation of, 227
   clear, 75, 97
   continuing, 290
   leading, 192
   relevant, 211
   strong, 136
averment, 308
avoidance, 58, 168–69, 177, 185, 191, 203, 209, 238–39, 242–43, 296
   remedy of, 155, 159, 167, 185, 239, 242

B

background expectation, 138
background knowledge, 72, 74
bad faith, 140, 149–50, 166, 183, 185–86
   constituted, 151

contract of insurance acts in, 157, 196
bad faith conduct, 139
bad faith manner, 149
balance, 60, 254, 273
bank, 13, 55–56, 59, 77, 137, 175, 184, 281, 285, 297
bank officer, relevant, 285
bar, 256
    statutory time, 245
bargain, 34, 139, 153, 158, 166, 176, 182, 222
    bad, 183
    extraordinary, 192, 292
bargaining power, 270
    unequal, 271
basis, 3, 16–18, 24, 52–53, 171, 174–75, 177, 195, 198, 218, 228–30, 236, 238, 240, 244
basis clause, 16–18, 53, 69, 175, 215, 228, 243
belief, 204–5, 247–49, 251, 253, 255, 257–58, 261, 263, 275–77, 281, 284–87, 293
    alleged, 285
    ill-founded, 277
    potential, 205
    real, 204–5, 284
    reasonable, 151
    subjective, 78
believing, 153, 158, 166, 176, 222, 255, 284
beneficiaries, 32, 252, 309
benefits, 2, 31, 96, 101, 120, 145, 149, 151, 153, 171, 176, 178, 180
    compensating, 30
    disproportionate, 177, 185
    mutual, 143
    pecuniary, 30
betterment, 26–27
beyond reasonable doubt, 299–300

bill, 45
    false, 285
    relevant, 110
binding, 9, 34
binding contract, 6, 19, 38, 42–43, 105, 171
    obligatory, 68
binding policy, 183
blood, 220
board, 114–16
body, 64, 136, 140, 142
    large, 133
boundaries, 40
    often-blurred, 271
brain specialist, 199
branches, 57
bridges, 99, 168, 297
broad overarching principles, enforcing, 134
brochures, 1, 61, 120
broker, 6–7, 34, 190, 197, 223, 225, 231, 233–34, 236
bronchial asthma, 122
bundle, 45, 273
burden of proving, 216, 229, 299, 306
burden shifts, 299
    evidential, 299
burglary policy, 172
business, 61, 86–87, 132, 164, 187, 190, 195, 221, 292
    adjusting, 227
    flouts, 87
    insurance broking, 227
    insurer's, 279
business efficacy, 86, 95, 137, 139, 141
business manner, 95
business people, 86
business sense, 81, 90, 107
    good, 81, 87
buyer, 1, 285
    potential, 1, 61

C

calculations, 27
cancellation, 184, 191
candour, 156, 274
cannot be mealy mouthed, 270
capacity, 228, 236
cardiomegaly, 122
cards, 133, 144
carefulness, 259
careless, 204–5, 231–32, 235, 247, 251, 253, 276, 284
carelessness, 204, 250, 255
cargo, 114, 203
caring, 253, 255, 263, 276, 281, 286
carriage, 108, 111, 152
carriage exempting liability, 109
carrier, 108–9, 281, 284–85
case Biggar, 235
case law, 145, 147
    modern English, 139
cases, 18–19, 28–29, 32–34, 56, 66, 91–92, 108–11, 140, 149–51, 201–2, 207–9, 237–42, 245, 248–49, 251–54, 256, 268–69, 273–74, 295–98, 300–301
    civil, 300, 304–5
    criminal, 300, 302, 304
    distinct, 284
    exceptional, 288
    party's, 298
    plain, 242
    subsequent, 184
cases policies, 172
cases turn, 66
causa causans, 119, 124
causal link, 246
causa proxima, 119, 124
causa sine, 119, 124
cause confusion, 132
cause harm, 246
caveat emptor, 167

celare, 166, 240
celare quicquid reticeas, 166
celebrated judgment, 154
century, 127, 130
certificate, 20–21, 44, 214
cessation, 227
character, promissory, 59–60
charge, 200, 282, 293, 302
cheat, 276, 281, 310
circumscribe, 145
circumstances
    limited, 245
    particular, 191
    present, 163
    relevant, 169, 310
    special, 36, 256
    surrounding, 14, 29, 77–78, 84, 87, 105, 119, 304
circumstances change, 261
civil burden, 303
civilian systems, 127
civil law systems, 133–34, 143
claim, 24–25, 32, 46, 55, 67, 115–16, 121–23, 157, 161–62, 169, 179–81, 184–86, 200–201, 213, 232–34, 285–86, 293–96, 298–99, 304, 306–7
    civil, 301–4
    dependent's death, 64
    likely to give rise to a, 67
    making false, 132
    may give rise to a, 67
    particular, 310
    plaintiff's, 45, 100, 110, 122, 273
    statement of, 306–7
claimant, 84, 208, 247, 254, 292
claimant bank, 285
claim damages, 241, 248
claim for damages, 57, 200, 286, 294
claim stage, 172
class, 27, 53, 170, 195, 286, 292

limited, 130
clause, 18, 21, 57, 68, 85, 87, 90–91, 93, 99–103, 106–17, 126, 138, 145, 193, 266–71
    ambiguous, 96
    bailee, 116, 126
    cancellation, 184
    covered, 200
    endeavours, 145
    exception, 98, 103, 111–12
    exclusion, 112, 266
    exemption, 110–11, 118
    forfeiture, 179
    framed, 269
    incontestability, 210, 214, 243
    particular, 87, 107
    police, 271
    relevant, 118
    single, 63
    subsequent, 114
    worded, 117
clear terms promulgates, 28
clerical staff, 34
client, 7, 223, 231
code, 23, 129
    territorial, 23
code words, 74
codification, 164
collateral matter, 239
collusion, 154, 227, 250
coming clean, 133, 144
commencement, 114, 169, 171
    subsequent, 64
commentary, 57–58
commentator, 58
commentators regard, 73
commerce, 87, 138
commercial behaviour, 145
commercial contracts, 87, 105, 135, 137–38, 191, 245
    ordinary, 137

commercial documents, 14, 53, 79, 81, 87
commercial import, 53
commercial intercourse, 244
commercially unacceptable, 139
commercial parties negotiating, 133
commercial principles, 81, 87
commercial purpose, 81, 105
commercial sector, particular, 151
commercial world, 268
commission, 169
common assumption, 139
common continuing intention, 42
common denominator, 91
common examples, 294
common form, 20, 264
common intention, 34–35, 37–40, 42, 44, 70, 78
    alleged, 39
common knowledge, 19, 100, 187, 279
common law, 36, 39–41, 63–66, 127–29, 131, 143, 146–48, 155, 164, 167–68, 177–78, 241, 247–48
common law duty, 150, 161, 169, 297
    applicable, 241
common law jurisdictions, 135, 145, 304
common law offence, 248
common law position, 225
common law principles, 128, 294, 301
common law remedies, 241
common law requirements, 161, 187, 227
common law sense, 255–56
common law systems, 135
common law tort, 248
common law world, 133
common methods, 68
common sense, 86–87
communication, 8, 10, 105–6, 141

company, 19–21, 34, 49, 94, 97–98, 170, 175, 179–80, 234–35, 245, 283
   defendant insurance, 102
   respondent, 308–9
   shipping, 110–11
company's asset, 308
company's policy, 21
compensation, 45–46, 63–66, 272
compensation policy, 62
   worker's, 82
competitive edge, 273
complain, 217, 292
complaint, 170, 204
completed Proposal Form, 205
completeness, 121
completion, 151, 171, 205
complex phrases, 92
compliance, 48, 51, 59, 144, 188, 228, 271, 279
   equitable, 52
   exact, 55, 60
   strict, 53, 92, 125, 187
   waived, 279
comprehensive definition, 249
compromise, 273, 295
computation, 212–13
concealment, 166, 183, 194, 209, 230, 238, 240, 248–49, 293
   active, 249, 292
   deliberate, 239
   underwriter pleading, 208
conceals, 194, 256
concept, 127, 129–31, 135, 142, 144, 146, 152, 157, 167, 246, 252
   broad, 29
   relevant, 144
conceptual difficulties, 130, 152
conclusion, opposite, 186
concurrence, 97

condition precedent, 17–18, 21, 47–50, 56–57, 59, 101, 175, 306
conditions, 1, 9, 17–18, 20–21, 25–26, 46–49, 53–57, 84, 91–92, 100–101, 113, 120–23, 162–63, 170–72, 174–75, 179–80, 187–88, 196–97, 215, 228–30
   additional, 200
   medical, 179
   personal, 179
   promissory, 54
conduct, 55, 61, 78, 84, 139–41, 144–45, 149, 246, 250, 252, 256, 274, 276
   base, 250
   criminal, 303–4
   defendant's, 252
   discretionary, 149
   honest, 252
   particular, 141
   post-contractual, 168
   relinquish, 162
   subsequent, 15, 80
   unreasonable, 155
   wilful, 275
conflict, 95, 224
   unresolved, 267
confusion, 132, 303
conjunction, 16, 80
connection, 24, 53–54, 86, 104, 131, 161–62, 295
   causal, 292
connivance, 227, 233, 249
connotation, 130
consensus, 39, 293
consensus ad idem, 4, 105–6, 293
consent, 142, 267
   mutual, 22, 173–74
   vitiate, 245
   written, 162

consequences, 47, 148, 157, 181–82, 216, 222, 236, 238, 291, 297, 304
   far-reaching, 159
   legal, 117
   lesser, 47
   unjust, 225–26
consequences flow, 81, 277
consequent delays, 151
consignee Hua Ho, 110–11
consignees, 109–11
   designated, 111
conspiracy, 248, 250, 303
construction, 7–8, 11–12, 52–53, 63, 65, 73–76, 82–88, 90, 93–95, 97, 99–104, 111–12, 114, 118–19, 137
   accepted canon of, 81, 87
   contractual, 268
   fair, 94
   favourable, 94
   matter of, 14, 23, 124, 139, 269
   natural, 13, 191
   ordinary principles of, 98, 103, 112
   particular, 49
   principles of, 83, 93, 96
   process of, 38, 142–43
   proper, 82, 88
   reasonable, 12, 94, 102, 139, 196, 216
   rival, 84
   rules of, 53, 83, 85–86, 89, 95, 125, 267
   true, 4, 11, 75, 113, 163
construction industry, 151
construction of contracts, 12, 73, 137
construed cl, 111
construed policies, 81
consultant urologist, 220
consumer, 168, 187, 227–28, 271

consumer contracts, 128
consumption, 202
contemplation, 270
contend, 200, 208
contention, 35, 42, 63, 120–21, 169, 180, 213, 219, 289, 308
   insurer's, 181
   respective, 211
contents, relevant, 144
contesting, 210, 213
context, 58, 62, 78, 82–83, 86–87, 89–90, 93, 105, 107, 111–13, 140–44, 251, 253
   legal, 155
   local, 145
   obvious, 15, 80–81
   particular, 141, 163
contextual approach, 73, 79, 271
   modern, 15, 80
continental paternalism, 135
contingency, 31, 51, 154
contingent chance, 153, 165, 221
continuance, 19, 175
continuation, 22, 172–73
contract, 1–15, 17–24, 27–31, 37–49, 51–61, 67–74, 76–80, 103–11, 129–46, 149–53, 155–61, 163–71, 173–75, 181–86, 191–96, 206–8, 221–24, 262–65, 267–75, 287–94
   altered, 180
   avoids the, 55
   the basis of the, 56
   bilateral, 47
   collateral, 117, 268, 287
   conditional, 52
   final, 34
   first, 6
   formal, 7, 117
   fresh, 22, 173
   implied, 290

interpreting, 73, 78
loan, 152
new, 23, 172, 174, 180, 212
non-marine, 239
oral, 268
original, 23, 40, 172, 174
partnership, 152
performing, 134
potential, 153, 176, 178
private, 77
reinsurance, 5, 68, 113
relational, 141
relevant, 278
standard form, 14, 79
subsisting, 22, 173
supplementary rider, 214
synallagmatic, 47
unaltered, 180
valid, 4, 293
void, 57
contract documents, 7, 268
contract exercise, 149
contracting, 143, 262
contracting parties, 13, 15, 47, 80–81, 116, 139, 143, 191–92, 262, 292–93
contracting party's decision, 293
contract law, 134–35
general, 153
contract repudiates, 54
contracts states, 135
contracts uberrimae fidei, 155, 166, 193, 200
contract terms, 76, 143
contractual contexts, 140, 144
contractual document, 7, 48, 52, 78, 91, 100, 102, 139, 271
contractual intention, ascertaining, 15, 80
contractual invalidation, 269
contractual objectives, 150

mutual, 149
contractual relations, 78, 150
contractual relationships, 117, 138, 141, 148, 152
continuing, 182
particular, 138
contractual terms, 117, 181
inferred, 152
contra proferentem, 102
construed, 83
verba fortius accipiuntur, 97
contra proferentem rule, 99
contra proferentes, 179
contra proferentum, 85, 91, 96, 100, 103, 125
construed, 101
contra proferentum rule, 16, 53, 84, 91, 96, 98–99, 101–2, 118, 120, 125
contravention, 188
control, 113, 162
control mechanism, 150
controversy, 55, 167
convenience, 107, 251
conversations, 288
convey, 72, 74, 282
conveyance, 110, 249
convictions, 172, 201–2, 279
cooperation, 141–42
co-operation, mutual, 145
cooperation, requiring, 140
copiousness, 147
core value, 140
corners, 77–78
coronaries, left, 122
correlative obligations, 66
correspondence, 4
cost overruns, 151
costs, 1, 40, 116, 162, 213, 238, 275
claimant's, 84
incurred, 162

321

insured's, 163
reasonable, 26
costs charges, 162
costs of proceedings, 116, 126
counsel, 215–16, 257, 271, 285, 309
    learned, 10, 213, 273
counter, 8, 113
court, 13–17, 23–26, 28–30, 34–38, 40–43, 75–83, 93–95, 100–105, 145–50, 215–16, 228–29, 232–34, 236–39, 244–45, 265–69, 271–74, 282–83, 297–99, 301–3, 305–7
    appellate, 237, 305
    interpreting, 77
    lower, 303
court's role, 76, 124
covenant, 151, 180
    implied, 151
coverage, 45–46
creation, 186
    artificial, 99
credibility, 273
credit, 77, 281, 285
criminal, 69, 299–303
criminal convictions, 202
criminal kind, 301
criminal offence, 69, 119, 248–49, 302
criminal proceedings, 302, 309
criminal record, 172, 189, 201, 237
crippling judgment, 28
cross-examination, 44, 236, 273, 300
currency, 20, 33, 66
customer relations department, 273

D

damaged items, 26
damages, 25–26, 29–31, 46–47, 52, 54, 61–66, 108–10, 175, 177, 203, 233, 240–41, 275–77, 286, 290–91
    awarded, 283
    general, 275
    recover, 193, 203
    sufficient, 63
    sustained, 276
danger, 253
    apprehended, 154
date, 9, 15, 54, 56–58, 60, 65, 113–14, 162, 167, 212–14, 286
    original, 212
    original issue, 214
    particular, 60
    settlement, 257
dearth, relative, 147
death, 29–30, 64, 67, 108, 119–22, 124
    cause of, 121–24, 126
    deceased's, 123
    event of, 120–21, 123
death certificate, 120
deceased's heart, 122
deceit, 138, 203–4, 221, 224, 247–48, 251, 255, 261, 276–77, 281, 284–86, 292
    action of, 254, 284
    tort of, 241, 246–48, 251, 254, 261, 275–76, 281, 310
deceive, 133, 140, 240, 246, 249, 252, 275, 292, 304
    intent to, 247
decency, 132, 155
deception, 250
decision, 75–76, 113–14, 117, 133, 136–38, 183–84, 212–13, 215–17, 223, 225–26, 228–29, 271, 284, 302–4, 306
    deliberate, 257–58
    insured's, 251
    insurer's, 295
    prior, 83, 88
    reinsurance, 182
    reported, 161

declaration, 15–16, 26, 40, 53, 59, 80, 101, 153, 174, 176–77, 189
    proposer's, 52
    subjective, 16, 80
    usual, 17
declaration forms, 1, 61
declaratory, 77, 158
deeds, 98, 104
defeating, 37, 110
defeats, 36, 111, 135
defence, 30, 35, 154, 180, 185, 227, 233, 248, 253, 282, 287, 293, 306–7
    complete, 181
    good, 48
    hospital's, 162
    statutory, 273
defendant beneficiary, 281
defendants, 44–46, 92, 108–11, 122, 150–51, 181–82, 184–85, 188–89, 212–15, 237, 256–57, 269, 273–76, 283–84, 299–300
    first, 233
    insured, 251
    second, 233
defendant's insurers, first, 233
defraud, 250
    conspiracy to, 248, 303
degree, 46, 132, 145–46, 157, 241, 259, 263, 265, 270, 302–3
    generous, 254
    high, 141, 157
    particular, 155
degree illiterate, 232
deleted words, 90–91, 125
deletion, 91
deliberateness, 240
delivery, 46, 110–11
    proper, 110–11
departure, clear, 302
depreciation, 26

deprive, 112, 179, 193, 203, 221, 224, 250, 269
deputy registrar, 275
destination, 44
detention, 31, 108
detriment, 84, 248, 250–52
devices, 253
    legitimate, 271
diabetes, 210, 219
dicta, 179, 245, 257, 282
dictionaries, 75–76
dictum, 244, 267
difference, 7, 18, 55, 59–60, 72–73, 91, 131, 144, 217, 229, 240
directors, 48, 308–9
disablement, 121
discern, 78, 192
discharge, 38, 56, 109, 171, 181, 292, 299–301
    effects, 56
disclosure, 156, 167, 169, 171, 177–80, 182, 184–87, 189, 191, 194–96, 198, 216, 218, 273, 275
    duty of, 154, 161, 164, 167–72, 175–77, 180–81, 184, 187–88, 190, 220, 223–24, 278–79
    general, 180
    honest, 193
    incorrect, 215–16, 228–29
    independent duty of, 193, 221
    insured's duty of, 167, 193, 278
    positive obligations of, 141, 158
    post-contract, 182
    requirement of, 167, 187
    requiring, 169
    voluntary, 168
    waived, 190
disclosure obligations, 191
disclosure of matters, 189, 216
discovery, 185

discretion, 42, 150, 186
discretionary remedy, 38, 43
disease, 64–65, 121–22, 174, 198, 209
dishonest knowledge, 253
dishonest mind, 254
dishonesty, 139, 240, 242, 245, 248, 252–55, 272, 277
    deliberate, 255
    finding of, 252–53
dispute, 7, 25, 149, 159, 162, 177, 230, 298
dispute resolution service, alternative, 128
dissenting judgment, 76, 136
divergence, 90, 206, 223
doctrine, 135–36, 145, 148, 152, 154–55, 168, 179, 240, 242
    equitable, 250
    established, 148
    fledgling, 145, 147
    general, 132
    independent, 148
    legal, 153, 177
document, 12–14, 39, 41–43, 45, 52–53, 74, 76–79, 89, 93, 100–101, 104, 117, 119–20, 214, 255
    incorporated, 104
    primary, 123
    relevant, 209, 308
    tender, 151
document prove, 255
document recording, 138
dominant bargaining position, 271
dominant cause, 123
dominant status, 127
doubt subject, 283
draft documents, 100
drafts, 79, 91, 181
    broker's, 6
draftsman, 58, 191, 193, 270
    parliamentary, 56

drug usage, 108, 201
    prolonged, 108
duration, 45, 67
duty, 49, 132, 134–37, 141–44, 146–47, 155–65, 167–69, 171–72, 175–78, 180–81, 183–88, 194–99, 202, 218–20, 222–23, 230–34, 296–97
    assured's, 185
    attendant, 158, 275
    continuing, 196, 198
    contractual, 136, 140
    fiduciary, 275
    implied, 143
    insured proposer's, 177
    insured's, 178, 218
    mutual, 159, 176–77, 179, 242
    particular, 105
    person's, 294
    positive, 199
    pre-contract, 184
    pre-contractual, 159, 178
    reciprocal, 154, 167, 177–78
    ship owner's, 165
    statutory, 160, 241
duty of care, 166, 296, 298
duty of disclosure of material facts, 195–96, 198, 209, 228
duty of good faith in relation, 153, 181

E

earning, 217, 229
editors, 246
    learned, 116
effect
    given, 112, 117, 268
    purported, 269
    retrospective, 37, 167, 181
effectiveness, 270
effect Lord Hoffmann, 139
election, 64

worker's, 64
employees, 45, 83
employer, 63, 65–66, 82
    agent's, 222
    insured, 83
employment, 109, 137, 216
encapsulates, 127
endeavours formulation, 145
endorsements, 174
enforceability, 17, 63, 230
enforcement, 63, 135, 149
English case, 165
English commercial law, 130
English contract, 146
English Contract Law, 132–33, 204
English Courts, 85, 129, 133, 179
English general common law, 152
English hostility, traditional, 134, 144
English judges, 130
English language, 11
English law, 105–6, 129, 133–35, 137, 140, 142–44, 148, 152, 246, 249, 291
English law of contract, 105
English law of insurance, 127
English law on inducement, 207
English lawyers, 74, 105
English Marine Insurance Act, 131
English policy, 85
English words, 74
    ordinary, 74–75
enquiries, special, 292
enquiry, 89, 239
entities, relevant, 187
entitle, 107, 159, 198, 206
entitling, 63, 116
entry, 29, 64
epieikeia, 152
epithets, 130, 139
equality, relative, 270
equitable principles, 250

equitable relation, 29, 31
    legal or, 29
equitable sense, 256
equity, 41, 148, 152, 246, 289
    court of, 34, 246, 288
equity Lord Macnaghten, 247
error, 39–40, 43–44, 191, 245, 297, 308
    negligent, 191, 245
    obvious grammatical, 81
escape, 185, 236, 238
estate, 32, 212, 309
estimated income, 217, 229
estoppel, 274, 287
etymological, 85, 102–3
evaluation, 301
    pecuniary, 29
event, 2–3, 19, 22, 31, 33, 44, 47, 55, 67, 100, 102, 214–15, 254, 305–6
    insured, 33
    particular, 22, 173
    specified, 2–3, 56
    subsequent, 95
eventuality, 78
    particular, 78
evidence, 12–15, 44–45, 75, 79–81, 118, 122, 175, 205, 208–9, 219–20, 224, 253–54, 273–74, 299–301, 305–6, 308–10
    absence of, 121, 207
    adducing, 299, 301
    available, 273
    better, 305
    clear, 38
    cogent, 39
    convincing, 38, 246
    counter, 288
    direct, 206, 304
    documentary, 12
    external, 75
    oral, 79, 219, 266

parol, 13
parole, 13
plaintiff's, 45
secondary, 12
evidence clause, 268
evidence rule, 267
   best, 12
   encapsulated parol, 266
eviscerates, 135
exaggerating, 132
exaggeration, 295
examination, 74, 122, 179, 192, 246, 282
exceptions, established, 291
excerpt
   first, 10
   second, 10
excerpts, 10, 156
exchange, 105, 110, 141, 151, 182
exclusion, 101, 108, 121, 191, 241
execution, 38, 93, 191, 268
exempt, 108–9
exempting, 109
exemption, 109, 111, 262, 266
exemption cl, 108
exercise, 22, 42, 75, 78, 150, 156–57, 159, 166, 170, 173, 184, 186
   circumscribe Zurich's, 162
exhaustive definition, 112, 295
exigencies, plain, 170
existence, 18–21, 67, 73, 136, 180, 184, 262, 269–70, 298, 305–6, 309
existence latent ambiguity, 13
exonerate, 94, 291
ex parte application, 131
expectations, 138–41, 149–50, 225, 258
   community, 136
   legitimate, 268–69
   normal, 151

reasonable, 142, 150–51
relevant background, 140
expense, incurring, 141
experience, 56, 61, 133, 178, 262
experts, 5–6
   legal, 300
expressions, 55, 58, 71–72, 74–76, 127–28, 130, 144, 275, 298–300
   mutual, 74
   nonexistent, 72
   outward, 35, 37, 42
   particular, 79
   relevant, 72
   symbols of, 72
   written, 38
extension, 22, 172–74, 295
extension betokens, 22, 173
no external injuries were noted, 120
extract, 10, 76, 204
extrinsic, 12, 267
extrinsic evidence, 12–16, 73, 78–81, 92, 99, 224, 271
   admissibility of, 14–15, 73, 79–80
   court's treatment of, 14, 79
   inadmissible, 267, 270
   seeking, 85
extrinsic matters, 79

F

fact-law distinction, 36
facts
   agreed, 273
   background, 38
   the matrix of, 77
   matter of, 260
   mistakes of, 35–36
   objective, 271
   real, 290
   relevant, 155, 178, 250
   special, 153, 165, 171, 221
   statement of, 59, 140, 259

suppress, 196
true, 290
undoubted, 55
unpleaded, 308
weighty, 94
facts material, 180, 194
fact uncertainty, 112
failure, 110, 150, 158, 180–81, 188, 190, 197, 201–2, 278, 297, 300
　insurer's, 188
　left ventricular, 120
　proposer's, 201
　total, 169
and fair dealing, 143
fairness, 132, 136, 145, 149, 155, 165
faith, 97, 152, 183, 288, 290–92
　full and perfect, 130
falsehood, 261, 292–93
false impression, 262
false pre-contractual statement, 264
false representation, 247–48, 251–52, 255, 258, 261, 263, 275–76, 281, 284, 286, 293
　involve a, 247
false statement, 251, 253, 255, 258–59, 262, 265, 276, 280–82, 284, 286, 295
false statement of fact, 262, 289
falsity, 254, 257–58, 264, 277, 280, 282–83
father's illnesses, 210
fault, 16
　actual, 109
favour employers, 83
fever, high, 219
fibres, 63–66
　asbestos, 64
fiduciary, 137, 151
fiduciary relationships, 140, 166
　special, 156
financial institutions, 187

financial interests, 67
financial involvement, 31
Financial Ombudsman Service, 127
financial positions, 159
financial stability, 187
finding, 116, 119, 204, 215, 237, 254, 273–74
　trial judge's, 283
first defendants claiming, 233
floating policy, 68
folded card, 6
forbearances, 72
Forbes, 27
force, 22, 29, 46, 118, 129, 173, 210, 214, 220, 232
　binding, 146
　contractual, 117
　equal, 176, 232
　greatest, 178
foreseeability, 32
form
　absolute, 244
　contractual, 267
　corrected, 38
　documentary, 271
　final, 269
　ordinary, 22, 173
　particular, 34
　present, 57
　printed, 91
　proposal/application, 53
　unqualified, 257
formation, 1, 3, 5, 9, 33, 37, 39–40, 43, 105–6, 155, 157, 223–24, 228
　contractual, 149
form part, 61, 82, 86, 151
formula, 117, 267
fort, 154
fortuitous, 32–33
foundation, 27
　reasonable, 285

frank, 158, 274–75
fraud, 69, 191–92, 194, 202, 204, 210–11, 240–41, 244–53, 255–56, 261–62, 275–77, 280–81, 284–87, 290–91, 301–10
    absence of, 191, 296
    absent, 268
    agent's, 291
    allegation of, 303, 305, 309
    alleged, 308
    amount to, 250, 255, 257, 261, 295
    a charge of, 248
    charge of, 247, 307, 310
    civil, 303–4
    claim in, 203, 240, 247
    common law, 251
fraud
    constructive, 240
    criminal, 301, 303
    defendant's, 292
    defining, 247
    element of, 69, 211, 247
    evidence of, 213, 255, 295
    general allegation of, 307, 309
    intentional, 246
    present purposes, 257
    proof of, 251, 253, 255, 281–82, 284, 310–11
    smell of, 309
    sufficient particulars of, 308–9, 312
    test for, 256, 310
fraud set, 69
fraudulent, 239, 241, 249–50, 253, 255, 258, 260, 263–64, 276–82, 284–85, 290, 294–95, 310
    ordinary consequences of, 192, 221
fraudulent claims, 157–58, 253
fraudulent concealment, 208
fraudulent conduct, 240
fraudulent inducement, 264
fraudulent insurance claims, 301, 305
fraudulent intent, 251, 304
fraudulent intention, 166, 222
fraudulent misrepresentation, 203–4, 224, 240, 243, 259, 261–62, 275, 277, 280–81, 286–87, 289, 292, 311
    actionable, 204
    nature of, 276, 311
fraudulent non-disclosure, 127, 239
fraudulent recklessness, 280, 311
fraudulent representation, 281, 286
fraudulent statement, 280
fraudulent suppression, 211
fraud unravels, 244
fraus omnia corrumpit, 244
freedom, 143, 146
    preserving, 271
freight, 114–16
fulfilment, 30, 47, 149
    exact, 17, 230
    literal, 53
full value, 26
    the, 26
function, 87, 90, 107, 185
    court's, 215, 229
    interpretative, 75
    legislative, 37
fundamental term aforesaid, 110

G

general duty, 133, 135
    independent, 162
generality, 270, 307
genesis, 104–5
good faith, 127, 129–36, 139–54, 156–62, 166–68, 176–77, 181, 185–86, 190–91, 221–22, 277, 295, 297
    complete, 181

contracts in, 133, 144
contracts of, 155, 157
doctrine of, 132, 134–36, 144–45, 147–48, 150, 153, 240
duty of, 133, 135–37, 142–44, 146, 155, 162–64, 177, 181–83, 186, 240–42, 296–97
duty of utmost, 152, 159–61, 164–65, 167–68, 172, 176, 180, 202, 223
general duty of, 146–47
general principle of, 130, 134
greatest, 130
implied duty of, 142, 145, 148, 157
the most abundant, 130
obligation of, 135, 150–51, 180, 272
perfect, 130
principle of, 129, 146, 165, 182, 186
principle of utmost, 131, 163, 168
requirement of, 96, 134, 137, 141, 149, 152
requirement of utmost, 132, 155, 158, 163
good faith manner, 150
goods, 25, 45–46, 68, 97, 108–11, 114–15, 119, 129, 184, 285
governor, 154
grammatical, 298
grammatical sense, 106
grant, 14, 96, 185
grantors, 96, 289
grant relief, 296
ground, 37, 94, 135, 154, 170, 190–91, 200, 210–13, 247, 257, 289–90
common, 102
first, 94, 237
reasonable, 255
second, 237
guide, 58, 106, 149

H

harm, 61, 246, 292–93
significant, 149–50
headaches, 199
casual, 199
ordinary, 199
ordinary casual, 199
particular, 199
headnotes, 90, 113
health, 198
declaration of good, 214
heart attack, 122
massive, 120
heart disease, 122
hypertension/ischaemic, 209
heightened burden, 254
held covered provision, 56
history, 57, 130
medical, 120, 122
home, 47, 85, 136
honest belief, 253, 255–58, 282, 284
absence of, 277, 280
honest non-disclosure, 242
honesty, 132, 138–40, 149, 155, 170–71, 186, 191, 245, 247, 252
requiring, 139
hospital, 162–63
house, 27, 35, 37, 134, 137–38, 146, 175–76, 181, 184, 192, 248
old, 27
plaintiff's, 232
human communications, 137
hundred years, 248
hypertension, 122, 209

I

identification, 107
identity, 22, 173
alternative, 120
singular, 120

ignorance, 151, 153, 158, 166, 176, 222, 255
    conscious, 257
illegality, showing, 307
illegitimate, 90
illegitimate restriction, 143
illiterate, 236
illnesses, prolonged, 218–19
illustrations, 69
immateriality, 55
implication, 73, 76, 95, 128, 131, 137, 139, 145, 168
    necessary, 95, 132
implied term, 95, 117, 125, 145, 150, 159, 161, 177, 181–82, 266
imposition, 165, 169
improbability, 254
impugned act, 69
imputed knowledge, 197
imputing, 225
inaccuracy, 231, 235
inadmissibility, 224
inadvertent, 81, 110
inapplicability, 112–13, 126
incapacity, 63–65
    consequential, 63
incidents, 137, 244
    legal, 244
incompetence, 255
inconsistencies, apparent, 76
inconsistency, 7, 123, 126
incontestability provisions, 211
    contractual, 214
    statutory, 214
incorporation, 20–21
incumbent, 179–80, 199, 218
indemnification, 175
indemnify, 25–27, 61, 163, 177, 185, 202
indemnifying, 84

indemnity, 24–25, 30, 63, 82, 84, 118, 129, 162, 233
    contract of, 23, 61, 68
    professional, 204
indemnity clause, 98, 118, 126
indemnity policy, 24–25, 112
    ordinary, 25
indifference, 218, 253
indispensable shield, 180
individualism, 134
inducement, 205–7, 243, 270, 287–90, 311
    establishing actual, 288
    operative, 289
    sole, 287, 289
inducement test, 205
inference, 91, 207, 253, 262, 288, 290, 297, 300, 304
    fair, 290
    legitimate, 26
    ordinary, 57
infirmity, 121–22, 174
influence, undue, 69, 307
Informa, 85
Informa Law, 168
information, 138, 140–41, 151, 168, 170, 175, 182–83, 189–90, 216, 218, 231–32, 235–36, 264
    correct, 231, 235
    critical, 151
    inadequate, 231, 235
    inconsistent, 151
    incorrect, 232
    insurer of, 193, 224
    new, 182
    possessed material geotechnical, 151
    relevant, 169
    sufficient, 257
    verified, 262
    volunteer, 178

withhold, 151, 250
Ingall, 202
ingredient
   necessary, 248
   new, 254
ingredients, 91
   required, 213
inhalation, 64
   time of, 63, 65
initialling, 183, 198
initio, 47, 159, 245, 250
injuries, external, 122
injury, 61, 63–66, 120–21, 179, 248, 250, 261, 277, 291
   bodily, 119, 122–24
   event of, 121, 123
   in the event of death or, 120
   pecuniary, 249
   for that, 65
   time of, 63–64, 66
inland transport clause, 100
innocent non-disclosure clause, 239
inquiries, reasonable, 178
instructions, 234
instrument, 14, 38–41, 43, 75, 79, 86, 88–89, 97–98, 104, 185
   formal, 42–43
   mercantile, 85
   written, 39–40, 42, 78–79
insurable interest, 3, 28–31, 70
   defined, 31
   embraces that, 28
insurance, 1–3, 6–12, 17–24, 27–34, 50–52, 54, 60–61, 68–70, 81–85, 103, 114–16, 129–32, 155–63, 169–75, 179–81, 193–95, 200–201, 217–19, 228–30, 232–33
   accident, 83, 103, 123, 126
   general, 278
   interim, 20

   life, 2, 83, 175, 199, 202, 211
   maritime, 167
   non-marine, 27, 61, 297
   original, 6, 113
   period of, 22, 173–74
   proposal for, 5, 11, 156, 171, 211–12, 236, 238, 272
   seeking, 169
   sekarang dikenali sebagai Tahan, 21
   vehicle, 23
insurance agent, 12, 189, 223–26, 228, 231, 235, 237
   country, 225
insurance broker, 5, 232–33, 236
insurance broker's knowledge, 237
insurance business, 34, 227
insurance certificate, 23
insurance claims, 123, 126, 216, 246, 279, 304
insurance company, 1–2, 5, 13, 16, 27–28, 94, 96, 98–100, 103, 184, 198–99, 223, 226, 232, 236
insurance context, 202, 239–40
insurance contracts, 1, 3, 5, 9, 44–45, 47–48, 71, 124–28, 152–53, 158–59, 163–64, 168–70, 176–77, 193–94, 223–24
   context of, 157, 163
   long-term, 68
insurance coverage, 46
insurance fraud, 132, 304, 312
Insurance Law, 2–3, 7–9, 19, 21–23, 29–33, 41–43, 47–55, 59–63, 81–83, 87–91, 103–7, 115–19, 127–29, 155–57, 167–69, 171–75, 193–97, 203–5, 229–31, 249–51
Insurance law in Malaysia, 127
insurance markets, 165
insurance matters, 187, 228

insurance money, 118
insurance monies, 118
insurance office, 34
insurance ombudsman, 127
insurance policy, 18, 20, 28, 32–34, 81–82, 87, 90–93, 98–99, 107–8, 112–13, 118–20, 188, 218, 228–29, 233
    combined, 172
    first, 212
    life, 67, 70, 219
    marine, 59, 128
    motor, 100, 102, 111, 125–26
    risks, 172
insurance policy exclusion clause, 112
insurance proposal, 153, 176–77
insurance proposal form, 225
insurance relationship, 161
insurance slip, 7
insurance transactions, 165
insured act, 161
insured claimant, 261
insured handling, 112
insured plaintiff, 120–21, 188, 201, 220, 263
insured plaintiff's claim, 120–21, 124, 162, 211
insured proposer, 177
insured respondent, 155
insureds, 2, 8, 152, 216
insured's activities, 112
insured's agent, 138
insured's interest, 200
insured vehicle, 200, 294
insurer appellant, 217, 229
insurer company, 201
insurer defendants, 18, 120–21, 175, 180, 188, 210–11, 220, 261, 296
insurer defendant's decision, 119, 121, 220
insurer defendant's liability, 263

insurer plaintiff, 188
insurer respondents, 48
insurers, 2–3, 5–11, 17–21, 24–27, 47–59, 81–84, 93–94, 98–102, 156–58, 160–65, 167–72, 174–82, 184–87, 189–90, 192–200, 206–11, 216–21, 223–25, 278–79, 293–98
    actual, 209, 293
    appellant, 229
    defendant, 201
    particular, 207, 209, 293
    reasonable, 198
insurers issue, 20
insurer's judgment, 169
insurer's knowledge, 165
insurer's mind, 210
insurer's questions, 53
insurers reserve, 25
insurer.When, 50
intent, 16, 80, 111, 240, 246, 249–50, 270, 281
    expressed, 269
    legislative, 37
    subjective, 15, 40, 77, 80
    true, 44–45
intention, 4, 14–15, 38–41, 43–45, 58–59, 71–73, 77–80, 83–84, 89, 102–6, 124–26, 248–51, 259–60, 264, 267–68, 276–77, 281, 286
    apparent, 4
    conscious, 78
    imputed, 77
    mutual, 119
    plaintiff's, 45
    presumed, 86, 137, 142–43, 176
    real, 45, 79, 86
    representor's, 281
    subjective, 142
    true, 38

unilateral, 119
interests, direct, 61
interests conflict, 162
interpolation, 76
interpretation, 12, 14–15, 53, 71–75, 78–80, 85, 88, 91, 118, 123, 125–26, 267, 271
   contractual, 72–73, 76, 124, 144
   general rules of, 85, 98, 100, 102–3
   his own private, 284
   legal, 40
   literal, 102
   normal canons of, 16, 80
   process of, 71–72
   reasonable, 53, 87
   requiring, 72
   rival, 49
   sound, 82
   ultimate, 16, 80
interpretation set, 73
interpretative controversies, 271
interpretative tool, 271
invalidating, 170
invention, 231, 235, 246
invitation, 8, 10
issuance, 20, 43–44

J

joint venture agreements, 141
judges, 7, 56, 58, 90, 97, 165, 168, 182, 192, 247–48, 254–55
judge's mind, 75
judgment, 62–63, 130–32, 145–48, 159, 161, 164–67, 170, 196, 198, 232–33, 237, 241, 244–45, 292–93, 297–99
judicial activism, 36
judicial formulations, 132
judicial impression, 46
judicial procedure, 40

judicial pronouncement, 225
juncture, 15, 80, 270, 306
juridical basis, 136
jurisdiction, 42, 133–34, 245–46
   equitable, 34
   fair and reasonable, 128
jurisprudence, traditional, 168
justice, 36, 149, 247, 250
justification, 157, 185, 272
   reasonable, 149, 151

K

knowledge, 153, 165, 170–72, 176–78, 194–95, 199, 218–23, 225–28, 235–37, 249, 253–54, 256–58, 261, 263, 276–77
   actual, 290
   conscious, 254
   defendant's, 280
   general, 292
   maker's, 261
   necessary, 253
   real, 264

L

lading, 110, 285
   bill of, 45, 108, 110–11, 286
language, 56–57, 72, 75–76, 78, 80, 82, 84, 87–89, 92–93, 96–98, 101, 112, 192, 240–41
   clear, 49
   contractual, 79
   equivocal, 73
   explicit, 100
   foreign, 75
   general, 192, 291
   interpreting, 73
lapsed policy, 212
law, 12, 14–15, 29–30, 35–37, 39–40, 54–55, 57–58, 71–75, 103, 127–30, 137, 146–47, 151–52,

    155–57, 159, 170, 244–47, 259–61, 264–65, 286–88
  applicable, 128
  civil, 127, 135
  current, 206
  developed, 128
  established, 100, 102, 136, 194, 218, 275
  general, 54, 58, 206, 209, 238, 277, 293
  mercantile, 128, 131, 167
  merchant, 23
  new, 227
  new common, 127
  relevant, 147
  settled, 55, 218, 222, 226, 301, 303
  trite, 43, 200, 208, 307
  unified European, 135
law merchant, 129
law rule, 37
  common, 56
lawyers, 100, 136, 180
  common, 143
leading underwriter initials, 6
legal analyst, 192, 292
legal burden, 299–300
legal commentators, 155
legal distinction, 60
legal document, 74
legal effect, 17, 74, 117, 267, 269–70, 292
legal obligation, 66, 168, 179
legal or equitable interest, 29
legal principles, 4
legal prism, 270
legal relations, 4, 31, 117, 222
legal responsibilities, 145
legal status, 245
legal systems, 133, 144
legal threshold, 274

legal transition, 223
legislation, 37, 134, 226–27, 301
legislative domain, 146
legislative intervention, 37, 226
legislative scheme, 83
letter, 41, 79, 188, 246, 250, 257, 274, 281, 285–86
  circular, 283
  official, 18
liability, 27–31, 47–50, 55–58, 61–67, 94, 99–100, 107–9, 111–12, 138, 152, 162–63, 177, 191–92, 223–25, 232–33, 257, 260–61, 270
  accrued, 66
  assured's, 61
  correlative, 222
  defendant's, 101, 299
  discharged from, 58
  disclaim, 48–50, 242
  employer's, 63–64, 66
  escape, 55
  establishing, 63
  excluded, 108
  exclusion of, 241
  exempting, 108
  incurred, 67
  legal, 27, 29–31
  maximum, 24
  pecuniary, 29
  potential, 29
  repudiating, 55
liability insurance, 31, 61–62, 67
liability insurance policy, 61–62, 70
liability policies, 29, 67
licensed insurer, 187–88, 201, 216, 228
licensed life insurer, 211
life, 19, 21, 24, 29–30, 60, 67, 174, 198–99
  ordinary, 40
  person's, 67

life assurance, 67, 158
life policy, 22, 173–74, 196, 211
life time, 214
limb, second, 210, 213
limbs, 102
    distinct, 253
limitations, 34, 59, 84, 186, 191, 256, 266, 282–83, 307
    implied, 162
    judge's, 241
limited amounts, 68
limited cases, 69
limited contractual remedy, 297
literal meaning, 81–82, 90, 107, 125
litigant desirous, 273
litigation, 180, 185–86
    hostile, 186
litigation stage, 172, 181
loading, 109, 114–15
logical postulation, 306
long-established principle, 96
long-term distributorship agreements, 141
loss, 8, 19–27, 29–33, 47–49, 60–61, 67–68, 108–9, 113–15, 118, 169, 175, 180–82, 207–8, 232–33, 306
    actual, 24–26
    direct, 113
    economic, 249
    financial, 31
    inflict, 179
    legal, 31
    partial, 25
    real, 26
    total, 25, 104, 233
loss policy, consequential, 306
lucid touch, usual, 39
lungs, 64–66

M

machinery, 25, 114–15
    new, 26
    refrigerating, 114–15
maker, 204, 252, 264, 287
manager, 273
    administrative, 44
mandatory statutory form, 82, 124
manifestation, 163
marine, 60, 131, 239
marine adventure, 29, 31
marine field, 60
marine insurance, 44, 47, 51, 54, 57–59, 83–84, 113, 116, 126–27, 129, 131
    contract of, 129, 131, 155, 167
    law of, 55, 60
    law relating to, 57, 128
marine insurers, 164
market, 1, 6, 61, 105
    foreign exchange, 187
market conditions, 26
market rivals, 273
market value, 26
material, 168, 172, 176–78, 181–83, 189–90, 193–99, 203, 209, 215–16, 218–19, 228–31, 239, 265, 287–88, 293–95
    accepted, 182
material act, 159
material advantage, 248
material change, 141
material circumstance, 132, 164, 166, 169, 178, 195–96, 220
material date, 263
material distinction, 51
material factors, 272
material facts, 153, 158–59, 174–77, 183–84, 186–87, 193–202, 208–11, 213, 216–20, 224, 228–29, 238, 249, 272–73, 311

material information, 151, 169, 171, 180, 195–96, 198, 208, 218
    volunteer, 168
materiality, 17, 54–55, 195, 205, 215, 217, 221, 229–30, 265, 287–88
    waiver negatives, 190
material matters, 156, 189, 196, 211, 213, 231, 235
material misdescription, 233, 236–37
material misrepresentation, 206–7, 239, 265, 296
material misstatement, 204
material non-disclosure, 172, 174, 200–201, 207, 223, 242, 274
material particulars, 200, 294
material representation, 209, 221, 288, 290, 293
material time, 44, 194, 196, 198–99
material words, 67
matrices, factual, 145
matrix, factual, 77, 87, 271
matters material, 165, 176
maxim, 81–82
maximum amount, 24–26
meaning, 57, 62–66, 71–72, 74–76, 78, 85–86, 89–90, 92–93, 104, 106–7, 115, 137–38, 255–56, 281–83, 296
meaning of the words, 74
meaning quoad hoc, customary, 86
measurement, 25
meat, 114–15
    freight of, 114–15
    frozen, 114–15
medical doctors, 209
medical treatment, 162
medicine chest, 165
medium, 8, 10, 271
member, 8, 10, 292, 308
    family, 202
    misled, 308

member states, 135
memorandum, 34, 183
mental defect, 174
merchandize, 114–15
mesothelioma, 64–66
metaphorical colloquialisms, 133
method
    alternative, 47
    primary, 106
    traditional, 46
    usual, 20
    wrong, 283
methodology, established, 137
midwife, active, 191
mind, 13, 53–54, 73–74, 77–78, 105, 192–93, 197, 209, 230, 246–47, 253–54, 258–59, 263–64, 284–85, 292–93
minority shareholder, 308
misapplication, 252
misapprehension, 42
misappropriation, 303
mischief, hidden, 199
misdelivery, 110
mislead, 153, 165, 221, 250, 262, 275, 291
misrepresentation, 69, 202–3, 206–7, 209–10, 240–41, 246, 257–59, 261–66, 272, 274–75, 277–80, 286–94, 296–97, 307, 310–11
    actual, 202
    alleged, 265, 307
    defendant's, 292
    dishonest, 192, 221
    false, 246
    ground of, 289, 294
    innocent, 158, 210, 261–63, 294
    intentional, 249
    making, 146
    negligent, 203, 281, 297
    operative, 265, 311

relevant, 253
wilful, 246
misrepresentation and non-disclosure, 128, 202, 275
misrepresentations in issue, 280, 296
misrepresentee, 265
misrepresenting, 249
misrepresentor, 265
misstatement, 17–18, 156, 197, 204, 259
   negligent, 296
mis-statement, positive, 166
misstatement, relevant, 254
mistake, 33–34, 36–41, 46, 70, 91, 135, 166, 218, 222, 290
   alleged, 33
   barring, 268
   common, 37–39, 42–43
   correct obvious, 38
   innocent, 240
   mutual, 39, 42–43, 45
   unilateral, 39
mistake of law, 35–37
mistake of law rule, 37
misunderstood, 94, 195, 231, 235
modern ascendancy, early, 129
modifications, 4, 187, 215
money, 2, 35–36, 41, 67, 303
money market, 187
moral delinquency, 253
moral hazard, 171
moral obligations, 30
moral turpitude, 250
motives, 190, 203, 239–40, 253, 262, 281
   efficient, 166
   representor's, 281
motoring offences, 172
motor insurance, 31, 172
   refused, 201
motor policy, 200, 294
motor vehicle policy, third-party, 62
multiplicity, 132

N

natural assumption, 8
natural meaning, 8, 92
nature, 1–2, 14, 23, 29–31, 45–46, 60, 62, 68–69, 79, 81, 161–62, 263, 265, 297–98, 302–3
   exact, 153, 176–77
   open-textured, 146
   particular, 51
   secondary, 46
   true, 274
negat incumbit probatio, 298
negligence, 65–66, 108–11, 231–32, 235–36, 238, 263, 272, 277, 280, 296–97, 299
   contributory, 299
   gross, 255, 257, 280
negligence action, 299
negligent acts, 81
negotiations, 4, 6, 40, 45, 79–80, 106, 116–17, 126, 146–47, 171, 178
   oral, 268
   pre-contractual, 117
   prior, 15
   protracted, 4
   protracted documentary, 4
neighbouring paragraph, 91
neque enim id, 166
nominee, 88, 119, 123
non-compliance, 15, 48, 169
non-delivery, 110
nondisclosure, 191
non-disclosure, 165–66, 168–70, 181–82, 188–89, 198–203, 207–8, 215, 217, 223, 225, 239–43, 272–73, 275, 293–94, 296–97
   allegation of, 216, 229
   alleged, 240

culpable, 241
effect of, 209–10, 243, 272, 294
established, 193
ground of, 211, 224
innocent, 209, 241
insurers allege, 208
negligent, 296–97
non-fraudulent, 239
partial, 202
pre-contractual, 216
relevant, 207
non-disclosure and misrepresentation, 189, 200, 243, 294
non-disclosure of material facts, 197, 200–201, 210, 213, 238
non-fulfilment, 47, 59
non-observance, 46, 179
non-payment, 22, 173, 214
norms, 28, 138
    cultural, 144
    general, 138
note, 7, 20–21, 127, 236–37
notification, 67, 160
nullifies, 149–50, 159
numerical strength, 192

O

object, 8, 73, 78, 87, 89, 111, 113, 115, 169, 180
    commercial, 90, 107, 126
    designed, 310
objection, 55, 58, 143
    fatal, 36
    first, 36
    insurmountable, 36
    second, 36
objective principle, 142
objective test, 4, 252
    normal, 15, 79
objective viewpoint, 15, 80
objectivity, 78, 124

obligations, 63–64, 133–34, 143, 145, 149–50, 152, 157, 175, 181–85, 190–91, 193, 195–96, 200–201, 297, 299–300
    continuing, 175
    contractual, 138, 152, 182
    general, 134, 145, 230
    implied, 157, 161
    mutual, 155
    necessary, 148
    onerous, 141
    positive, 141, 158, 199
    principal's, 191
    reciprocal, 152
    special, 297
    tortious, 155
obligatory, 180
    open, 68
obliquity, 69, 248
    moral, 253
obscure, 161, 218
observance, 46–48, 101, 139
observer, informed, 89
occasions, 5, 96, 116, 127, 146, 167, 180, 182, 242, 244, 295
    particular, 104
    repeated, 57
occlusions, 122
occupation, true, 217, 229
occurrence, 2–3, 31, 55–56, 65, 67, 254
offence, 169, 303
offer, 1, 3–5, 8–11, 25, 106, 223
    formal, 9, 11
    original, 5
offeree, 4–5, 105
offeror, 4–5, 105
office, 34, 75, 204
officer-in-charge, 44
ombudsman, 128
    new, 128

omissions, 16, 191, 211, 218, 245, 250, 265
   deliberate, 140
onerous, 143, 184
onus, 178, 208, 243, 301
open cover, 68
openness, 157, 185
   requiring, 144
operation, 47, 79, 160, 172, 242
   possible, 113
operative part, 212
opinion, 58, 72–73, 97, 186, 191–92, 195, 233, 236, 238, 260, 264, 269, 294–95
   academic, 36
   judicial, 206, 224
   legal, 223
   statement of, 259, 264
opinion impinge, 191
order, 42, 46, 103, 141, 186, 244, 260, 294, 307
   delivery, 109–10, 281
order rectification, 40
original policy, 113, 172, 174, 306
original proposal form, 174
original purposes, 149–50
ought to know, 256
outward acts, 43
owners, 62, 109, 119, 151, 233, 251, 256
   potential policy, 227
owner's knowledge, 151

P

pamphlets, 1, 61
parol evidence rule, 12–13, 73, 78, 267–68
participation, 154
   insured's, 178
particularise, 308
particulars, 10, 216, 234, 301, 307, 310

necessary, 307
sufficient, 308–9
particulars set, 237
parties, 1–2, 4, 13–20, 32–35, 37–46, 71–74, 76–81, 83–87, 95–98, 103–6, 113–17, 133–46, 148–61, 165–68, 176–78, 191–94, 247–49, 259–65, 267–71, 298–301
   aggrieved, 28, 159, 270, 272
   assured, 297
   commercial, 192, 292
   contending, 149
   deceived, 248
   definite, 4
   injured, 248
   innocent, 38, 46–47, 54, 157, 196
   litigating, 273
   negotiating, 134, 147
   opposite, 35, 42, 146, 183, 307
parties antecedent, 42
parties contract, 42
parties misunderstand, 39
partners, 137, 204
partnership, 130, 140, 149, 156, 166
party acts, 149–50
party complaining, 277, 290
party labours, 151
party pleading, 307
party's perception, 141
passage, 10, 14, 44, 50, 57, 60, 75, 134, 165, 253, 255
passenger, 13
   appellant's pillion, 13
payment, 2, 9, 19, 36–37, 48, 63–64, 67, 162, 175, 285–86, 295–96
   making, 25
payment of premiums, 9, 19
payment systems, 187
penetration, 65–66, 135
   initial, 64

perceptively, 117
perchance, 203, 240
performance, 54, 135–36, 139–42, 148–49, 151–52, 155, 175, 182, 307
    complete, 49
performance of contracts, 134–35, 142, 144
perils, 60, 115–16, 129
    relevant insured, 65
period
    fixed, 174
    new, 22, 173
    relevant, 66
    specified, 22, 173
person, 13–14, 28–31, 72, 109, 139–40, 168–70, 191, 204–5, 227–28, 230, 234, 236, 238, 249–50, 252–53, 255–56, 260, 276, 278–81, 290–91
    honest, 252
    insured, 28, 84, 124, 171, 174
    ordinary, 100
    particular, 29
    reasonable, 4, 11, 72, 74, 78, 187, 217, 279, 283, 285
    unauthorised, 111
personal accident policies, 24, 198
personal characteristics, 171
personal embarrassment, 295
personal knowledge, 44–45
personal representatives, 32
person guilty, 281
person's consciousness, 202
person's entitlement, 247
person signs, 11
perspective, 269
    evidential, 270
    legal, 270
petitioner, 308–9
philosophic, 102

phrase, 75–76, 82, 85, 88–89, 106, 126, 130–31, 189–92, 241, 247–48, 300, 305, 312
physical characteristics, 171
physical defect, 121
    pre-existing, 121–22
physical hazard, 171
piecemeal solutions, developed, 133
plaintiff, 26, 44–46, 100–102, 110–11, 150–51, 161, 188, 204–5, 220, 232–33, 263–65, 269, 272–77, 280–81, 286, 289, 292–93, 299–300, 302, 306
    first, 213
plaintiff company, 14
plaintiff's disability, 161
plaintiff's goods, 44
plaintiff's questions, 120
plaintiff's shipments, 45
plaintiff's warehouse, 46
playing fair, 133, 144
plea, 208–9, 293
pleadings, 58, 209, 273, 306–8, 312
pneumoconiosis case, 65
police, 147, 248
policy, modern, 48
policy agree, 17
policy contra proferentem, 83
policyholder, 197
policy insurance, 89
policy owner, 211
policy period, 65
policy perspective, 269
policy words, 62
pollution discharges, 112
ports, 114–15
position, 8, 10, 76, 78, 133–34, 161–62, 223, 225–26, 231–32, 235–36, 264–65, 288–89, 303–4
    adversarial, 134
    adverserial, 146

    current, 226
    hallowed, 266
    legal, 158, 226, 231
    mutual, 249
    true, 58, 140
possession, 6, 31, 170
post-contract, 184
post-contract development, 184
post-contract situation, 185
post-contract stage, 128, 172
post-formation, 155
post-mortem, 120
post-mortem report, 108, 120
Post Office, 61–62
power, 11, 22, 38, 142, 162, 173, 222
    legal, 222
practicalities, 225
practice
    modern, 129
    sharp, 69
    unworkable in, 134
preamble, 187, 227
precautions, reasonable, 81
precedent, 48, 179
precipitate, 45
pre-contract situation, 182
pre-contract stage, 172, 181
pre-contractual stage, 128
predecessor, 57
preexisting, 121
preferred method, 134
prejudice, 34, 50, 56–57, 182, 191, 270, 290, 307
    but without, 57
premises, 45, 209
premium, 2, 6, 9–10, 18–22, 24, 164, 166, 169–70, 173, 181–82, 185, 187–88, 196–98, 206, 273–74
    additional, 200
    rate of, 6, 194
    single, 63

premium fund, 273
preponderance, 254
presentation, 285
preservation, 61
pressures, 73, 135
presumption, 8, 12, 19, 21, 34, 89, 206–7, 230, 268, 287
    basic, 92
    rebuttable, 15, 79
principal criteria, 137
    in principle at least, 143
Principles
    basic, 77
    broad, 136
    first, 51
    fundamental, 23, 118, 161
    ordinary, 60, 105, 112
printed clause, subsequent, 115
privity, 28, 109, 222
probabilities, 154, 254, 302–3, 305
    balance of, 121, 124, 206–8, 251, 254, 274, 301–5
    on the balance of, 299–300
    high degree of, 302, 305, 309
probably can, 122
problem, 76–77, 100, 128, 295
    current, 239
proceedings, 63, 116, 126, 147, 299–300
    civil, 301, 303–4
    instituted, 233
    present, 271
process, 7, 25, 63, 71–73, 92, 137, 144, 178, 180, 271
    analytical, 14, 79
    continuous, 301
    contractual, 149
    fourfold, 11
    tendering, 151
professional manner, 178
profit, 23, 27

prohibition, 15, 80
prolongation, 22, 30, 173
promises, 2, 4, 53, 105–6, 117, 236, 238, 249
   contractual, 4
   insurer's, 48
promissory undertaking, 54
proof, 12, 15, 35, 40, 246, 287, 290, 298–301, 303–6, 309, 312
   burden of, 32, 208, 298–301, 303, 306
   convincing, 39, 42
   degree of, 305, 309
   disallowing, 268
   onus of, 208, 301
   standard of, 39, 251, 254–55, 299–305
   strong burden of, 34, 42
proof beyond reasonable doubt, 305
property, 20, 25–26, 29, 31, 40, 175, 179, 249–50, 252, 294, 296
   company's, 293
   insurable, 31
   insured, 28, 201
property insurance, 29
proposal, 1, 3, 8–11, 16, 19, 21, 49, 52, 222, 226, 228–32, 234–38
proposal form, 8–12, 16–17, 93, 123, 174–75, 179–80, 188–89, 196–97, 200, 204–5, 215–20, 223–25, 227–29, 231–38, 294
proposer, 3, 8–10, 19–20, 168–69, 172, 186, 188–89, 197, 201, 216, 224–25, 230–32, 235
proposition, 18, 23–24, 49, 64, 75, 83, 94, 108, 159, 167, 284
   general, 283
   principal, 75
proprietary interest, 119
proscribed purpose, 295
prosecution, 300

prosecution inquest, 92
prospective policyholders, 195
prosperous offices, 67
prostate cancer, 220
protagonists, 274
protection, 61, 174, 242
protracted journey, 57
prove, 34, 46, 207–9, 211, 213, 254–55, 280–81, 286, 288, 293, 299–301, 306, 308–10
prove contributory negligence, 299
prove inducement, 206–7
prove non-disclosure, 208, 219
proving beyond reasonable doubt, 305
proving facts, 299
proving fraud, 298, 301, 303, 311
provisions, 22, 24–25, 48–50, 56, 59, 81–82, 91–93, 101, 107–8, 128–29, 160, 267–68, 270
   contractual, 107, 241
   first, 91
   general, 121, 213
   particular, 37, 42, 66
   relevant, 16, 23, 80, 85, 214
   self-contained, 91
   worded, 269
proviso, 15, 80, 98, 102–3, 111–12, 126, 214, 266
proximate cause, 122, 129
prudent, 98, 187, 198, 287, 305–6
   ordinary, 230
prudent insurer, 132, 164, 170, 176, 195–97, 209, 293
prudent investigations, 178
pulmonary tuberculosis, 201
purchaser, 289
purposes, obvious, 267

Q

qualification, 79, 206, 285, 295
   temporal, 162

quod tuscias, 166
quorum intersit id scire, 166
quoted case, 153

R

rates/premiums, 217, 230
rationalise, 245
read over and checked are true, 237
reasonableness, 84, 149, 155, 270
reasoning, 64, 117, 190, 297
    commercial, 60
    inadequate, 245
    legal, 225
    succinct, 114
rebuilding, 2, 25
rebut, 209, 293
receipt, 19–21, 64, 92
    interim, 20–21
recesses, inner, 105
recital, 52
    first, 82
reckless, 209, 275, 293
recklessness, 204, 253, 257
recognition, 60, 143
    clear, 136
    judicial, 148
reconciling, 76
record, 33–34, 38
recorded use, first, 131
recourse, 28, 75, 90–91
recover, 24–26, 28, 33, 116, 158, 166
recovery, 47–48
rectification, 16, 33–34, 37–40, 42–43, 45–46, 70, 73, 81
    equitable remedy of, 37, 39
    judicial, 40
    party claiming, 34
    seeking, 34, 39, 42
reduction, 27
    formal, 123

reference, 3, 6, 9, 12, 14, 20, 23, 28–29, 75–76, 107, 155, 175, 179–80
regulation, 103, 135, 187, 227
reinstate, 25
reinstatement, 25–26, 100, 214
    cost of, 26
    last, 212, 214
reinstatement basis, 25
reinstating, 25
reinsurance, 5, 7, 113, 207
    obtaining, 190
reinsurance policy, 81
reinsurance treaty, 185
reinsurer, 207
rejection, 5, 170
relationship, 30–31, 87, 137–38, 140, 152, 157, 161–62, 166, 181–82, 186, 267
    continuing, 154
    incident of the, 161
    legal, 244
    longer-term, 141
    quasi-fiduciary, 151
reliance, 160, 216–17, 226, 246, 260, 267, 275, 284, 292, 311
relief, 246, 261
relieve, 192, 230, 291, 299
re-litigation, 37
remedy, 47, 155, 159, 177, 181–82, 185–86, 203, 210, 234, 239–42, 294, 296–97
    contractual, 182
    inadequate, 52
    procedural, 186
    sole, 177
    supplementary, 297
renders the contract void, 55
renewal, 19, 22–23, 172–74, 213
    reserving continuous rights of, 22, 173
renewal certificate, 174

renewal period, 19
renewed policy, 174–75
repetition, 22, 173
replacement, cost of, 26
replacement value, 26
representation, 51–52, 165, 203, 205, 256, 258–65, 267, 269, 275–77, 280–83, 285–90, 292, 294, 296, 310–11
    continuing, 290
    intentional, 248
    positive, 202
    second pre-contractual, 269
    word, 258
representation of fact, 259, 276, 286
representation test, 282
representee, 246, 259–60, 264–65, 281–82, 286–88, 290, 292, 311
    normal, 261, 264
representee thought, 288
representor, 246, 256–59, 262–64, 277, 281–82, 311
representor's state, 259, 263
repudiate, 46, 54–55, 201, 210, 294
    insurer to, 49, 52, 54
repudiate liability, 55, 156, 232, 304
repudiation, 47, 54
    subsequent, 44
request, 140, 216, 231
    proposer's, 235
requirement, 139–41, 153, 157, 161, 170, 172, 182, 185, 266, 270, 294
    core, 143
    general, 134
    reasonableness, 270
    statutory, 186, 242
    uberrimae fidei, 275
rescission, 203, 240–41, 264, 296
researched article, 130
resolution, 112, 149

resources, massive, 100
respective purposes, 91
responsibility, 109, 111, 189, 299, 301
restitution, 35, 37, 159
restoration, 25
restraint, 34, 242
result, 2, 5, 59–60, 82, 84, 180–81, 225, 231, 235, 240, 265, 268, 286–87
    fairer, 87
    irrational, 112
    particular, 99
    reasonable, 49
    unanticipated, 81, 90
    unreasonable, 49
resulting directly and naturally, 32
result non-disclosure, 240
retention, 19, 21, 36
retrocession, 190
retrograde step, 165
rhetorical appeals, 132
rights, 7, 20, 28, 40, 66, 78, 129, 149, 185, 193, 203
    contractual, 175
    legal, 274
    mutual, 38
    respective, 42, 193
rights revest, 22, 173
risk, 3, 6–7, 19, 31–32, 54–56, 59–60, 68, 114–15, 118, 164–65, 169–71, 176–78, 182–84, 187–89, 193–96, 198, 217–18, 220–22, 230, 292–94
    actual, 153, 194
    additional, 169, 182
    at, 169
    chief, 81, 90
    inescapable, 129
    marine, 68
    moral, 169
    original, 182

particular, 32
sole, 109
third-party, 28
risk of errors, 191, 245
risk of loss, 52, 171
risque, 165–66
robbery, 247, 276
room, 72–73
root, 47, 52–53, 240
route
  first, 85
  second, 85
  technical, 85
  third, 85
rules, 3, 12, 14, 35–37, 39, 53–54, 91, 93, 95–96, 98, 169–70, 192, 267–68, 297–99, 306–7
  ancient, 298
  broad, 53
  cardinal, 103
  default, 137
  distinct, 12, 14
  down, 246
  far-reaching, 131
  fast, 29
  first, 12
  fundamental, 222
  general, 8, 10, 14, 78, 86, 202, 234, 236–37, 288, 291, 293
  good, 101
  modern, 129
  new, 36
  peculiar, 88
  procedural, 185
  second, 12
  strict, 78
  third, 12
  traditional, 259
ruling, 148, 165

S

safety, 31, 61
sail, 51, 60, 190
sailing, final, 114–15
sale, 14, 47, 152, 251, 289, 308
salutary reminder, 255
salvage charges, 115
scheme, coherent, 181
schemes, new, 246
scope, 28, 36, 53, 68–69, 129, 143, 163, 200
  extended, 82
scrutiny, 15, 80, 91, 112
sea, 108, 115, 129, 131, 152
seaworthiness, 165
seaworthy state, 165
section
  interpreted, 227
  interpreting, 213
security, intended, 203, 224
self-interest, 134
sendings, regular, 68
sense consensual, 245
sentence
  last, 58
  second, 57
servants, 108, 110
settlement, 62
shades, 69, 249
shadow, 305, 309
shared values, 138
shed light, 81
shew, 14
  surrounding contemporaneous circumstances, 86
ship, 2, 51, 68, 108–9, 114–16, 165–66, 222, 251
  arrived, 165
shipment, 44, 110, 114
  fictitious, 285
shipping agent, 109

shoes, 187, 237
signature, 6, 40, 205
signed proposal, 20
signed proposal form, 234
signification, primary, 86
signs, 53, 69, 74, 100, 205, 231–32, 234–35
silence, 202, 207, 240, 248, 250, 275–76
slip, 6–9, 34, 44, 121–22, 183, 198
    initialled, 6
    printed, 113
slip binding, 183
social policy, 37
sole cause, 288
sole effective cause, 207
sole inducing cause, 293
solicitors, 204, 274
    plaintiff's, 274
something more, 282
sound, 10, 81, 87, 101
source, 128, 134, 152
    first, 128
    new, 128
species, 1, 68, 246, 253
specificity, 132
speculation, 130, 153, 165
speech, 24, 130, 137, 142, 192, 204, 250, 291
    ordinary, 247
springboard, 136
square brackets, 57
stages
    first, 7
    initial, 185
standard documents, 100
standard form, 20
standard of proof beyond reasonable doubt, 301, 303
standard printed clause, 113
standard printed policy, 82

standards, 1, 139, 144, 252, 304
    applying, 136
    community, 149, 155
    moral, 252
    ordinary, 252
statement clause, truth of, 193, 203, 242
statements, 7–9, 16–17, 48, 52–53, 55, 58–59, 196–97, 204–5, 211–13, 236–38, 257–60, 263–65, 275, 280–85, 287–88
    alleged, 17
    dishonest, 296
    generalised, 166
    insured's, 225
    lucid, 165
    particular, 55, 260
    untrue, 53, 204, 240
    witness, 273
statute, 65–66, 75–76, 127, 245
    relevant, 307
statutory evidential scheme, 268
statutory policy, 63
statutory provisions, clear, 215
statutory restriction, 211
stipulate, 22, 173, 212, 230
stipulated amount, 67
stipulation, 17, 46, 95, 97, 230
    collateral, 57
    contractual, 231, 235
    particular, 49
    suggested, 95
stipulations, reasonable, 87
stolen goods, 201
strain, 84, 92, 253
stress, 237, 253
sub-contractors, 8, 29
subject, 20, 24–25, 28–29, 55–56, 58, 83, 100, 102–3, 128, 131, 133, 174, 258, 265–66, 270–71
subjective understandings, 105

subject matter, 3, 18, 30–31, 89, 104, 113
subject-matter, 14, 30–31, 110
    proper, 73
    real, 61
submission, 3, 45, 63, 216, 248, 297, 309
    hearing, 275
    respondent's, 75
    written, 63
subrogation, 129
subscribers, 7
subsections, 187, 228, 278
subsidiary questions, 35
subsisting, 22, 173
substance, 63, 102, 112, 157, 263–64, 298
substratum, 47, 60
subtract, 15, 78–79, 219
subtracting, 12, 73
sum of money, 2, 67
superseding, 269
supervision, 187
    judicial, 40
suppression, 166, 197, 222
surrounding circumstances turn, 74
symbols, 72
symptoms, 170, 202
synallagmatic, 47
syntactical analysis, 87

T

tablets, 220
temptation, 183
tenderers, 151
    prospective, 151
tenure, 156, 159
terms, 1–13, 15, 19–23, 28–30, 38–41, 43, 45–54, 56–57, 68–71, 73, 78–80, 88–89, 95, 101, 120–24, 137–45, 160–62, 173–74, 206–7, 266–71
    agreed, 20
    ambiguous, 271
    deliberate, 30
    erudite, 146
    exact, 5
    fundamental, 110–11
    general, 308
    improved, 146
    jurisprudential, 271
    monetary, 25
    new, 5
    particular, 46–47
    plain, 49
    prove, 267
    standard, 20
    true, 34
    usual, 20
    written, 13
terms set, 12
test, 4, 40, 52, 63, 105, 141, 150, 253, 256, 277, 282
    combined, 252–53
    common-sense, 123
    reasonableness, 270
    relevant, 253
    subjective, 252
    subjective standard, 252
    traditional prudent insurer, 205
    urine, 220
testify, 44–45
testimony, 219, 273–74
text, 4, 7, 60, 72–73, 78
    relevant, 10
textbooks, leading, 167
theft, 200–201
third parties, 28, 40, 61, 67, 82, 86, 116, 118, 222, 237, 302, 308
    injured, 28
third party goods, 118

time, 29, 38, 44–46, 54–55, 62–66, 105, 170–71, 173–76, 183, 197–98, 208–9, 218–19, 222–23, 261–62, 288
    long, 95
time policy, 23
titles, 7, 289
topic, 15, 80
tort, 62, 152, 177, 257, 261, 275, 281, 284, 286–87, 293, 296–97
    civil, 248
tortfeasor, weak, 28
trace, 5, 45, 127
trade, 3, 27, 86, 89, 96, 129, 172, 270
    particular, 104, 138
trade secret, 273
transaction, 36, 41, 77–78, 86, 130, 170, 244–45, 249–50, 252, 264–65, 288–91
    arm's length, 251
    closed, 36–37
    commercial, 139
    completed, 37
    sham, 251
transfers, 40, 153, 176–77, 310
transport, 74, 109
treatise Templeman, 44
trespassing, 146
trial, 84, 247, 274, 288, 301, 306
trial judge, 219, 228–29, 283
    learned, 200, 216, 294
trivial, 54, 170
trust, 138, 145, 303, 307
    mutual, 141
trust assets, 252
trusteeship, 140
truth, 17, 204–6, 215, 225, 228–31, 247–49, 251, 253, 255–58, 261–63, 275–77, 281–84, 286–87
    subject of, 257–58
truthfulness, 18

truth support, 186

U

ultimate interests, 151
unambiguous wordings, 14
uncertainty, 2–3, 36, 134, 144–45, 147
    element of, 2–3
    excessive, 144
    legal, 146
uncomfortable co-existence, 266
underground, 256
undergrowth, 116
under-writer, 153, 165–66
underwriters, 5–6, 95, 114, 154, 178, 180, 182–83, 206, 208, 217, 221–22
    bound, 101
    leading, 6–7
    particular, 6
underwriter's mind, 180
underwriter trusts, 221
under-writer trusts, 153, 165
unilateral act, 60
unlikelihood, 254
unreasonableness, 285
unstated shared understandings, 137
upfront, truthful, 158
up-river warehouse, 184
usage, 53
    general, 54
    known, 89
user, relevant, 118
use words, 14, 89
utmost good faith, 127, 130–32, 152, 155–61, 163–68, 171–72, 175–76, 178, 180, 183, 193, 195–96, 202, 205, 297
utmost importance, 263
utmost particularity, 307

V

vagueness, 310
  general, 308
validity, 27, 47, 167, 210, 213, 236
value policy, agreed, 24
variance, 23, 79, 267
variation, 181–82
  purported, 269
vehicle, 99–100
  commercial, 23
  motor, 103
  private, 23
vehicle involuntarily, 99
vendor, 147, 289
venture, 292
  joint, 86, 93
verdict, 62–63
vessel, 114–16, 233, 251
  sinking, 165
victim, 203, 249
vigour, extreme, 32
violent, 119–21, 123–24
  accidental, 121, 124
vitiates, 194, 198, 250
vitiates judgments, 244
vitiating element, 268
voyage, 115, 166, 222
  outward, 114
voyage clause, 45–46
voyage destination, 46
voyage policy, 23

W

waiver, 60, 188–91, 242
  subsequent, 58
warranty, 46, 48–49, 51–60, 70–71, 128, 217, 228–29, 267, 290
  collateral, 116–17, 266–67, 270
  implied, 58
  promissory, 56, 58–61
weight, 107, 134
well-trodden principle, 98
wilful, 253, 257–58, 307
wilful act, 233
wilful blind eye, 202
wilful suppression, 275
wit, 110
witnesses, 44, 188, 273, 300
  defendant's, 44
wording, 6–8, 14, 26, 28, 87, 90, 92, 96, 100, 104, 107, 267–68
words, 11–12, 14–16, 27–28, 33–34, 51–55, 62–63, 66–67, 71–72, 74–78, 80–93, 97, 100–107, 114–25, 138–39, 227, 250, 256, 282–83
  ambiguous, 98
  clear, 49
  foreign, 74
  particular, 76, 271
  technical, 75, 92
  trade, 74
  wrong, 16, 81
worker, 65–66, 83
work hardship, 27
writ, 185
  letter claim, 92
writer, 12, 14
writing, 12, 79, 92, 100, 105, 113–14, 123, 266, 268, 308
written contract, 13–15, 38, 69, 72–73, 77, 79, 81, 83, 234, 266–67, 270
  subsequent, 38
written document, 78, 85, 98, 100, 102–3, 267
written policy, 51, 59
written words, 15–16, 80–81

Y

years period, 212–13

Printed in Great Britain
by Amazon